Patent Exhaustion and International Trade Regulation

World Trade Institute Advanced Studies

VOLUME 13

The titles published in this series are listed at *brill.com/wtia*

Patent Exhaustion and International Trade Regulation

By

Santanu Mukherjee

BRILL | NIJHOFF

LEIDEN | BOSTON

The open access publication of this book has been published with the support of the Swiss National Science Foundation.

The Library of Congress Cataloging-in-Publication Data is available online at https://catalog.loc.gov
LC record available at https://lccn.loc.gov/2022060712

Typeface for the Latin, Greek, and Cyrillic scripts: "Brill". See and download: brill.com/brill-typeface.

ISSN 2405-9331
ISBN 978-90-04-54280-8 (hardback)
ISBN 978-90-04-54281-5 (e-book)

This book is printed on acid-free paper and produced in a sustainable manner.

Contents

PART 2
Multilateral and Regional Trade Regulations and Patent Exhaustion

Foreword

International Trade Regulation, right from GATT 1947 Agreement to the present day has witnessed a sea change as modes of trading changed with time. The shift from GATT 1947 to GATT 1994 introduced Intellectual Property Rights (IPR) in an effective manner through long years of negotiations. The Agreement on Trade Related aspects of Intellectual Property Rights (TRIPS) became a pillar of the World Trade Organisation (WTO). Directly interfacing between GATT and IPR, TRIPS addressed number of issues and forcing many WTO members to change their laws, but one of the issues that remained open, was 'Exhaustion' of IPR.

This book addresses this issue of exhaustion most vividly, explaining the rationale of patents, managing ubiquity through patent exhaustion. The evolution of exhaustion principle in different jurisdictions is remarkable. Gradually bringing readers to WTO regulation, not only different modes of exhaustion and treatment of parallel trade is established, but the exegesis of exhaustion principle under TRIPS as well as GATT and GATS is unprecedented. The book's analyses of MFN and National Treatment and the exceptions to them, supported by detailed elaboration of GATT Panels and Appellate Body Reports is noteworthy. As the author moves to the negotiation history of TRIPS, the meticulous detail, literally takes one back to the negotiations. Interesting to note that the author does not stop at that but studies exhaustion in the plethora of regional trade blocs. Further, the link between Trade Regulations, IPR and Competition Policy which is often overlooked is also well captured. Finally, one of the most critical aspects of public policy, the interface between patents and international trade is captured in every aspect of international trade, leading to the TRIPS amendment.

I commend the author for his painstaking research, robust arguments and vast comparative analyses of different legal jurisdictions. The author's grasp over the subject speaks about his in-depth knowledge and experience, his ability to explain lucidly is indeed laudable. Such a comprehensive book that covers one of the most complicated issues of patent law, as well as TRIPS, GATT and GATS, undoubtedly makes an indispensable reading for those engaged in legal practice, academia and policy making on IPR and WTO. I congratulate the author for this valuable contribution to international trade law and IPR scholarship.

Ambassador Dr. Mohan Kumar
Chairman Research and Information System for Developing Countries, New Delhi
Former Ambassador of India to France,
Former Ambassador of India to the Kingdom of Bahrain &
Former India's lead negotiator at the GATT, later at the WTO
New Delhi, September 2022

Preface

Parallel trade of products protected by intellectual property, in particular patents, has been a long-standing and unresolved issue in intellectual property law. International trade in original goods put lawfully on a market abroad and imported at lower prices to the benefit of consumers has been considered detrimental to intellectual property. Despite an overall commitment to open market and free trade, parallel trade is met with persistent resistance and often called grey imports, suggesting unlawfulness, or at least illegitimate trade impairing monopoly rights and rents. It challenges the tradition of nationally defined and protected intellectual property rights.

With the advent of the TRIPS Agreement and the incorporation of intellectual property standards and enforcement in the multilateral trading system of the World Trade Organization and in bilateral or plurilateral agreements, the problem of parallel trading was linked to the broader agenda and framework of international trade and the principles of WTO law. The present thesis explores the wider implications of provisions of the TRIPS Agreement beyond Article 6 and includes a detail assessment of the implications of GATT and the GATS Agreements. It links the problem not only to international trade regulation but also to regional trade agreements, in particular EU law, and disciplines of competition law and policy.

Since parallel trade goods relates to the geographical origin of the product, and not the nationality of the right holder, restrictions are subject to national treatment and the ban on quantitative restrictions, exceptions from which required detailed justification under Article XX GATT and Article XIV GATS. They have to meet the necessity test and thus call for the least restrictive manner in pursuit of a public policy goal. The thesis draws attention to this wider regulatory field and takes issue with the widespread opinion among intellectual property lawyers that Article 6 TRIPS exhaustively deals with the matter and leaves it to full discretion of Members of the WTO.

The thesis concludes that the doctrine of international exhaustion offers a convincing answer within the multilateral trading system, and that the doctrines both of national and regional exhaustion do not stand the legal test of international trade regulation. In light of persistent and long-standing insistence on national exhaustion and the territoriality of intellectual property rights in the patent field by industries affected, this is a challenging, but well-founded and well-argued proposition. The thesis succeeds to support the proposition with a multitude of legal and policy arguments. It doing so, it offers the most comprehensive analysis of the subject of parallel trading and exhaustion of rights ever produced. It makes an important contribution to the debate.

Accompanying Dr Santanu Mukherjee over many years in the pursuit of his research has been most rewarding. The thesis was developed by the author next to a busy professional life as a practising lawyer in India, and upon completing the MILE programme at the World Trade Institute, University of Bern, Switzerland. Despite a busy schedule, he persistently pursued his academic work and sets and example to all those in comparable circumstances. I am particularly glad and happy to see this volume added to the World Trade Institute Advanced Series.

Thomas Cottier
Bern, September 2022

Acknowledgments

This book is the culmination of my doctoral research at the University of Bern, Switzerland. I am deeply indebted to my doctoral supervisor Prof Dr Thomas Cottier, my guru, for his academic guidance and continuous moral support, without which I would have never reached the closure of my research. I thank him from the bottom of my heart for being a pillar of support right from conceptualising the research and going through challenging periods until the end. Thanks for all the discussions on the topic and especially when I was preparing the foundation of my arguments. His encouragement to think more deeply on the subject from different perspectives and not narrowly on TRIPS, has opened my thought process and changed my outlook.

I would like to thank the Max Planck Institute for Intellectual Property and Competition Law (MPI) in Munich for their support to undertake the initial research. Special thanks to Dr Christopher Heath, for all the enriched discussions while at the Institute (now with the Board of Appeals, European Patent Office). Thanks to Professors Dr. Joseph Straus, Dr. Ansgar Ohly, Dr Reto Hilty and Dr Josef Drexel for their guidance and also thanks to, Ms. Elfride Stangl at the MPI administration office for her kind help and assistance. Thanks also to the National Law University, New Delhi (NLUD) for allowing me to use their library facilities. My friends, Prof. Yogesh Pai at NLU, Delhi and Prof. Arul George Scaria, now with NLSU, Bangalore for all the discussions and debates about my research.

I dedicate this book to my parents, wife, sister, aunt and maternal cousin for their constant support and inspiration and my young son for coping with shortened play time. I wish my father who had been a constant inspiration was there with us today to share my joy. I am thankful to each one of them for helping me balance family responsibilities, professional work and the doctoral research that emanated in this book. Thanks to all my friends who had helped me always with their positivity and support.

Santanu Mukherjee

Figures and Table

Figures

Table

Abbreviations and Acronyms

AB	Appellate Body
AIDS	Acquired Immune Deficiency Syndrome
AIIPI	International Association for the Protection of Industrial Property
AP	Andean Pact
ASEAN	Association of South East Asian Nations
CACM	Central American Common Market
CET	Common External Tariff
CGC	Gulf Co-operation Council
CL	Compulsory License
CU	Customs Union
CUSFTA	Canada-US Free Trade Agreement
DABMP	Dutch Assessment Board for Medicinal Products
DIAC	Draft International Antitrust Code
DSB	Dispute Settlement Body
EC	European Community
ECJ	European Court of Justice
ECOWAS	Economic Community of West African States
ECSC	European Coal and Steel Community
EEA	European Economic Area
EEC	European Economic Community
EFTA	European Free Trade Association
EMR	Exclusive Marketing Rights
EPC	European Patent Convention
EU	European Union
FTA	Free Trade Agreements
GATT	General Agreement on Trade Tariffs
GATS	General Agreement on Trade in Services
GSP	Generalised System of Preferences
HIV	Human Immunodeficiency Virus
ICC	International Chamber of Commerce
IMF	International Monetary Fund
INTA	International Trademark Association
IP	Intellectual Property
IPC	Intellectual Property Rights Committee
IPRS	Intellectual Property Rights
ITO	International Trade Organisation
LAFTA	Latin American Free Trade Area

LAIA	Latin American Integration Agreement
LDC	Least Developing countries
MNC	Multinational Corporations
MFN	Most Favoured Nation
NAFTA	North American Free Trade Agreement
NT	National Treatment
NTB	Non-Tariff Barrier
PAFTA	Pacific Free Trade Area
PMASA	Pharmaceutical Manufacturers' Association of South Africa
PTA	Preferential Trade Area
QC	Queen's Counsel
QR	Quantitative Restrictions
RTA	Regional Trade Agreements
R&D	Research and Development
SAARC	South Asian Association for Regional Cooperation
SADCC	Southern African Development Coordination Conference
SAFTA	South Asian Free Trade Agreement
SKF	Smith Kline & French Laboratories Ltd.
S & DT	Special and Differential Treatment
TRIPS	Trade Related aspects of Intellectual Property Rights
UK	United Kingdom
UN	United Nations
UNCTAD	United Nations Conference on Trade and Development
UNESCO	United Nations Educational, Scientific and Cultural Organisation
UNHCR	United Nations Commission on Human Rights
US	United States
USPTO	United States Patent and Trademark Office
USTR	United States Trade Representatives
WHO	World Health Organisation
WIPO	World Intellectual Property Organisation
WTO	World Trade Organisation

Introduction

The General Agreement on Tariffs and Trade (GATT) 1994 reinforced a comprehensive trade liberalisation agenda under the World Trade Organisation (WTO) covering trade in goods, services as well as intellectual property (IP). The Agreement on Trade Related aspects of Intellectual Property Rights (TRIPS) aims not only at restricting trade in counterfeits and pirated goods but also harmonises the minimum level of protection of intellectual property rights (IPRS) within the WTO membership. The fundamental goal was to remove illegitimate barriers to trade and create a level playing field where IPRS were protected as well as could be used for dissemination of knowledge through technology transfers. In such a scenario it would have been ideal to address the issue of exhaustion of IPRS under the WTO regime and install an appropriate mode of exhaustion of IPRS for its different forms. The members negotiated on the exhaustion issue but could not come to any conclusion resulting in a status-quo where each member retained their practice of exhaustion. It was an agreement to disagree and leave the matter to policy space of WTO members.

With the introduction of TRIPS Agreement within the WTO regulatory regime, a uniform minimum level of IP standards was incorporated into the multilateral trading system. With a spill-over effect the IP standards were not only linked to different WTO agreements by way of cross-reference but also stretched onto bilateral and plurilateral agreements. For this reason, parallel trade of goods protected by patents cannot be addressed just by analysing TRIPS but need to be assessed from a broader framework in a wholesome manner under the WTO regulatory regime. It is divided into three sections and a concluding part, each with different chapters that build up the research analysis and discussion of various aspects before suggesting an ideal mode and means to install an appropriate mode of exhaustion.

Part 1 of the book offers an introduction to patent rights, its history, rationale and special characteristics within the broader gamut of IPRS leading to the unique characteristics of ubiquity in patents. Elaborating on how important it is to balance ubiquity, through exhaustion of patents. In this process, both the doctrines of exhaustion and implied licensing are extensively discussed, from conceptualisation of the doctrines, their expression in different forms to underlying economic reasoning. The next chapters in this part then addresses the economics of patents and the economic rationale for exhaustion in international trade elaborating the economic reasoning of each mode of exhaustion. Subsequent chapters of the book, then analyses the evolution of the doctrines in different jurisdictions of the world. Initiating in countries where

DOI:10.1163/9789004542815_002

the exhaustion doctrine developed in a distinct manner in some form or the other to some of the developing countries (with comparable IPRs and trade interests). The last chapters of this part then establish the link between patent exhaustion and multilateral trade through the treatment of parallel imports and briefly discusses exhaustion in some other modes of IPRs.

Part 2 elaborates patent exhaustion from the perspective of multilateral and regional trade regulations. It provides an in-depth analysis of the negotiating history of TRIPS within GATT and the negotiation on exhaustion in particular within TRIPS. This is followed by analysis of the Preamble and different Articles of the TRIPS Agreement interpreting them from the perspective of patent exhaustion. The next chapter provides analysis of different relevant Articles of GATT and their interpretation by different panels and the Appellate Body of the WTO and assessing the mode of exhaustion as per these interpretations. In the next chapter the interface between GATS and exhaustion is analysed under different relevant Articles. Then the discussion shifts to regional trade regulations in relation with the WTO regulatory regime analysing FTAs, RTAs and studies the exhaustion modes practiced in some of the prominent regional blocs.

Part 3 of the book expands on the policy dimensions of patent exhaustion with specific relevance to access to essential patented pharmaceutical drugs. It highlights how the debate dominated the WTO global rule making scenario as well as some of the affected countries. This part also analyses the development of competition policy at the multilateral level and how the exhaustion doctrine fits into the dynamics and interface of IPR-Competition law/policy to determine treatment of parallel imports.

The book finally draws its conclusion and recommendations from the research undertaken and detailed analyses provided to determine the most appropriate mode of exhaustion. Assessing the purpose of patents, addressing ubiquity and studying the historical evolution of patent law as well as interpreting multilateral regulations under TRIPS, GATT 1994 and other relevant WTO Agreements, the book supports international exhaustion to be uniformly adopted in the WTO. In the process while it analyses different regional blocs, it finds that adoption of international exhaustion within WTO can be extended to the CUs too. Further, from a competition policy perspective too, the analysis presents that international exhaustion is the most appropriate mode of exhaustion. With this recommendation, a draft text for amending *Article 6* of the TRIPS is proposed, expounding as to why the right time has come to negotiate the amendment effecting international exhaustion globally.

PART 1

Patents and Exhaustion

CHAPTER 1

Intellectual Property Rights and Patents: Introduction to Intellectual Property Rights

Intellectual Property Rights (IPRs) are legal rights that result from intellectual activity in the industrial, scientific, literary and artistic fields.[1] It is essentially a western concept based upon Roman law foundations of property allocation. Culturally and historically, the eastern oriental culture had never placed private rights over any type of knowledge property. In ancient India, the cultural and philosophical practice was in freedom of knowledge as mandated in the Rig Veda (one of the ancient Indian philosophical texts of the Hindus). It was believed that there should not be any restriction or bondage on knowledge as it is universal and free. Hence inventions or creations of human beings were to be utilized for the development and well-being of the human society at large.[2] In China, imitation was considered as a high compliment to the artist (the logic being, the work is so good that it has inspired others to imitate or replicate the work) and in ancient Java (Indonesia) community values and hence community rights were greater than private rights.[3]

IPRs are legal rights that were exported to the eastern countries by their colonial rulers and as a result of this, Intellectual Property (IP) legislation conferring private rights to IP were established in countries that had never followed the philosophy of such private rights. In some other countries (in erstwhile Soviet Union and those which were part of the Soviet bloc until its breakdown) private rights on means of production were totally withdrawn due to the influence of Bolshevik Revolution. As a result, rights for intellectual creations were said to be people's rights, which effectively meant that they were owned by the State. Individuals were limited to be recognised and honoured, short of being able to dispose of their work.

1 WIPO, "The Concept of Intellectual Property" in WIPO Intellectual Property Handbook: Policy, Law and Use, paragraph 1.1, 2001.

2 Mukherjee Santanu, "The Journey of Indian Patent Law towards TRIPS Compliance", 35 (2) IIC pg. 126, (125–150) 2004.

3 Gerster Richard, "Patents and Development Lessons Learnt from the Economic History of Switzerland", Intellectual Property Rights Series, pg. 2, No. 4, Third World Network 2001. Available at, http://www.gersterconsulting.ch/docs/TWN_Patents_and_Development.pdf.

DOI:10.1163/9789004542815_003

IPRS are statutory rights assured to the moral and economic aspirations of the creator of the IP to provide incentive to the inventor by way of providing legally protected exclusivity against rival enterprises in direct competition, for a certain restricted period.[4]

Different IPRS protect different types of IP, e.g. patent rights deal with the protection of scientific and technological inventions while copyright deals with protection of literary and artistic creations and trademarks to distinguish one's goods from similar other goods.[5] There are more types of IPRS to protect different other types of IP, in particular trademarks and related rights which seek to distinguish products from each other. This book focuses on the patent system and the nature of the right elaborating on the doctrine of exhaustion in relation to international trade rules under the aegis of the World Trade Organization (WTO).

One needs to understand that the main reason for having patents is economic gains wherein the inventor discloses the invention and the process to work it instead of adopting secrecy and in return gets market exclusivity.[6] In return, the patent system allows the owner market exclusivity and even restricted monopoly under a mandatory contractual agreement through an elaborate application and grant procedure that requires meeting certain specific requirements. Thus, such agreement requires the invention to be new or novel, to make an inventive step, to be industrially applicable and to disclose the patent in a manner to enable a person skilled in the art to work the invention. This balances the monopoly right on one hand and public welfare on the other through dissemination of knowledge and technology, enhancing social progress.[7] In other words, to ensure that the general public at large can benefit from the invention that is being accorded market exclusivity through the patent, the inventor is mandated to fully disclose the invention. The patent rights are wide in nature allowing the right owner to exclude others from making, using, selling, offering to sell or importing the patented invention.[8] Hence it becomes important to ensure effective disclosure so that a person with ordinary skills in the particular field to be able to make and practice the

4 Cornish William, "Intellectual Property and Monopoly" in "Intellectual Property: Patents, Copyright, Trade Marks and Allied Rights", 4th edition, Sweet & Maxwell, pg. 40, 1999.

5 Abbott Frederick, Cottier Thomas, Gurry Francis, International Intellectual Property in an Integrated World Economy 4th edition, Aspen Case Book Series, Wolter Kluwer, pg. 8, 2019.

6 Penrose Edith Tilton, "Economics of the International Patent System", Johns Hopkins Press, pg. 101–107, 1951.

7 Moore Adam, "Intellectual Property: Theory, Privilege, and Pragmatism" 16 Canadian Journal of Law and Jurisprudence at pg. 198 (191–216), 2003.

8 Barett Margrett, "Intellectual Property cases and materials", West Group, pg. 115, 2001.

invention. This on one hand incentivises the inventor by protecting the efforts of the inventor and as well as encourages others to enhance innovation beyond the invention.

1.1 Brief History of Patents

Historically, the first statutory recognition of monopoly right for inventions (and can be termed as ancestor of 'patents' due to the nature of protection to inventions) was provided by the Venetian Senate through its ACT of 1474.[9] This legal right provided the author with a licence to exclude others from making the protected product, for ten years provided the inventor could prove the usefulness and novelty of the invention to qualify for protection.[10] It also had a provision for penalty against infringement wherein the infringer could be summoned by the city Magistrate and obliged to pay hundred ducats and the counterfeit destroyed.[11] This type of continental patent law moved to England in the form of royal grants for inventor privileges where, although the grants provided market monopoly, the aim was more to reward political creditors through issuance of '*Litterae Patentes*' or 'Letters Patent' (open letters – '*patentes*' meaning open) rather than for promoting inventions.[12] The grant of letters patents carrying the message of the monarch under his/her seal became popular under the English crown. Early records show that William Cecil, chief advisor of Elizabeth I used patents to encourage foreign innovators to come and work in Britain by assured protection of their creative work.[13] During the period 1561–1590 of Queen Elizabeth I, England granted about 50 patents.[14] In 1610 '*The Book of Bounty*' was issued and the first judicial precedent can be attributed to the *Cloth worker of Ipswich Case* of 1614 where the ambit of patent as a monopoly right was determined.[15] In 1623 the Statute of Monopolies was

---

9 Mandich Giulio, "Venetian Patents" (1450–1550), 30 J. Patent & Trademark Off. Society, pg. 166, 177, 1948.

10 May Christopher and Sell Susan, "Intellectual Property Rights: A Critical History", Lynne Reinner Publishers, pg. 89, (66–111), 2006.

11 Ibid at 9.

12 Holyoak Jon and Torremans Paul, "Themes in Intellectual Property" in "Intellectual Property Law", pg. 6, Butterworths 1995.

13 Walterscheid Edward, "The early evolution of the United States Patent Law: Antecedents", 76 J. Patent & Trademark Off. Society, Part 1 pg. 697, 1994; Part 2 pg. 849, 1994; Part 3 pg. 771 & 847, 1995 and Part 4 pg. 77, 1996.

14 Graff Garrett, "The Patent Trap" in The Harvard Magazine, July–August 2005.

15 Young David, Watson Antony, Thorley Simon and Miller Richard, "Terrell on the Law of Patent", pg. 2, 3, 14th Edition, London Sweet and Maxwell 1994. The *Clothworkers of Iswich*

promulgated by King James I in England although it gradually lost importance as it became more of a royal favour to well-placed courtiers.

In the United States of America (US), before George Washington signed the United States Patent Grant on 31st July 1790, all inventions by the natives of the colony were owned by the British monarch. Hence if the inventor wanted to protect his invention, he needed to make a special appeal to the governing body of the colony. The first recorded grant of such right was made by the Massachusetts General Court, in 1641, to Samuel Winslow for the novel method of making salt.[16] The US Constitution was the first ever to accord constitutional rights on creative arts and scientific inventions. In *Article 1, Clause 8* it states,

> Congress shall have the power ... to promote the progress of science and useful arts, by securing for limited times to authors and inventors the exclusive right to their respective writings and discoveries.

After the signing of the United States Patent Grant in 1790 under the New Constitution recognising patents for the first time in such a document, the first patent under the statute was granted to Samuel Hopkins of Pittsford, Vermont, for making potash (a chemical used in industrial production of soaps, fertilisers, gunpowder and glass).[17]

Later when the US Patent Act of 4th July 1836 was introduced, patents were numbered and the first patent to be granted under this law was for the invention of traction wheels by John Ruggles in 13th July, 1836.[18] It is interesting to note that even then, questions were raised on the role played by patents on innovation, thus raising doubts as to the purpose of the monopoly in first place. This is clear from a letter of none other than the first examiner of patents in the United States, Thomas Jefferson to Isaac McPherson in 1813.

Case stated, "But if a man hath brought in a new invention and a new trade within the kingdom in peril of his life and consumption of his estate or stock, etc. or if a man hath made a new discovery of anything, in such cases the King of his grace and favour in recompense of his costs and travail may grant by charter unto him that he shall only use such a trade or trafique for a certain time, because at first people of the kingdom are ignorant, and have not the knowledge and skill to use it. But when the patent is expired the King cannot make a new grant thereof".

16 See, https://constitution.congress.gov/browse/article-1/section-8/; https://cambridge.dlconsulting.com/cgi-bin/cambridge?a=d&d=Sentinel19420926-01.2.46 for further discussions.

17 For details of the first patent see, http://www.philly.com/philly/blogs/TODAY-IN-PHILADELPHIA-HISTORY/Samuel-Hopkins-granted-first-patent-in-the-United-States.html.

18 For the first US patent for the invention of traction wheels that was registered see, http://www.patentstation.com/mdm/tractionwheels.htm.

It states,

> He who receives an idea from me, receives instruction himself without lessening mine; as he who lights his taper at mine, receives light without darkening me. That ideas should freely spread from one to another over the globe, for the moral and mutual instruction of man, and improvement of his condition, seems to have been peculiarly and benevolently designed by nature, when she made them, like fire, expansible over all space, without lessening their density in any point, and like the air in which we breathe, move, and have our physical being, incapable of confinement or exclusive appropriation. Inventions then cannot, in nature, be a subject of property. Society may give an exclusive right to the profits arising from them, as an encouragement to men to pursue ideas which may produce utility, but this may or may not be done, according to the will and convenience of the society, without claim or complaint from anybody. *Accordingly, it is a fact, as far as I am informed, that England was, until we copied her, the only country on earth which ever, by a general law, gave a legal right to the exclusive use of an idea. In some other countries it is sometimes done, in a great case, and by a special and personal act, but, generally speaking, other nations have thought that these monopolies produce more embarrassment than advantage to society; and it may be observed that the nations which refuse monopolies of invention, are as fruitful as England in new and useful devices.* (*Emphasis added*)[19]

By early nineteenth century, IP legislation was already established as municipal law in most of the western countries. IP legislation gained international importance from the early 19th century by means of bilateral agreements securing IP protection in neighbouring countries, protecting inventors from unfair competition. It becomes the subject matter of the first multilateral treaties in international economic law with the signing of the Paris Convention for the Protection of Industrial Property in 1883 (Paris Convention) and the Bern Convention (Bern Convention) for the protection of literary and artistic works in 1886, building upon the stock of bilateral agreements and domestic legislation. During the passage of time, different other international conventions and multilateral agreements were signed modifying old rules and introducing changes in new ones to suit the need of the day. However, although there was

19 Thomas Jefferson's letter to Isaac McPherson see, https://founders.archives.gov/documents/Jefferson/03-06-02-0322.

considerable internationalisation of the IP legislation, the essentially municipal character of the law was never questioned. In the modern day, internationalisation of IPRs has reached a stage that countries can hardly resist the contemporary IPRs model, which can no longer be identified solely as a western concept. Today, alienating from the IPRs system would actually mean exclusion from profitable foreign markets as well as barring the home market from efficient products and advanced technologies that can benefit the consumers at home.[20]

1.2 Rationale for Patents

The patent system in a sort of monopoly rights, was known to be first developed by German miners who invented new processes for mining in the Alps, but evolved in the form of statute later in the Venetian state.[21] As it evolved since then, the first Venetian *Act of 1474* had been enacted, it was based on the Faustian exchange.[22] The inventor committing to disclose details about the invention and the way to work it while in exchange the government providing legally protected exclusive rights over the invention.[23] This means that the government contracts to grant restricted market exclusivity to innovators as a reward for the innovation. This provides incentives to them with an intention to enhance innovation and help technology dissemination in return of the knowledge of how to make the invention work.

This rationale of 'private gain in exchange of public good' is clear from the text of the statute enacted by the senate of Venice on 19th March 1474 and quoted below:

20 Hamilton Merci, "The TRIPS Agreement: Imperialistic, Outdated and Overprotective" in Adam D. Moore (eds.), "Intellectual Property: Moral, Legal, and International Dilemmas", Lanham, MD: Rowman & Littlefield, pg. 243, 1997.

21 Ibid at 12, pg. 33, 34, 1995.

22 In the 'Faustian Exchange', often also referred to as or 'Faustian Pact' or 'Faustian Bargain', there is a 'give and take' arrangement. As the legend goes, Dr. Johann Georg Faust or popular in English as Dr. John Faustus, a 15th century alchemist was said to have traded his soul to Mephistopheles (a demon in German folklore acting on behalf of the Devil) to obtain 24 years of unrestrained creativity.

23 Daniele Archibugi and Filippetti Andrea, "The Globalisation of Intellectual Property Rights: Four Learned Lessons and Four Theses", Volume 1, Global Policy, London School of Economics and Political Science and John Wiley and Sons Ltd., Issue 2, pg. 138, May 2010.

> Therefore it is enacted by the authority of this body that whoever makes in this city any new and ingenious device not previously made within our jurisdiction, is bound to register it at the office of the Provveditori di *Comun* as soon as it has been perfected, so that it will be possible to use and apply it. It will be prohibited to anyone else within any of our territories to make any other device in the form or likeness of that one without the author's consent or license, for the term of ten years. But anyone should act thus, the aforesaid author and the inventor would be free to cite him before every office of this city, by which office the aforesaid infringer would be prepared to pay one hundred ducats and his artifice would be immediately destroyed. But our government will be free, at its total pleasure, to take for its own use and needs any of the said devices or instruments, on this condition, that others than the authors may not employ them.

It will also be noticed that in case any proposed invention or technological improvement was presumed to impact the '*guild monopoly*', this government authorised monopoly could be breached on grounds of '*socioeconomic utility*'. Further, the Venetian legislators explicitly excluded some monopolies in fields for public utility, e.g. the manufacturing of eye glasses so that public could access reading glasses through their wide distribution. It is also interesting to note that there was a possibility of revoking the monopoly if the invention did not work. E.g. the right for windmills.[24]

Edith Tilton Penrose's seminal work regarding the international patent system in 1951 addresses the fundamental balance between economic costs and gains.[25] The modern patent system is not restricted to a single country jurisdiction but is more global in nature while the rights are acquired and enjoyed nationally in each jurisdiction. Based on her fundamental work on the international patent system and its rational, Penrose states that there are many factors to be considered while assessing the costs and gains from a patent system. She states that the incentives gained through acquiring the patent for the invention is negligible (for the community) if considered in respect of its global contribution, and only some firms gain. She concludes that, considering the patents system of incentivising is based on restricting the use of new inventions to enable the patentee earn monopoly rent, heavy social costs are incurred. According to her, the costs are not only due to the monopoly rents by

24 Ibid at 10, pg. 59, 60.

25 Ibid at 6, pg. 101–107.

way of royalties but also due to the production lost through use of less efficient technology as the patent restricts use of newer more efficient technology.[26]

One might indeed raise valid concerns regarding the patent system and the possibility of costs overrunning the gains, but the patent system provides time-tested mechanism to incentivise the inventor. One needs to look at the possibility of the internal checks and balance of the system that enables the society through the intervention of the State to regulate the grant and use of the patents in a balanced manner.[27] To balance the private monopoly rights and public interest in an effective manner the patent system embeds several processes. For example, a proper patent examination procedure that caters to the strict patentability criteria helps in maintaining a balanced approach. It must be admitted that in today's complex nature of scientific innovation, a strong patent system without compromising on the public interest in the technological advancement is necessary.[28]

The patent system is based on clear philosophical foundation that has helped it grow in a systematic manner. There are number of philosophies that influenced the development of IP legislation in general, as illustrated below.[29]

1.2.1 *Libertarian*

This approach is based on concepts developed by the British philosopher John Locke. John Locke wrote the "*Two Treatises of Government*" in which he primarily argues that people form governments through social contract for preservation of their natural rights.[30] According to this approach, all people have natural rights to life, liberty and property, which the government of the land is duty-bound to protect. Because this philosophy highlights the natural right of a person, it is often referred to as '*natural right*' philosophy. According to Locke, if a person removes a property from nature and works on it ('mixed his labour') to add value to it, the result is his property. It is in this context that intellectual property would deserve protection.

26 Ibid at 5, pg. 119–124.

27 Ibid at 12, pg. 35, 36.

28 Organisation for Economic Co-operation and Development (OECD) "Overview of recent trends in patent regimes in United States, Japan and Europe" Working Party on Innovation and Technology Policy of the Directorate for Science, Technology and Industry, pg. 5, June 2003.

29 Resnik David, "A pluralistic account of intellectual property", 46 Journal of Business Ethics, Kluwer Law pg. 319–335, 2003.

30 See, https://www.thefederalistpapers.org/wp-content/uploads/2012/12/Two-Treatises-of-Government-by-John-Locke.pdf.

1.2.2 *Self-expression*

This approach is based in the German philosopher Friederich Hegel's philosophy regarding freedom, self-expression and property. It also drew support from other philosophers like S. Avineri, J. Waldron, M. Radin, and John Rawls. According to this view, intellectual property can act as a medium for a person's self-expression and development because it helps a person to identify himself or herself with the outside world and allow control over his or her expression and creativity as his or her property.

1.2.3 *Utilitarian*

The utilitarian approach can be said to be the main foundation of IPRs today, propounded by the English philosopher Jeremy Bentham in 1780.[31] According to his utilitarian philosophy, an act can be considered as utility based on whether it brings more pleasure, happiness or prevents pain or unhappiness than any other alternative. The characteristics of bringing more pleasure or removing pain can be stated to result in more welfare enhancing for people. Patents protection is hence justified since they increase utility in society by encouraging artists, authors and inventors through rewards and incentives; thus, they contribute to the enhancement of arts, science and technology. To be more precise, Bentham justifies patents as a way of reward for labour, where he categorises labour as the physical labour needed to bring an effect and the skill and mental power needed for the labour. After considering different possible incentives, he concludes that a temporary monopoly to the author of the invention in exclusion of all others is the appropriate '*recompense*' for such industriousness, genius and ingenuity that goes into the invention.

This philosophy also influenced economist John Stuart Mill who even argued from a human rights perspective and stated that allowing others to freely use the inventor's works without his consent would be immoral. According to him the inventor needs to be both compensated and rewarded. He states that although at times pecuniary grants are made to the inventor, it cannot suffice and an exclusive privilege for certain period is preferable.[32]

1.2.4 *Human Rights*

Further expanding on the human rights aspect of the Utilitarian philosophy that was influenced by economist John Stuart Mill as discussed earlier in

---

31 Bentham Jeremy, "Introduction to the Principles of Morals and Legislation" written in 1780 and published in 1789. See discussion, https://www.utilitarianism.com/bentham.htm.

32 Fisher Matt, "Fundamentals of patent law: Interpretation and scope of protection", Bloomsbury, pg. 69, 70, 2007.

this chapter, there has been contemporary efforts in linking IPRs and human rights. The logic being, ability to use an inventor or creator's works without his/her consent would be immoral and against his/her human rights. It is important to address the human rights approach since it is increasingly becoming important and relevant. The development of doctrinal human rights as a legal discipline has been more in public international law and has evolved in national jurisdictions locally as part of Constitutional law, only after the World War II. On the contrary patents and copyrights as two of the mainstream IP protection has been well-established since very long time as human creativity involves reward from one's labour and cannot be delinked from rights of the human. Further, it will be noticed that international agreements like the TRIPS Agreement provides a direct link between sustainable development goals and human rights through the objectives of Article 7 and 8 of the Agreement of societal gains and public interest.[33]

On a broader perspective if one considers IPRs in perspective of multilateral trade laws, it is important to consider the similarities and differences between multilateral trade regulations and human rights. In both general approach and substantive rights between the principles of human rights covenants and the international trade regulations there are distinct similarities. The covenants on human rights ensure individual freedom, non-discrimination, equal opportunities and respect for rule of law while on the same note, principles of non-discrimination, most-favoured nation national treatment and rule-based dispute settlement mechanisms are the fundamentals of the multilateral trade regulations.[34] However there are some differences between the two too, the main aim of the multilateral trading system is to create welfare enhancing economic environment. Although it can be said that this economic welfare would result in a conducive human rights atmosphere, this has never been established with an aim to enforce human rights.[35] It has also been argued that given the recognition of IPRs as individual rights hence considering it as human rights would justify application of interpretation methods for human rights to certain IPRs to balance private rights and public interests.[36]

33 Ibid at 5, pg. 172, 173, 184.

34 Petersmann Ernst-Ulrich, "The WTO Constitution and Huma Rights", Journal of International Economic Law, pg. 19–25, 2000.

35 Lim Hoe, "Trade and Human Rights: What's at Issue?", 2 Journal of World Trade, Volume 35, pg. 5, 2001.

36 Helfer R. Lawrence, "Adjudicating Copyright Claims Under the TRIPS Agreement: The Case for a European Human Rights Analogy", in 39 Harvard International Law Journal, pg. 396, (357–441), 1998. Available at, https://scholarship.law.duke.edu/cgi/viewcontent.cgi?article=2648&context=faculty_scholarship.

The human rights approach bases its philosophy on owning property being a fundamental right and as such includes both tangible and intangible property. It evolves from the United Nations' recognition of one's right to own property, provided in *Article 17.1* of the Universal Declaration of Human Rights. But it must also be noted that it does not specifically mention IPRs in any manner, hence interpretation varies.[37] *Article 17* of the Universal Declaration of Human Rights states:

(1) Everyone has the right to own property.
(2) No one shall be arbitrarily deprived of his property.

One also needs to take into consideration that although protected, the nature of property rights and its treatment given by sovereign states differ from one another. For example, the Indian Constitution was amended in 1977 (given effect in 1978) to remove the right to acquire, hold and dispose of property as a fundamental right. At the same time, the right to property was not totally abolished in India, it was made statutory right through insertion of *Article 300 (A)* to assure that a person would not be deprived from owning a property, '*... save by authority of law.*' Hence, while the state has authority to take over a citizen's property, it needs to be through due process of law where the person owning the property has the right of appropriate compensation.[38]

It is noteworthy that irrespective of the nature of property rights that is accorded by a sovereign state, the United Nations also recognises the underlying moral and material interests resulting from one's creativity.

Article 27 of the Universal Declaration of Human Rights states:

(1) Everyone has the right to freely participate in the cultural life of the community, to enjoy the arts and to share in scientific advancement and its benefits.
(2) Everyone has the right to the protection of the moral and material interests resulting from any scientific, literary or artistic production of which he is the author.[39]

Similarly, the Covenant on Economic, Social and Cultural Rights of 1966 also provides in *Article 15*:

37 Peter Drahos, "Intellectual Property and Human Rights", Intellectual Property Quarterly, pg. 6,7, 1999. Available at, https://www.researchgate.net/publication/285855355_Intellectual_property_and_human_rights.

38 https://www.india.gov.in/my-government/constitution-india/amendments/constitution-india-forty-fourth-amendment-act-1978.

39 https://www.un.org/en/about-us/universal-declaration-of-human-rights.

1 (c) To benefit from the production of the moral and material interests resulting from any scientific, literary and artistic production of which he is the author.

2. The steps to be taken by the States to the present Covenant to achieve the full realisation of this right shall include those necessary for the conversation, the development and diffusion of science and culture.[40]

Even the more recent Declaration of Rights of Indigenous People of 2007 protects traditional knowledge and traditional cultural expressions where *Article 31* states:

1. Indigenous people have the right to maintain, control, protect and develop their traditional cultural expressions, as well as the manifestations of their sciences, technologies and cultures, including human and generic resources, seeds, medicines, knowledge of their properties of fauna and flora, oral traditions, literatures, designs, sports and traditional games and visual and performing arts. They also have the right to maintain, control, protect and develop their intellectual property over such cultural heritage, traditional knowledge, and traditional cultural expressions.
2. In conjunction with indigenous peoples, States shall take effective measures to recognise and protect the exercise of these rights.[41]

From the above one might be tempted to question whether '*the moral, legal, political and economic justifications of human rights appropriate for intellectual property rights? Has the TRIPS Agreement been influenced by the 'human rights revolution' of the 1990s?*' Such analogy needs to be considered however, considering that human rights are not mentioned in any WTO regulations and that '*moral rights*' had been specifically kept outside the TRIPS, there was no intention of linking the public interest clauses related to IPRS with human rights.[42]

40 https://www.ohchr.org/en/professionalinterest/pages/cescr.aspx.

41 https://www.un.org/development/desa/indigenouspeoples/wp-content/uploads/sites/19/2018/11/UNDRIP_E_web.pdf.

42 Petersmann Ernst-Ulrich, "The WTO Constitution and the Millennium Round", in Bronckers M. and Quick R. eds. "New Directions in International Economic Law", Kluwer, pgs. 125, 131, (111–133), 2000.

1.2.5 *Distributive Justice*

This approach advocates that the creator of something new, e.g. inventors and authors, should be rewarded by the granting of some exclusive rights since they provide a service to society through their contribution. It would be unjust to allow people who have not contributed to the new creation to 'free ride' on the work done by the creator.

1.2.6 *Privacy*

This approach supports some specific types of IPRs, such as trade secrets and confidential business information. According to this view, intellectual property protection for business and trade secrets is justified since they accord protection to commercially valuable confidential information. However, such a justification is exclusively applicable to confidential information and would not qualify for other types of intellectual property rights, e.g. patents (where disclosure is necessary) or trademarks (which are required to be seen by people).

1.2.7 *Egalitarian*

This approach deals with how intellectual property rights affect the distribution of the protected property. It brings in a balance between the philosophy of individual rights on one hand, and the Marxist philosophy on the other, which is against private property rights (irrespective of whether they are tangible or intangible). This philosophy was propagated by John Rawls (although not specifically from the intellectual property perspective). His '*Theory of Justice*' states that justice is an essential of well-ordered societies that are based on basic liberties and equal rights for all which should emanate into equal opportunities to the least advantaged. In his own words,

> the guiding idea is that the principles of justice for the basic structure of society are the object of the original agreement. They are the principles that free and rational persons concerned to further their own interests would accept in an initial position of equality as defining the fundamental terms of their association. These principles are to regulate all further agreements; they specify the kinds of social cooperation that can be entered into and the forms of government that can be established.[43]

---

43 Rawls John, "A Theory of Justice", Library of Congress Cataloging-in-Publication Data 1921, Revised Edition, Harvard University Press, Pg. 10, 1971. Available at, https://giuseppecapograssi.files.wordpress.com/2014/08/rawls99.pdf.

The '*Utilitarian approach*' and the '*Natural rights*' or '*Libertarian approach*' are the two philosophies that play the most important roles among the different ones that has been enumerated above. The utilitarian approach is based on the economic perspective to generate the greatest welfare for society at large and to create suitable incentives for investment. Accordingly, the rights of inventors need to be protected to prevent third parties who have not contributed to the invention, from copying the work. Thus, profiting on the inventor's cost can be restricted and at the same time the innovator can be provided incentives.

In the latter approach, rights are justified from the perspective of the creator's moral rights. This is based on the notion that since the creator has put in labour to create something new, the creator should be allowed to restrict others from using or enjoying it without his or her prior consent. As elaborated earlier in the utilitarian philosophy and as propagated by economist John Stuart Mill, it is argued that considering the physical and mental labour that goes into an invention, the inventor should be able to protect the invention. Any unauthorised use of such invention would be a violation of the inventor's moral rights, hence his or her human rights.[44]

Both philosophies aim to support incentives for further innovation through patents. The problem arises when one group wants the rights to be the mandatory representation of their moral and economic aspirations while others view them as public rights inappropriate for private ownership. In such circumstances, the most appropriate path can be a balanced approach by which IPRs are allowed for innovation but regulated for purposes of social and economic policy.[45] Apart from this, the argument that patents are not essential for innovation needs to be examined too.[46] One of the prominent arguments detaching innovation from the patent system is that there are complex motives for inventors to invent and hence it cannot be said that only patents encourage invention. One might even argue that instead, it facilitates investors to invest in manufacturing and distribution of the patented products.

> The question is no longer whether the patent system stimulates inventive talents to use more of their time and energy than they otherwise would for the development of new technology, but rather whether it stimulates

44 Ibid at 32, pg. 69.

45 Maskus Keith, "Globalisation and the Economics of Intellectual Property Rights: Dancing the Dual Distortion", in "Intellectual Property Rights in the Global Economy", Institute for International Economics, Washington D.C. pg. 27, 28, August 2000.

46 Gutterman Alan, "Innovation and Competition Policy", Kluwer Law, pg. 36, 37, 1997.

business corporations to hire more of these talents than they otherwise would for this task.[47]

Whether patents encourage innovation through direct incentives or because of attracting investments, the impacts of such innovations need to spill over industry and contribute to society positively.[48]

1.3 Specific Characteristics of Intellectual Property Rights

On careful study it will be noticed that IPRs have some specific characteristics. They are:

a. Negative rights – IPRs are intangible property rights that protect innovations and provide incentive to the innovator. It is important to note that like any (physical) property right, IPRs are also negative rights which mean that it excludes third parties from using, enjoying or in any way exploiting the rights.[49] This means that this is a right given to the owner of IPRs to restrict others from using, selling or doing any other activity with the IPRs without the owner's prior consent.
b. Exclusive rights – IPRs allow certain amount of exclusivity in the market for a limited period to encourage creative intellectual output, both in the field of science and technology and art and culture. Protection is required to restrict competitors from usurping the creators work without taking permission of the creator. For this reason, the IP owner is allowed lead time against competitors and enable them to commercially gain by way of a justified but restrictive exclusivity.[50] This time-bound exclusivity enables the IP owner to gain sufficient exclusivity to generate some additional market power through restricting output, however it cannot create monopoly sufficient to drive out competing alternatives from the market. It must also be

47 Machlup Fritz, "An Economic Review of the Patent System", Study No. 5, "Study of the Subcommittee on Patents, Trademarks and Copyrights of the Committee on the Judiciary, US Senate", pg. 36, 1958.

48 Moir Hazel, "What are the costs and benefits of patent systems?", in Arup Christopher and Caenegem William van (eds.), "Intellectual Property Policy Reform", Edward Elgar Publishing Ltd., pg. 31, 36, (29–54), 2009.

49 Ibid at 9, pg. 12.

50 Cornish William, D. Llewelyn and T. Alpine, "Intellectual Property: Patents, Copyrights, Trade Marks and Allied Rights", Sweet & Maxwell, pg. 6–8, 2010.

noted that unlike unlimited duration of trademarks or long tenure of copyrights, patents are of limited nature for 20 years from grant (filing) specifically to enable diffusion of the scientific and technological invention thus balancing private rights and public interests. From this perspective, IPRS also are qualified as private rights. They deploy their effects among competitors and do not primarily establish a vertical relationship. The point of view does not consider the nature of patents as publicly granted monopoly rights by government.

c. Ubiquitous in nature – A careful study of IPRS will show that they are 'Ubiquitous' in nature, which means that the intellectual property aspect of the physical goods exists independent of the goods incorporating such rights. Since the rights occur simultaneously for all goods irrespective of where the goods are being marketed, all the products manufactured in a single batch will be protected at the same time even if they are physically located in different places (subject to the condition that protection is accorded to them through due process of law). In other words, the IPRS follow the product downstream and as such the owner of the IPRS would be able to control the movement of the product. Hence this ubiquitous nature of IPRS enables it to be a broad right with far-reaching effects that can control many markets at the same time.[51] Hence the ubiquitous nature of the right might result in distortion of the market in favour of the right holder.

From the above it will be clear that each of the different approaches set certain values and goals and as such, are important. Each has its own strengths and weaknesses thus they can complement each other if addressed from a pluralistic approach. One of the major characteristics of patent law and IPRS in general, is that they are non-exclusive in nature. This means that two persons can acquire, possess and enjoy the intangible property at the same time without preventing each other from doing the same. Moreover, most of the time when a product is marketed under a trademark often along with a logo and even a trade-dress. While the technology in the product may be protected by patents, the brand and logo of the product may be protected trademark law. Considering that trademark law protects the brand name and logo and not used for market segregation, in most jurisdiction the trademark exhausts internationally. Profit motive can influence a patent holder to extend the legitimate patent exclusivity to a dominant monopoly beyond its ambit, leading to a

51 Ibid at 5, pg. 99, 100, (98–102).

situation of patent abuse. Any such attempt would distort the market and have anti-competitive effect and as such need to be regulated. In such scenario, a pluralistic approach to such IPRs become important in order to balance private rights and public interests and restrict possibilities of adverse effect on market competition.

CHAPTER 2

Ubiquity and Exhaustion Doctrine: Ubiquity in Patents

The patent right allows the right holder to restrict manufacture, use, sell or distribute it by any other way without the permission of the owner. The ubiquitous nature of the right enables it to exist independent of the physical product itself in each of the product at any given time. Hence a single patent right can effectively restrict the use or commercialisation of the product at any given time even if the patent is limited to a particular component of the product. This is because the patent can control the entire supply chain of the product at any given time since they exist in different markets at the same time, thus providing significant market power in the hands of the patent holder.

Given the enormous power in the hands of the patent owner to control the use, sell or any form of distribution of the product, the profit motive can entail possibility of misuse or abuse of such power. For example, a patent holder 'A', licenses the patent to 'B' to manufacture it in country 'Yellow' and to 'C' in country 'Blue' against payment of negotiated royalties. B and C respectively manufactures the products in a legitimate manner under the patent licenses and tries to sell it in the international market. But as soon as B and C tries to sell it in a different market e.g. in countries 'Green', 'Red', and others, A can stop B and C by exercising his patent rights at any given time simultaneously, unless controlled through checks and balance measures. Thus, the ubiquitous nature of the patent enables A to restrict competition at multiple places simultaneously and in this case, even after B and C pays royalty in lieu of the innovator's lead time. One needs to note that the royalty received is for the innovation introduced and not for profiteering through different market allocation.

For this reason, it is important to address ubiquity in patents in an appropriate manner so that it does not restrict free movement of goods in the market. To this effect, the doctrine of exhaustion (Erschöpfung) was developed and introduced by the German professor Kohler in the 19th Century and eventually adopted by courts and legislation, inherently limiting such powers. However at the time of propounding the concept, he did not spell out the geographical scope of exhaustion leading to some contradicting interpretations.[52]

52 Reichgericht in Zivilsachen (RGZ) 50, 362 – "*Duotal*", cited by Heath Christopher, "Legal Concepts of Exhaustion and Parallel Imports", in Heath Christopher (ed.), "Parallel

© SANTANU MUKHERJEE, 2023 | DOI:10.1163/9789004542815_004

Exhaustion of the patent right provides the necessary balance needed in the patent system to address ubiquity by restraining enforcement of patents for distribution of the patented product after first sale.[53] According to the '*doctrine of exhaustion*', if any product protected by IPRS is put on the market by way of use, sale or any other form of distribution including licensing, by the right holder or by someone else with his/her consent, then the right holder exhausts the ability to exercise his IPRS over the goods and restrict its further sale or use. This can happen by way of the first sale of the patented goods and known as the '*first sale doctrine*' in the US.[54] By way of addressing ubiquity in patents, exhaustion of patents establishes itself as an available policy balance between private ownership rights on one hand and public interest via consumer access on the other hand.[55] In case the exhaustion is applied globally, it enables consumers greater access of patented products in any market of the world after they are legitimately distributed in any market.[56]

Patent exhaustion or non-exhaustion developed in different jurisdictions and got established with certain variations. In the United Kingdom (UK), the practice was not based on general exhaustion of the IPRS but on contractual agreement between the holder of the IPRS and the buyer as to the after-sale treatment of the IP in the product. In absence of any contractual restriction, an '*Implied License*' to the buyer over the IP in the product would result. In Germany, the country of origin of the doctrine of exhaustion, and in other European countries, it developed as '*Exhaustion*' of the IPRS. It was eventually adopted also by the European Union. In the United States, the concept emerged as the '*First Sale*' doctrine.

Imports in Asia", Kluwer Law International, 2004. Also see, Cottier Thomas, "Parallel Trade and Exhaustion of Intellectual Property in WTO Law Revisited", in Ruse Khan Grosse Henning & Metzger Axel (eds.), "Intellectual Property Ordering Beyond Borders", Cambridge University Press, pg. 192 (189–232), 2022.

53 Cottier Thomas and Stucki Marc, "Conflit entre importations paralléle et propriéte intellectuelle? Actes du colloque de Lausanne, comparativa no. 60" translated by Meitinger Ingo as, "Parallel Imports in Patents, Copyrights and Industrial Design Law – The Scope of European and International Public Law", and reprinted in The International Intellectual Property System Commentary and Materials –Part 1, Kluwer Law International, pg. 606, 1999.

54 Ibid at 50. pg. 58.

55 Ganslandt Mattias, Maskus Keith, "Intellectual Property Rights, Parallel Imports and Strategic Behaviour", Journal of Economic Law, pg. 1, 2, 2007.

56 Meitinger Ingo, "Parallel Imports into Switzerland – A Spot of Global Free Trade amidst Fortress Europe?" in Cottier Thomas and Mavroidis Petros (eds.), "Intellectual Property: Trade, Competition, and Sustainable Development", Michigan University Press, pg. 21, 219, 2003.

Exhaustion or implied license or first sale doctrine, is an affirmative defence in a patent infringement action often with claims of equitable estoppels (also known as legal estoppels). The three variations are discussed in greater detail in Chapter 4 while elaborating the exhaustion practice in different legal jurisdictions of the world.

2.1 Doctrine of Implied License

The doctrine of implied license as practised in the UK was later exported to different commonwealth countries through the colonization route. It was also adopted by other countries, however, with the passage of time some of these countries changed their exhaustion or non-exhaustion regime through legislative amendments or judicial interpretation. As per the doctrine, once an IPRS product is sold or distributed legally in any manner, it is implied that the IPRS embedded in the product is licensed for life of the patent to the buyer along with the transfer of the right to the physical property. As such, if the holder wants to retain control over the IPRS in that product, the holder needs to put specific notice on the product informing the buyer that IPRS has not been licensed or have a contractual agreement specifically restricting the license of the patented product. The doctrine flows from the decision of the English High Court in *Betts v. Willimott*[57] and further elaborated in *National Phonograph Co. of Australia v. Menck*[58] where it allowed the patent holder to control further distribution only if expressly notified to the purchaser.[59]

In any situation where there is no contractual restriction by the patent holder determining further sale of the patented product, the sale of the physical product would imply that the IP in the product is automatically licensed to the purchaser. This means, if the patent holder does not put a written notice, restraining further sale of the patented product or determining the market, it would be implied that the patent holder does not intend to restrict further distribution of the patented product. It is interesting to note that in jurisdictions where the doctrine of implied license is practiced, contractual law supersedes IPRS laws. In some jurisdictions, if there is a statutory provision for specific exhaustion of rights, any restriction imposed via contracts based on

57 *Betts v. Willimott*, [1871] 6 L.R.Ch. 239, 245.

58 *National Phonograph Co. of Australia v. Menck* [1911] 28 R.P.C. 229.

59 Heath Christopher, "Patent Exhaustion rules and self-replacing technologies", in Calboli Irene and Edward Lee (eds.), "Research handbook on Intellectual Property Exhaustion and Parallel Imports", Edward Elgar Publishing Ltd., pg. 291, (289–307), 2016.

the doctrine of implied license would not stand good. This was practiced in the UK before it absorbed the EPO practice. It is now to be seen after Brexit takes effect, whether UK would continue with the European practice of regional exhaustion or would return to its old practice of implied license. So far, the UK government has engaged in stakeholder consultations as to the way forward without any determination yet.

2.2 Doctrine of First Sale

As per the first sale doctrine, once the patent owner sells the patented product, s/he cannot exercise the patent rights to restrict others from using, selling or distributing the patented product further down the chain. In other words, with the first unrestricted sale of the patented product, the patent owner exhausts the market control over distribution of the original product through patent rights. This means that the patent holder can enjoy from the patented product including selling it, restrain unauthorised manufacturing of it, or even destroy it, but cannot enforce the patent to restrain others from further selling or distributing it.[60]

An important criterion of the patent system is the enabling disclosure that helps the technological innovation to be available to the public for further innovation. In order to obtain a patent grant, the applicant needs to disclose details of the patent sufficiently enough so that a person skilled in the art can perform the patented technology. The idea is to allow a person to build on the invention from the description of the patent and it's working, as provided in the patent without application of further inventive step.[61] It is important to note that the enabling disclosure enables a person to understand the patented technology and how it works. However, it does not allow any third party to work the patent without the patentee's authorisation. As such, disclosure does not in any way exhaust the rights held by the patentee or in case of an implied license it does not nullify the rights to restrain others from manufacturing. In exhaustion of patents or in case of implied license only the rights of distribution exhaust or is licensed.

An important logic to have an exclusivity-based incentive system is that it can provide the inventor, the patent holder, with a legitimate reward based balanced legal regime. The patent system provides with a time-bound exclusivity

60 Haedicke Maximilian and Timman Henrik, "Patent Law A handbook on European and German Patent law", C.H. Beck, pg. 22, para 74, 2014.

61 Ibid at 50, pg. 225, 2003.

to the inventor when s/he applies for a patent, so that the patented invention can be exploited within a stipulated time while at the same time, restraining others from using it without permission. The doctrine of first sale acts as checks and balance measure as to what extent the patent owner can exploit the invention in the market. The doctrine establishes that once the patent owner places the product in the market the first time, s/he is rewarded sufficiently in the form of patent royalty, hence s/he cannot seek royalty again. Seeking royalty multiple times shall result additional profiting through market segregation and distort the market.

2.3 Exhaustion of Patent Rights

The doctrine of '*Exhaustion*' is based on the principle that once the patent owner uses the patented product or places it in the market by sale or any other means s/he loses the right to restrict the purchaser from further use or sale of the IPRS embedded product, thus the patent right exhausts. The main intention of the exhaustion principle is to restrict the control of markets and of collection of multiple rewards by enforcing the patents more than once through market segregation. Fundamentally, once the patented product is used or sold, it already collects the financial reward by way of royalty / license fees and is converted into an economically realisable, marketable commodity. Allowing further exercise of the same patent would be essentially against the principle of free movement of goods. However, it is important to note that exhaustion only applies to original goods. IP rights continue to be effective in relation to counterfeits and items produced under violation of exclusive rights. This is of particular importance in trademark and copyright, but also applies to patented products.

From purely IPRS perspective, there can be two different modes of exhaustion, '*National Exhaustion*' and '*International Exhaustion*'. A third form of exhaustion, namely '*Regional Exhaustion*', was introduced by the European Court of Justice (ECJ) through its interpretations and judgements and later got codified.[62] The ECJ harmonized exhaustion regime within Europe to facilitate trade between the members resulting in the regional exhaustion, the third form of exhaustion, a hybrid of national and international exhaustion.

The three different types of exhaustion for all IPRS are elaborated below:

62 Slotboom Marco, "The Exhaustion of Intellectual Property Rights, Different Approaches in EC and WTO Law", 6 The Journal of World Intellectual Property, pg. 425, 426, 2003.

> National Exhaustion – IP rights cannot be used to restrict the marketing of products that have been placed on the national market by or with the consent of the IP right holder within that national market. However, the IP right holder can prevent parallel imports of his product from a foreign country.
>
> Regional Exhaustion – IP rights cannot be used to prevent the marketing of goods anywhere in a certain region (e.g. A free trade zone or a customs union, such as the EC) once the goods have been put on the market somewhere in that region by or with the consent of the IP right holder. The IP right holder can, however, prevent the importation of these goods from outside the region in question.
>
> International Exhaustion – IP rights cannot be used to prevent the marketing of a good by other persons anywhere in the world once his good has been placed on the market by or with the consent of the right holder.[63]

From the above explanation in all the three cases of exhaustion, a right holder exhausts her/his IPRs once s/he puts the IP protected goods in the market. The difference in the three modes of exhaustion is that while in national exhaustion the right exhausts only to the extent when the goods are placed in the national domestic market. In regional exhaustion the geographical boundary extends to not just the national domestic market but within the whole region, a free trade area or a customs union (CU). In case of international exhaustion, the right owner relinquishes his right on putting his good on any market irrespective of whether it is domestic or the international market. The argument that, as patent laws of different countries vary considerably and are held by unconnected owners, uniform exhaustion might distort the market. Such argument stands outdated with the Agreement on Trade Related aspects of Intellectual Property Rights (TRIPS) of the World Trade Organisation (WTO) being operational. The TRIPS has brought in a minimum level of protection that does not hinder adoption of a single form of exhaustion for the WTO members, in fact such adoption would facilitate multilateral trade.

It has been highlighted that patent holders often sell their products at different prices in different markets. Prices also differ in different markets due to low manufacturing costs and other comparative advantages when produced

63 Merwe Van der L. A., "The Exhaustion of Rights in Patent Law with specific emphasis on the issue of parallel importation", 3 Intellectual Property Quarterly, pg. 288, 2000.

under licensees, resulting in arbitrage. Based on such arbitrage, an independent trader can acquire IP products legitimately from where it is cheaper and sell them in a market where the price of such IP products sold through authorised distributor is costlier. In the process, sell it at a price lower than that of the authorised distributor in that market and financially gain from the arbitrage.

CHAPTER 3

Economics of Patents and Economic Rationale for Exhaustion in Relation to International Trade

3.1

3.1.1 *The Economics of Patents*

In the earlier chapters while discussing the rational for the patent system, the economic incentive for the inventor became most prominent among all reasons. It was also discussed by Edith Tilton Penrose where it was very clearly stated that patent protection is based on economic costs and gains. So, the loss from restricting the use of inventions and creating a monopoly situation can be balanced depending on factors like size of the national market, nature of national industry, motivation of inventor and the method of financing available to the inventor.[64] However the nature of knowledge being a public good, irrespective of its use by any person at any given time would not restrain use by others, once placed in the market. Hence once made public, it is not possible to restrict use and enjoyment by others. In such scenario even when the inventor puts in labour and spends time and money, others can ride on the invention without bearing any of the costs or in other words, free ride on the inventor's efforts. Thus, the intangible nature of the IP makes it easily vulnerable to copying and replication creating inherent externalities. These inherent externalities invariably lead to market failure and as a result, attract only low levels of inefficient innovation. The patent system helps avert such market failure by curving out property rights for the inventions of the inventors.[65] These property rights on human creativity leading to invention are in line with traditional property rights and based on freedom of choice, as it should be in the case of any standard goods and services.[66]

---

64 Ibid at 5, See "The Summary and Conclusions" chapter of Penrose Edith Tilton, "Economics of the International Patent System" reproduced, pg. 121.

65 Arrow Kenneth, "Economic Welfare and the Allocation of Resources for Invention", in the "Rate and Direction of Inventive Activity: Economic and Social Factors", Nelson (ed.), pg. 609, 1962. Also see, "The Summary and Conclusions" chapter of Edith Tilton Penrose, "Economics of the International Patent System" reproduced. Pg. 8, 2019.

66 Barzel Yoram, "Economic Analysis of Property Rights", Cambridge University Press 2nd edition, 1989.

DOI:10.1163/9789004542815_005

Microeconomics models are based on perfect market competition wherein price is the sole criteria that determines competition. This is based on the concept that such markets are completely homogenous and there are number of suppliers in the market. Such market situation leads to perfect competition wherein there is social surplus consisting of consumer's surplus and producer's surplus. However, in the real market situation the scenario is different, there is hardly perfect competition. The products are not homogenous in nature and thus price does not solely influence the consumer's market behaviour, quality also plays a vital role. Mandatory enabling disclosure to obtain patents enables opening up of primary research through such processes and encourages follow-up innovations while reducing wasteful innovation races.[67] In such a situation patent enhances market performances by excluding products (resulting from innovative technologies and thus promising better quality) from market competition for a short period.

Early works of the noted economist Fritz Machlup in his report to the US Senate states that the most relevant economic reason for the patent system is the possibility of commercialisation of new products. Considering the economic case in favour of the patent system, the fundamental issue he says, is more commercial than the incentive to the inventor.[68] He argues that the patent system provides the possibility of the inventors to obtain investments to enable production based on the invention and that is the fundamental economic reason for the patent system to sustain and succeed. Interesting to note that he discounts the importance of enabling disclosure as a social good and argues that it is the possibility to protect the invention from unauthorised use that is most crucial.[69]

The fact that one of the economic reasons for the patent system is to provide legal protection from copies, inventors would invariably try to protect their inventions and in absence of patents would opt for some other means. D. D. Friedman, W. M. Landes and R. A. Posner argues that in absence of patents there would be a tendency of protecting the inventions through trade secrets. This would take away transparency and the possibility of enabling disclosure and foreclose possibilities of enhanced research and innovation based on published patent data.[70] Even if we accept Machlup's position for argument's sake,

67 Kitch Edmund, "The Nature and Function of the Patent System", Journal of Law and Economics 20, pgs. 265–290, 1977. Available at, http://www.law.nyu.edu/sites/default/files/upload_documents/Kitch.pdf.

68 Ibid at 47, pg. 36.

69 Ibid at 5, pg. 119.

70 Friedman David, Landes William and Posner Richard, "Some Economics of Trade Secret Law", Journal of Economic Perspectives, pg. 61–72, 1991.

that the enabling disclosure is nothing but an illusion, the fact that throughout ages many patents have built on published patent data and by means of patent landscaping, disclosure remains crucial to the patent system.

To correct market failures, countries use their IPRs in a manner that is best suited to their industries and markets. Here it must be noted that laws on IPRs including patent law is territorial in nature, thus there are often differences in the patent law of one country from another. For this reason, trade between countries having different parameters in their patent rights could face market distortion. For example, if a country's patent protection is weak while in another it is stricter, competitors of the patent holder in a country with weaker protection would be able to gain undue benefit. They would prefer to piggyback on the investments made by the patent holder without any substantial investment and gain commercially when these products are traded internationally. IPRs were brought within the purview of WTO through the TRIPS Agreement based on this reason. The TRIPS Agreement introduced minimum standards of protection of IPRs, harmonising the bottom floor of protection of IPR laws of members. Through this harmonisation the transaction costs incurred in operating in different regulatory jurisdictions is reduced (although not eliminated since TRIPS does not bring 100% harmonisation of IP laws).[71]

Patents are granted to inventors as lead-time over competitors by way of market exclusivity for their contribution to scientific and technological development. It also helps to recover fixed costs incurred in research and development. It is found that when the fixed costs are high and it is easier to invent around the patent or copy the invention, greater patent protection is needed to provide sufficient incentives.[72] As discussed earlier, the secondary reason for patents is based on the logic that if the inventor was not provided with legal protection, then free riding on the invention would lead to unfair gain at the expense of the inventor. The patent holder is thus provided sufficient market exclusivity that act as monetary incentive enabling supra-normal profit. The main economic reason is that when the elasticity of demand is low due to lack of competition, the patent holder would be able to charge more and cover its expenses as well as make monetary gains. Here it should not be ignored that countries might not have economic interest in defending inventions via patents if the monetary gains from such inventions accrue to inventors in other

71 Braga Carlos Primo and Fink Carsten, "The relationship between intellectual property rights and foreign direct investment", Duke Journal of Comparative and International Law, pg. 168, 169, (163–186) 1998.

72 Landes William and Posner Richard, "The Economic Structure of Intellectual Property Law", The Belknap Press of Harvard University Press, pg. 300, 2003.

countries. For this reason, there will be a big tendency to make copies of the invention at marginal cost of follow up R&D investment.[73]

The main reason for providing patents is to balance the externalities in producing new technologies at one hand, and the '*collective good*' character of these technologies on the other hand since the social value is often higher than the private value resulting in market failure even in perfect competition.[74] In such circumstances the role of patent is to correct the market failure by creating incentives to invest and by increasing the private value of the new technology. However, there is also a counter argument that knowledge assets like new technology are products of the mind and are hence public goods that should not be privatised. Subsequently the argument follows that governments should intervene in production of such knowledge assets and maintain them as public goods, mainly by funding research in Universities or R&D related to defence. They can themselves create knowledge (which can be funded by taxes) and make it available free of cost to the public or provide subsidies to private individuals or bodies to produce such knowledge (the subsidies can be financed by taxes).[75]

Richard Nelson elaborates on this further and states that profit-seeking firms might not be able to capitalise on all the investment made in fundamental scientific research due to uncertainties resulting from imitators. Hence as these profit-seeking firms are basically risk-averse, they would be constrained to invest in fundamental research.[76] True, profit-seeking firms might be averse to investing in fundamental research and such research would likely be conducted in Universities and R&D institutions. However even in such cases of public funded research, role of patents would still be crucial. There might not be an interest in private proprietorship of public-funded research *per se*, but when such research would need to move to the next stage, transforming the invention to a new product, patents would help in technology transfer through

73 Maskus Keith and Reichman Jerome, "The Globalization of Private Knowledge Goods and the Privatization of Global Public Goods", 7 (2) Journal of International Economic Law, pg. 285, (279–320) 2004.

74 Dijk Theon van, "The Economic Theory of Patents: A Survey", MERIT Research Memorandum 2/94–017, Maastricht Economic Research Institute on Innovation and Technology, Netherlands, pg. 7, 1994.

75 Dasgupta Partha, "The Economic theory of Technology Policy: An Introduction" in Dasgupta Partha and Stoneman Paul (eds.), "Economic Policy and Technological Performance", Cambridge University Press, Pg. 7–20, 1987.

76 Nelson Richard, "Introduction to the Rate and Direction of Inventive Activity: Economic and Social Factors" in Nelson Richard (ed.), "The Rate ... Factor", Princeton University Press, pgs. 1–16, 1962.

licensing or assignment of the technology. Typically, patents would help in market valuation of the research in a manner that the private party interested in the invention can use the patent to transition from laboratory to the market via licensing or assignment.[77]

It must not be ignored that since patents are related to knowledge assets, they enhance appropriability of knowledge and boost investment in R&D. For this reason, they are the solution to the '*quasi-public good*' characteristic of knowledge assets. On the other hand, they can also cause market distortion since the market exclusivity can lead to an abusive monopoly, inappropriately increasing the patent holder's market power. Thus, it is important to note that although patents are granted to increase the private value of the new technology, certain checks and balances are necessary to make sure that the private value does not supersede the social value. From the above analysis it can be stated that the basic requirements of enabling disclosure, inventive step and utility are the essentials to minimise the social costs. Similarly patent rights have restricted duration of 20 years from grant (filing) with the same intention of balancing private rights and public interests. This book presents that '*exhaustion of patents*' further helps create a balance between the two in addition to the restriction on the patent rights imposed through a fixed duration of 20 years.

3.1.2 *The Economic Arguments for Free Trade in Relation to Exhaustion of Patents*

Arguments in favour of free trade are based on the Ricardian theory of comparative advantage, introduced by David Ricardo nearly 250 years back.[78] According to this theory, in two national markets where two different commodities are traded, if one market has an absolute cost advantage over the other in one product and the other country has absolute cost disadvantage in the second product, one product is manufactured at a relatively higher price in each of the two countries. Hence if a country is more efficient in producing one product while not so in the other product, it can choose to produce only the one in which it is efficient and import the other product. There is a trade-off for the country to produce what is more efficient in that country

77 Langinier Corinne and Moshini Gian Carlo, "The Economics of Patents: An Overview", CARD Working Papers, pg. 6, 2002. Available at, https://lib.dr.iastate.edu/cgi/viewcontent.cgi?Article=1317&context=card_workingpapers.

78 Ricardo David, "On The Principles of Political Economy and Taxation", 1817 (third edition 1821), Batoche Boohenerks Kitc 2001. (Available at https://socialsciences.mcmaster.ca/econ/ugcm/3ll3/ricardo/Principles.pdf).

and import what is not, instead of producing every product locally even when the country does not produce it efficiently. In economic terms, this trade-off is called '*Opportunity Cost*'.[79] If the opportunity cost is lower in producing certain product than importing from other countries, then the country will have comparative advantage in producing it locally. The comparative advantage establishes that it is economically more advantageous for a country to produce the goods and services in which it is efficient and not produce those in which it is least efficient. Each country can then trade with the other countries on their efficient produce and both benefit from trade.

Thus, if both the markets relinquish autarky[80] and adopt international trade then consumer welfare in both the countries will increase. It is known that consumers benefit as market competition brings down price, resulting in economic efficiency. This fundamental argument in favour of removing trade barriers is to generate economic surplus based on comparative advantages.

The Ricardian theory is based on the concept that international price differences are solely caused because of cost differences. However, in real life circumstances this is not necessarily the case, Ricardo did not consider number of factors, e.g. transportation that would affect pricing. Moreover, if there is no perfect competition due to external factors, or monopolies, or preferential differences towards the commodities that are traded between one country and another, there will be artificial price differentiation where this theory would not work. One might argue that firms adopt price differentiation to cater to different markets with different levels of wealth and income so that the products are available in both the markets. However, in Arthur Cecil Pigou's seminal work on externalities, he describes that the sellers adopt price differentiation to maximize profits.[81] So one might conclude that a market of people with low income and low wealth will not be catered to even by lowering the price if economies of scale cannot be achieved. In such situation international exhaustion to import the products from any other country market where it is available at a cheaper price could be a viable option.

It has been already discussed that patents are market exclusivities that can become restricted monopolies but have the sanction of law. In terms of the

79 Krugman Paul and Obstfeld Maurice, "International Economics Theory and Policy", Pearson Education, pg. 12, 2000.

80 Autarky has its roots in the Greek meaning 'self-sufficiency'. It is usually referred to trade policies that aim in maximising trade within the country and minimising trade with other countries.

81 Pigou Arthur Cecil, "The Economics of Welfare", Macmillan and Company Ltd., pg. 175, 176, 4th Edition 1932. Available at, http://files.libertyfund.org/files/1410/Pigou_0316.pdf.

Ricardian theory this means that such exclusivities or monopolies will affect the price of the patented commodities. Thus, the international price difference between commodities manufactured in different countries will not solely depend on differences in costs, but also be influenced by these patents. In such circumstances where the patent holder is authorised to have market monopoly for a restricted time, he would benefit most if he assesses the price elasticity of demand for the patented product in different markets and prices the product differently. This would allow him to increase his profit not only from working the patent but also from the consumer's surplus in each market.[82]

All this will lead to different prices for the patented products in different markets. Naturally, if these patented products are cheaper in one country than the other, some people will buy such products in the country where it is sold at a cheaper price and sell it at a higher price in the country where the price is high. This type of activity is defined in economic terms as '*arbitrage*'. Such arbitrage will balance the act of the patent monopoly from exceeding its mandate since it will restrict the monopolist's gain from the consumer's surplus although not restricting his benefits from the patent. Obviously, patent holders would not prefer to reduce their financial gains and might argue that, in general the patent allows him to exclude competition and thus s/he should be allowed to restrict competition from her/his licensees. It is debatable whether the exclusion from price competition should include those products that are brought to a different market by the patent holder himself.

3.2 The Economic Reasoning for Patent Exhaustion

The fundamental reason for adoption of exhaustion of patents is to place a checks and balances means to control possibilities of excessive market power gained due to ubiquitous nature of patents. Ubiquity allows patent rights over multiple number of units of a product situated at different places at the same time. Hence the patent holder can exercise control over the patented products in different markets even without having any physical control over the products, thus, bringing the much-needed legal security in trade and commerce.

Exhaustion of patents enable mitigation of the deadweight loss that occurs due to the exclusivity of the IP resulting in the ability to price above market

82 Ganea Peter, "A comparative study on parallel imports in patented and trademarked commodities in Japan and in the EU, discussed in the light of economic theory", Institute of Intellectual Property, Japan, pg. 4, 5, March 2001.

competitors.[83] As mentioned earlier, exhaustion of patent right allows minimising the social costs, thus balancing the private value and social value of an invention. The exhaustion principle as such is generally accepted without much debate, however the issue at the centre of all debates is not whether the patent right should exhaust, but on how and when such exhaustion should be.

Some economists tend to support price discrimination to the extent that different groups of consumers are ready to pay different prices at different length of the demand curve. Hence, where the demand curve is relatively inelastic the price can be high and where the demand is elastic price can be low. Arbitrage would result not only with the exhaustion of patent but also if the prices have been artificially manipulated due to government control, hence it is important to address it carefully to avoid any unintended market distortion.[84]

Here it is important to note that exhaustion would enable parallel trading of original patented products placed on a foreign market by the same right holder. Such product should not in any manner be confused with illegitimate products that have been manufactured without the permission of the right holder. Hence the essence of IPRs to exercise enforcement restraints on such infringed products would remain unhindered in any manner since the right is not existing in the first place, cannot exhaust when the product is paced in the market. There needs to be a definite policy as to how such arbitrage is to be treated. Details of different economic reasoning are analysed below to elaborate the three types of exhaustion and highlight the ideal mode of exhaustion.

3.2.1 *Economic Reasoning for 'National Exhaustion' of Patent Rights*

'*National Exhaustion*' of IPRs enables arbitrage but restricted within national boundaries of the market. Some economists support such exhaustion since they support the exclusive territories that this exhaustion establishes.[85] This exhaustion restrains arbitrage to the national boundaries. This help in maintaining exclusive market territories that are argued to encourage investments in local services and beneficial price discrimination, thus enhancing economic welfare. They are more inclined to favour patent holders who argue that the

83 Katz Ariel, "The economic rationale for exhaustion: distribution and post-sale restraints" in Calboli Irene and Lee Edward (eds.), "Research handbook on Intellectual Property Exhaustion and Parallel Imports", Edward Elgar Publishing Ltd., pg. 25, (23–43), 2016.

84 Vautier Kerrin, "The Economics of Parallel Imports", in Heath Christopher and Sanders Anselm Kamperman (eds.), "Industrial Property in the Bio-Medical Age – Challenges for Asia", Kluwer Law International, pg. 187, 2003.

85 Rey Patrick and Stiglitz Joseph, "The Role of Exclusive Territories in Producers' Competition", 26 (3) Rand Journal of Economics, pg. 431–451, 1995.

restrictions on arbitrage are necessary to provide legitimate protection to patents. According to them, since national exhaustion allows the patent holder to maximise profit in each market, they allow overall increase of their profit and thus benefit the patent holders.[86]

In addition, it is stated that by following national exhaustion, the patent holder can control the movement of the goods by controlling the imports of the patented products.[87] Thus according to this school of thought, arbitrage should be restricted to any economic free riding on the promotional and advertising expenses incurred by the authorised distributor based locally. In such cases it is argued that the parallel exporter free rides on the externality, which reduces efficiency especially in products tied with after-sales service. Further, if there is any material difference between the products sold in the parallel channel and the authorised channel there is obvious welfare reduction.[88]

It is also argued (although not from a purely economic perspective) that if unrestricted arbitrage is allowed, there may be consumer confusion wherein the consumers will be deceived as to the origin of the product. Here it must not be ignored that in case of re-imports, the same firm manufactures the products and only the markets in which they are sold are different. Thus, this argument can be made only in cases where the products are manufactured by the patent holder and the licensee separately and marketed in tandem. In any such case whether the country of origin is mentioned or not would not make any difference so far patent exhaustion is concerned. It would only be an issue in case of the exhaustion and can be dealt with appropriately. However, in such cases the patents would not exhaust if the producer is different, the exhaustion will only trigger when the patented product originates from the same company or its subsidiaries (holding company).

Considering this argument from the perspective of patents, such notion is based on the belief that confusion may occur since there is a high quality product, manufactured by the patent holder and a low quality product manufactured by the licensee of the patent holder.[89] It is argued that if the manufacturer prefers price differentiation for different markets then there cannot

86 Fink Carsten, "Entering the Jungle of Intellectual Property Rights – Exhaustion and Parallel Imports", Department of Economics, University of Heidelberg, Germany, pg. 13, 14 (2–23) 1999.

87 Maskus Keith, "Intellectual Property Rights in the Global Economy", Institute for International Economics, Washington D.C., pg. 214, 2000.

88 Crampes Claude and Hollander Abraham, "The pricing of pharmaceuticals facing parallel imports", Journal of Economic Law, University of Montreal, pg. 8, 2003.

89 Anderson Simon and Ginsburgh Victor, 7 (1) Review of International Economics, pgs. 126–139, 1999.

be different products in the same market and thus there cannot be confusion between the two products in the same market. Here it is indeed important to note that if there is material difference between the locally originated goods and the parallel imports of inferior quality, they can be restricted from being marketed.

There is a well-established legal practice in Trademarks law in most countries that does not allow exhaustion if there are material differences in the goods.[90] Similar restriction on exhaustion, i.e. same treatment as in the case of trademarks can be accorded to patented products that are materially and physically different. However, the burden of proving inferior quality would be on the complainant, hence the authorised distributor in the country or the licensor of the patent. This would be rather tricky, as it would acknowledge that the patent holder markets inferior quality products in some markets even when it has the capacity to market better quality. Restricting licensee's products through restriction on parallel import is beyond economic reasoning. It can be argued that imposing restrictions on arbitrage to restrain intra-brand competition of patented products through restraints on parallel imports only curtails spread of innovation through technology transfer.

Critics argue that arbitrage decrease global economic welfare since it restricts price discrimination.[91] It is argued that price discrimination where different price is charged for different price groups help in profit maximisation. However, such arguments are often based on the assumption that the patent holder's product is different in quality than that of the licensee, which need not be the case. It is also noticed that if arbitrage is allowed, since both the patent holder's product and the imported product would be on the market, in case of less demand in the low-income country, the patent holder will not be interested in supplying this market, hence the low-income market would only get the (supposedly) inferior products. On the other hand, if there is less demand in the high price market, the patent holder would try to monopolise

90 This provision of restraining exhaustion in case of imported products being materially different was first established in USA in the Lever Brothers case interpreting Section 42 of the Lanham Act which statutorily allows parallel imports of trade marked products. Due to their material differences the products were not considered as genuine. Hence although marketed under identical trademark to that registered in USA were not considered exhausted due to their material and physical difference. *Lever Brothers Co v United States of America, eta al.*, 877 F.2d 101 (D.C. Cir. 1989) and *Lever Brothers Co v United States of America, eta al.*, 981 F. 2nd 1330 (D.C. Cir. 1993).

91 Malueg David and Schwartz Marius, "Parallel Imports, Demand Dispersion, and International Price Discrimination", 37 Journal of International Economics, pgs. 167–195, 1994.

the high-income market thus low-priced products manufactured by the licensee will not reach this market. In such a pareto-inferior situation neither the consumers in the low-income country, nor in the high-income country would be better off. The consumers in the low-income country would not get the better product while the consumers in the high-income country would not get the cheaper products, thus restricting access to the products in poorer countries. However, it needs to be reiterated that imports of inferior quality products can be restricted based on their material difference.

Some others argue that restraining arbitrage is welfare enhancing since this would allow the patent holder to cater to the markets of the high-income country as well as the low-income country by differentiating the prices of the same product. They state that when the transaction costs are low, low-priced buyers would try to resell the products at high-price markets and due to this the patent holder will try to opt for uniform pricing and this will be detrimental to consumer welfare in general.[92] Thus according to them, consumers in both the countries would be better off if price differentiation is allowed. It is argued that there will be a tendency by the patent holder to decrease the price in the high-income country to enable competing with the parallel imports. Hence to recuperate the loss, there would be an increase in the price of the product in the low-income country from where it is being sourced. This would result in equalising the price of the patented product in different international markets, thus reducing the welfare in low-income countries. Others take a more liberal view and state that although one might argue in favour of restricting re-imports that are priced low and meant for low-income markets, there is no reason to restrict parallel imports in general.[93]

Price-differentiation is based on the relative elasticity of demand where in the relatively elastic market consumers will be charged lower price and in the relatively inelastic market consumers will be charged higher. Hence the economies of scale matters too, higher demand for the product also affects price. In such scenario, it is also argued that in cases where low-income countries benefit from lower price due to price competition, if the inflow of parallel import is from another low-income country, the exporting country might experience a price rise. This is because there would be a tendency to disallow arbitrage by

92 Hammer Peter, "Differential Pricing of Essential AIDS Drugs: Markets, Politics and Public Health", 4 (2) Journal of International Economic Law, Oxford University Press, pgs. 886, (883–912), 2002.

93 Ibid at 55, pgs. 18.

the patent holder and not cater to a particular country market, however such conditions also need to consider remedies of CL available.[94]

One might also argue that restricting arbitrage and setting prices independently in each country to allow charging a mark-up price over marginal distribution costs based on '*Ramsey pricing*'[95] is beneficial.[96] The sunk costs in R&D (which although benefits users in different markets) are borne locally and can be recovered efficiently if the mark up is fixed in different national markets according to the elasticity of demand in that market based on Ramsey pricing. Accordingly, prices will be set differently in each country in a manner that the mark-up of price over the original cost, rise with a fall in the elasticity of demand, so as to cover the sunk costs. Thus, market segmentation can help in financing new R&D but here it is important to note that this treatment should be specific to re-imports rather than generically applied to all imports based on national exhaustion of patents.

It needs to be highlighted that often the reasoning provided by the proponents of national exhaustion are based on theoretical simulation models on economic assumptions since sufficient empirical data is not available. In absence of specific data, Glanslandt and Maskus prepared an econometric model and deduced on instrumental-variables estimation.[97] The aim was to determine effect of exhaustion but there are a lot of assumptions made, based on hypothetical situations that might not reflect the actual situations. In such scenario, given that these models can provide quite different results if there is even slight change in the variables, these models are not reliable.

3.2.2 *Economic Reasoning for 'International Exhaustion' of Patent Rights*

The basic economic reasoning for international exhaustion lies from the very nature of the exhaustion doctrine itself. International exhaustion enables restraint-free distribution of the patented products once financial compensation gained either through sale or royalty/license fees on distribution. Supporters of international exhaustion view that allowing arbitrage would restrict the possibility of patent exclusivity being extended to unrestrained

94 Watal Jayashree, "Intellectual Property Rights in the WTO and Developing Countries", Oxford University Press, pgs., 301, 2002.

95 First introduced by British economist Frank Ramsey, the concept of 'Ramsey pricing' states that the mark-up price should be inverse to the price elasticity of demand. Thus, with an increase in the demand for the product, the price mark-up should be reduced.

96 Danizon Patricia, "Pharmaceutical Price Regulation: National Policies versus Global Interests", The American Enterprise Institute, Washington D.C., 1997.

97 Ibid at 55, pg. 38, 39.

monopoly that is susceptible to abuse. On the other hand, while it puts a check on the unrestrained use of patent exclusivity, given the fact that the patents are still enforceable against infringers, it does not compromise the welfare introduced by the patent. It is argued that allowing unrestrained arbitrage prevents the possibility of collusive tendency that might arise in the patent holder due to private territorial restraints. Moreover, international exhaustion enabled parallel imports counterbalances against abusive price-discrimination when government enforcement on territorial rights causes rent-seeking behaviour.[98]

One needs to consider that parallel trade can happen only when there is not just international price difference, but only if the difference is sufficient to cover the transportation costs leading in profitable arbitrage.[99] Critics of international exhaustion argue that if international exhaustion is adopted, the patent holder would not price discriminate geographically hence the importer would not be able to import at a lower price. This would thus increase the price of the patented goods in the import market, negatively affecting the consumers.[100] In other words, the patent holder might try to increase the price in the low-priced markets to bring in a uniform price thus killing the welfare enhancing possibility of international exhaustion if introduced without any control mechanism. This argument may hold ground only in cases where the patented goods are manufactured in States having similar economies like in the European Union (EU). If the markets are large while the consumers are not financially able to pay higher costs of the patented goods, the patent holder will adopt lower price for this market especially when the market is big and seek profit by scaling up sales.

They also argue that countries often achieve low prices only by price regulation and not through efficient production hence distort production efficiency.[101] This argument completely ignores the fact that the lower price might be not be due to price regulation but because of lower cost of production in

98 Maskus Keith, "Benefiting from Intellectual Property Protection", in Bernard Hoekman, Aaditya Mattoo and Philip English edited, "Development, Trade and the WTO – A Handbook", The World Bank, pg. 377, 2002.

99 Maskus Keith, "Parallel imports in pharmaceuticals: Implications for competition and prices in developing countries", Final Report to World Intellectual Property Organisation, pg. 8, April 2001.

100 Drexel Josef, "EU competition law and parallel trade in pharmaceuticals: lessons to be learned for WTO/TRIPS?", in Jan Rosén edited, "Intellectual Property at the Crossroads of Trade", Edward Elgar Publishing Ltd., pg., 6, 7, 12, (3–24), 2012.

101 Danton Patricia, "The Economics of Parallel Trade", in Towse Ruth and Holzhauer Rudi (eds.), "The Economics of Intellectual Property", Edward Elgar Publishing Ltd., pg. 365, (358–370), 2002.

a country. One cannot undermine the fact that the patent holder (as a price-discriminator) would obviously try not to allow arbitrage so that it can make maximum profit.

Another argument is that arbitrage does not bring welfare effects for the consumers, it allegedly benefits only the intermediaries. But such arguments are not supported with sound empirical data.[102] Although there has been some empirical research in the pharmaceutical sector, it has been restricted only within the European Economic Area (EEA). As such, the parameters considered for the empirical research would not give the same results if extrapolated to other geographical areas. Even then, studies have shown that moving from a national exhaustion regime to regional exhaustion regime in Sweden had led to significant reduction of pharmaceutical prices which made it clear that the welfare is enjoyed by the consumers and not just the intermediaries. Conclusions of this sort often fail to consider the importance of the size of the market and issues like economies of scale and the bargaining power of the consumers. It is already recorded that, patented products are often more expensive in smaller developing country markets than in bigger developed country markets.[103] International exhaustion, stimulates competition neutralising the effectiveness of price differentiation and enhancing free trade. Hence one cannot negate the fact that based on real life situation, many developing countries are opting for international exhaustion.[104]

It is further argued that the parallel importer free rides on the promotional and advertising expenses incurred by the authorised distributor. In today's global reach of media, advertisements travel beyond borders even if they might be locally oriented. Hence even if the advertisement expenses are borne

102 Maskus Keith, "Economic perspectives on exhaustion and parallel imports" in Calboli Irene and Lee Edward (eds.), "Research handbook on Intellectual Property Exhaustion and Parallel Imports", Edward Elgar Publishing Ltd., pg., 110, 111 (106–124), 2016.

103 WHO, "More Equitable Pricing for Essential Drugs: What do we mean and what are the issues?", pg. 3, Background Paper prepared by the WHO Secretariat for the WHO – WTO Secretariat Workshop on Differential Pricing and Financing of Essential Drugs, Hosbjor, Norway from 8th11th April 2001. The paper states that because pharmaceutical purchases in developing and LDC are mainly financed by individuals where they are negotiated individually prices of medicines are often higher than those in developed countries where the prices are often negotiated by insurance companies or the government.

104 Cottier Thomas, "Parallel Trade and Exhaustion of Intellectual Property in WTO Law Revisited", in Ruse Khan Grosse Henning & Metzger Axel (eds.), "Intellectual Property Ordering Beyond Borders", Cambridge University Press, pg. 193 (189–232), 2022. Also see, Clugston Christopher, "International Exhaustion, Parallel Imports and the Conflict between the Patent and Copyright Laws of the United States", 3 Beijing Law Review, Vol 4, pgs. 95–99, 2013.

exclusively by the authorised distributor the benefit is enjoyed globally by the patent holder. Moreover, often the manufacturer itself also incurs promotional and advertisement expenses. This is internalised by all the distributors (authorised as well as the unauthorised) hence the argument of free riding does not hold ground.

It is important to note that the patent holder's products as well as the parallel importer's products both are legitimate and so it is not clear how restrictions on arbitrage would be pro-competitive. There is no empirical data to determine that arbitrage can harm authorised distributors through their free riding, as often claimed. If the parallel imports manufactured by the licensee are materially different and inferior from the patented products then the issue of consumer deception can occur.[105] In any such case the burden should be on the patent holder to prove the difference in quality standards through systematic quality tests. In other circumstances the issue of free riding can only be justified to some extent when the authorised distributor provides a product take back guarantee or free service warranty in any country where there are authorised distributors. In such a case it is important to notify the buyer that the product has come through the parallel channel wherein the tied-up service-warranty or product guarantee is not available. It is up to the consumer to choose whether to opt for a low-priced product without service-warranty or a high-priced local product that comes with tied service-warranty.

3.2.3 *Economic Reasoning for 'Regional Exhaustion' of Patent Rights*

Conceptually there was no existence of '*Regional Exhaustio*n'. Regional exhaustion is a blend of national and international exhaustions, introduced in Europe through case law fundamentally based on free movement of goods within a CU. It is based on the economics of barrier free trade in the European Union market, a CU and was created through judicial pronouncements by the ECJ prior to codification in secondary legislation (directives and regulations) in shaping the common market. In spirit, the practice of regional exhaustion in Europe, more specifically within the EEA is based on *Article 34* of the Treaty on the Functioning of the European Union (EU Treaty) which states,

> "[q]uantitative restrictions on exports, and all measures having equivalent effect, shall be prohibited between Member States." read with the exception for, "... the protection of industrial or commercial property."

105 Hilke John, "Free Trading or Free-Riding: An Examination of the theories and available empirical evidence on gray market imports", 32 World Competition, pg. 80, (75–91), 1988.

Hence it is well established that the aim had always been to uphold the free movement of goods and services within the European Union where IPRS could not become non-tariff barriers.[106]

Within a multilateral trade regime, regional exhaustion for the CU draws its validity from *Article XXIV* of General Agreement on Tariffs and Trade (GATT) that provides the internal and external requirements crucial for its formation. *Article XXIV 5 (a)* restricts the external duties and other regulations imposed on its formation from being higher or more restrictive than that before the CU was formed. *Article XXIV 8 (a) (I) & (II)* while elaborating the internal requirements of the CU, requires duties and other regulations are eliminated on substantially all products being traded within the territories. Additionally, the members of the CU need to apply substantially the same duties and other regulations of commerce to trade of other non-parties. However, although regional exhaustion was based on the free movement of goods by removing the possibility of IPRS becoming a non-tariff barrier within the CU, it was initially not introduced for such purpose.

The regional exhaustion mode started as a competition law measure against anticompetitive market power gained due to national exhaustion in the Grundig, Consten Case of 1966.[107] In this case Grundig, an electronic goods manufacturing company selling under its trademark registered in Germany and other EU states, appointed Consten SaRL for exclusive distribution of its goods in France. UNEF, a third-party vendor in France bought the products in Germany and imported and sold them in France. Grundig and Consten alleging infringement of their trademark and copyright in name and logo, complained before the EC. The EC declared that under *Article 85* of the Treaty of Rome (now *Article 101* of the Treaty of the Functioning of the European Union), intra-brand trade would support free movement of goods within the members. This decision of the Commission was challenged by Consten and Grundig before the ECJ and was joined by Germany and Italy. The ECJ considered carefully all arguments and decided in favour of the EC deciding that the anti-cartel aspect in European competition law would supersede national trademark laws about the common market.[108]

---

106 Ghosh Shubha, "Incentives, contracts and intellectual property exhaustion" in Calboli Irene and Lee Edward (eds.), "Research handbook on Intellectual Property Exhaustion and Parallel Imports", Edward Elgar Publishing Ltd., pgs., 153–154 (125–170), 2016.

107 *Consten SaRL and Grundig GmbH v Commission of EEC* (1966), Case 56/64. Available at, https://eur-lex.europa.eu/legal-content/EN/TXT/PDF/?uri=CELEX:61964CJ0056&from=EN.

108 Cottier Thomas, "Parallel Trade and Exhaustion of Intellectual Property in WTO Law Revisited", in Ruse Khan Grosse Henning & Metzger Axel (eds.), "Intellectual Property

It is interesting to note that while regional exhaustion became an established practice in Europe, a comparative analysis will show that other regional blocs did not adopt regional exhaustion. NAFTA members did not specify regional exhaustion neither any mode of exhaustion and each member followed their own.[109] Even in case of ASEAN, regional exhaustion was not adopted. Since its establishment in 1967, there was never an attempt to create EU-like regional institutions hence one would not expect regional exhaustion of IPRS too. However, in 2007 the ASEAN Charter was adopted to establish an integrated single market, ASEAN Economic Community (AEC) and the AEC was launched in December 2015.[110] It will be noticed that even when there were efforts to eliminate tariff and non-tariff barriers through adoption of a Common Effective Preferential Tariff Scheme for the ASEAN Free Trade Area[111] (AFTA),[112] IPRS were kept outside the purview of non-tariff barriers through an exception.

From an economic perspective, it has already been stated that it is incorrect to assume that restricting arbitrage is welfare enhancing. In fact, the welfare trade-offs in regulating arbitrage are circumstantial hence proponents of regional exhaustion try to show that countries with lower trade barriers which are in a region would gain from allowing arbitrage. Because when the cost of allowing arbitrage is less, it is beneficial to allow arbitrage while if such cost were high then imposing a restriction would be better. Arguably this mode of exhaustion was adopted since on one hand it encourages unobstructed trade between the member countries of the EU and at the same time does not

---

Ordering Beyond Borders", Cambridge University Press, pg. 192 (189–232), 2022. Also see, Ebb Lawrence, "The Grundig-Consten Case Revisited: Judicial Harmonisation of National Law and Treaty Law in The Common Market", 6 University of Pennsylvania Law Review, Volume 115, pg. 856–859 (855–889), 1967.

109 Ibid at 106, pgs., 158 (125–170).

110 The ASEAN Members committed to accelerate the establishment of the ASEAN Economic Community in the Cebu Declaration on the Acceleration of the Establishment of an ASEAN Community by 2015. ASEAN, CEBU DECLARATION ON THE ACCELERATION OF THE ESTABLISHMENT OF AN ASEAN COMMUNITY BY 2015 (Jan. 13 2007). The ASEAN Community consists of three pillars of the ASEAN Security Community, ASEAN Economic Community (AEC), and ASEAN Socio-Cultural Community and this form the roadmap for an ASEAN Community 2009–2015.

111 Agreement on the Common Effective Preferential Tariff (CEPT) Scheme for the ASEAN Free Trade Area (AFTA), Jan. 28, 1992, art. 5, WIPO Lex. No. TRT/AFTA/001 [hereinafter CEPT-AFTA].

112 But *Article 8(d)* of the ASEAN Trade in Goods Agreement (ATIGA) stipulates that the protection and enforcement of trademark rights (IPRS) may constitute a general exception to the prohibition to non-tariff barriers within ASEAN. ATIGA, Feb. 26, 2009, WIPO Lex. No. TRT/ASEAN/001. ATIGA replaced the earlier CEPT-AFTA scheme signed in 1992.

restrain the patent holder's right to exploit the patent. It restricts the possibility of patent rights being used as a quantitative restriction but only within the EU. The ECJ relied on this economic reasoning as it was determined to remove trade barriers even if it was in the form of IPRS.[113]

It is interesting to note that the exhaustion is restricted within the EU region and not extended beyond EU countries, the member countries hence do not permit international exhaustion. As a result, the patent holder can restrict parallel imports from outside EU even when it is being imported from a country where the patent holder had consented manufacture of the patent product.[114] Thus the basic economic reasoning of the ECJ acknowledges that arbitrage can enhance welfare but restrains it within the regional bloc. Thus, regional exhaustion is like international exhaustion with the difference that it restricts the exhaustion within the regional bloc rather than internationally.

Here regional exhaustion applies to only CUS and not to FTAS, the fundamental premise being the difference between the two in treatment of tariffs, an exception being the EEA Agreement. A case in point on copyright exhaustion is *Polydor Ltd. and RSO Records Inc. v Harlequin Record Shops Ltd. and Simons Records Ltd.* (*Polydor case*). This parallel import case raised question as to whether enforcement of copyrights held in UK by the right holder against its own licensees in Portugal would result in such measure being quantitative restrictions on imports within the meaning of *Article 14*(2) of the Agreement between EEC and Portugal and was arbitrary discrimination between identical products. It is interesting to note how in a conflict between two private parties in a domestic court, international agreements prevailed in a way giving horizontal direct effect to international agreement, thus directly enforceable by individuals in the EEC.[115]

In right another distinct case on exhaustion of trademarks was the issue of contention within EEA was the *Mag Instrument Inc. v California Trading Company Norway* (*Maglite Case*).[116] Before addressing the case, it must be mentioned that the EEA Agreement allows their laws to be interpreted homogeneously in-sync within the EU, thus following ECJ jurisprudence through the 'Court of the EFTA members' (EFTA Court) without adhering to the jurisdiction

113 Ibid at 60, pg. 56.

114 Ibid at 60, pg. 57.

115 *Polydor Limited and RSO Records Incorporated v Harlequin Record Shops Ltd. and Simons Records Limited*, Case 270/80 [1982], ECR 329. Available at, https://eur-lex.europa.eu/legal-content/EN/TXT/?uri=CELEX:61980CJ0270.

116 *Mag Instrument Inc. v California Trading Company Norway*, Case E-2/97 [1997], EFTA Ct. Rep. 129. Available at, https://eftacourt.int/cases/e-02-97/.

of ECJ. In the *Mag Instrument Inc. v California Trading Company Norway* (*Maglite Case*), the EFTA Court under the EEA Agreement allowed Norway to follow international exhaustion irrespective of the exhaustion followed within the EU. It opined that the EEA is undoubtedly an enhanced free trade agreement but distinct from the EU which is a CU.

Albeit these are old cases, but nothing has changed for courts using international agreements for dispute resolution. Today with large number of new trade agreements proliferating the multilateral trading arena, disputes are bound to rise and intellectual property rights is expected to be a crucial component. In such scenario instead of each of these RTAs and PTAs adopting different dispute settlement mechanisms, extending the WTO dispute settlement regime could be best suited. In such premise, restraining parallel imports would not be in any way different than the *Polydor case*.[117]

3.2.4 *Ideal Mode of Patent Exhaustion among the Three Modes*

The doctrine of exhaustion in any of its modes is aimed at controlling the re-distribution and commercialisation, rather than the re-production of patented goods. Hence it

> neither prohibits IP owners from, achieving the benefits that post-sale restraints might bring about, nor does it totally impair their ability to do so.[118]

The foundational reason to grant IPRs is to enable the inventor or creator to get the market returns related to the invention by restraining competitors from using the patented invention without consent and thus provide incentive to innovate further. This would result in net efficiency gain and allow efficient market operation only if such exclusivity does not supersede the benefits of enhanced innovation. International exhaustion establishes this benefit-cost optimisation by allowing the purchaser of the patented goods to develop a secondary market competitively, restraining the patent owner to enforce exclusive rights in this second market.[119]

---

117 Cottier Thomas, "Intellectual Property and Mega-Regionals Trade Agreements: Progress and Opportunities Missed", in S Griller, W. Obwexer, Erich Vranes (Eds.), "Mega-Regional Trade Agreements: CETA, TTIP and TiSA", Oxford University Press, pgs. 151–174, 2017.

118 Ibid at 83, pg. 34.

119 Chiappetta Vincent, "Working toward international harmony on intellectual property exhaustion (and substantive law)", in Calboli Irene and Lee Edward (eds.), "Research handbook on Intellectual Property Exhaustion and Parallel Imports", Edward Elgar Publishing Ltd., pg. 129 (125–144), 2016.

Based on comparative advantages to the parallel importer, the mode of exhaustion enables reduction of national welfare loss through arbitrage. By allowing some of the profits from the sale of patented products to be shared by nationals, it becomes welfare enhancing.[120] However, sometimes it is argued that if arbitrage is allowed, the patent holder will not be accorded legitimate protection to his products due to the deception caused by the parallel imports. Such an argument fails any justification since the patent holder himself authorises the production of licensed products under the patent. Thus, only because the products are manufactured by the licensee outside the country cannot make them infringed products. It is the patent holder's conscious decision to license the product and further it follows only after a negotiated royalty is paid, hence the question of deception does not rise.

There is no doubt that the patent holders would be able to maximise profits when they are able to segregate markets and differentiate price as per local demand. This would be possible if there is a single price in each market, but if it is a heterogeneous market with differentiated prices depended on different factors (e.g. quick access to the patented goods), then it would only be possible if the price equations allow higher profits. However, the argument put forward by the proponents of national exhaustion is due to fact that different markets bear different prices, depending on social and economic welfare of a country at large. These results in differences between rich and poor hence need for price differentiation according to different markets, particularly in the pharmaceutical sector, but also in others like in copyright industry, undermining prices in rich markets. Typically, parallel trade, based on international exhaustion of patents would usually occur at the wholesale level and very limited at the retail consumer level. This is mainly because often goods imported at parallel would not be tied with complementary services and sometimes even lack warranties. In such scenarios it would be erroneous to consider that parallel trade would take place only because there is price discrimination.[121] Hence even when international exhaustion is followed, there are many other factors that would determine if parallel trade would be possible.

Apart from the arguments that have been discussed, there is a general reasoning that arbitrage permits local consumers to avail patented products at a lower price through enhanced market competition. The parallel imports

120 Watal Jayashree, "Parallel Imports and IPR-Based Dominant Positions: Where Do India's Interests Lie?" in Cottier Thomas and Mavroidis Petros (eds.), "Intellectual Property: Trade, Competition and Sustainable Development" The Univ. of Michigan Press, pg. 200, (199–209) 2003.

121 Ibid at 102, pg. 115, 116.

are based on the principles of free trade that allows efficient allocation of international resources in a way helping developing country licensees. It dismantles trade barriers and thus helps relocation of production bases to developing countries given their low establishment and overhead costs. As a result, it enhances the production ability of number of countries as they receive new technology promoting local entrepreneurship.[122] Legitimizing parallel trade by adopting international exhaustion would enable greater competition, as distributors would compete with each other. Given that parallel trade would reduce the profits of the patent holder instead of maximising profits, it is natural for patent holders to set the wholesale prices to limit or eliminate possibilities of parallel trade.[123] The result would be influenced by the size of the market, the ability of the licensee to negotiate and finally the legal regime as to whether it would allow or disallow international exhaustion. However, sometimes completely different arguments are raised like parallel trade would discourage investments in new technologies. These arguments are not supported by empirical data and are unjustified reflection of favourable bias towards patent holders.[124]

The argument in favour of restricting arbitrage based on Ramsey pricing also does not hold, given the fact that such pricing can only be beneficial if it can regulate the returns. In Ramsey Pricing (named after economist Frank Ramsey, 1927), economic welfare maximises when firms achieve their pre-set profit targets wherein as the elasticity of demand increases the optimal tax decreases.[125] Thus, if there is a single regulator that can restrict firms to make only normal returns to cover the sunk costs, restricting arbitrage based on Ramsey pricing will be efficient. However, the situation is different, in most cases firms try to earn more than the '*normal returns*' and due to the independence of different markets, there is no single regulator that can set the prices globally. In such circumstances, banning arbitrage based on Ramsey pricing will not be supportable.

Further, it is argued that market segmentation is best for R&D i.e. arbitrage affects R&D negatively and that parallel trade reduces the profit that exercise of the IP (in this case, patented good). As such, given that profitability depends

122 Frederick Abbott, "First Report (Final) to the Committee on International Trade Law of the International Law Association on the subject of Parallel Importation", 1 JIEL 4, pg. 607, (607–636), 1998.

123 Ibid at 102, pg. 117.

124 Ibid at 102, pg. 118.

125 See Oxford dictionary of Economics, https://www.oxfordreference.com/view/10.1093/oi/authority.20110803100403450.

on the willingness to invest in new technologies, parallel trade enabled through international exhaustion reduces investment in R&D.[126] The most relevant industry in this case is perhaps the pharmaceutical industry but even in such a sensitive industry, evidence on parallel imports does not support such claims. In the 1990s, R&D in the pharmaceutical industry in Sweden and Denmark showed considerable increase even when they were high parallel import recipient countries. On the other hand, Canada on restricting parallel importation of pharmaceuticals, experienced increase in R&D activities. This shows that allowing or disallowing arbitrage (enabling or disabling parallel trade) does not necessarily affect R&D or in other words, does not affect introduction of new medicines negatively.

On the contrary, it is international exhaustion that facilitates attraction of more capital since it allows the lender to dispose of licensed IP products after the first sale as the rights are exhausted. Lenders usually prefer to have control of the patented products that are to be manufactured with the help of their money (until such borrowed money is repaid). In case of international exhaustion, the licensor of the patent (i.e. the patent holder) cannot control the movement of the product after the first sale.

Thus, the lender can use the patented products that are manufactured as collateral security,

> Lending on goods incorporating associated intellectual property in a given jurisdiction would be promoted if the jurisdiction adopted the exhaustion doctrine, either in its intellectual property law regime or its secured transactions regime, in a formulation that gives secured lenders greater certainty that they may realize on their security rights in the genuine goods, lawfully made copies, and goods made and transferred with the authority of the patent owner, without permission by the licensors of the associated intellectual property.[127]

126 Ibid at 102, pg. 118.

127 Commercial Finance Association (CFA), "Intellectual Property Issues Affecting a Secured Transactions Regime", March 2004.

CHAPTER 4

Evolution of Exhaustion: Patent Exhaustion in Different Jurisdictions

Exhaustion or non-exhaustion of IPRS in general and patents have developed in different ways in different jurisdictions. For academic research, this book has analysed the evolution of the exhaustion doctrine and as well the contracts-based alternate in four main jurisdictions, the UK, Germany moving into the EU position, the US and Japan. Subsequently it has also elaborated a group of developing countries that have similar position on IPRS and are all emerging economies with similar economic problems.

The UK is studied since it established common law principles not only in its own territories but also in all its colonies and distinctly developed a contracts-based practice. The German practice of exhaustion is important to note since this was the country of origin of the doctrine before gradually spreading to other countries through judicial interpretations of their courts. As European countries came together to form the EU, the German position changed to adapt to the regional exhaustion position – a hybrid of national and international exhaustion, established by the ECJ. Based on the doctrine of exhaustion, US courts developed the '*First Sale doctrine*', an international exhaustion doctrine with the possibility of contractual intervention like doctrine of implied license. Japan is one of the rare countries so far that has managed to move up the ladder from a developing country to an industrialised country while remaining highly advanced in IP-based technological innovation. Hence Japan is the other industrialised country studied in this book.

Finally, the group of developing countries analysed in this book are Brazil, China, India and South Africa. This is a group of countries with significant participation in international trade, a group that has gradually moved into contemporary IPRS laws and policies. They are part of similar group of negotiating bloc in different international negotiations (e.g. G20 in WTO, BASIC in UNFCCC). They have similar socio-economic problems and takes similar positions in different international trade issues including IPRS. Often, they use IPRS as a policy tool to address health and other public issues, hence considered worth analysing.

DOI:10.1163/9789004542815_006

4.1 The United Kingdom and the Doctrine of 'Implied License'

Patent right is a territorial right in all Anglo-Commonwealth jurisdictions thus they are limited to the territory of the jurisdiction granting the patent. This means that a patent granted in one jurisdiction would not automatically be honoured outside this jurisdiction.[128] Historically the patent system was first codified as early as 1624 as, '*The Statute of Monopolies*' and granted exclusivity to inventions for 14 years. It is worth noting that the inventor who was accorded protection also included importers of the invention, hence the importers were authorised to apply for patents in their own name in their countries.[129]

In Britain the relation between the patent holder's rights and the right of distribution of the patented goods were predominantly contractual and the doctrine of exhaustion was unknown. The rights to distribute after the first sale depended on whether the owner of the patented product was contractually allowed to do so under a license agreement.[130] Hence, historically, before the doctrine of exhaustion was known due to joining the European Single Market and the EU, Britain followed the '*doctrine of implied licence*'.[131] Under this doctrine it is considered that once a certain good is sold or distributed legally by the original owner, it is '*implied*' that along with the product the owner also '*licences*' all rights attached to the product. This obviously includes IPRs, subject to the condition that the sale of the product does not include any specific pre-condition, whereby the said implied licence would then be nullified.

Later, the effect of this principle was confirmed by the English case *Betts v Willmott* where the doctrine of implied licence was upheld, although often it is erroneously referred to as an example of '*doctrine of exhaustion*'.[132] In this

128 Warwick Rothnie, "Parallel Imports", Sweet & Maxwell, pg. 112, 1993.

129 Khan Zarina and Sokoloff Kenneth, "Historical perspectives on Patent Systems in economic development", in Netanel Neil Weinstock (ed.), "The Development Agenda Global Intellectual Property and Developing Countries", Oxford University Press, pg. 216, 217 (215–243), 2009.

130 Ibid at 50, pg. 45.

131 In *Crane v. Price*, 1842, mentioned in 1 Webster's Patent Cases 377, Webster's comments (413) were, "For a particular Article … Hence it is obvious, that a person legally acquires, by licence or by purchase, title to that which is the subject of letters patent, he may use it or improve upon it in whatever manner he pleases; in the same manner as if dealing with property of any other kind".

132 In *Betts v. Willmott*, 1871 L.R. 6 Ch. App. 239, Lord Hatherley L.C. stated, "Unless it can be shewn … that there is some clear communication to the party to whom the Article is sold, I apprehend that in as much as he has the right of vending the goods in France, or Belgium or England, or in any other quarter of the globe, he transfers with the goods necessarily the licence to use them wherever the purchaser pleases. When a man has purchased an Article he expects to have control over it and there must be some clear and

case, it was held that if the British patent holder himself marketed his patented goods abroad, he could prevent their importation back to Britain only if there was an express embargo attached to the sale by way of contract.[133] The implied licence regime was now established in the UK, wherein the owner of the IPRs in UK could restrict entry of product manufactured by the licensee situated outside the country only if the license agreement restricted it specifically. Hence, if the license agreement restricted the licensor to produce and sell/market the product only in the foreign country or in a pre-defined market, that did not include the originating (IPR owner/licensor's) country, then the IPRs owner/licensor could restrict entry of the product. If there was no express limitation in the license agreement, then the licensee could not be restricted from exporting the product to the licensor's country.[134]

A case in point is the famous *Tilghman's* case, wherein the territorial nature of the patent rights was in question.[135] In this case, Tilghman who held patents for cutting and grinding hard substances, also used to make frosted glass lamps in England and Belgium, had granted license to the plaintiff to manufacture glassware in the patented process in Belgium. The plaintiff ignored the contractual restrictions imposed on it and not only sold in Belgium, but also started selling the glassware products in England. Tilghman then sent '*Cease and Desist*' notice that was responded by an application for interim injunction against Tilghman from sending such notices. The notices were alleged to be uncalled for, since they intended to settle the dispute through the arbitration dispute resolution provision in the license contract.

The High Court refused injunction based on the English and Belgium patents held by different entities. Further, the Court of Appeal refused the injunction on ground that given the different owners of the Belgian and English patents, the license under the former is distinct from the latter. Hence the patent holder of the English patent is authorised to restrain the import of the patented glassware into England. Here the most important factor was that the patented glassware was sold by the licensee who was licensed only to manufacture and not sell. Had the English patent holder sold the patented product without express restrictions and the purchasers re-sold it or exported it to

explicit agreement to the contrary to justify the vendor in saying that he has not given the purchase his licence to sell the item, or to use wherever he pleases as against himself".

133 Ibid at 4.

134 Brown Jeremy, "International Exhaustion in Europe", Les Nouvelles, pg. 108, September 1997.

135 *Société Anonyme des Manufactures de Glaces v Tilghman's Patent Sand Blast Company* (1883) 25Ch. D1 (CA).

England, the patent holder would not have been able to enforce the patent. In this case, Tilghman could not excuse the clear terms in the license contract.[136]

In most cases the practice was governed more by contract law and later it was codified under the Sale and Goods Act 1893 (of the UK), establishing that the buyer of goods would also be guaranteed the enjoyment of the goods in all forms. But as mentioned earlier it was possible for the seller of the goods to restrict further distribution of goods covered by the IPRs by way of placing a notice to the purchaser (maybe in the sale voucher or on the package or on a label placed on the body of the product), which would restrict the doctrine of implied licence to take effect. Thus, Britain did not practice exhaustion in its literal term. In fact, there was never a case of automatic exhaustion, rather the approach varied with the subject matter and in all cases the patent holder's licences determined the treatment.

This practice of implied licence was followed in the UK all through, even after the doctrine of exhaustion became well established in Germany and some other countries of continental Europe. It will be noticed that there was hardly a case when the patent holder sold the patented goods without placing such notice (thus although implied licence could be evoked, parties managed to avoid it). Since with the sale of the patented goods, further use, sale or distribution of the patented goods could be contractually restricted, the restriction bound not only the purchaser of the goods, but also all recipients of the goods.

Two prominent cases in point are, *Dunlop v Longlife and Goodyear v Lancashire Batteries*.[137] In the first case the court held that where the licensee of a patent held only limited licence, the licensee had to follow the limitations imposed by way of the licence. Hence if a certain retail price were marked then selling below the marked price would be considered as an infringement of the patent. In the second case that dealt with selling automobile tyres at price below the marked price, it was held that since it was expressly mentioned in the contract that the selling price should not be below the marked price, it was a case of infringement. Thus, it can be noted that in both cases it was possible to limit the nature of the licence by way of contract.

After this, the practice of the doctrine of implied license was influenced by the Resale Prices Act 1964. Few years later the House of Lords passed their judgment in the *Beecham* case which put checks on what would be implied

136 Sothers Christopher, "Patent Exhaustion: the UK Perspective" in "Parallel Trade in Europe: Intellectual Property, Competition and Regulatory Law", Hart, Oxford, pgs. 40, 41, 2007.

137 *Dunlop v Longlife* (1958) R.P.C. 473 and *Goodyear v Lancashire Batteries* (1958) L.R. 1 R.P. 22 at 35.

in the license contract.[138] In this case, Bristol-Myers had a patent license from Beecham covering whole world excluding the British Commonwealth. '*International Products*' bought Penicillin covered by Bristol-Myers in US and imported it into Kenya (a Commonwealth member) violating the restrictions imposed through the license contract. This infringement case initially decided by the High Court in Kenya, held that the moment a patented product was sold, it was from the restrictions imposed by the patent and hence,

(a) a sale by the agent of a patent holder acting within the scope of his authority confers on the purchaser the same rights as a sale by the patent holder, but
(b) in the case of a sale by a licensee, the extent of the release depends on the scope of the license agreement.

In this case there was no confusion as to the terms of the license hence the interim injunction was granted.[139]

The Patents Act 1977 addressed infringement provisions in *Section 60* in *sub-section (1) and sub-section (4)*. It was considered to give effect to regional exhaustion in compliance with the Community Patent Convention 1975. It is however interesting to note that even before *Section 60(4)* could come into effect as soon as there was a possibility to take the provision out under the Community Patent Convention, it was removed in the Patents Act 2004 (effective from 2005).

In a later case, *United Wire Ltd. v Screen Repair Services (Scotland) and others,* the House of Lords decided that a patent holder cannot restrict any third party to conduct repair on a patented product. However, such repair of the patented product cannot be to such extent that it becomes equal to a new product. Such repairs would not be allowed on the basis that the patent rights have been exhausted or such repairs would result in patent infringement.[140] The practice of implied licence gradually gave way to regional exhaustion, with UK joining the European Economic Community (EEC). The Treaty of Rome bound the UK along with its continental neighbours by the decisions of the ECJ that all members needed to adhere to. However, it will be very interesting to note that the conservative attitude of the English Courts continued with the old practice of implied licence as long as it was possible. We still find examples of cases where the rights were still not exhausted with the sale of the goods since restrictions

138 Beecham Group Ltd. v International Products Ltd., (1968) R.P.C. 129 and FSR 162.

139 Ibid at 102, pg. 117, 2016.

140 *United Wire Ltd. v Screen Repair Services (Scotland) and others*, House of Lords, 4 All E R 353 (2000).

could be placed through the licence agreement and would likely be considered in violation of the EU requirements.

4.2 Patent Exhaustion in Germany and Some Countries in Continental Europe

The credit of introducing the principle of exhaustion goes to Josef Kohler of Germany. His view differed from that of implied licence practised in England and in different papers written by him he stated that with the first sale of every single copy of a product legally, the owner relinquished his right over the intellectual property embedded in the product.[141] Kohler regarded that the common proprietary right of the owner of a product should prevail over the IP right of the product. Closely following this development published by Kohler, the Reichgericht in Germany (former German Imperial Supreme Court) used the term '*Konsumtion*' in the *Duotal* case in 1902 and thus was responsible for the conceptual doctrinisation of the exhaustion Principle.[142] The doctrine stated that the first time when the holder of an IPRS sold his product, he immediately lost his right to restrict the buyer from enjoyment of that product through enforcement of the IPRS in the product.

The fundamental difference between '*implied licence*' and '*exhaustion of the rights*' is that in the former, there is no exhaustion of the IPRS but with the distribution of the physical product, the IPRS embedded is also licensed to the buyer unless such implied license is expressly barred through contract. In the case of the latter, the effect is rather automatic as soon as the IPRS embedded product is put into any distribution channel, i.e. the right to enforce the IPRS is exhausted irrespective of any contractual bindings. In fact, this was perhaps the first time when the right of the consumer found precedence over IPRS through indoctrination. It is also noted that even at that time when the phenomenon was introduced, the lookout was to remove barriers to trade within the German federated states (later known as 'Länders').[143]

It is interesting to note that although Germany had a tradition of following exhaustion within the federated states, it has changed to the EU regional exhaustion in the present day.[144] The scope of exhaustion is crucial since it

141 Ibid at 52, pg. 16, (13–23).

142 Reichgericht in Zivilsachen (RGZ) 50, 362 – "*Duotal*", cited by Christopher Heath, ibid at 141, pg. 16.

143 See Chapter 4.2 of this book for detailed discussion.

144 Ibid at 60, pg. 805.

defines the limits of the patented product in circulation. While any mode of distribution of the patented product would be considered legitimate, unauthorised manufacture of the patented product would be considered as an infringement. The scope of exhaustion also brings into its ambit the effect of repairs, maintenance and replacement of spare parts subject to wear and tear. It is regarded that even when the entire product with all its parts is patented, repairs, maintenance and replacement of parts would be allowed so far it is within the scope of permissible repairs and replacement based on the exhaustion doctrine.[145]

The practice of the doctrine of exhaustion propounded by Kohler became well established not only in Germany but also in some other countries like Switzerland, Austria, Netherlands and some other Nordic countries. Switzerland followed its own mode of exhaustion since it was not part of the EU. As far as the exhaustion issue is concerned in Switzerland, there are five cantonal decisions (cantons are sovereign geographical territories like states or provinces within the Confederation) out of which two were in favour of international exhaustion while the other three were not. However, jurisprudence set the path on exhaustion and the most noteworthy is the *Kodak* case by the Commercial Court of Zurich Canton that favoured international exhaustion later overruled by the Federal Court of Switzerland.[146]

In this case, the Swiss supermarket Jumbo imported Kodak films and single use cameras from England instead of buying it from the authorised Swiss licensor of Kodak photographic goods. Since there was no specific treatment of the exhaustion in the Swiss Patent Act, the Commercial Court of the Zurich Canton chose to decide in favour of the parallel importation from England, allowing international exhaustion. This decision was appealed before the Federal Supreme Court of Switzerland where the court differentiated trademarks and copyrights from that of patents and favoured the mode of national exhaustion in case of patents. In effect the Court stated that patent rights are for shorter period than copyright and trademarks and it was more expensive to maintain patents, hence the patent right needed to be stronger than the other forms of IPRs. This differentiated approach was adopted also in consideration of the interests of the research-based pharmaceutical industry in Switzerland.[147]

145 Ibid at 60, pg. 809.

146 *Kodak v Jumbo-Markt AG*, 4C.24/1999/rnd, 7 December 1999 on appeal from, Zurich Commercial Court, "Kodak Photographic Material" case, 23 November 1998.

147 Ibid at 5, pg. 260–262. Also see, Cottier Thomas and Oesch Matthias, "International Trade Regulation", pg. 953–958, Cameron May & Staempfli, Bern & London 2005.

After this judgement, Switzerland followed the mode of national exhaustion in cases of patents whereas international exhaustion for other IPRs.[148]

Here it must be mentioned that Swiss patent law governed Liechtenstein and as such, they followed a unique bilateral exhaustion with Liechtenstein for patents. The practice of differentiated exhaustion for different IPRs continued even after Switzerland joined the EEA. It changed to regional exhaustion within the EEA with the revision of the Swiss Patent law in 2009. The amended patent law explicitly states,

> 1. If the proprietor of the patent has placed patent-protected goods on the market in Switzerland or within the European Economic Area, or consented to their placing on the market in Switzerland or within the European Economic Area, these goods may be imported and used or resold commercially in Switzerland.[149]

This means that if the point of first distribution of the patented product is outside the EEA, importation of such product into Switzerland would infringe the patent law. There are however certain exemptions from regional exhaustion in certain specific cases where national exhaustion prevails, or where the patented products have been subjected to price control through government interventions.[150]

Although the principle of common market and free movement of goods within the EU gradually took precedence, initially there was no clear policy on the issue of exhaustion and different countries of the EU carried on their individual '*exhaustion*' regimes. This became a growing problem as IPRs became a non-tariff barrier to trade, prompting the ECJ to introduce the regional exhaustion policy through its decisions and a common exhaustion policy popularly referred to as '*Regional Exhaustion*' was established.[151]

---

148 Correa Carlos, "International Exhaustion of Rights", in "Trade Related Aspects of Intellectual Property Rights A commentary on the TRIPS Agreement", Oxford University Press, pg. 79, 80, (78–90), 2007.

149 Article 9a: Federal Acts of Patents for Invention (Patents Act PatA) as on 1st April 2019. Available at, www.admin.ch/opc/en/classified-compilation/19540108/201904010000/232.14.pdf.

150 Ibid at 147.

151 Here it must be noted that the common exhaustion mode in patent law followed throughout Europe is more a result of case laws introduced by the ECJ eg., Case 78/70, Deutsche Gramophone ECR 487 (1971), Case 15/74, *Centrafarm v. Sterling Drug* ECR 1147 (1974) and was not through codification. There were repeated efforts to harmonise the Patent Laws in within the EC through codification and as a result of which the two Community Patent Conventions were introduced. However, since Conventions are not based on the EC Treaty, they were not adopted pursuant to EC legislation procedures and they never became enforceable since all members of the EC did not ratify them.

4.3 Patent Exhaustion in the United States of America

In the US, exhaustion flowed from judicial decisions interpreting a blend of patent, antitrust and common law principles.[152] The exhaustion of patent rights is practised based on the doctrine of '*first sale*' where the rights to distribution of the patented product gets transferred to the buyer of the patented property with the first sale of the product. The rationale for the first sale doctrine is the same in any conventional exhaustion doctrine where the right of the patent holder to exclude others from exploiting the patent ends since he has already been rewarded with the first sale of the product. The only possible difference between the doctrines of '*first sale*' and '*exhaustion*' is that while the former is controlled by laws of contract for sale while the latter establishes out-right exhaustion without any possibility of opt-out.[153] Finally, whether in case of exhaustion doctrine or that of implied license, the practice of these doctrines emphasize the need to impose necessary market bound restrictions on the patent rights beyond the legislative requirements of patent law, namely '*enabling disclosure*' and limited monopoly.

The principle of first sale in patent law was developed in the US through case law as early as 1873.[154] In one of the early cases the patent holder, Merrill & Horner had assigned all rights, title and interest pertaining to the patent (for improvement of coffin lids) to Lockhart & Seelye of Cambridge in Middlesex County, Massachusetts but was restricted to manufacture, use and sell the patented products within a radius of ten miles of Boston. Lockhart & Seelye again assigned their patent right to a person named Adams.

Here the defendant, Burke was an undertaker in the business of arranging and supervising burial of the dead and preparation of graves in the town of Natwick (which was approximately 17 miles from Boston, hence outside the mentioned circle). As a part of his work Burke often bought coffins from suppliers and sold them to the personal representatives of the deceased person who instructed him for organising the burial. In this case, he bought coffins and used the same for his work on payment by a party. The plaintiff, Adams found this and got hold of a Bill of costs confirming the sale of the coffin by Burke and produced the bill to file a case before the court alleging infringement of the patent right by the defendant Burke (since he sold the coffin with

152 Ibid at 106, pgs., 16 (3–22).

153 Kieff Scott, "Quanta v LG Electronics: Frustrating Patent Deals by taking Contracting Options off the Table?", John M. Olin Program in Law and Economics, Stanford Law School, Working Paper No. 366, pg. 321, September 2008.

154 *Adam v Burke*, 84 U.S. 453 (1873).

the patented coffin-lid). The defendant pleaded before the court that he had not used or sold any coffin that contained the patented invention and claimed that he had bought the coffins from Lockhart and Seelye (who had been assigned the patent right by the original patent holder hence the product was not a counterfeit). The Circuit Court had dismissed the plaintiff's claim that took the case to the Supreme Court on appeal.

It must be noted here that an earlier case *Bloomer v McQuewan*, confirmed the right of the purchaser to use the patented product after he bought it, relinquishing the patent rights of the seller. In this case Mr. Chief Justice Taney had stated that when the machine (whether covered by a patent or free from patents) passed hands and went to the hands of the purchaser, it was no longer within the limits of the patent.[155] *Adams v Burke* was a step ahead of *Bloomer v McQuewan*, while delivering the opinion of the Supreme Court Mr. Justice Miller was of the opinion,

> When the patentee, or the person having his rights, sells a machine or instrument whose sale value is in its use, he receives the consideration for its use and he parts with the right to restrict that use. The Article, in the language of the court, passes without the limit of the monopoly. That is to say, the patentee or his assignee having in the act of sale received all the royalty or consideration which he claims for the use of his invention in that particular machine or instrument, it is open to the use of the purchaser without further restriction on account of the monopoly of the patentees.[156]

Although the Supreme Court affirmed the decision of the Circuit Court dismissing the plaintiff's bill, there were dissenting views among the other judges on the bench. In a way this was the first case of parallel trade of patented goods decided by the US judiciary. Although the right of Lockhart & Seelye to manufacture, sell and use the coffin-lids was limited to a particular area (restricted within a circle of ten miles around Boston), it was made clear in this judgment that a purchaser who had purchased a single coffin from them did not only purchase the coffin but the right to use the coffin and all rights which came with it. Specifying the rights acquired by the purchaser, it was stated that as the patent holder had received his consideration the product was no longer within the monopoly of the patent. Determining the doctrine of '*exhaustion*' or the

155 *Bloomer v. McQuewan*, 14 How. 539.
156 *Bloomer v. McQuewan*, 14 How. 539.

'first sale' doctrine very clearly, the judgement was stated that imposing a limitation on the sale of the patented product would be extension of the monopoly beyond its statutory mandate. It also mentioned that even if the patent holders might subdivide their patents territorially and restrict further manufacture or sale within a specified area contractually, as in this case, if such products are manufactured or sold legally, even such contractual limitations would not hold good once the product was sold.

In the case of *Holiday v Mattheson* where the patents were held by Holiday in US and the UK, the patents of Holiday were considered exhausted based on the doctrine of *'first sale'*.[157] In this case, the importer bought the patented product from a third party who had purchased the same in England (which was on sale without any specific restriction as to the market in which it was to be sold), imported it to US and sold it. The court emphasised on the fact that since the patent holder had not imposed any contractual restriction, the patent holder was unable to restrict the sale of the product based on the patent right. There was abject clarity in the decision as to international exhaustion where the sale of the patented product in England, exhausted the patent rights in US and the patent holder was not allowed to stop the defendant from using or selling the product in the US.[158]

It was in 1890 that the nature of exhaustion in the US was reconfirmed by the *Boesch v Graff* case.[159] In this case there were three issues in conflict but the one which was relevant from the perspective of the doctrine of exhaustion was the question as to whether a dealer residing in the US could buy patented products from a legitimate seller in another country (from a licensee) and import and sell them in the US (where there was an existing patent on such product) without any further licence or permission from the US patent holder. The Court opined that foreign law could not control US patents. Hence, following the territoriality principle, it decided that if an existing patent in the US protected a product, the US dealer could not import and/or sale the patented product without a permission or licence from the US patent holder. This was a clear case of limiting exhaustion within the national boundaries thus establishing the mode of national exhaustion.

---

157 *Holiday v. Mattheson*, 24 Fed. 185–1866 (C.C.S.D.N.Y. 1885).

158 Rothchild John, "Exhaustion of intellectual property rights and the principle of territoriality in the United States", in Calboli Irene and Lee Edward (eds.), "Research handbook on Intellectual Property Exhaustion and Parallel Imports", Edward Elgar Publishing Ltd., pg. 241, (226–245), 2016.

159 *Boesch v. Graff* 133 US 697 (1890).

A few years later in a case in which the patent owner restricted the assignee's rights to a great extent through different assignment contracts (which the defendant alleged to be in violation of the act of congress) the court discussed in detail the act of congress and allowed a defence on the part of the defendant but decided that the contracts were not in violation of the said act of congress.[160] Thus, the Supreme Court allowed restrictions to be imposed by way of contract (both through assignment and licence). In such cases, the patent holder could control the ambit of their patents contractually if such limitations were not illegal in nature and provided the licensee agreed to the contract.[161] This was again a turning point from earlier case law where a pure form of exhaustion was established to a practice that was more in the nature of an 'implied licence'.

Another important decision by the Supreme Court of US in favour of the first sale doctrine effectively establishing the exhaustion of patent rights is *United States v Univis Lens Co. Inc.*[162] In this case, Univis Lens Company Incorporated (Univis), owned the method and product patents on multifocal optical lenses. Univis sold these patented multifocal optical lenses as lens blanks and licensed both wholesalers and retailers to grind and polish them, as required to sell them as prescription lenses for correction spectacles. The District Court had earlier held while deciding patent infringement of the Univis Lens that if the patent over an unfinished product requires certain essential features to be completed by the licensee without violation of the patent as such, then the patent holder exhausts his/her rights over the patent and the licensee's actions would not be considered an infringement of the patent. The Supreme Court upheld the decision of the District Court as the lens blanks manufactured by the patent owner, Univis could only be used as prescription glasses for which it was essential to be grinded and polished. It is interesting to note that the case was brought in as a violation of the Sherman Act (Antitrust Law), where the question raised was that the license contract was anti-competitive. This decision is a distinct

160 26 Staat. at L 209 dated July 2, 1890.

161 *E. Bement & Sons v National Harrow Co.*, 186 U.S. 70, 91 (1902).

162 *United States v Univis Lens Co.*, 316 U.S. 241 (1942). In this case the Supreme Court upheld the judgement of the district court and stated, "The patentee may surrender his monopoly in whole by the sale of his patent or in part by the sale of an article embodying the invention. His monopoly remains so long as he retains the ownership of the patented Article. But the sale of it exhausts the monopoly in that Article and the patentee may not thereafter, by virtue of his patent, control the use or disposition of the Article". The apex court had confirmed in this case that there was no violation of the Sherman Act and the features of the contracts do not come under the exceptions of the Millers-Tyding Act in any way.

example of a case in which imposing restrictions to the first sale doctrine by way of binding the purchaser through a contract did not hold ground since it was proved to be anti-competitive.

It is found that with the passage of time, the principle of first sale became an established rule in the US by virtue of case law. But at the same time the Courts decided the eligibility of the restrictions imposed on the exhaustion of patent rights on case-by-case basis. Hence the Court allowed contractual restrictions in cases where such restrictions were not in violation of any competition law. It is important to mention that although case law established the principle of first sale, the mode of exhaustion national or international was not yet decided. In the unique case of *Sanofi S.A. v Med-Tech Veterinarian Products Inc.* decided by the US District Court of New Jersey, it was held that although the foreign patent holder owned a product patent in US, it could not restrict re-sale of the patented products in the US. This was because it did not put any restrictions in the sale contract by way of notice and it sold its products in a country where it did not have any patent over its products.[163]

This case established that in case of unrestricted first sale by the patent holder or the licensee outside the US, the US patent holder would exhaust his rights.[164] However, if the first unrestricted sale was not by the US patent holder or his licensee, then it would not exhaust. In this case the patent holder had drawn out an exclusive licence in favour of a company (American Home Products Corporation) in the US. As an exclusive licensee it had the right to injunctive remedy against any unauthorised distribution of the patented goods in the US. In case of the patented goods being imported from abroad (parallel imports), the licensee could treat them as unauthorised and considered as infringed goods. The verdict of this case enabled the licensee to restrict the sale of the imported goods. As a matter of fact, different courts in the US started following this line and although in principle they follow the doctrine of first sale, they allowed the patent holder to impose restrictions. In most cases it was noticed that there was a clear indication since 1988 towards national exhaustion in cases of process patents while interpreting *Section 35 USC Sec 271(g)*.[165] Thus, if any patented product is manufactured outside the US by its

163 *Sanofi S.A. v. Med-Tech Veterinarian Products Inc.* 565 F. Supp. 931 (1983).

164 Turton Michael and Mills Aleta, "The first sale doctrine and parallel imports in the United States after Jazz photo", Comments 3 E.I.P.R., pgs. 149, 150, (148–152) 2004.

165 *35 USC Sec 271* states, "(g) Whoever without authority imports into the United States or offers to sell, or uses within the United States a product which is made by a process patented in the United States shall be liable as and infringer, if the importation, offer to sell, sale, or use of the product occurs during the term of such process patent. In an action for infringement of a process patent, no remedy may be granted for infringement on account

licensee and then imported into the US, it will be treated to be an infringed product (even if it is manufactured by a subsidiary). Here it is important that the process in which it is made needs to be covered under a process patent in US. Thus, process patents will not exhaust internationally but only nationally.

In 1998, the US Supreme Court judgement on Quality King relating to the exhaustion of copyrights caused a good amount of introspection that it might even influence other modes of IP, including patents. The judgement was contrary to the US government's much advocated national exhaustion policy taken in global trade negotiations. In this case the Court held that if the US copyrighted products were exported, they could be freely imported back. This meant that international exhaustion was accepted and thus parallel import in the form of re-import was allowed. Here it is worthy of note that the US government not only strongly advocates a national exhaustion policy, but this is its position beyond its boundaries. Recently it influenced five small countries (Cambodia, Ecuador, Sri Lanka, Tobago and Trinidad) into treaty obligations to provide protection against parallel imports.[166] The first such instance was the US – Morocco Free Trade Agreement.[167] Further this is evident from the position taken by the office of the USTR, which strictly advocates the position of national exhaustion, well reflected in all their representations at the WTO and all other international bodies. The USTR's position against parallel imports is not based on any analytical study but because of industry pressure.[168]

It must be carefully noted that although the US Supreme Court had decided in favour of the international exhaustion mode in copyright related matter, a later judgement by the US Court of Appeals for the Federal Circuit was against international exhaustion in a patent related matter.[169] In this case Fuji Photo Film Company owned US patents in different inventions related to single use

of the non-commercial use or retail sale of a product unless there is no adequate remedy under this title for infringement on account of the importation or other use, offer to sell, or sale of that product. A product which is made by a patented process will, for purposes of this title, not be considered to be so made after- (1) it is materially changed by subsequent processes; or (2) it becomes a trivial and nonessential component of another product."

166 Jehoram Herman, "Prohibition of Parallel Imports through Intellectual property Rights", 30 (5) IIC pg. 150, 1999.

167 See, https://ustr.gov/sites/default/files/uploads/agreements/fta/morocco/asset_upload_file797_3849.pdf.

168 Ibid at 5, pg. 177, (177–187).

169 Barrett Margreth, "A Fond Farewell to Parallel Imports of Patented Goods: The United States and the Rule of International Exhaustion", pgs. 571–577, Issue 12 E.I.P.R. 2002. See discussion on *Jazz Photo Corp. V. International Trade Commission*, 264 F. 3d 1094 (Fed. Cir. 2001), U.S. Supreme Court No. 01–1158, filed February 6, 2002.

disposable cameras sold by the company and its licensees. After the film was completely exposed, the photo processor (in the studio) opened the plastic shell of the camera, removed the film for processing and discarded the shell. Fuji did not intend to use these camera shells again, however third-party firms in China started obtaining and refurbishing large number of such cameras for re-use. In this particular case a company named '*Jazz Photo*' bought such refurbished cameras and re-imported them into the US for resale attracting infringement action. Such act of refurbishing could not qualify as repair of the cameras since they were basically re-constructed without permission of the patent holder.

Here the dispute was whether the doctrine of exhaustion should apply or it would be considered infringement of the patent. Further Fuji also argued that it had imposed contractual restrictions on reuse of the camera. In its contention it argued that the doctrine of exhaustion did not apply to process claims and was restricted only to apparatus claims under the US laws and as such the process and design claims of Fuji's patent was infringed. It is interesting to note that the Federal Circuit Court did not find Fuji to have effectively imposed any contractual restriction on the re-use of the camera and also the defence of repair of the camera would apply not only to the apparatus claims but also to the process, design and utility claims.

The Court raised a different issue, ultimately deciding in favour of national exhaustion.

> Fuji states that some of the imported … cameras originated and were sold only overseas, but are included in the refurbished importations by some of the respondents. The record supports this statement, which does not appear to be disputed. United States patent rights are not exhausted by products of foreign provenance. To invoke the protection of the first sale doctrine, the authorized first sale must have occurred under the United States patent law. Our decision applies only to [cameras] for which the United States patent right has been exhausted by first sale in the United States. Imported [cameras] of solely foreign provenance are not immunized from infringement of United States patent by the nature of their refurbishment.[170]

Two recent judgements by the US Courts are of utmost importance for considering patent exhaustions. The first, a landmark judgement by the Supreme

170 Ibid at 169.

Court of USA, *Quanta v. LGE.,*[171] where the court not only decided in favour of the first sale doctrine but also established exhaustion of patents in specific terms. It further clarified that conditional sale was disallowed and contractual restrictions were annulled. In this decision, the court relied heavily on a previous case, *United States v. Univis Lens Co.*, (discussed earlier).[172]

In *Quanta,* LGE alleged infringement of three of its method patents on computers that LGE had licensed to Intel Corporation (Intel). Intel makes and sells semiconductor chips at multiple levels of the supply chain and as is often the practice, LG executed a portfolio license in favour of Intel. Equipped with the license agreement, Intel manufactured computer systems embedding chips that were made under patent license from LG and sold them without restrictions to third parties from further using the chips in combination with non-Intel products.[173] In a separate Master Agreement, Intel mentioned to its customers that the Intel product was under license from LGE it did not violate any of its patents. However, it was also mentioned that it did not cover any combination that combined Intel's product with any non-Intel product, although that would not breach the contract and result in termination of the Patent License.[174]

Quanta purchased microprocessors and chipsets from Intel and combined them with non-Intel memory and buses and although it did not modify Intel's components, it worked the LGE patents. At this, LGE filed a complaint against Quanta alleging infringement of its three patents since it combined the Intel and non-Intel products. Quanta pleaded defence of non-infringement based on the doctrine of exhaustion, claiming that the LGE patents had exhausted. The District Court held in its interim judgement that LGE forfeited the rights to

---

171 *Quanta Computer, Inc., et al. v. LG Electronics, Inc.* (No. 06–937) 453 F. 3d 1364, reversed (Supreme Court, 9 June, 2008).

172 Ibid at 162. In this case the Supreme Court upheld the judgement of the district court and stated, "The patentee may surrender his monopoly in whole by the sale of his patent or in part by the sale of an Article embodying the invention. His monopoly remains so long as he retains the ownership of the patented Article. But the sale of it exhausts the monopoly in that Article and the patentee may not thereafter, by virtue of his patent, control the use or disposition of the Article". The apex court had confirmed in this particular case that there was no violation of the Sherman Act and the features of the contracts do not come under the exceptions of the Millers-Tyding Act in any way.

173 Paul John, Freeman Kia, Gerstenblish Bart and Underwood Jessica, "The U.S. Supreme Court clarifies Patent Exhaustion", Les Nouvelles, pgs. 154, 155, 156, (149–157), September 2008.

174 Painchod Francois and Cebron Claire, "Overview of the implications of the Quanta Computer Inc. v LG Electronics Inc. Decision on the drafting of License Agreements from a Canadian Perspective", les Nouvelles pgs. 99, 100, (99–104), June 2009.

infringement action based on exhaustion, since Quanta was a legitimate purchaser of the Intel Products. In a subsequent order limiting the interim judgement, the court however decided that since LGE patents included method claims, exhaustion would not apply. According to the court, exhaustion applied only on products and not to process,

> patent exhaustion applies only to apparatus or composition-of-matter claims that describe a physical object, and does not apply to process, or method, claims that describe operations to make or use a product.[175]

On appeal at the Court of Appeals for the Federal Circuit, the earlier decision was affirmed in part and revised in part where the court agreed that the exhaustion doctrine did not apply to process claims. At the same time concluded that the exhaustion did not apply in the Quanta case because LGE did not license Intel to sell the Intel products to Quanta for use in combination with non-Intel products.

The Supreme Court relied on the earlier *Univis* judgement and opined that the licensed products sold by Intel did not infringe the patents even if they had read on the patent claims. It would have exhausted irrespective of the contractual restrictions since there were no other non-fringing alternatives, it is only those combinations with non-Intel products that were infringing. The court held that although it is true that patented process might not be sold in the same way as a patented product, but since the patented process is embedded in the product itself, the sale of such patented products/devices would exhaust the patents. Hence it is erroneous to state that only product patents would exhaust while process or method patents would not exhaust (internationally).[176]

The court went on further to lay down the reasoning behind such decision,

> Eliminating exhaustion for method patents would seriously undermine the exhaustion doctrine. Patent holders seeking to avoid patent exhaustion could simply draft their patent claims to describe a method rather than an apparatus. Apparatus and method claims 'may approach each other so nearly that it will be difficult to distinguish the process from the function of the apparatus'. By characterizing their claims as method instead of apparatus claims, or including a method claim for the

175 Ibid at 171.

176 Verbraeken Erik, "Recent U.S. and EU developments: The Exhaustion Theory is not yet exhausted", les Nouvelles, pg. 157 (148–161), September 2009.

> machines' patented method of performing its task, a patent drafter could shield practically any patented item from exhaustion.[177]

In the second contention between the parties as to whether by combining the Intel and non-Intel products, there was infringement of the LGE patents, the court found similarity with *Univis*. In *Univis* it was found that the lenses could only be used as prescription lenses after they were grounded and polished, hence grinding and polishing the lenses were essential features, and working them did not result in infringement of the patents. In this case it was established beyond doubt that the Intel microprocessors and chipsets could work only if they were attached to memory and buses and Quanta did not modify Intel's products in any manner by combining them with non-Intel products. Here it must be noted that LGE could not provide any alternate use of Intel's microprocessors and chipsets manufactured by the patented method other than that used by Quanta.

The Intel products were specifically designed to function only when memory or buses were attached; Quanta was not required to make any creative or inventive decision when it added those parts. Quanta had no alternative but to follow Intel's specifications in incorporating the Intel Products into its computers because it did not know their internal structure, which Intel guards as a trade secret.

Hence the court established that Intel's products embedded the patents.

Finally, the court considered the nature of the license agreement between LGE and Intel and found that the agreement did not specifically bar Intel to sell its microprocessors and chipsets to any purchaser who intended to combine their products with those are not their products. Further, although there was a provision requiring notice to Intel's purchasers barring them from combining Intel products with non-Intel products, the agreement did not mention that breach of that agreement would constitute breach of the License Agreement between LGE and Intel. As a result, although Quanta used Intel products in combination with non-Intel products thus in violation of the notice provided by Intel, that did not disturb the master agreement between LGE and Intel. There were no conditions imposed on Intel to sell the patented products, hence, with LGE licensing Intel to use the patented processes to manufacture the microprocessors and chipsets, LGE had exhausted its rights to restrict any third party from using Intel's products manufactured under the patented process under license from LGE. The court also held that the issue of notification

177 Ibid at 171.

of restriction against implied license does not hold ground since Quanta has claimed exhaustion of patents as defence and has not raised the defence of implied license. The Supreme Court reversed the judgement of the Court of Appeals and established a clear case of exhaustion of patents in US jurisprudence. Given the fact that the court dwelt on whether there were contractual conditions imposed by the patent holder, the influence of the doctrine of implied license cannot be ignored.

Following Quanta, a more recent case, *Bowman v Monsanto*[178] decided by the Supreme Court, dealt with exhaustion of patents without allowing restrictions through contractual terms. In this case, Monsanto restricted the purchasers of its genetically modified, pesticide resistant, soya bean seeds from planting the seed beyond one season; from supplying the seed to any other grower for planting; from saving the crop for replanting or transfer to a third party for replanting; from using it for the purpose of research; and crop breeding or crop production. Bowman, a farmer, obtained second generation soya bean seeds from grain elevators and planted them to be sued by Monsanto of patent infringement of two patents on type of gene and synthase before the US Court of Appeals for the Federal Circuit.[179]

Bowman claimed that the patents have exhausted on sale, based on the Quanta decision but the Federal Circuit rejected the defence. The Federal Circuit stated that the exhaustion doctrine would not apply to self-replicating technologies since it would result in re-use. Exhaustion permitted reselling but not copying of patented technology, which Bowman did by growing third generation plants from the seeds. Bowman contended that Monsanto's seeds had all future generation seeds hence embodying the patents hence the only reasonable and intended use was to replant them to create new seeds. However, the Federal Circuit disagreed with Bowman and held that reproduction of a new plant from the seed created a new Article hence infringement of the patent. It also stated that the only intended use could not be to replant them to make new seeds since it can be used as livestock feed. The Court also rejected the exhaustion defence on grounds that this is a special technology that recreates itself hence creating an exception from Quanta for *sui-generis* technologies hence deciding in favour of Monsanto. However, the Court did not address the exhaustion claim 15 on '*method*' or process enabling natural propagation given that there is no clarity as to how process patents would exhaust.[180]

---

178 *Bowman v Monsanto Co.*, 133 S. Ct. 1761, 1766 (2013).
179 *Monsanto Co. v. Bowman*, 657 F.3d 1341 (Fed. CIRC. 2011).
180 Ibid at 59, pgs. 295, 296.

On appeal before the Supreme Court, Bowman still could not defend the infringement suit. However, the most important is the analysis of the Supreme Court on exhaustion, the Court held that if Bowman not just consumed the seeds as livestock feed, but had resold the patented soya bean seeds that he had purchased from the grain elevator, there would not have been any infringement. The doctrine of exhaustion as enumerated through a number of case laws in US is restricted to re-distribution and would not allow him to make additional patented soya beans. Hence the Supreme Court still held that contractual terms and conditions would not defeat the doctrine of exhaustion.[181]

Usually, the trend in the decision of the US courts have been to follow the doctrine of first sale where parties can restrict international exhaustion contractually, however, in the most recent Supreme Court decisions like *Quanta v LGE Inc. and Bowman v Monsanto Co.* have shown that parties might not be able impose contractual restriction to stop parallel importation. Thus, establishing exhaustion of patent rights in its purest form.[182]

It is Important to note that specific Insertions were made to the US Patent Act through The Uruguay Round Agreements Act 1994[183] followed by the US President's Statement on Administrative action which includes the exhaustion issue by its mention of parallel imports.[184] Here it can be stated that '*import*' means importation of licensed products to the country of patent holder. The above study of the juridical practice on exhaustion in the US shows that the tendency is to allow international exhaustion through the '*first sale*' doctrine unless it is not restricted contractually. This has been discussed in this book and needs to be mentioned that it's in dilution. In other non-physical IP goods like digital products, the US has shown tendency to follow international exhaustion. A case in point is the recent decision of the *US International Trade Commission* (*ITC*) affirming that electronically transmitted information constitutes an '*Article*'.[185] Hence, as patent protection would be available for

181 Ibid at 106, pgs. 20, 21 (3–22).

182 Ibid at 171.

183 The Uruguay Round Agreements Act, Pub. L. No. 103–465, § 532, § 533, 108 Sat. 4809, 4983–90, 1994.

184 Shanker Daya, "Brazil, the Pharmaceutical Industry and the WTO" 5 (1) The Journal of World Intellectual Property Law pgs. 74, (53–104) 2002. "Other areas of U.S. intellectual Property law are unaffected by the Agreement on TRIPS. For example, the Agreement does not require any change in current U.S. law or practice with respect to parallel importation of goods that are the subject of intellectual property rights".

185 Frankel Suzy and Gervais Suzy, "International intellectual property rules and parallel imports", in Calboli Irene and Lee Edward (eds.), "Research handbook on Intellectual Property Exhaustion and Parallel Imports", Edward Elgar Publishing Ltd., pgs. 86, (85–105), 2016.

inventions that are transmitted via electronic medium, e.g. digital models that can be 3D printed, the exhaustion principle would similarly be applicable.[186]

In one of the recent cases, *Impression Products v. Lexmark International*, the US Supreme Court decided in favour of international exhaustion of patents. In this case, Impression Products Inc. bought used ink cartridges of Lexmark, refilled and replaced the microchip on it and resold them. Lexmark alleged infringement of their patent rights over the ink cartridges and won the lawsuit at the Federal Circuit. On appeal before the Supreme Court, international exhaustion was established as defence and the sale was considered legitimate and not an infringement of the patents. However the Court did not bar the possibility of enforcing any contractual limitations over marketing of the products separately as a breach of contract and not as patent infringement.[187] The two important take-away from the Supreme Court judgment reversing the Federal Circuit's decision, decided in interpretation of statute alone without taking into account international law were, I) violation of a contractual restriction on purchaser's right to reuse or resell the patented product would not be considered a patent infringement and II) patents exhausted by sale of the patented products outside USA.[188]

As discussed earlier in this book, in certain products (e.g. pharmaceuticals), US still tries to impose a ban on parallel imports of patented products through other laws. In this regard, the foremost law to impose such ban is the Prescription Drug Marketing Act, 1987. This law imposes restriction of imports of counterfeits as well as parallel imports on health grounds and also restricts re-importation. It is difficult to understand how drugs manufactured by a US patent holder and exported outside the country can be a health hazard if re-imported. The argument is based on the premise that parallel imports often are difficult to distinguish from counterfeits hence parallel trade also fosters the import of counterfeited products. However, the same argument can be made that the counterfeits are difficult to distinguish from the original imports of patented products. This prompts an argument that the ban is actually a disguised protection to the local pharmaceutical industry rather than a health issue.

186 In the matter of "*Certain Digital Models, Digital Data and Treatment Plans for Use in Making Incremental* DENTAL *Positioning Adjustment Appliances, the Appliances Made Therefrom and Methods of Making the Same*", Inv. No. 337-TA-833, April 10, 2014.

187 *Impression Products Inc. v. Lexmark International Inc.*, 137 S Ct. 1523 (2017). Available at, https://www.supremecourt.gov/opinions/16pdf/15-1189_ebfj.pdf.

188 Ibid at 5, pgs. 253–258.

It is also interesting to note that although judicial interpretation in US has tilted towards international exhaustion, the US Federal government tends to push for national exhaustion as government policy, including in their free trade agreements (FTA) with other countries. Typically, US would restrict parallel importation through imposing national exhaustion or through contractual restrictions. E.g. *Article 16.7(2) of the Singapore United States Free Trade Agreement* (*SUSFTA*) *2003*. The SUSFTA allows the patent holder to restrain parallel trade contractually.[189]

4.4 Patent Exhaustion in Japan

In Japan the post war laws reflect exhaustion of patents in *Articles 2(3) and 68* of the Japanese Patent Act (April 1959). Initially the practice of Patent exhaustion was specifically national in nature and the rule of territoriality was followed in letter and spirit. E.g. A Japanese patent owner or exclusive licence holder could initiate the Customs Bureau to issue a sanction on parallel imported products patented in Japan. However legal history shows that the Japanese legislation never had to deal with the issue of parallel imports as primary concern, although statutory provisions were there to restrict parallel importation based on national exhaustion of patents. Some other Japanese legislation that addresses the issue of exhaustion are *Article 21 of the Customs and Tariff Law, Article 113(1) of the Copyright Act* prohibiting infringement, *Article 1(2)* of the Unfair Competition Act prohibiting unauthorised use, *Article 23 of the Antimonopoly Act and Article 6 of the Unfair Competition Act*.[190]

Irrespective of the above statutes and different provisions which could have been interpreted as to the exact mode of exhaustion, the clarity is provided through case law and hence exhaustion in Japan is often identified as judge-made law.[191] As far as case law is concerned, there are only two court cases concerning parallel imports of patented products. One is the *Brunswick case* in which the Japanese court addressed the parallel importation of patented goods regarding automatic installing device for bowling pins. In this case, Brunswick

189 Kaunpoth Jakrit, "Intellectual Property Protection after TRIPS: An Asian experience" in Mallon Justin and Lawson Charles (eds.), "Interpreting and implementing the TRIPS Agreement Is it Fair?" Edward Elgar Publishing Ltd., pgs. 85, 86, (71–96), 2008.

190 Heath Christopher, "From "Parker" to "BBS" – The Treatment of Parallel Imports in Japan", 24 (2) IIC, pgs. 182, 1993.

191 Kawaguchi Hiroya, "Exhaustion of Patent right" in "The Essentials of Japanese Patent Law", Kluwer Law International, pgs. 64, 65, 2007.

was the owner of patents for the product in Australia as well as in Japan. A sub-licensee sold the products in Australia and the defendant purchased twenty-two products in Australia and imported them into Japan. The matter was decided by the Osaka District Court strictly on the principle of territoriality, which treated the issue of parallel import as a matter of infringement and rejected the principle of international exhaustion.[192] Here it must be noted that in the field of Trade Marks the scenario in Japan had already changed with the *Parker case*, wherein international exhaustion was followed (parallel imports of Parker pens from Hong Kong was allowed).[193] Later this became a usual practise and the Court followed international exhaustion in another case setting the trend that was picked up by the other decision in trademark law.[194]

The second and the most prominent case related to the issue of exhaustion of patents is the BBS Aluminium Wheel case. In this case, *BBS Kraftfahrzeug Technik A.G.* held both a German and a Japanese patent on one of its products, aluminium hubcaps for automobile wheels. BBS manufactured and sold these products as well as licensed another company named Rorinser to manufacture the products in Germany through a licensed dealership. The defendant, a Japanese company, Jap Auto Products Kabushiki Kaisha (K.K.) and Lacimex Japan K.K. bought these products in Germany from Rorinser and then imported them in Japan for sale. BBS alleged that this was a case of infringement and filed an injunction suit before the Tokyo District Court claiming damages. Similar to the Brunswick case the District Court refused to admit international exhaustion and found the parallel importation as infringement of the patent law of Japan.[195]

Aggrieved with the decision of the High Court, the defendant appealed before the Tokyo High Court and in an interesting manner the decision was overturned.[196] The Tokyo High Court over-ruled the District Court's decision and allowed parallel import of patented products. In its judgement the High Court held that there could not be any specific distinction between the distribution of a patented product within the country or outside and thus if the patented product is of the same make, on importation it would not be treated as infringed product. The most important point to be noted in the decision is

192 *Brunswick Corp. v Orian Kogyo Kabushiki Kaisha* (1969), 1 Mutai / Saishu 160, Osaka District Court, 9th June, 1969.

193 Tokyo District Court's decision of 29th May, 1965 in *Parker I* case.

194 Tokyo District Court's decision of 7th December, 1984 on the *Lacoste* case is worth mention.

195 Tokyo District Court's decision in *BBS Wheels*, Wa-No. 16565 of 1992.

196 Tokyo High Court's decision in *BBS Wheels*, Ne-No. 3272 of 1994.

the Court's acceptance of the fact that BBS had received a royalty for the patented products once and so, in the court's opinion they should not be allowed to receive a second royalty for the same product only because it is imported by traders of another country.

The High Court opined that once the products were sold and the patent holder was duly compensated, the patent holder did not have any right over the action over the third party that bought the patented products which should be treated as legitimate goods and not infringed ones (thus established international exhaustion). However, the Court also mentioned that in case any limitation was imposed on the IP (e.g. by way of compulsory licence, etc.), then the exhaustion of the right would depend on the case and the treatment of the goods might differ depending on the circumstances. As such there should not be a '*one size fit all*' approach but must be regarded on a case-by-case basis. The High Court decision supports those who are of the opinion that patent law aims at providing incentive for innovation that is attained by its first sale. Here they also stress that in such cases parallel importation can be allowed only when there is an existing patent and the owner of the patent had freely set the price of the patented goods first sold (there was no government control or other manipulative measure to influence the price against the will of the patent holder in this case).[197]

Later the matter was appealed before the Supreme Court where in a landmark judgement the Supreme Court of Japan, upheld the decision of the Tokyo High Court strongly establishing international exhaustion in Japan even for patented products.[198] In this case the Supreme Court however acknowledged the fact that parallel importation could be avoided by way of an explicit agreement between the buyer and the patent holder specifying the markets where the concerned patented products were to be sold (that is binding by restrictions imposed through contract). Thus, once the patent holder who held a patent in another country in addition to one in Japan (over the same invention), sold the patented product (even outside Japan), the purchaser of the product would be allowed to import the product into Japan unless it was barred by an express notice to the purchaser in the other country.[199] In other words, the

197 Naoko Nanao, Takahiro Koyama and Hiromi Sudo, "Decisions on Parallel Imports of Patented Goods", The Journal of Law and Technology, 1996.

198 Supreme Court of Japan decision in *BBS Wheels*, Wo-No. 1988 of 1997.

199 Matsushita Mitsuo, "Issues Regarding Parallel Importation of Trademarked and Patented Products and Competition Policy in Japan", in Cottier Thomas and Mavroidis Petros (eds.), "Intellectual Property: trade, Competition and Sustainable Development", The Michigan University Press, pg. 193, 2003.

Supreme Court allowed conditional exhaustion that is more in line with the doctrine of implied license than exhaustion.

The Supreme Court found it reasonable to support a policy of implied license because of the international nature of the business wherein legal stability was important. Hence it can be noticed that although it is often cited as a case of international exhaustion, the Supreme Court did not establish a pure form of international exhaustion. Sometimes this reasoning of the Supreme Court, leading to the possibility of superseding the exhaustion principle as a doctrine of IPRs through contracts, is criticised.[200]

International exhaustion provides the necessary incentives to the patent holder as well as allows the consumers of the patented product to access the products at a reasonable price. Thus, this limited exclusivity of patents through international exhaustion, balances between the interest of the patent holder and that of the public since such limited exclusivity will invite more parallel imports, resulting in lower price. The judgement is indeed appreciated by those who support international exhaustion but one is unable to reason why the Supreme Court placed the exception to international exhaustion through a contractual clause. It might be that since the issue of parallel importation is not just an IPRs issue but also involves international trade, obviously controlled through contracts between the patent holder and the licensee, the court preferred to allow the patent holder an option to control distribution through contracts.

At times it is also questioned whether following international exhaustion affects the patent system negatively since the patent holders might prefer not to license the patents in Japan. However, the approach of the Supreme Court while reviewing the decision of the High Court makes it clear that this was not the case. The court seemed to consider the interest of the patent holder in a highly industrialised country like Japan where technology-based industries rule the scenario and allowed the doctrine of implied license condition the mode of international exhaustion.

In this case there were no such contractual restrictions imposed by the patent holder, hence the patent rights should be deemed to have exhausted. However, it might not have been exhausted had the patent holder restricted the entry to defined markets in the license contract. It is important to mention that Japanese government's representations at the international forums (e.g. the WTO) always adhered to the exhaustion framework provided by their domestic courts.

---

200 Ibid 198.

4.5 Patent Exhaustion in Some Developing Countries

Many of the developing countries of today were colonies of different industrialised countries and their municipal laws were usually modelled on the laws of their colonial rulers. The UK practice of '*implied licence*' was exported to their colonies where they ruled and that became a conventional practice in many other common law countries until some countries changed the practice in course of time.

The divide among developing countries in adoption of implied license, one or the other mode of exhaustion or absence of it can be observed in many Asian and African countries where the Spanish or French colonies ruled. In these countries usually there was no mode of exhaustion or implied licence as were popular in erstwhile English colonies where it was exported. Further, the other reason why any such practice was never promoted was mainly because it would have not served the colonial rulers. They would never want their rights to exhaust in any manner whatsoever since that would be detrimental to their business interests. It is much later that some of these countries moved to form international associations and became bound to treaties and agreements that motivated them to adopt specific modes of exhaustion.

As elaborated in the case of South Africa, many developing countries have amended their patent laws to allow international exhaustion and some are in a process of doing so to enable parallel importation. There is a strong belief that blocking parallel importation will be unfavourable to developing countries. It will maintain high price of the patented products since multiple royalties will be charged resulting in patents acting as non-tariff barriers to trade.[201] Parallel imports entering the country would help to keep the price of patented products low under competition and parallel exports of patented products manufactured under license would allow making use of the comparative advantage of manufacturing the product in a low-cost developing country.

Practice of exhaustion of patent rights in some of the fast-growing developing countries leading the group of twenty countries (G 20) bloc in the WTO,[202] are enumerated hereunder:

201 Xintian Yin, "Parallel Importation as viewed from the Chinese Patent Law", 2 China Patents & Trademarks, pg. 28, (25–28) 2001.

202 The 'fast growing developing countries' in this text refers to the leading countries of the G 20 bloc, namely Brazil, China, India and South Africa (G 20 comprises of twentyone countries – Argentina, Bolivia, Brazil, Chile, China, Cuba, Egypt, Guatemala, India, Indonesia, Mexico, Nigeria, Pakistan, Paraguay, Phillipinnes, South Africa, Tanzania, Thailand, Uruguay, Venezuela and Zimbabwe).

4.5.1 *Brazil*

Brazil's patent law dates to 1809, a founding member of the Paris Convention in 1882, since then Brazil had always been a member. The present patent law *Brazilian Federal Law 9.279/96*, came into effect in 1997 after Brazil's obligation to the TRIPS Agreement was incorporated into the law.[203] Brazil allows both civil and criminal action for patent infringement but parallel imports are not considered infringement from criminal action perspective hence can be addressed only by civil action.[204]

According to *Article 42* of the patent law the patent holder can restrict importation by third parties of a product that is made by the patented process and according to *Article 43* the patented product can be restricted from being imported by third parties without the consent of the patent holder in Brazil. This clearly shows that Brazil follows the mode of national exhaustion.[205] However there are two exceptions wherein parallel imports are allowed. Under *Article 68 Sections 3 & 4* of the law, to check abuse of market power if CL is granted under which the person holding the CL imports the patented product from abroad, third parties can also parallel import simultaneously.[206]

Article 68 (4) states,

> In the event of importation, in order to exploit a patent or importation in the preceding paragraph, third parties shall also be allowed to import a product manufactured according to a process patent or a product patent, provided it has been placed on the market directly by the patent owner or with his consent.

This shows that parallel imports can be restricted under national exhaustion mode while international exhaustion can be adopted as a remedy against abuse of market power. Further, parallel imports are also allowed if manufacturing

203 Barbosa Denis, "The Brazilian Legal System" available at https://www.dbba.com.br/wp-content/uploads/empresarial09.pdf.

204 Article 184.

205 See Report by AIPPI on Brazil's Exhaustion mode based on their questionnaire available at: https://www.aippi.fr/upload/Totonto2014/sumrep_q240_e_120814.pdf. Also see WIPO Standing Committee on the Law of Patents, WIPO SCP/21/7 October 6, 2014. Also available at http://www.wipo.int/edocs/mdocs/scp/en/scp_21/scp_21_7.pdf. Please note that due to unavailability of any details on the Brazilian Patent Law in English, the AIPPI questionnaire and the WIPO Secretariat document are the main source of information.

206 Ibid at 203.

of the patented product under patent would not be economically viable for Brazil.[207]

In addition to following national exhaustion of patents, it is also possible to restrict parallel imports contractually. In such a case the licensing agreement needs to specifically define the market in which the licensee is authorised to distribute the patented product produced under the licensing agreement. Thus, if the licensee exports the patented product in violation of the licensing agreement, it will be a breach of contract and will not be considered a breach of IP law or an infringement.[208] Here it must be noted that unlike many common law countries where similar cases fall under the doctrine of implied licence and a specific notice as to the applicable market in which the patented product is to be given, there is no such requirement under the Brazilian law.[209]

4.5.2 *China*

In China, the issue of patent exhaustion has witnessed changes as the Patent Act has been amended from time to time. The present Chinese Patent Act 2008 in its third revision allows international exhaustion of patents. The State Intellectual Property Office (SIPO) of China confirmed it,

> Article 69(1) Chinese Patent Act provides that where the sale of a patent product or products directly obtained from a patented process is made by the patented or under the authorisation of the patented, any other person may use, offer to sell or import that product.

The provision of international exhaustion has been specifically introduced to address availability of pharmaceutical medicines at lower price. It has never been a matter of contention.[210]

---

207 See Report by AIPPI on Brazil's Exhaustion mode based on their questionnaire available at: https://www.aippi.fr/upload/Totonto2014/sumrep_q240_e_120814.pdf. Also see WIPO Standing Committee on the Law of Patents, WIPO SCP/21/7 October 6, 2014 (53–104). Also available at http://www.wipo.int/edocs/mdocs/scp/en/scp_21/scp_21_7.pdf. Please note that due to unavailability of any details on the Brazilian Patent Law in English, the AIPPI questionnaire and the WIPO Secretariat document are the main source of information.

208 Ibid at 203.

209 Ibid at 203.

210 Bailey Christopher and Wang Lucy, "Exceptions and Limitation", in Luginbuehl Stefan and Ganea Peter (eds.), "Patent Law in Greater China", Edward Elgar Publishing Ltd., pg. 128, 129, 296, 297, 2014. Also see, Si Xiangjun (Jay) and Wang Stephanie, "Chinese Patent-Law and Implementation Amendments Bring Key Changes, Interpretive Challenges", Davis Wright Tremaine LLP. Available at,

Historically, the Patent Act of the People's Republic of China was adopted in 1984 and became effective from 1985. Later it was replaced with the Patent Act of 1992 that again got amended by the Patent Act of 2000. The Patent Act of 1985 or of 1992 did not explicitly prescribe any mode of exhaustion or determine whether parallel imports would be allowed. In Patent Act of 2000, *Section 62* that determined patent exhaustion by reference to treatment of parallel imports was not deleted. It was changed to *Sections 63 and 11* was revised again to delete paragraph 3 and the subject content of this paragraph incorporated in paragraphs 1 and 2. It read,

> After the grant of the patent right for an invention or utility model, except as otherwise provided for in the law, no entity or individual may, without the authorisation of the patentee, exploit the patent, that is, make, use, offer to sell, sell or import the patented product; or use the patented process or use, offer to sell, sell or import the product directly obtained by the patented process, for production or business purposes.
>
> After the grant of the patent right for a design, no entity or individual may, without the authorisation of the patentee, exploit the design, that is, make, sell or import the product incorporating its or his patented design, for production or business purposes.

The above language led to confusion as some interpreted it in favour of national exhaustion since importation without authorisation was not possible, while others interpreted it as international exhaustion since if it was legitimate in the country of source it could be imported.[211] Further, *Section 12* required a written license contract between the patent holder and the licensee, where the licensee of the patent needed to draw up a contract for the particular jurisdiction, thus international exhaustion was rather difficult to establish in reality. However, the presence of *Section 63* related to parallel trade continued causing anomaly and confusion as to the exact exhaustion mode followed in China.[212]

The *Chinese Patent Act of 2008* clearly introduced international exhaustion of patents as an exemption from infringement. It states that patented products or products made by patented process can be imported once such products are

---

https://www.dwt.com/advisories/Chinese_PatentLaw_and_Implementation_Amendments_Bring_Key_Changes_Interpretive_Challenges_02_22_2011/.

211 Yu Xiang, "Exhaustion and Parallel Imports in China" (The *Patent Act of 2000*, adopted on 25th August 2000, entered into force on July 2001 reproduced in English); 26 European Intellectual Property Review, pg. 26, 2004.

212 Ibid at 211.

sold by the patent owner or its authorised companies or individuals without being considered as infringement of the patent.[213] It is only very recently on 28th March 2018 in a landmark judgment deciding *Iwncomm v Sony*, the Beijing High Court confirmed that exhaustion of patent was applicable only for product patents. In this Standards Essential Patent (SEP) related infringement case it ruled against international exhaustion defence raised by Sony even when explicit language of the same was in the Patent Act 2008.[214]

4.5.3 *India*

India's Patent Law dates to 1856 when it was introduced by the British and later modified by the legislation of 1911.[215] Subsequently after India attained independence there were number of studies commissioned by the Indian government that resulted in the *Patent Act of 1970*.[216] This patent law focused on developing a strong indigenous pharmaceutical industry to cater to the needs of the huge Indian poor population. Backed by the Indian drug policy of 1978, the patent law achieved its goal by successfully establishing a strong generic pharmaceutical industry and provide easy access to medicines.[217] In the past 15 years there have been some amendments to the *Patent Act 1970* to cater to the industrial needs of the country and to bring it in line with the nation's commitment to international rules, regulations and treaties.

Under the Patent Act 1970 that came into effect in 1971, India did not have any specific exhaustion regime since the law was inherited from the British where there was no practice of the exhaustion of IPRs. However, since the Indian Patent law of 1970 was similar to the English Patent Act of 1949, it can be presumed that the doctrine of implied licence as practiced in UK would have prevailed in India too. It is not possible to ascertain the mode of exhaustion, since there is no precedent related to exhaustion under this patent law. The first amendment to the Indian Patent Act 1970, in 1999 was mainly done to introduce the exclusive marketing rights (EMR) for product patent applications in line with India's TRIPS commitment. There was a strong opinion persisting

---

213 Ibid at 211.

214 Zhang Hui, Mengling and Yang James, Wolters Kluwer Patent Blog, May 29, 2018. Available at, http://patentblog.kluweriplaw.com/2018/05/29/beijing-high-court-upholds-chinas-first-ever-sep-injunction-iwncomm-v-sony/.

215 Ibid at 2.

216 Baldia Sonia, "Exhaustion and Parallel Imports in India", Heath Christopher eds., "Parallel Imports in Asia", Kluwer Law International, pgs. 64, 65, 2004.

217 Dhar Biswajit and Rao Niranjan, "Transfer of Technology for Successful Integration into the Global Economy – A case Study of the Pharmaceutical Industry in India" (1–10), Document No. UNCTAD/ITE/IPC/Misc.22, UNCTAD New York and Geneva 2002.

in the country that pharmaceuticals would cost more once product patent was introduced.[218] By the time India moved The Patent (Second) Amendment Bill of 1999, international public health issues were being debated in the country as well as in the international forums. The Bill was referred to a joint select committee of eminent professionals, academics and it also solicited views from the general public at large.[219] There were long and serious discussions before India finally passed the Bill.

Meanwhile the WTO ministerial meeting at Doha had already come out with the Doha Declaration on Public Health that confirmed number of flexibilities that are available to the WTO members.[220] One such discussion was on the exhaustion doctrine that applied to patents and the members confirmed the possibility of using any mode of exhaustion that the country deemed fit. Subsequently, the Patents (Amendment) Bill 2002 introduced specific provision for following international exhaustion. The concerned clause that introduces international exhaustion is *Section 107A(b)* and it states,

> importation of patented products by any person from a person who is duly authorised by the patent holder to sell or distribute the product, shall not be considered as an infringement of patent rights.

The Patent (Second) Amendment Act 2002 got the President's assent on 25th June 2002 and after operationalisation of the Patent Rules it became effective from 2003.

It must be noted that the wording of this particular section of the law being restrictive, it went against the purpose of the provision, practically making it impossible to allow international exhaustion in letter and spirit as was intended. Let us consider a hypothetical case of why it would have been impossible to allow international exhaustion under the given language of the statute. 'A' holds the patent for a particular product in India and Nepal and sells the patented product at Rs. 500 in India and through its authorised licensee in

---

218 Chaudhuri Shubham, Goldberg Pinelopi and Jia Panle, "The effects of extending Intellectual Property Rights Protection to Developing Countries: A case study of the Indian Pharmaceutical Market", pg. 33, National Bureau of Economic Research Working Paper 10159 Cambridge MA 2003. Available at www.nber.org/papers/w10159. In this paper it is concluded that in certain pharmaceutical medicine segments, "... patent enforcement would result in a total annual welfare loss of U.S. $713 million for the Indian economy."

219 The Committee on Patents (Second) Amendment Bill 1999.

220 Doha Declaration on the TRIPS Agreement and public health, adopted on 14th November 2001. WTO Doc. No. WT/MIN(01)/DEC/2 available at, http://www.wto.org/english/thewto_e/minist_e/min01_e/mindecl_trips_e.htm.

Nepal at Rs. 100. To enable '*Max Bazar*' a retail store in India, buy the product in Nepal at the local price at Rs. 100 and then import it to India to sell at a price less than Rs. 500 at which it was being sold by the patent holder in India under this provision of the Indian law, Max Bazar would need to buy it only from the seller authorised by the patent holder (*importation of patented products by any person from a person who is authorized by the patent holder*). It is obvious that as soon as the patent holder realised that its patented product was being sourced from its authorised licensee in Nepal at a lower price, it would restrict the licensee from exporting it to India. If a third party bought the patented product from the Licensee in Nepal and exported to Max Bazar for sale in India, that would not qualify under *Section 107A (b)* since the third party would not be a person '*authorized by the patentee*'.[221] Since the law did not specify who was a '*duly authorised*' person it would lead to unnecessary confusion and the above analysis was the only legal analysis that would perhaps deem merit.

To address this problem, *Section 107A(b)* was amended in the Patents (Amendment) Act 2005 and the language was changed to give effect to international exhaustion and enable parallel importation. Post amendment of the Act, *Section 107A(b)* read,

> importation of patented products by any person from a person who is duly authorised under the law to produce and sell or distribute the product, shall not be considered as an infringement of patent rights.

This clearly denotes that the third party need not be compelled to buy the patented product from the patent holder or his authorised representative but any third party who can legally sell it in the country.[222]

In application of the amended section of the Act in today's scenario, if we take the same hypothetical case where 'A' holds the patent for a particular product in India and Nepal and sells the same, patented product at Rs. 500 in India and through its authorised licensee in Nepal at Rs. 100. Max Bazar in India, can buy the product in Nepal at the local price (Rs. 100) either from the authorized retail outlet of the patent holder or from any other third-party seller in Nepal

221 Basheer Shamnad and Kochupillai Mrilani, "'Exhausting' Patent Rights in India: Parallel Imports and TRIPS Compliance", Journal of Intellectual Property Rights, Vol. 13, pages 486–497, September 2008.

222 The official press release of the Government of India on ... stated that Section 107 A (b) had been amended, "... to say that the foreign exporter need only be 'duly authorised under the law', thus making parallel imports easier. A parallel import is a mechanism that helps in price control." referred to by Basheer and Kochupillai.

who had bought it from the authorized retail outlet in Nepal. However, if the Indian patent holder does not hold a patent in Nepal for the product because either because it has not filed for patent or if the Nepalese Patent law does not mandate patents (under the TRIPS exemption for least developed nations), generic versions of the patented product cannot be imported to India since the patent in India would be valid while the generic version would be legitimate only in Nepal. In any case, the patent right would not exhaust given that the product would not be protected under a patent. For the patent to exhaust, the patent needs to exist in the first case, hence there cannot be a case of parallel importation of generics into India. The patent holder would have the legal right to restrict entry of such imports through infringement action.

It might be interesting to note that in the amended language of the Section, the word '*produce*' have been added. Often it is noticed that manufacturers of patented products prefer to manufacture the products in countries where the establishment costs are low and hence allow considerable comparative advantage. While in many others which do not have the manufacturing capacity, the patent holder might prefer to export at a lower price mainly to capture the market through price differentiation. Although it is not clear if there is any specific reason for inclusion of the word '*produce*' (*'... authorised under the law to produce and sell ...') emphasis added*, in the amended section of the patent law, it can be construed to include both that are locally manufactured under license as well as imports (for further re-importation).

The main intention of the amendment was to allow international exhaustion in a manner that patented products could be sourced via parallel importation to reduce costs. It must be noted that the entire process was initiated following the Doha Declaration of WTO pertaining to TRIPS and the debate over patented medicines and access to them in developing and least developing countries. In this regard, it is noteworthy to reflect on the political intent of the government as recorded in the parliamentary debates. Mr. E.V.K.S. Elangovan, Minister of State for Commerce and Industry, while answering a question on the probable impact of the new patent legislation on drug prices, specifically refers to the intent being, to allow parallel importation of patented medicine,

> As a result thereof, the existing law effectively balances and calibrates intellectual property protection with public health, national security and public interest concerns.

> The existing law has effective provisions: ... d. The provision relating to parallel import of patented product for ensuring availability of patented products at cheaper price to the consumers. [Section 107A(b)].[223]

Further, there was no specific limitation or qualification as to when parallel imports might be allowed. This means that parallel imports would be allowed by the practice of international exhaustion hence it would not be possible to restrict parallel imports contractually, i.e. statutory provisions would supersede contractual obligations. It might also follow the doctrine of implied licence wherein parallel imports would be allowed only if it was not restricted contractually through specific notice. In such a case where the sale of the patented product was restricted through contract i.e. conditional sales, the intention of giving effect to international exhaustion and as such allowing parallel imports would fail. Another interpretation is that the *Section 107A(b)* enables not only international exhaustion but parallel importation from a country *per se*, i.e. if the product has been legitimately produced in that country. This means that parallel importation would prevail irrespective of the fact that such imports have been subjected to price control or compulsory licensing (CL) or where the patent does not even exist as might legitimately be the case in a least developed country because of the language used in the section, i.e. " ... *legitimately placed in the market*".[224]

Until date there has been a single patent case heard by the Delhi High Court in *Strix Ltd. v. Maharaja Appliances Ltd.* that has been linked to exhaustion of patent but unfortunately without much clarity on the mode of exhaustion. The plaintiffs in this case, Strix held a patent for kettle heaters with sensors and

223 Parliamentary debate held in the Rajya Sabha (At the upper house of the Indian Parliament on March 3, 2005, answering a question posed by Mr. Karnendu Bhattacharya).

224 Ibid at 221. September 2008. "107B. ... amendments are proposed: ... Parallel Importation and Exhaustion of Rights. (a) For the purposes of this Act, the rights of a patentee or anyone claiming through such patentee shall stand exhausted after an Article covered by a patent has been sold once anywhere in the world (including within India), by or with the authorization of such patentee. (b) The provisions of section 107B (a) shall apply in case of sale of any patented Article, notwithstanding: (I) any contractual stipulation to the contrary by the patentee or her authorized representatives. (II) The specific form of the transaction between the patentee or her authorized representative and the buyer. Any attempt to classify what is in essence a 'sale' of an Article as a license shall be ignored for the purpose of this section. (III) any notice in relation to the Article placed by the patentee or her authorised representatives or any other party selling the patented Article; unless such notice is absolutely essential to ensure public health or safety." (Footnotes omitted). Basheer and Kochupillai.

were selling them in India, including to the defendants, Maharaja.[225] Later the defendants on finding cheaper kettles allegedly of improved quality, started importing and selling them until restrained by the plaintiffs through a suit for infringement, before the Delhi High Court.

The defendants argued that the Chinese imports were patented hence exhausted under *Section 107A (b)*. Here it is important to note that the patents allegedly held by the Chinese supplier was not licensed by Strix or held by any of its international subsidiaries hence there was no parallel existence of rights that could have exhausted. Surprisingly the defendants claimed parallel existence of patents on same invention in China by a different owner and initiated revocation of the patent held by the plaintiff in India. However, since the defendant could not substantiate its case even by presenting the valid patent number, the Single Bench at the Delhi High Court granted injunction in favour of the plaintiff. The case attracted public interest with the intention to ascertain the mode of patent exhaustion in India and a '*Public Interest Litigation*' (PIL) was filed before the division bench of the Delhi High Court but it was not entertained for lack of *locus standi*. The court considered it to be a private dispute and refused to admit it in public interest as a PIL.[226]

In fact the above case has proved wrong the interpretation that irrespective of the existence of patent in the importing country, if a parallel product is legally put in the exporting country, it can be imported to India under *Section 107A(b)*.[227] At the same time this case does not establish that if Strix held a patent in China subsequent to the Indian patent or vice versa in India and the defendant or any other third party imported it from China leveraging lower costs, the exhaustion defence would not be allowed.

4.5.4 *South Africa*

Like many other commonwealth countries, South Africa does not explicitly define its exhaustion regime. Under the Medicine Act 1965, provision for parallel importation was made but interestingly *Section 45(2) of the Patent Act* did not specifically allow international exhaustion. However, a reading of *Section 45* of

225 *Strix Ltd. v. Maharaja Appliances Ltd.* (2008) I.A. No. 7441 of 2008 in C.S. (OS) No. 1206 of 2008 (India).

226 Pai Yogesh, "The hermeneutics of the Patent exhaustion", in Calboli Irene and Lee Edward (eds.), "Research handbook on Intellectual Property Exhaustion and Parallel Imports", Edward Elgar Publishing Ltd., pg. 328 (324–340), 2016.

227 Basheer Shamnad, "India's Tryst with TRIPS: The Patents (Amendment) Act, 2005", 1 The Indian Journal of Law and Technology, pgs. 30, 31, 2005.

the South African Patent law can be interpreted in favour of implied licence.[228] But the issue of parallel imports of patented pharmaceuticals became a highly debated one and attracted a lot of international media exposure not because of its patent law but because of another law. Given the fact that South Africa is plagued with number of diseases, there is a specific law to control medicines and related substances and their availability at affordable prices. This law was first promulgated in 1965 and amended from time to time. The Medicines and Related Substance Amendment Act 1997 was successfully brought in by the Health Minister Ms. Nkosazana Dlamini-Zuma and President Nelson Mandela gave his assent to it.[229] The Act included provisions under which the Health Minister could ascertain whether parallel importation of medicines and related substances would be allowed and if so, the parameters binding such imports.[230] Different provisions of the law allowed different measures to make medicines and related substances available to the South African people at an affordable price.

The judicial interpretation in *Stauffer v Agricura* confirmed national exhaustion. This raised economic concerns and subsequently in May 2003 pharmaceutical companies in consultation with the Federal government of South Africa, introduced *Section 15C* along with supporting *Regulation 7*. This enabled parallel importation of medicine on basis of a permit under certain criteria and in June 2003 the guidelines for allowing parallel importation of medicines, was confirmed. This is a specific case of evolution of the patent exhaustion regime in a common law country from non-exhaustion to national exhaustion and then to international exhaustion (restricted to certain sectors and subject to certain conditions).[231]

This included not only parallel imports but also taking other measures like CL. *Section 15C* of the Medicines and Related Substance Amendment Act 1997

228 Section 45 of South African Patent Law: Effect of Patent, "(1) The effect of a patent shall be to grant to the patentee in the Republic, subject to the provisions of this Act, for the duration of the patent, the right to exclude other persons from making, using, exercising, disposing or offering to dispose of or importing the invention, so that he or she shall have and enjoy the whole profit and advantage accruing by reason of the invention. [Subsection amended by Act 38/1997 to include "offering to dispose of" and "importing"] (2) The sale of a patented Article by or on behalf of a patentee or his licensee shall, subject to other patent rights, give the purchaser the right to use and dispose of that Article."

229 Bond Patrick, "Globalization, Pharmaceutical Pricing and South African Health Policy: Managing Confrontation with U.S. Firms and Politicians", 29 (4) International Journal of Health Services, pg. 2, 1999.

230 UNCTAD – ICTSD, "Resource Book on TRIPS and Development", Cambridge University Press pg. 111, 2005.

231 *Stauffer Chemical Co. v Agricura Ltd.* 1979 BP 168 (CP).

specifically provided for parallel imports and became a matter of contention between the South African government and the government of US. *Section 15C* states,

> The Minister may prescribe conditions for the supply of more affordable medicines in certain circumstances so as to protect the health of the public, and in particular may
>
> (a) notwithstanding anything to the contrary contained in the Patents Act, 1978 (Act No. 57 of 1978), determine that the rights with regard to any medicine under a patent granted in the Republic shall not extend to acts in respect of such medicine which has been put onto the market by the owner of the medicine, or with his or her consent;
>
> (b) prescribe the conditions on which any medicine which is identical in composition, meets the same quality standard and is intended to have the same proprietary name as that of another medicine already registered in the Republic, but which is imported by a person other than the person who is the holder of the registration certificate of the medicine already registered and which originates from any site of manufacture of the original manufacturer as approved by the council in the prescribed manner, may be imported;
>
> (c) prescribe the registration procedure for, as well as the use of, the medicine referred to in paragraph (b)[232]

40 pharmaceutical companies got together under the banner of the Pharmaceutical Manufacturers' Association of South Africa (PMA) and moved against the Act before the South African High Court in Pretoria.[233] Among many allegations, one was that *Section 15 C* of the Medicines and Related Substance Amendment Act 1997 overrides the South African Patent Act of 1978 and thus is in violation of the TRIPS Agreement and the language used in drafting this section of the Act was objectionable. They challenged the constitutional validity under *Article 231(2) and (3)* of the amendment alleging that it

232 *Section 15 C of the Medicines and Related Substance Amendment Act 1997.*

233 Notice of Motion in the High Court of South Africa, (Transvaal Provisional Division) Case No. 4183/98. 27% of the South African pharmaceutical market was controlled by US pharmaceutical companies and their subsidiaries.

was based on an impermissible delegation of powers from the legislative to the executive branch of government.[234]

The matter was not just brought in before the national court but the pharmaceutical industry lobby managed to put diplomatic pressure on South Africa through the government of US. The USTR designated South Africa as a '*Special 301 Watch List*' country on its annual review of IPRS both in 1998 and 1999 stating that it lacked adequate IPRS protection. To exert additional pressure, the US White House declared that the four items that South Africa had requested preferential treatment under the Generalised System of Preferences (GSP) would be suspended because of South Africa's laws on IPRS.[235]

The pharmaceutical companies strongly opposed the South African government and took this stand against the particular law, not only to influence their interpretation of *Article 6* of the TRIPS Agreement but also to create a precedent that will discourage other countries to opt for parallel imports.[236] But ironically the language of the particular section of the law was in fact not a creation of South African drafters in the government but was provided to the South African government by the WIPO Committee of Experts.[237] Further, the interpretation of *Article 6* of the TRIPS Agreement in relation to exhaustion of IPRS was also unbalanced since this Article did not compel any member country to follow national exhaustion. The case was widely publicised and there was a strong public opinion against the pharmaceutical industry. Finally, the pharmaceutical companies withdrew the case unconditionally in 2001. Till date South Africa follows international exhaustion in case of pharmaceutical substances as provided under this law and the common law practice shows that in general the country follows implied licence (although there is no specific mention of this anywhere).

This study shows that the exhaustion principle did not develop in a uniform manner in different jurisdictions of the world. Some followed the exhaustion principle whereas some others followed the exhaustion principle with variations, while some tried to control movement of the patented product after sale, through contracts and some did not have any system at all. With increased

---

234 Abbot Frederick, "Toward a new era of objective assessment in the field of TRIPS and variable geometry for the preservation of multilateralism", 8 (1) Journal of International Economic Law, pg. 86, (77–100) 2005.

235 Barber Simon, "U.S. Witholds Benefits Over Zuma's Bill", Africa News, July 15, 1998.

236 Fisher William III and Rigamonti Cyrill, "The South Africa AIDS Controversy A Case Study in Patent Law and Policy", The Law of Business of Patents, Harvard Law School, pg. 5, Feb 2005.

237 Abbott Frederick, "WTO TRIPS Agreement and 1st Implications for Access to Medicines in Developing Countries", Study Paper 2a, Commission on IPR, pg. 53, 54, 2002.

participation in international trade, linkages between most of the legal jurisdictions, the need to establish a common exhaustion principle is important. International exhaustion can play a central role of balancing IPRs on one hand and free trade on the other where customer benefits is paramount.

4.5.5 *Indonesia*

The first Indonesian post-independence Patent law is quite recent, replacing the 1910 law of patents and Regulation of Industrial Property of 1912, introduced in 1989 and became effective in 1991.[238] The Law excluded inventions related to the production of food and beverages, new types of animals or plants and methods of treating animals and humans. It restricted the validity for 14 years' tenure renewable for another 2 years and mandated working of the patent locally.[239] The Act allows not only parallel imports of patented medicines but also generics.[240] Further the explanatory memorandum allows what is mentioned as '*copy products*', referring to generics rather than infringed copies.[241] The provision of '*copy products*', instead of providing clarity sometimes resulted in confusion with counterfeits although the drafters never intended so.[242]

Indonesia enacted a new patent law that came into force in August 2001.[243] In the amended law it removed reference to '*copy products*' but generally remained silent on exhaustion or treatment of parallel imports. However, given that patent violations are actionable both by civil suit and criminal prosecution, the law provided specific reprieve from criminal action in cases of parallel import of pharmaceutical products. *Article 135* states,

---

238 Law No. 6 of 1989. Available at, http://www.wipo.int/wipolex/en/text.jsp?file_id=256035.

239 Endshaw Assafa, "Intellectual Property in ASEAN: A Survey" in "Intellectual Property in Asian Emerging Economies", Ashgate Publishing Ltd., Pgs. 17, 18 (13–42), 2010.

240 Section 21 states, "… importation of patented products or of products made by a patented process or their equivalents by someone other than the patent holder."

241 Antons Christoph and Priapantja Cita Citrawinda, "Exhaustion and Parallel Imports in Indonesia", pg. 9, 102 (101–111). Illustration of Bambang Kesowo, "Perkembangan Pengaturan Paten dalam Rangka Pembangunan Sistem Hak I Nasional (Beberapa Catatan tentang Kemungkinan Pengaruhnya terhadap Industri Obat di Indonesia)" [The Development of Patent Regulation within the Framework of the Establishment of a National Intellectual Property System (Some Remarks about Possible Effects on the Pharmaceutical Industry in Indonesia)] Jakarta, 1999.

242 Lau, Laurence J., "The sources of East Asian economic growth" in F. Gerard Adams and Shinichi Ichimura (eds.) "East Asian Development: Will the East Asian Miracle Survive?" Praeger, London, pgs. 17, 18 (13–42), 1998.

243 Patent Law No. 14 of 2001 – Lembaran Negara Republik Indonesia 2001 No. 109 www.dgip.go.id (website of the Directorate General of Intellectual Property).

(a) Import of a pharmaceutical product which is protected by patent in Indonesia and sold in a country by the rightful patent holder under the condition that the said product is imported in accordance with existing laws and regulations.

Hence remains without any changes in the new amendment of 2016.[244]

Unfortunately, instead of providing clarity, this has still not removed confusion as to the meaning of the exemption, whether it means that no criminal action can be taken but civil action would be allowed or parallel imports would not be considered as infringement. So far Indonesia had been more a source of parallel exports rather than parallel imports so the issue has not been litigated. However, if the trend reverses and cheaper parallel imports are available, there might be disputes and it is to be seen how the courts would interpret *Article 135(a)* in terms of allowing or restricting parallel imports into Indonesia.

4.5.6 *Malaysia*

The British controlled the administration of IPRs in what was known as '*The Straits Settlements*' (Penang, Malacca and Singapore) by re-registration of patents for the region after they were granted in the UK. As a result, even the applications from the three States needed to be filed and subsequently granted in the UK.[245] With passage of time an independent IP regime was introduced based on the UK model and The Patent Act of 1983 (Act 291) was enacted. This law governs patent issues in Malaysia effective since 1986 and was amended in 2000. The amended law came into effect in 2001 and replaced the old one with the main aim to address the issue of access to patented pharmaceuticals including HIV/AIDS drugs at reasonable price.

The Act indirectly touches upon exhaustion but does not define market as to whether it is national or international, hence it is difficult to conclude whether the mode of exhaustion would be national exhaustion or international exhaustion. However, under *Section 43(1)* of the Patent Act it is possible for the patent holder to restrict the licensee from further exporting the product or binding the market of the product via licence contract. *Section 43(1)* states,

(1) In the absence of any provision to the contrary in the licence contract, the licensee shall be entitled to do any or all of the acts referred to in paragraph 19a), and subsection 36(3), within the whole

244 Indonesia: Massive Amendments to the Patent Law, https://adipven.com/en/2016/09/06/indonesia-massive-amendments-to-the-patent-law/.

245 Ibid at 242.

> geographical area of Malaysia without limitation as to time and through any application of the invention.[246]

Here it must be noted that *Section 36(3)* provides all the rights of the patent holder. The provision in this Section only elaborates the rights that would flow to the licensee unless contractually restricted. So, a patent holder can authorise anyone to sell under this provision. It however does not restrict third parties to buy the patented product in a different country from the authorised seller of the patent holder and then import it back into Malaysia.[247]

Growing concerns about rising prices of pharmaceuticals in Malaysia and worries about access to drugs for HIV/AIDS prompted a revision of the patent law to specifically allow parallel imports of patented pharmaceuticals. The Patents (Amendment) Act 2000 came into effect from 1st August 2001 introduced *Section 58A*, and states

> (1) It shall not be an act of infringement to import, offer for sale, sell or use –
> (a) any patented product; or
> (b) any product obtained directly by means of the patented process or to which the patented process has been applied, which is produced by, or with the consent, conditional or otherwise, of the owner of the patent or his licensee.
>
> (2) For the purposes of this section, 'patent' includes a patent granted in any country outside Malaysia in respect of the same or essentially the same invention as that for which a patent is granted under this Act.[248] (Emphasis added).

The above provision in the present law thus clearly confirms a move towards international exhaustion of patent rights wherein parallel imports of patented products are allowed.

4.5.7 *Singapore*

One might question as to why the Singapore has been included in the study on developing countries with high gross national per capita and other parameters

246 The legal provision in Section 43(1) is available at, http://www.myipo.gov.my/wp-content/uploads/2016/09/PATENT-ACT-1983-ACT-291.pdf.

247 Chong John, "Exhaustion and Parallel Imports in Malaysia", in Heath Christopher (ed.) "Parallel imports in Asia", Kluwer Law International pg. 126, (123–135), 2004.

248 *Section 58A* is introduced afresh in the Patent (Amendment) Act and was not there in the old Act. It is available at, http://www.wipo.int/wipolex/en/text.jsp?file_id=128830#P63_4459.

that are different from other developing countries.[249] However Singapore does not declare itself as a developed country and there is no globally mandated threshold to determine which country is developing and which is developed. Singapore has been included since it is an ideal case of a growing economy that has come out of its third-world shackles. As mentioned earlier, historically IPRS in Singapore was directly governed by UK as one of the Straits. Historically, the British introduced patent law in Singapore through the United Kingdom Patents Ordinance 1937 and the patents for protection in Singapore were registered in UK followed by re-registration in Singapore.[250]

Even after Singapore became independent in 1965, the practice of registration of patents in UK under the UK patent Act 1977 and then its re-registration in Singapore continued. Later it is only in 1994 things changed and the new patent law became effective from 23rd February 1995.[251] It is interesting to note that although the new law is modelled after the UK Patent Act 1977, it did not opt for a practice of '*implied licence*'. It may be argued that in UK implied license is more a practice that was introduced by common law jurisprudence while interpreting contractual obligations rather than being indoctrinated in any manner of codification. However, it is interesting to note that with time Singapore chose to follow the contrary and opt for international exhaustion as expressed in the consideration of what would entail infringement.

Section 66(2)(g) of the Singapore Patents Act 1995 elaborates what would not be considered as infringement and states,

> *the import*, use, disposal or offer to dispose of, of any patented product, or of any product obtained by means of a patented process or to which a patented process has been applied, which is produced by or with the consent (conditional or otherwise) of the proprietor of the patent or any person licensed by him, and for this purpose, 'patent' includes a patent granted in any country outside of Singapore in respect of the same or substantially the same invention as that for which a patent is granted

249 World Bank data on Singapore, https://www.worldbank.org/en/country/singapore/overview#1.

250 Ibid at 242. Pgs. 34, 35.

251 Loon Ng-Loy Wee, "The exhaustion doctrine in Singapore: different strokes for different IP folks", in Calboli Irene and Lee Edward (eds.), "Research Handbook on Intellectual Property Exhaustion and Parallel Imports", Edward Elgar Publishing Ltd., pgs. 193, 194 (185–1), 2004.

> under this Act and 'patented product', 'patented process' and 'licensed' shall be construed accordingly. (Emphasis added).[252]

This text makes it clear that international exhaustion is preferred whether the patent holder manufactures and/or markets the product directly, or the patented product is manufactured and/or marketed by the licensee. Further, the market may be the home market of the patent holder or the international market. More important here is the fact that even if the product is manufactured by a party under a CL, it would still exhaust.[253]

Singapore is the most active patent applicant country among the ASEAN nations and its filings at the United States Patent and Trademark Office (USPTO) are also on the rise and from the perspective of trade, the US is the largest foreign investor in Singapore.[254] Obviously, Singapore's option to follow international exhaustion and allow parallel imports was not liked by the US industries with exports of patented products coming from US as also from their licensees in other countries. Parallel imports enabled through international patent exhaustion would restrain their possibility to gain additional market-specific profits hence they were opposed to it. The negotiations between Singapore and US for a FTA started and in the detailed provision on IPRs, exhaustion was subtly included in the signed text of 6th May 2003.[255] Chapter 16 of the FTA requires that, there should be means to prevent importation of patented pharmaceutical products that breach licence contracts between the patent holder and the licensee. However, there is no case law on parallel imports. This shows that the FTA has been a successful deterrent to restrain parallel imports or managed to keep parallel imports off from litigation.

4.5.8 *Thailand*

Thailand was never a colony of any other country hence the focus of Thai law in general, addressed indigenous requirements although the common law approach was generally followed until 1924 when there was a shift to civil law system. As a result, while other ASEAN countries adopted their colonial rulers' patent laws, Thailand did not have any law to protect inventions until as

252 Section 66 (2) (g) available at, https://sso.agc.gov.sg/Act/PA1994?ValidDate=20171030&ProvIds=pr66-.

253 Ibid at 251, pg. 138, 139; Ibid at 242, pgs. 54, 55.

254 S. Said, "U.S. Free trade pact to boost S'pore GDP by 0.5 Pct", Malaysia Economic News, May 7 2003.

255 Details of the Free Trade Agreement is available at, https://ustr.gov/sites/default/files/uploads/agreements/fta/singapore/asset_upload_file708_4036.pdf.

late as 1979.[256] This Patent Act of 1979 of Thailand was amended in 1999 mainly to make its law compliant to the TRIPS Agreement. In the previous law there was no specific provision for exhaustion of rights but the new law addressed it.

Section 36(7) of the Thai Patent Act 1999 states,

> the use, sale, possession with the intention for sale, offering for sale or importation of a patented product when it has been produced or sold with the authorisation or consent of the patented holder.[257]

Here consent is expected to include licences beyond borders, thus it can be considered to allow parallel imports.[258] However there was lack of clarity as to whether international or national exhaustion mode would be applicable. It was also not clear if the exhaustion would be restricted to only patents and petty patents or would also cover other IPRs.[259]

It is important to note that although it is presumed that parallel imports of patented products are allowed, there is no case law to support this interpretation. In case of trademarks the courts have not been consistent in allowing or restricting parallel imports, and in case where it was restricted, it was so by way of contracts.[260] In 1996 Thailand established the Central Intellectual Property and International Trade Court that started functioning in 1997.[261] In case of trademarks this court has opined in favour of international exhaustion.[262] The Supreme Court also has later confirmed this decision.[263] No such decision has come on patents hence one would have to wait and see how the court would

256 Ibid at 242, Pg. 40, 41.

257 The Patent Act 1999 is available at, http://www.asianlii.org/th/legis/consol_act/pa19991/.

258 Ariyanuntaka Vichai, "Exhaustion and Parallel Imports in Thailand", in Heath Christopher (ed.) "Parallel imports in Asia", Kluwer Law International, pg. 97 (95–100), 2004.

259 Supasiripongchai Noppanun, "Parallel Importation of Patented Products in Thailand: The need for the New Patent Exhaustion Regime in the light of ASEAN Economic Community (AEC)", Volume 7 Queen Mary Journal of Intellectual Property, Issue 4, pg. 370, (366–415), 2017.

260 Kosolkitiwong Punjaporn, "The legend and practical measures to prevent parallel imports", Special Topic Report to Anti-Counterfeiting Committee of Asian patent Attorneys' Association (APAA), 60th & 61st Council Meetings, 27–31 October 2012.

261 The Act for the Establishment of and Procedure for Intellectual Property and International Trade Court 1996 was passed by the National Assembly and promulgated in the Government Gazette on 25th December 1996 and was passed to inaugurate it by Rozal Decree on 1st December 1997. For salient features and other details of the court see, Ariyanuntaka Vichai, "Intellectual Property and International Trade Court: A New Dimension for IP Rights Enforcement in Thailand".

262 Thailand Court Decision No. 16/2542 (1999).

263 Supreme Court of Thailand's Decision No. 2817/2543 (2000).

interpret the law dealing with conflicts related to parallel imports of patented products.

4.5.9 *The Philippines*

The Spanish colonial rulers imposed their IP laws in the Philippines, through the Royal Decree of May 1887. Later this continued under the treaty of transfer of sovereignty between Spain and the USA until 1913 before being replaced by US patent law. The Patent law of 1947 (Republic Act No. 165) had provisions that were contemporary to many industrialised nations with validity of 17 years. An amendment was introduced in 1953 to include second-tier utility models with 5 years' validity. Later in 1997 the IP laws were strengthened and '*The 1997 Intellectual Property Code*' with 20 years validity for patents and 7 years' validity for utility models were introduced.[264]

In the present day, the Intellectual Property Code of the Philippines is the relevant IP law, providing necessary protection and administration of IPRs.[265] There is nothing in this code that allows or disallows exhaustion or deals with parallel imports. *Section 71* of the code restricts importation of patented products without the authorisation of the patent holder. This is interpreted to be a restraint on importation of counterfeits however it is not clear whether parallel imports would be considered as counterfeits.[266]

The courts in the Philippines have considered the issue of parallel imports from the point of contract law rather than IP law. Given the absence of specific exhaustion provision in the statute, it depends on any specific reference of importation from a licensee who has consent from the patent holder in determining the market for the patented product. A prominent case in this regard is the '*Mayfair*' case before the Supreme Court of the Philippines where the petitioner was party to an exclusive distributorship contract with the House of Mayfair in England (dating back to 1987).[267] The respondent bought the product from the House of Mayfair through FNF trading in West Germany and sold it in the Philippines.[268] The Court restricted the parallel importation on the

---

264 Ibid at 242, Pgs. 26, 27, 29.

265 Republic Act No. 8293.

266 Fider Alex Ferdinand, "Exhaustion and Parallel Imports in the Philippines", in Heath Christopher (ed.) "Parallel imports in Asia", Kluwer Law International, pg. 114 (13–121), 2004.

267 *Yu v. Court of Appeals*, 217 SCRA 328–333 (1993).

268 A commentary in English is available at, https://www.lawphil.net/judjuris/juri1993/jan1993/gr_86683_1993.html.

basis of the exclusive contract and not on the basis of IP law, thus not considering it as an infringement but as a breach of contract.

In yet another case in 1995, the Court of Appeals relied on the Mayfair case and restricted parallel imports.[269] In this case, Ariancorp was the exclusive distributor of '*Murata*' fax machines in the Philippines and U–Bix imported different models of the Murata fax machine and sold it in Philippines. Even in this case, the court relied on the exclusive distributorship contract rather than IP law. However as far as policy issue is concerned, there is a growing trend in the government to allow parallel imports, especially in the area of pharmaceutical products.

The Republic Act No. 8293 or the IP Code allows exhaustion of patents specifically as a limitation to patent rights. *Section 72* states,

> Limitations of Patent Rights – The Owner of a patent has no right to prevent third parties from performing, without his authorization, the acts referred to in Section 71 hereof in the following circumstances:
>
> 72.1 Using a patented product which *has been put on the market in the Philippines by the owner of the product, or with his express consent*, in so far as such use is performed after that product has been so put on the said market; (*Emphasis added*).

The provision tends to follow the international exhaustion mode where once the patented product is distributed in Philippines either directly by the patent holder or by the licensee then further distribution cannot be restrained through enforcement of the patents.[270]

4.5.10 *Vietnam*

In Vietnam, patent law is evolving and in the process of synchronising with international standards.[271] Patents are not only governed by patent law but also by the Civil Code of 1995 under government decrees and circulars and are treated in conjunction. The present law does not mention about exhaustion of patent rights, neither is there a practice of referring to earlier precedents for guidance.[272] According to *Section 796* of the Civil Code a patent owner has

269 *U–Bix Corporation v. Ariancorp International Inc.* CA – G.R. No. 41260, 1995.

270 Republic Act No. 8293 (IP Code) available at, https://www.lawphil.net/statutes/repacts/ra1997/ra_8293_1997.html.

271 The Lien Hoang (eds.), "Commentary of the Civil Code", The National Politics Publishing House, Hanoi pgs. 12–20, 1998.

272 Pham Duy Nghia, "Exhaustion and Parallel Imports in Vietnam", in Heath Christopher (ed.) "Parallel imports in Asia", Kluwer Law International, pg. 86 (85–93), 2004.

exclusive rights over the patented product to use it, transfer the right to others and protect from infringers. *Section 34(I)* of the *Decree 63/CP* of 1996 further confirms that the patent rights not only allow manufacture of the patented products, but also allows other rights like that of advertising, offering for sale and distribution and importation. However, it is silent on the rights of third parties to import from a second source of authorised patented products.

On the other hand, regarding licenses and importation, territoriality of the licence is accepted but at the same time licences cannot contractually restrict the licensee from exporting the product.[273] Hence even in case of technology transfers, the transferor cannot contractually restrict the transferee from exporting the products manufactured under licences nor the quantity unless the importing country restricts it through its municipal laws.[274] This means that the law allows parallel exports although it is silent on parallel imports. If a product has already been marketed by the owner of the patent inside the country or internationally, then its use by a third party would not be considered as infringement.[275] This can however be deduced as international exhaustion allowing parallel imports.

There is a growing trend to allow parallel imports more specifically for at least pharmaceuticals drugs to keep their price low. However, given that after opening of Vietnam's economy, there has been considerable interest among pharmaceutical multinational companies to market their products in Vietnam, there is strong resistance from the global industry towards international exhaustion. It is interesting to note that the '*Agreement between the United States of America and the Socialist Republic of Vietnam on Trade Relations*', popularly known as US-Vietnam FTA, does not specify any exhaustion mode to be followed. Chapter 2 of the agreement elaborates '*Intellectual Property Rights*' and *Article 7* provides for Patents in details but completely omits any mention of exhaustion of patents or refers to parallel importation.[276]

The comparative study of independent patent laws in the ASEAN countries in this chapter shows that in most cases, patent law or industrial property law in general is a recent introduction. It will thus take time to absorb different doctrines and concepts of the law into their legal system. The process started

273 Para 17.3 and 17.4 of Circular 3055/TT/SHCN (1996).

274 *Section 13 (III)* Decree 45/1998/ND-CP.

275 *Section 52 (1) (b)* of Decree 63/CP (1996).

276 See the text of the US-Vietnam FTA, the Agreement between the United States of America and the Socialist Republic of Vietnam on Trade Relations, http://vcci-ip.com/wp-content/uploads/2017/06/Agreement_between_the_United_States_of_America_and_the_Socialist_Republic_of_Vietnam_on_Trade_Relations.pdf.

with TRIPS as all these countries have become part of the international regime and are forced to have a quick transit from their past. On the other hand, reality also presents that the socio-economic growth pattern of the different ASEAN members are considerably diverse.[277] Hence the nature of innovation also varies from one member to another significantly.

Considering the need for industrial progress, ASEAN has prepared an action plan to move ahead on issues related to IPRS through an Action Plan.[278] The ASEAN Intellectual Property Action Plan is designed to co-ordinate the efforts of each ASEAN member and enhance collaboration among all members as well as establish regional cooperation in this field.[279] The ultimate goal is to involve dialogue partners of ASEAN as well as civil society organisations in the quest for social, economic and technological development. The Action Plan has identified simplification and harmonisation of IP laws of the Members. In this regard, considering a harmonised exhaustion of IPRS policy allowing international exhaustion might be valuable from the perspective of ASEAN's role in multilateral trade.

277 Lam Ngo Van and Wattanapruttipaisan Thitapha, "Intellectual Property Rights and Enterprise Development in ASEAN" 7 (1) The Journal of World Intellectual Property, pg. 92 (53–93) 2004.

278 ASEAN Intellectual Property Rights Action Plan (Under the Hanoi Plan) 2004–2010 available at, http://asean.org/?static_post=asean-intellectual-property-right-action-plan-2004-2010.

279 ASEAN Intellectual Property Rights Action Plan (Under the Hanoi Plan) 2004–2010 available at, http://asean.org/?static_post=asean-intellectual-property-right-action-plan-2004-2010.

CHAPTER 5

Exhaustion and Parallel Trade: Patent Exhaustion

5.1 The Effect of Patent Exhaustion on Parallel Trade

On careful study of the evolution of the doctrine of '*exhaustion*' it is recognised that even in the early 19th century when the doctrine of exhaustion was propounded by Josef Kohler, the aim was to *facilitate free trade* within the German '*Länders*'.[280] Today as distinct forms of exhaustion can be identified it might seem that since the principle of exhaustion referred to by Kohler was within Germany, it was '*national exhaustion*' commensurate with the understanding of a Nation State. However, given the fact that Kohler had no objection in exports being re-imported to the local market, it would be erroneous to categorise the mode of exhaustion as national exhaustion.[281]

The most important question which is related to the issue of exhaustion of patent rights is regarding its effect on international trade since it determines whether a country would allow or disallow parallel importation.[282] It is quite prevalent among multinational companies to licence their patent rights to manufacturers in different countries on payment of royalty/licence fee, whereby the goods produced in the second country are then legitimately manufactured often at a considerably lower price. The producer might choose to sell the product at different prices in different markets as a marketing strategy. In such scenario the manufacturer in the second country might also export the patented products manufactured under license outside its own country. Further, a third party might buy the patented product in the country where it is cheaper and export it to the country where it is more expensive. Thus,

280 During the period 1871 to 1918, the form of government was the German Empire, a federal monarchy in which there were different federated monarchs each ruling their kingdoms, Grand Duchies, Duchies and Principalities as well as Free cities. These all together formed the federated states or 'Bundesstaaten' and later during the Weimer Republic was termed as 'Länders'. Here the reference is made regarding free trade between these federated states. (https://www.britannica.com/place/German-Empire).

281 Ibid at 140.

282 Govaere Inge and Demaret Paul, "The TRIPS Agreement: A Response to Global Regulatory Competition or an Exercise in Global Regulatory Coercion?", in Esty Daniel and Damien Geradin (eds.) "Regulatory Competition and Economic Integration", Oxford University Press, pg. 379, 2001.

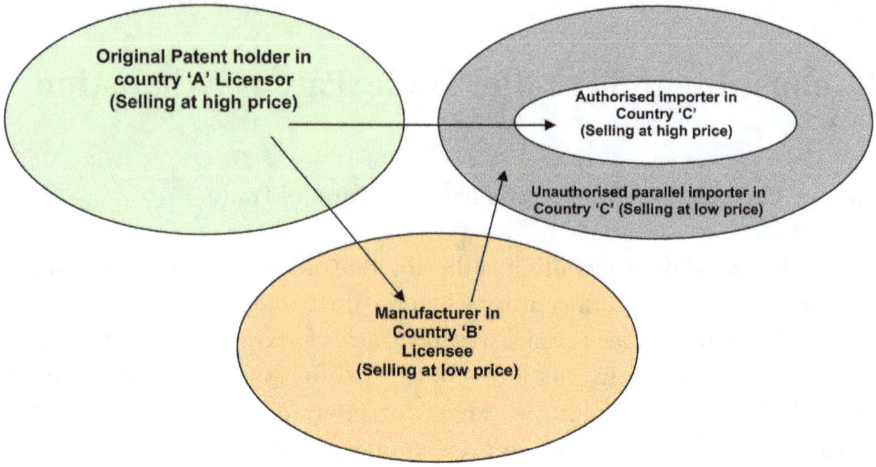

FIGURE 1 Case 1

establishing a parallel channel of distribution of a legitimate product separate from the authorised distributor.

Some of the illustrations of '*Parallel Imports*' below can provide clarity and practical effect on the markets:

In Case 1 the original patent holder in country 'A' manufactures the patented products in country 'A' and at the same time grants non-exclusive patent license to a manufacture it in country 'B'. Parallel trade occurs when importer in country 'C' imports the patented product from the licensee in country 'B' at a much lower price and sells it in country 'C' at a price lower than that of the authorised importer from country 'A'. Usually, this type of parallel importation takes place since the cost of importing from country 'C' even after paying transportation and ancillary costs is much lower in terms of the price at which the authorised importer from country 'A' sells it in Country 'C'.

In Case 2 the patent holder manufactures the patented product in country 'A' and exports the product through its authorised distributor to country 'B', at one price and to country 'C' at a higher price than in county 'B'. An unauthorised trader in country 'C' buys it from the authorised distributor in country 'B' and imports it back to country 'C' to sell it at a price cheaper than being sold by the authorised distributor. Unlike the previous case based on comparative advantage of the licensee in country 'B', this is a case of price differentiation in different markets by the manufacturer.

In Case 3 the patent holder manufactures the patented product in country 'A' and sells it through an authorised distributor. It also exports to country 'B' through its authorised distributor/licensee at a lower price than in country 'A'.

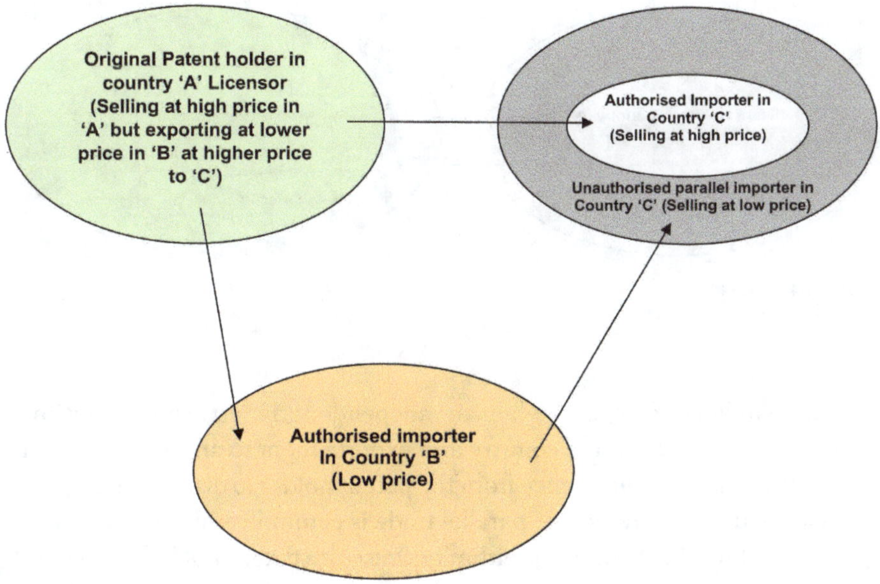

FIGURE 2 Case 2

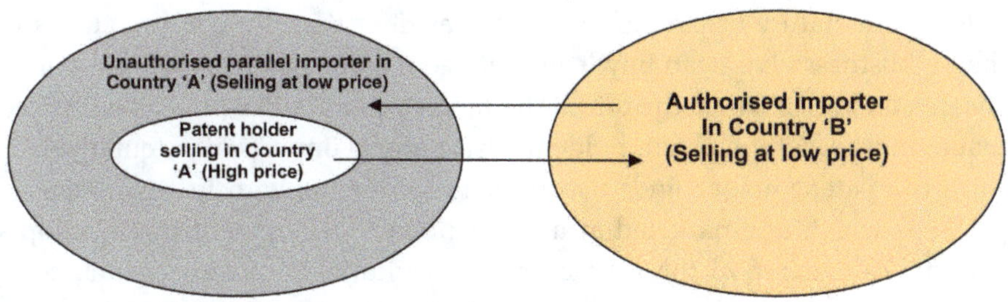

FIGURE 3 Case 3

An unauthorised importer in country 'A' buys the patented product in country 'B' at the lower price and re-imports back to country 'A' to sell it in an unauthorised outlet at a lower price.

Case 4 is when the patent holder manufactures the patented product in country 'A' and sells it through an authorised distributor. At the same time, it exports the product to country 'B' at a higher price and where it is sold through its authorised distributor at a higher price than in the home country (country 'A'). An unauthorised importer in country 'B' buys the patented product in country 'A' (at the lower price) from the authorised dealer of the patent holder and imports back to country 'B' to sell it in an unauthorised outlet at a lower price.

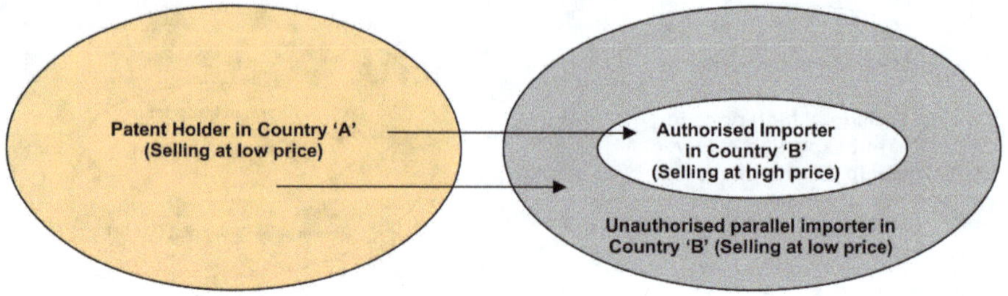

FIGURE 4 Case 4

Thus, parallel trade occurs when an independent trader acquires legitimate (IP protected) goods in one country and exports them to another country for sale without any specific licence from the patent holder to distribute the goods. As we have noticed the case of parallel trade is common and can occur due to variations of market conditions either because the patent holder licenses others the rights or adopts price differentiation. The trade in IP protected products that are sold through a channel parallel to the authorised channel is then referred as '*Parallel trade*' and the imports as '*Parallel Imports*'.

From the nature of parallel trade, it is evident that if a country allows it, then a business chain can buy legitimate goods from any market where it is cheaper and sell it where the price is higher at a competitive price. It is noticed that in most cases the patent holder resists parallel imports of patented goods since the patent holder finds its products competing with its own licensed products which are marketed at a lesser price.[283] The patent owner adopts national exhaustion of the IPRs based on territoriality to restrict such competition using IP enforcement mechanisms treating the legitimate imports as infringed products.

In countries that follow national exhaustion mode, since the patent owner relinquishes his right to restrict others from selling or distributing or manufacturing his product within the boundaries of the country, exhaustion is limited nationally and as such he would be able to restrict parallel imports from third countries. The argument in support of this is that parallel traders must be restricted because markets are different in nature and so different markets require different levels of promotion and support which is reflected on the price of the patented product. The parallel trader can avoid this cost and as

283 Some cases of parallel trade have been already discussed earlier in chapter 4 while elaborating on the evolution of the exhaustion principle in different countries and also in Chapter 8.2 on the EU regime of regional exhaustion.

such is able to produce at a competitive price which according to the advocates of this mode is an unfair exploitation which should not be allowed.

On the other hand, in countries that follow the international exhaustion mode, since patent rights are exhausted internationally, the patent holder relinquishes his/her rights as soon as the patented product is put on the market, whether within the country or abroad. This means that in case of international exhaustion, a patent holder would not be able to restrict parallel trade and as such parallel imports might be marketed side by side with the original product enjoying same status as the product of the patent owner in that country. The purpose of patent rights is to incentivise innovation and not to artificially partition markets and maintain high price that distorts markets. On comparing international exhaustion and regional exhaustion from the perspective of multilateral trade, the former stands out as more trade-friendly. By enabling intrabrand competition and restricting multiple monetary gains from same patent, international exhaustion removes the possibility of IPRs becoming a non-tariff trade barrier.

The third mode of exhaustion, the regional exhaustion is a hybrid of both national and international exhaustion to allow parallel trade within a regional trade bloc at the same time restrict parallel trade from outside the bloc. Based on the principle of regional market or community market, in case of regional exhaustion, a patent holder from one of the member countries of the regional block exhausts the patent right when the patented product is placed in the community market. However, the patent does not exhaust when it enters the market from outside the bloc, i.e. the patent holder can restrict any import of the patented product from any country outside the regional bloc.

On 7th January 2000, the International Chamber of Commerce (ICC) published its survey on the views of its members on exhaustion of IPRs. After looking into the details of the background of the exhaustion issue in the context of international trade and investment and based on the response to its questionnaire it decided against the principle of international exhaustion. According to the report there was no single global market like that of the European market hence there were no reason to introduce international exhaustion. However, there was a small group of members within the target of the study that supported international exhaustion which opined that it would allow more market competition and hence would be beneficial to the consumers as well as would support international trade by removal of trade barriers. The matter was also brought up in the Melbourne Congress of the International Association for the Protection of Industrial Property (AIIPI) where the views of different countries were different thus the matter was not taken further and the status quo of not supporting any mode of exhaustion was accepted.[284]

As far as trademarks are concerned, there is strong opinion in several countries that parallel imports should not be restricted unless it causes confusion in the minds of the consumers. Here it is worth considering the final report of the Committee on International Trade Law of the International Law Association where it was stated,

> In case of trademarks, no persuasive argument or data has been presenting for treating the EC market and the WTO market differently. Vertical allocation of distribution markets by manufacturers may have a positive effect on consumers by strengthening inter-brand competition. In both contexts, parallel imports will police against price discrimination.[285]

The owners of IPRs obviously try to achieve as much profit as possible from their IPRs and since it is gradually becoming difficult to partition the markets through trademarks, they are trying to obstruct parallel imports through copyrights and patents. Here, it is worth noting that even in case of copyrights there is a growing tendency to allow parallel imports given the market has expanded internationally.[286]

The issue of parallel trade and its importance is widely felt in relation to multilateral trade under the auspices of the WTO. Before analysing exhaustion of patents and its effect on parallel imports from the perspective of multilateral trade under the WTO regime, it is important to understand how the exhaustion of some of the IPRs other than patents can influence parallel imports.

5.2 The Effect of Exhaustion of Other IPRs on Parallel Trade

Different types of IPRs have different characteristics and so the effect of exhaustion in each case will differ. As mentioned in the introduction (Chapter 1), this book analyses only the exhaustion of patents and how it affects the possibility

284 See International Chamber of Commerce Policy Statement issued by the Commission on Intellectual and Industrial Property, dated 7th January 2000. Also, Ganguli Prabuddha, Pgs. 268–269, Summary Report of the International Association for the Protection of Intellectual Property (AIPPI) released at the AIPPI Congress in Melbourne 2001.

285 Ibid at 122, pg. 607, (607–636).

286 Moens Annelis, “IP Rights loosening grip on parallel imports”, Les Nouvelles pgs. 26–29, March 1999.

of parallel trade. Here it is also important to mention that '*patents*' refer exclusively to conventional patent rights which are conferred for a period of 20 years. Exhaustion of any patent right which is for shorter period (e.g. Petty Patents or Utility Models or any similar type of *sui-generis* protection) may have different impact and hence is not studied. However, given the fact that patented products are often marketed under trademarks and the get-up on packaging might be copyright protected, exhaustion of different other IPRs affect parallel trade. For this reason, trademarks and copyrights have been briefly discussed in relation to parallel trade to present it in appropriate perspective.

5.2.1 *Exhaustion of Trademarks*

Trademarks are different from patents or copyrights because, while patents and copyrights are granted as a reward for innovative work, trademarks are not awarded for any such innovation. Trademarks are marks or words that are coined to distinguish products of different manufacturers portraying the quality of the product. Thus, it is more of a marketing tool in the hands of the manufacturer of the product. If the quality of the product is good and/or there are inherent characteristics of the product uncommon to the others, it will be distinguished from the product by its trademark or the coined trade name. For this reason, once these good quality products are identified with their trademarks for some time, the marks create certain goodwill of their own and ascertain the origin of the product.

By the nature of trademark right, it will be clear that a patent holder or copyright owner can expect royalty or license fee for the invention, the innovation. A trademark owner on the contrary, can expect such royalty or license fee only when the trademark has acquired sufficient goodwill attached to the product marketed under the trademark. There is no reward to the trademark owner for coining the mark, the mark is just a tool. It is only when someone else tries to dishonestly pass of another product as that of the trademark owner, that the law is enforced and such unfair competition restricted. This type of infringement of one's trademarks can very well occur after the first sale of the trademark product or any time later. For this reason, exhaustion in trademarks is not the same as that of patents or copyrights. In case of trademarks when the owner of the trademark authorises another person to use the same trade mark through a license contract, the issue is settled contractually. So legitimately the licensee of the trademark can sell his or her products under that trademark anywhere in the world. The question is whether such ability to market the product globally, practicing international exhaustion should be allowed to be restricted via contracts.

Article 15 of the TRIPS Agreement while elaborating the protectable rights in a trademark, states that a trademark would constitute in any sign, combination of signs that distinguishes a goods and services of one undertaking from another and acquired through registration.[287] The intention of according protection to the trademark is to uphold the quality of goods and services by identifying them with the concerned mark. Hence the same trademark can be registered in different member countries of the WTO. In terms of WTO's legal principles as established through TRIPS *Article 15*, given that the same owner registers the trademark in different member countries of the WTO, there cannot be any consumer deception in case parallel importation of the trademark goods and services. This results in de facto international exhaustion and following any mode of exhaustion other than international exhaustion, thus restricting parallel imports, would amount to a non-tariff barrier. One might argue that under *Article 16(1)* of the TRIPS Agreement, a trademark owner can prevent third parties from non-consensual use. However, given that the parallel imports are legitimately licensed intra-brand goods, it is untenable that such goods are non-consensual unless its due to their inferior quality subject to proof of the same.[288]

Within the EC and the EFTA member states, there are also consistent ideas about what constitutes the specific subject matter of the respective property rights. In addition, the agreements were signed after the ECJ judgment in the *Deutsche Gramophone* case. Moreover, since the case law on the exhaustion was already established by the ECJ at the time the free trade agreement was concluded, different interpretations could have also been presented. It should have been clarified that adoption of regional exhaustion over international exhaustion was essentially based on the principle of free movement of goods within the internal market. However, the free trade agreements of the EC are also international agreements with third countries for which the international interpretation rules apply. According to *Article 31(1)* of the Vienna Convention on the Law of Treaties (VCLT), a contract is to be interpreted in good faith in accordance with the ordinary meaning of its terms in their context and not regarding its aim and purpose. It is questionable as to whether it is enough

287 Article 15: Protectable Subject Matter. https://www.wto.org/english/docs_e/legal_e/27-trips_04_e.htm.

288 Cottier Thomas, "Current and Future issues related to the TRIPS Agreement: A European Perspective" in "Trade and Intellectual Property Protection in WTO Law Collected Essays", Cameron May, pg. 321, (317–330), 2008.

to rely only on the corresponding or similar relevant EC regulations on exhaustion.[289]

For these reasons, practically there is no reason to restrict parallel imports of trademark goods. Parallel import of trademark goods is consumer friendly and restricts partition of markets. But trademark owners usually often try to justify restricting parallel imports on the grounds that costs of different markets are different, promotion and advertising expenses for the marks also vary in different countries and are locally borne.[290] Such an argument cannot hold ground since even if there is localisation of promotional expenses for the trademark identified product, it promotes the trademark of the product. All expenses (in different countries) are used to promote the trademark and parallel imports do not affect the trade mark negatively as counterfeits do. Moreover, the restriction of parallel imports can be considered as a constraint on competition and given the purpose of trademarks to identify the products, it is extremely difficult to support maintenance of such exclusive territories.[291] The products that are manufactured and/or marketed by the authorised licensee cannot be held different from that of the parallel importer since both have the legitimate trade mark. In case there are material differences between the products marketed by the parallel importer and the authorised licensee then the onus is with the authorised licensee to prove that the quality of the parallel product is inferior. There is no legitimacy in restraining products from being marketed under the trademark if they are not of inferior quality.

One of the early cases and an important case of parallel import of trade marked products is the *Habanos Cuban Cigars* case.[292] Decided by Justice Fysh at the Patents County Court in UK (which stands as the High Court in the relevant jurisdiction), it required the plaintiff to establish trademark infringement. The matter went to the Court of Appeals where the decision was overturned. The decision was a move towards international exhaustion although more in line with the doctrine of implied licence since Lord Justice Jacob opined that this was a case of implied consent. Here it cannot be overlooked that given

289 Freytag Christiane, "Parallelimporte nach EG und WTO Recht", pg. 99, (98–100), Dunckler and Humblot, Berlin 2001.

290 Prahl Dennis, "Exhausted and gray, but still going strong: A comparative view of parallel imports from the trademark perspective", pg. 1, 26–35, presentation at the Intellectual Property Association's Annual Meeting of 2001.

291 O'Toole Francis and Treanor Colm, "The European Union's Trade Mark Exhaustion Regime", 25 (3) World Competition, pg. 302, (279–302) 2002.

292 *MasterCigars Direct v. Hunters & Frankau* and *Corporacion Habanos v. MasterCigars Direct and Christopher Kenyon*. Details of the facts of the case is available at, https://www.lawgazette.co.uk/law/law-reports/4308.Article.

the fact that because of its EEA wide effect, the judgement is of utmost importance, laying down a path for others to follow.

The case involves Hunters & Frankau a company established in 1790 in the UK and MasterCigars Direct which was only 5 years old. Under an agreement with a partly Cuban government owned company, Corporacion Habanos, Hunters & Frankau was the exclusive importer and distributor of Cuban Cigars in the UK. Corporacion Habanos had the exclusive dealership in authentic Cuban cigars as well as owned some UK and European Community trademarks for different brands of cigars. Seven years earlier a Franco-Spanish tobacco company had bought 50% stake in Habanos and also bought some cigar distributorships in different parts of Europe. The price of a box of 25 Cuban Esplendidos cigars was less than US $170 whereas the price of the same in UK was about US $1240. MasterCigars imported Cuban cigars directly from Cuba and sold them in the UK markets at a price nearly 40% less than the marked retail price of Hunter.

Cuba followed the doctrine of international exhaustion and as a Cuban company there was no restriction on exporting or importing legitimate goods. As a matter of policy, Habanos sold cigars to foreigners through specific outlets (casas) and allowed them to purchase cigars worth US $ 25,000 in a single transaction, wherein the official identity documentation of the foreigner (passport number, etc.) was recorded. A consignment of cigars imported by MasterCigars legally purchased and well within the allowed quantity was confiscated by the Customs and Excise department of the UK on charges that they were counterfeits or illegal parallel imports of cigars imported by Hunters & Frankau. The matter was taken up first at the patent county court which held the importation as infringement. However, on appeal it was held that the county court erred in its decision.

The court considered that the trademark owner allowed foreigners to purchase cigars worth of US$ 25,000 (maximum) at a single time. It was clear that with such high amount of money large number of cigars could be bought legally and such large numbers obviously could not be intended solely for personal consumption. This meant that the company had given implied consent to the export of the cigars. By deciding on this line, the court specified the scope of the implied consent.

It was also an established fact that the sale was authenticated by issuance of invoices for both the parties (purchaser and the vendor) as well as for the customs department. The invoices had been printed not only in English but also Spanish, French and German catering to purchasers from different European countries and their documentation requirements for importation. This also established that the sale was controlled and legitimate and not as if a third party had purchased it from the open domestic market and imported it to their respective countries in Europe. Further, the defendant could also establish the fact that Corporacion Habanos had exercised control over the commercial market of Cuban cigars (Minutes of internal meetings of Corporacion Habanos was presented to substantiate such claims).

It must be noted here that although this case seems to be following the doctrine of international exhaustion, it is not so. The practice of regional exhaustion was still very much relevant however the judgment made it clear that the parallel imports could be legitimate in the EEA if the trademark owner consented to such imports (whether contractually or by implied consent). In any other case the parallel imports would be considered illegitimate and thus can be restricted through measures provided under the trademark laws and directives. Here it is worth mentioning that the European Parallel Importers Coalition (EPIC) had been making concerted efforts in re-introducing international exhaustion of trademarks in the EU.[293]

5.2.2 *Exhaustion of Copyrights*

Like patents, copyrights are exclusive rights that are awarded for new literary contributions and protection granted from unauthorised copying of such work. A unique character of copyright not common to patents is that the protection is available to the creator of the innovative work immediately from the time of creation without any registration or other formality.

The issue of exhaustion of copyright can be complicated since copyright is a bundle of rights that not only includes the right to sell or distribute it, but also to reproduce it or even adapt it or make a public display of it. The literary work need not necessarily be sold in the form of hard copies in printed form. For such reasons, depending on circumstances the copyright might not exhaust with the first sale or distribution if such sale did not comprise sale of hard copies. Further, in case of additional rights or related rights that are often bundled with a copyright, the copyright would not be exhausted with the first sale or distribution.

With reference to parallel importation of copyrighted products, some jurisdictions follow the doctrine of '*split distribution rights*' which is like exhaustion principle and the principle of implied licence but based on the right to distribute. This is because parallel imports can take place only when there is a parallel exporter holding copyright or exclusive licence to market the copyright materials in the exporting country. Thus, the parallel importer holds the same right

293 European Parallel Importers Coalition (EPIC), "The Case for re-introducing Global Trademark Exhaustion in EU legislation", Position Paper, EPIC January 2001.

as that of the parallel exporter. So, if the distribution rights are retained by the copyright owner or granted to the parallel exporter by the copyright owner or licensee, then parallel import would be allowed. But if the distribution rights to the parallel exporter is split between the exporter and importer, then it is not possible.

5.2.3 *Exhaustion of Trademarks and Copyrights in Relation to Patent Exhaustion and Effect on Parallel Trade*

The importance of the effect of the other IPRs on parallel trade can be significant. In case of patented products if a country follows international exhaustion of patents and national exhaustion of trademarks, copyrights, or others, it would still be possible to restrict parallel trade of the patented products if they are packaged under trademarks where the trademark followed national exhaustion. On the other hand, international exhaustion in trademarks can be undermined if there is a patent component in the product in cases of differentiated exhaustion regimes for trademarks and patents.

Proponents of national exhaustion of copyrights base their arguments on restriction of free-riding of parallel importers on authorised dealers.[294] They state that the copyright owners should be allowed to control parallel imports of copyright products because otherwise there would not be sufficient incentive for further creativity. Arguing that restricting parallel imports promotes competition and encourages local copyright-based industries.[295] It is difficult to argue how parallel trade would restrict the growth of local copyright-based industries, except the fact that the parallel imports would add competition in the market. On the contrary, parallel importation would allow considerable price competition in international markets and thus it is beneficial.[296] Research, particularly in the sound recording market has already shown that parallel imports can provide a competitive force via intra-title competition.[297]

---

294 Unauthorised distributors obtain the copyright products from outside the local market and thus do not reflect the legitimate costs of the authorised distributors who needs to consider pre-sale marketing and service costs.

295 Barfield Claude and Groombridge Mark, "The Economic Case for Copyright Owner Control over Parallel Imports", 1 (6) The Journal of World Intellectual Property, pg. 905 (903–939) 1998.

296 Ibid at 122, pg. 607, (607–636).

297 Theo Papadopoulos, "The Economic Case against Copyright Owner Control over Parallel Imports – The Market for Sound Recordings", 6 (2) The Journal of World Intellectual Property, pg. 356 (329–357) 2003.

For this reason, following a uniform policy of exhaustion across different IPRs is essential. However, industry lobbies try to exert pressure on governments to take a position that help them in profit maximisation through the IPRs to the extent that the country accepts such policies often overlooking consumer interests. Sometimes such influence can result in differentiated approach to exhaustion for different IPRs in the same jurisdiction. For example, Switzerland which has very strong pharmaceutical and precision instrument (e.g. watch and scientific tools) industries that depend heavily on patents, had convinced their government to follow national exhaustion in case of patents while international exhaustion for others. Given that it does not have a strong manufacturing base of retail consumer products, it followed international exhaustion in case of trademarks and copyrights. This allowed the traders in Switzerland to import products protected by trademarks and copyrights from the cheapest source in the world. It is noticed in the Kodak case (discussed later in this book) although the Zurich Commercial Court had relied on the uniformity of exhaustion of patents, trademarks and copyrights, this was not accepted by the Federal Supreme Court of Switzerland in Lausanne.[298] However later with codification of exhaustion within EU, the Swiss practice of exhaustion was also brought in-sync with EU.

From the above one can deduce that on narrow interpretation from exclusively an IP perspective, one might sometimes be prompted to argue in favour of national or regional exhaustion given the territorial nature of the rights. However, all such arguments ignore the perspective of international trade that completely changes the dimension. With the TRIPS Agreement in operation, one cannot ignore the effect of international trade law and hence this needs to be analysed from the perspective under the multilateral trade regime of the WTO.

As has been discussed in this book, the foundational basis of international trade law lies in the economic principle of '*Comparative Advantage*'. This theory is based on price mechanisms where every country produces goods and services and the price for these goods and services depend on the different factors of production. It is efficient and obvious that when the price of goods in a particular country is less than that for the same goods in another country, there will be a tendency to manufacture more of these products where it is cheaper and trade with the countries where they are more expensive. Thus, the producers in both countries will shift from producing less efficient and less cost-effective areas of production to those that are more efficient and

298 Zurich Commercial Court, 23 November 1998 in *Kodak Photographic Material* case.

international trade will thrive. Based on this, one would need to assess how the different WTO Agreements can impact the exhaustion regimes of WTO members and what should be the ideal exhaustion mode.

PART 2

Multilateral and Regional Trade Regulations and Patent Exhaustion

CHAPTER 6

TRIPS Agreement: The Negotiating History of the TRIPS Agreement and Patent Exhaustion

Different aspects of IPRS are governed and administered by different international inter-governmental organisations (IGO) under the aegis of number of international treaties and multilateral agreements. The World Intellectual Property Organisation (WIPO) is the specialised organ of the United Nations (UN) to administer IPRS globally, however the United Nations Educational, Scientific and Cultural Organisation (UNESCO) also addresses certain issues of IPRS like Copyright.[299] In today's context, amidst a broad array of multilateral agreements on IPRS, one important agreement is the TRIPS. With the signing of the GATT 1994 and establishment of the WTO, TRIPS Agreement became a founding pillar of the GATT 1994. GATT 1947 had nominally covered issues related to IPRS without any effectiveness and were taken up first as a matter of serious discussion only in the Tokyo Round of GATT Ministerial Conference in 1978.

The TRIPS Agreement does not introduce anything fundamentally and conceptually new as far as protection of IPRS is concerned since it is framed on existing international treaties on IPRS and encompasses them.[300] *Article 2* of the TRIPS Agreement establishes the link with the previous international covenants. It states,

---

299 WIPO was earlier known by its French acronym 'Bureaux Internationaux Réunis pour la Protection de la Propriété Intellectuelle' (BIRPI) or as 'United International Bureau for the Protection of Intellectual Property'. It administers different international Treaties and Conventions in the area of patents. Under the auspices of the BIRPI and later WIPO (after its establishment in 1967), the 'Paris Convention' for Protection of Industrial Property signed in 1883 and updated in the later years, 'The Patent Co-operation Treaty' signed in 1970, 'The Strasbourg Convention on the International Classification of Patents' signed in 1971 and the 'Patent Law Treaty' of 2000 were signed. They provide the basic guidelines and rules for member countries to opt for and follow to enhance protection of IPR in the member countries.

300 Yusuf Abdulqawi, "TRIPS: Background, Principles and General Provisions", in Correa Carlos and Yusuf Abdulqawi (eds.), "Intellectual Property and International Trade – The TRIOS Agreement", Walters Kluwer 2nd Edition, pgs. 19, 20, 21 (3–21), 2008.

DOI:10.1163/9789004542815_008

Intellectual Property Conventions

1. In respect of Parts 2, 3 and 4 of this Agreement, Members shall comply with Articles 1 through 12, and Article 19, of the Paris Convention (1967).
2. Nothing in Parts I to IV of this Agreement shall derogate from existing obligations that Members may have to each other under the Paris Convention, the Berne Convention, the Rome Convention and the Treaty on Intellectual Property in Respect of Integrated Circuits.

Along with the GATT and General Agreement on Trade in Services (GATS), the TRIPS Agreement forms one of the pillars of the WTO-based multilateral system. In that it continues to follow the fundamental principles of non-discrimination through an elaborate and transparent regime of Most Favoured Nation (MFN) and National Treatment (NT) that existed in Paris and Rome Conventions.[301] However, deviating from the Paris Convention, which allows members to determine the subject matter of patents, the TRIPS Agreement elaborately defines patentable subject matter and also exceptions to patentability.[302] Further, a significant move from status-quo with the TRIPS Agreement coming into effect was its inclusion in WTO dispute settlement mechanism. The issue of counterfeit trademarked products along with copyright piracy as problems hindering multilateral trade, were widely discussed right from the Tokyo Ministerial Round. Through protruded negotiations, it took the shape of TRIPS at the Punta del Este round culminating elaborate enforcement mechanisms within the Agreement itself.[303]

The fundamental reason for introducing MFN and NT in the multilateral trading system under the WTO is to have equal conditions of competition to determine that like products are treated equally.[304] The importance of this agreement lies in the fact that it established a uniform minimum standard

301 Braga Carlos Primo, "Trade-related intellectual property issues: the Uruguay Round Agreement and its economic implications", in Maskus Keith (ed.), "The WTO, Intellectual Property Rights and the Knowledge Economy", Edward Elgar Publishing Ltd., pg. 6, (3–41), 2004.

302 Kaur Annette, "Limitations and exceptions under the three-step test – how much room to walk the middle ground?" in Kur Annette and Levin Marianne (eds.), "Intellectual Property Rights in a Fair World Trade System", Edward Elgar Publishing Ltd., pgs. 220, 221 (208–261), 2011.

303 Cottier Thomas, "The Prospects for Intellectual Property in GATT", 28 Common Market Law Review, pg. 386, 387, (383–414), Kluwer Academic Publishers 1991.

304 Cottier Thomas & Schneider Lena, "The philosophy of non-discrimination in international trade regulation", in Sanders Anselm Kamperman edited, "The Principle of National Treatment in International Economic Law Trade, Investment and Intellectual Property" Edward Elgar Publishing Ltd., pg. 13 (3–33), 2014.

of protection of IPRS,[305] as well as directly connected IPRS with multilateral trade. Thus, the TRIPS Agreement provides a harmonised bottom floor of protection of IPRS for all members while allowing the members to decide the upper level of protection they prefer to provide.

The other significance of the TRIPS Agreement is that while a multitude of different treaties on IPRS catered to the governance and administration of IPRS, the linking of them with trade is through the TRIPS Agreement and it brought IPRS within the realm of the dispute settlement mechanism of the WTO. The Understanding on Rules and Procedures of Governing the Settlement of Disputes in the WTO, commonly referred to as Dispute Settlement Understanding (DSU), covers the TRIPS.[306] The mandatory surrender to the dispute resolution mechanism of the WTO with appeal provisions before the Appellate Body (AB) of the WTO, a permanent standing body, made the TRIPS unique in comparison with any of the other treaties on different IPRS.[307]

This completely changed the scenario since it was no longer just the industrialised nations that would need to provide effective protection of IPRS, but all members would need to have a common minimum threshold of protection (subject to certain transition time flexibility). This minimum threshold was much higher than that followed in the municipal laws of many GATT members at the time when TRIPS became part of the WTO system with the signing of GATT 1994. At the time TRIPS was signed, many of the member countries restricted patent protection only to processes and not products. Further, in many countries, protection was lower than 20 years and over 40 countries did not provide patent protection to pharmaceuticals.[308] With the introduction of TRIPS that was all set to change.

The TRIPS Agreement did not replace the existing international covenants on IPRS that started evolving since late 19th century to address cross-border protection. The distinct drawback that was observed was these international conventions lacked effective rules on implementation and enforcement at the right-holders level. There was absolute dependency on national court system

305 Otten Adrian, "Implications of the TRIPS Agreement for Dispute Settlement in Industrial Property" in Cottier Thomas and Widmer Peter (eds.), "Strategic Issues of Industrial Property Management in a globalising Economy", Hart Publishing, pg. 103, 1999.

306 Nolff Markus, "The relevance of TRIPS for Patent Law", in "TRIPS, PCT and Global Patent Procurement", Kluwer Law International, pg. 29, 2001.

307 Land Molly, "Adjudicating TRIPS for development", in TRIPS and Developing Countries Towards a New IP World Order? Edward Elgar Publishing Ltd., pgs. 146, 147 (142–162), 2014.

308 Vivekanandan V. C., "The Indian Patent Matrix: issues in patent amendment 2005", in Bird Robert and Jain Subhash (eds.), "The Global Challenge of Intellectual Property Rights", Edward Elgar Publishing Ltd., pg. 137 (135–152), 2008.

for enforcement of the IPRs. There were efforts in addressing enforcement of IPRs through adjudication by the International Court of Justice (ICJ),

> Since the 1967 Stockholm Revision, the Paris Convention contains a rule on dispute settlement (Art. 28), according to which, as first step, negotiations between the disputants should take place, and then, in the absence of a mutual agreement, the matter is to be brought before the International Court of Justice. This regulation is to be seen as a special, contractual submission to the jurisdiction of the International Court of Justice. It is applicable to all Union countries unless they have declared that they do not consider themselves bound (Art. 28.2)

However, even with such regulations, adjudication by the ICJ was not effective.[309]

The TRIPS Agreement stands unique from the other WTO Agreements by way of acknowledging individual rights.[310] Thus at one end it precludes discrimination between international trade[311] and on the other it allows the members necessary flexibility to countries to interpret crucial substantive issues like '*novelty*', '*inventive step*', '*disclosure*', '*grace period*', while according individual rights. Interesting to note that while the rights are elaborated at great extent, the TRIPS Agreement does not mandate any specific mode of exhaustion even when exhaustion is covered in *Article 6* of the Agreement. Apparently, it allows the members to adopt any mode of exhaustion it prefers. This, although seems to provide flexibility to the members, only adds to the confusion and hinders seamless removal of barriers to multilateral trade.

6.1 Intellectual Property Rights under the GATT and the Negotiating History of TRIPS

One will note that the WTO Secretariat does not maintain any institutional record of the negotiating history of GATT 1994 as it evolved into WTO, a new

309 Stoll Peter-Tobias, Busche Jan and Arend Katrin, "WTO – Trade-Related Aspects of Intellectual Property Rights", Max Planck Institute for Comparative Public Law and International Law, Martinus Nijhoff Publishers, pgs. 2, 3, 4, 2009.

310 Haugen Hans Morten, "TRIPS and compatible protection", in "The right to food and the TRIPS Agreement", Martinus Nijhoff Publishers, Boston, pg. 216, (213–253), 2007.

311 McGinnis John & Movsesian Mark, "The World Constitution" 114 Harvard Law Review at pg. 511, (524–526) 2000.

institution. However, scholars of international trade regulation who had either been involved in the negotiation themselves or through their interactions with negotiators, have tried to enumerate the negotiating history of TRIPS in various writings. We find considerable part of negotiating history of the TRIPS Agreement discussed as reflections of negotiators' perspectives revisited on the silver jubilee celebrations of establishment of the WTO in 2015. The keynote speech of ambassador Lars Anell, Chairman of the negotiating group at the TRIPS Symposium of 26th February 2015 is noteworthy.[312] While explaining how the negotiations started and progressed, he contributes to the negotiating history. It is interesting to note that while USA, Japan, the Nordic countries Switzerland, Canada, Australia, New Zealand, Singapore, Malaysia, Uruguay and Colombia were keen to start a trade round, the EC was initially less enthusiastic to push for it. The essence of his speech is found at the end where he says,

> First and foremost, I am convinced that it would be very serious if protection of IP were to stifle and prevent research. In a sense it would be self-defeating. There would be less genuine progress to protect. My other concern is more general. I think both politicians and the business community should consider the obvious need to demand a clear, visible, inventive step in order to award 20 years' protection from competition.[313]

Apart from such published memoirs, this book has also sourced the negotiating history from such scholarly works and through the author's personal interactions with some of the negotiators of the TRIPS Agreement where published records were not available.

From the beginning there was scepticism as to whether IPRs as a non-trade issue should have been linked with trade issues under the new WTO regime. There was a strong belief that IPRs under TRIPS were significantly different from other trade issues such as the labour and environment standards. Also, in effect, trade liberalisation undertaken on a multilateral platform produces positive efficiency where IPRs are trade restrictive. This is since IPRs can lower

312 The negotiating draft of Ambassador Lars Annell (of Sweden) is discussed at length later in this chapter. See, https://www.wto.org/english/res_e/booksp_e/trips_agree_e/chapter_4_e.pdf.

313 Anell Lars, "Keynote speech at the TRIPS Symposium 26 February 2015" in Watal Jayashree and Taubman Antony (eds.), "The Making of the TRIPS Agreement Personal Insights from The Uruguay Round Negotiations" WTO, pg. 366, 371 (365–371), 2015. Also available at, https://www.wto.org/english/res_e/booksp_e/trips_agree_e/chapter_4_e.pdf.

the economic welfare by increasing costs due to the monopolistic nature of the IPRs.[314]

At the time when the GATT was negotiated after World War II, even strong technology-based exporting countries like the US had less than 10% percent of its exports tied to IP.[315] For this reason there was initially not much interest even among the industrialised countries to link up international trade and IPRs internationally. On the other hand, developing countries did not have any interest in linking IPRs and international trade issues since they were mainly IPRs importing countries. They preferred not to increase the cost of the products through enhanced transaction costs due to protection of IPRs. For this reason, although IPRs were referred to in the original GATT 1947 Agreement, they were not so elaborate.[316] They were in terms of rights and obligations related to goods. In fact, some other international agreements like the '*Customs Valuation Code*' and the '*Standards Code*' had more elaborate provisions.[317]

Much later, during the US president Ronald Reagan's tenure, the US government decided on linking international trade and IPRs at that 98th US Congress. As a result of this, number of measures were taken to examine the level of IPRs that are maintained by the trade partners of US and how it affected trade with these partners.[318] This led to the promulgation of The Trade Act of 1984 in US, wherein different policy issues to address protection of IPRs were introduced. Initially steps were taken on the bi-lateral front wherein the US managed to effectively change the IP regimes of some of its partners (e.g. Korea, Taiwan and Singapore). By this time the US government also started moving the IP issues at the international front and it was taken up at the GATT negotiations as an issue of trade in counterfeit goods. In fact, the issue of commercial counterfeiting was first taken up at the end of the Tokyo Round of the GATT 1978 Ministerial meeting. But due to lack of consensus it had to be dropped from

314 Panagariya Arvind, "TRIPS and the WTO: An uneasy Marriage", in Maskus Keith (ed.), "The WTO, Intellectual Property Rights and the Knowledge Economy", Edward Elgar Publishing Ltd., pg. 43 (42–47), 2004.

315 Gadbaw Michael, "Intellectual Property and International Trade: Merger or Marriage of Convenience?" in Brown Lonnie and Szweda Eric (eds.), "Trade-Related Aspects of Intellectual Property", pg. 232, 1990.

316 *Article IX* of GATT 1947 established marks of origin and *Article XX* (*d*) allowed enforcement against infringements of IPR.

317 Braga Carlos Primo, "The Economics of Intellectual Property Rights and the GATT: A View from the South", Brown Lonnie and Szweda Eric (eds.), "Trade Related Aspects of Intellectual Property", Vanderbilt Journal of Transnational Law, William S. Hein and Co. Inc., pg. 247 (243–264) 1990.

318 U.S. Trade Representative, National Trade Estimate, Report, pgs. 222–237, 1985.

the agenda. Later the matter came up again in the Ministerial Declaration of the GATT in 1982.

The first time IPRs came up for discussion was regarding the need for stricter enforcement measures to restrict counterfeit of trademarked products and copyright piracy. The USA and the EEC tried to initiate negotiations on a draft '*Anti-Counterfeit Code* (*ACC*)' at the end of Tokyo round but did not pick up any traction due to lack of support from other industrialised countries.[319] Further, although the issue of higher protection of IPRs had come up in the Tokyo Round, it did not bring any impact. The US was not satisfied with the results and in the early 1980s, protectionist tendencies had already been rising in the US Congress.[320]

In the GATT, a group of IP experts was formed in 1984 to assess the situation given that there were differences on many issues (e.g. whether GATT was the right forum to address IPRs issues, what should be covered in the IPR protection code), however the core issue generally remained IPRs. There was a consensus that the problem in trade in counterfeit goods had to be tackled and the matter was taken up again in the mid-term review meeting at Montreal in 1986, wherein the US government mainly aimed at stopping piracy. The US government exerted tremendous pressure on specifically countries which accorded weaker protection of IPRs through its '*Special 301*' unilateral punitive measure under '*Omnibus Trade and Competitiveness Act*' of 23rd August 1988.[321]

Most of these were developing countries that were severely impacted with serious public health and access to affordable medicine problems. They used weaker patent laws that supported legitimate reverse-engineering to locally manufacture pharmaceutical drugs but did not necessarily have weak trademark laws or their enforcement. It is interesting to note that a perception was created by vested interests that developing countries were counterfeiters while the accuser industrialised countries were the sufferers. This narrative was deliberately expanded and propagated pushing the developing countries to a defensive position and making the way for enhanced demands for stricter protection norms under the GATT umbrella.[322]

319 Ibid at 303, pg. 386. Reference to Draft Agreement on Measures to Discourage the Importation of Counterfeit Goods, GATT Doc. L/8417 (31 July 1979).

320 Ostry Sylvia, "Intellectual Property Protection in the WTO: Major issues in the millennium round", Fraser Institute Conference Santiago, Chile, pg. 1, 19th April 1999.

321 Molly Land, "Adjudicating TRIPS for development", in TRIPS and Developing Countries Towards a New IP World Order? Edward Elgar Publishing Ltd., pgs. 146, 147 (142–162), 2014.

322 Watal Jayashree, "From Punta del Este to Doha and Beyond: Lessons from the TRIPS Negotiating Process", SSRN Electronic Journal, pg. 3, 2011. Available at https://www.researchgate.net/publication/228122380_From_Punta_Del_Este_to_Doha_and_Beyond_Lessons_from_the_TRIPS_Negotiating_Processes.

Some members presented fifteen subjects on the negotiation agenda but the members failed to gain consensus on four issues, of which the issue of trade in counterfeit goods was one.[323] The developing country members resisted inclusion of trade in counterfeits for some time, but gradually yielded. The first signal of yielding was noticed when fourteen developing country members presented their position on enforcement of trademarks and copyrights.[324] There were many other issues including some on which there were differences between the industrialised countries that kept the debate going, but finally the mandate to introduce regulations on trade in counterfeit goods was given at the Punta del Este, 1986 Ministerial meeting in Uruguay.[325]

The Industrialised countries had formed the '*Quad*' group, which pushed for stricter enforcement of IPRS included in the GATT regime with a wide coverage of IPS. This was countered by another group of 10 developing countries led by India and Brazil with Argentina, Cuba, Egypt, Nicaragua, Nigeria, Peru, Tanzania and Yugoslavia also joining. They resisted formation of a comprehensive code on IP within the GATT.[326] Finally, a ten-plus-ten group was formed and under the leadership of the chair of the negotiating group and assistance of the secretariat, negotiations proceeded to the July 1990 text.

The July 1990 text was the most controversial text since for the first time there was an official proposal that expanded beyond trade in counterfeits and pirated goods. '*Approach A*' proposals from developed countries included all aspects of IPRS and '*Approach B*' proposal from developing countries that restricted reference only to counterfeits and pirated goods. Eventually '*Approach B*' moved up to the Brussels text but was dropped as a separate alternate text since it was not considered credible. In fact, '*Approach B*' was incorporated in the comprehensive text including all IPRS hence it became redundant.

The role played by the private sector in pushing the IPRS issue in the GATT negotiations was very crucial at this stage. Practically they were the driving force in moving the issue of protection of IPRS beyond the debate on trade in counterfeit goods. The pharmaceutical, software and entertainment industries

323 Hartridge David and Subramanian Arvind, "Intellectual Property Rights: The Issues in GATT", 22 Vanderbilt Journal of Transnational Law, pg. 894, (893–910), 1989.

324 Communication from Argentina, Chile, Brazil, China, Colombia, Cuba, Egypt, India, Nigeria, Peru, Tanzania and Uruguay, (later joined by Pakistan and Zimbabwe), MTN.GNG/NG11/W/71 (14th May 1990).

325 Molly Land, "Adjudicating TRIPS for development", in TRIPS and Developing Countries Towards a New IP World Order? Edward Elgar Publishing Ltd., pgs. 146, 147 (142–162), 2014.

326 Bradley Jane, "Intellectual Property Rights, Investment and Trade in Services in the Uruguay Round: Laying the Foundations." 23 Stanford Journal of International Law, pgs. 57–98, 1987.

played a vital role, led by the Chief Executive Officer of the prominent US pharmaceutical giant, Pfizer as the Chairman of the Intellectual Property Rights Committee (IPC). Within two years the IPC managed to create a coalition of international multinational corporations (MNC) which comprised not only industries from the US but also from Europe and Japan. This coalition exerted influence on their governments to go beyond restriction on trade in counterfeit goods. As a result, issues like '*minimum standards of IPRs protection*', '*strict enforcement mechanisms*' and '*dispute settlement*' under the new GATT rules were laid on the table. This was objected by the developing countries led by Brazil and India, gradually depicting a larger North-South divide.

The issue of IP protection had caused a good bit of tension not just two camps with India and Brazil on one side and the US and EU on the other, but in general it polarised industrialised nations on one side and the developing world on the other. It even took the turn of an ideological dispute since the industrialised members pushed its ideology on the developing countries. This is because the industrialised countries tried to follow the line of natural justice wherein they tried to argue that they should not be robbed off their technological and literary innovations. While the developing countries felt that the IPRs would increase their costs since protection of IPRs would transfer wealth from their countries without providing proportionate social and economic gains.[327]

One of the main objections by developing nations to introduce IPRs protection measures, beyond trademarks and copyrights that would address counterfeits and pirated goods was because they would lose the ability to use reverse-engineering as a mode of technology dissemination. The developing nations believed that strict patent rights would hinder technology-transfer since they would increase the difficulty as well as costs in absorbing new technologies. They felt that there were double standards since their present position is not different to what many of the developed countries had in the last eighteenth and nineteenth centuries.[328] Further, the TRIPS Agreement placed a significant burden on the developing countries in terms of completely reforming the IPRs legal regime in most developing countries. This increased the transaction costs in introducing and implementing the changes on one hand and with the harmonised bottom level of protection on the other. It also imposed negative

327 Stern Richard, "Intellectual Property" in Finger Michael and Olechowski Andrzej (eds.) "The Uruguay Round – A Handbook for the Multilateral Trade Negotiations", World Bank publication pg. 205, 1987.

328 Christopher May, "A Global Political Economy of Intellectual Property Rights – The New Enclosures?", Routledge pg. 86, 2000.

economic implications in the short run where rents got transferred from developing to developed nation.[329]

India which was in the forefront of resistance against including IPRS, objected, based on the belief that enhanced protection of IPRS would retard the pace of the country's economic development because India had witnessed a tremendous growth in the generic pharmaceutical sector by removing product patents on pharmaceuticals.[330] But still in India the debate regarding IP protection was divided between definite groups but not effectively organised via associations or organisations as was noticed at later times. Some industries that would possibly be affected by a new stricter regime was against it, while others which had a more global stake was in favour of the need for enhanced protection.[331] It is well known that Brazil and India took the leading role on behalf of the developing countries in the debate on IPRS and tried to keep TRIPS issues outside the GATT framework or to maintain a status quo because they had industries that would be negatively affected.

Amidst all the heat on the IPRS, the Uruguay Round of the GATT started on 20th September 1986 at Punta del Esté. In the initial stage the Ministers representing the different Members issued the Ministerial Declaration to establish guidelines regarding the topics to be covered by the negotiations that included subjects like tariffs, non-tariff measures, safeguards, textiles and clothing, agriculture, subsidies and countervailing measures, dispute settlement and the most important among few others were that on IPRS.[332] There was a strong opinion that bringing IPRS into GATT was actually stretching GATT into the domains of WIPO and UNESCO.[333] However once the negotiations picked steam, it was clear that there was no possibility of preventing IPRS to be included along with the GATT agreement. India tried to block the MFN and NT in GATT from applying to IPRS on the grounds that since the obligations were

329 Anell Lars, "Keynote speech at the TRIPS Symposium 26 February 2015" in Watal Jayashree and Taubman Antony (eds.), "The Making of the TRIPS Agreement Personal Insights from The Uruguay Round Negotiations" WTO, pg. 393, 2015. Also available at, https://www.wto.org/english/res_e/booksp_e/trips_agree_e/chapter_4_e.pdf.

330 Ibid at 2.

331 Michael R. Gadbaw and Timothy J. Richards, "Intellectual Property Rights in the New GATT Round", Westview Press, pg. 189, 1988.

332 Dwyer Amy, "Trade-Related Aspects of Intellectual Property Rights" in "The GATT Uruguay Round: A Negotiating History (1986–1994), Volume IV: "The End Game", Stewart Terence (ed.), Kluwer Law International pg. 20–21, 1999. See, Ministerial Declaration on the Uruguay Round, GATT Doc. No. MIN(86)/W/19 DEC (20 September 1986) available at, https://www.wto.org/gatt_docs/English/SULPDF/91240226.pdf.

333 Cottier Thomas, "The Prospects for Intellectual Property in GATT", 28 Common Market Law Review, pg. 393, Kluwer Academic Publishers 1991.

related to goods and not rights of persons, these should not apply. However, although most of the developed countries had already settled to accept IPRs in the agenda, India's efforts were side-lined and it too like others agreed to include IPRs to restrict trade in counterfeits and pirated goods.

Finally, as elaborated earlier, in Punta del Esté, Uruguay Round of Ministerial Meeting in 1988, a broader text of trade related aspects of IPRs featured in the '*Negotiative Objective*' that read,

> In order to reduce the distortions and impediments to international trade, and taking into account the need to promote effective and adequate protection of intellectual property rights, and to ensure the measures and procedures to enforce intellectual property rights do not themselves become barriers to legitimate trade, the negotiations shall aim to clarify GATT provisions and elaborate as appropriate new rules and disciplines.
>
> Negotiations shall aim to develop a multilateral framework of principles, rules and disciplines dealing with international trade in counterfeit goods, taking into account work already undertaken in the GATT.
>
> These negotiations shall be without prejudice to other complementary initiatives that may be taken in the World Intellectual Property Organisation and elsewhere to deal with these matters.[334]

After nearly eight years of trade negotiations, the GATT 1994 agreement establishing the WTO was signed and became effective from 1st January 1995. The overall issue of IP was covered by a separate agreement – Agreement on TRIPS, covered under GATT 1995. The TRIPS Agreement became part and parcel of the WTO system as soon as it came into existence.[335] A transition period of one year was allowed[336] to all countries that needed to amend their domestic laws to bring them in compliance with TRIPS. Developing countries were provided an additional ten years to comply to TRIPS, but were required to introduce mechanisms to accept applications for patents from 1st January 2000 either

334 Cottier Thomas, "The Prospects for Intellectual Property in GATT", 28 Common Market Law Review, pg. 393, Kluwer Academic Publishers 1991. See, Ministerial Declaration on the Uruguay Round, GATT Doc. No. MIN(86)/W/19 DEC (20 September 1986) reprinted.

335 Although the WTO was established in 1995, since all member countries were provided one year's, transition under *Article 65* to implement TRIPS provisions into their domestic laws, it became effective in 1996. *Article II* (2) of the WTO Agreement, Final Act Embodying the Results of the Uruguay Round of Multilateral Trade Negotiations, GATT Doc. MTN/FA, 15, December 1993.

336 Under requirements of *Article 65* (1) of the TRIPS Agreement.

immediately or through a mailbox for deferred examination of patent while providing an immediate EMR to these applications.[337]

After long and protruded negotiations and consistent resistance, the developing countries finally agreed to the TRIPS Agreement once certain important flexibilities were incorporated into it.[338] The TRIPS Agreement introduced a common minimum standard of IPRS for all members and further, it brought IPRS in direct relationship with multilateral trade for the first time. It became the most comprehensive agreement on IP without replacing the different international conventions and treaties that had been signed earlier.

6.2 The Negotiating History of Exhaustion

It is important to note that at the time of negotiating TRIPS Agreement, industrialised countries were already generators of IP while the developing countries were not, but both were net users. Hence the obvious divide between developed and the developing nations where the developed countries wanted strictest level of IPRS protection and the developing countries wanted to treat IPRS goods as knowledge goods thus public products, to be used for economic development rather than private gains.[339] IPRS were introduced in the negotiations with the sole intention to restrain trade in counterfeit goods and it was obviously difficult to oppose. In the beginning, on 20th September 1986 when the ministers adopted the initial declaration, a very prominent objective outlined by the declaration was that, the measures and procedures to protect IPRS themselves should not become barriers to legitimate trade.

At the outset it must be mentioned that exhaustion of IPRS was not dealt with in any of the earlier conventions like the Paris Convention or Bern Convention. Perhaps keeping this at the background there was no mention of the exhaustion issue in the ministerial meetings until in the Uruguay round. However, the issue of parallel imports was discussed and in 1988 the GATT Secretariat came up with a text compiled from submissions by different members.

337 Under requirements of *Article 65* (2) of the TRIPS Agreement.

338 Ibid at 322.

339 Ross Julie and Wasserman Jessica, "The GATT Uruguay Round: A Negotiating History (1986–1994), Trade Related aspects of Intellectual Property Rights", Volume II: Commentary in Stewart Terence (ed. pg. 11, Kluwer Law, 1993).

> 27. The question has been raised as to what would be the substantive intellectual property norms by reference to which counterfeit goods should be defined. In this regard the following points have been made:
> – parallel imports are not counterfeit goods and a multilateral framework should not oblige parties to provide means of action against such goods.[340]

This also reflected in the notes prepared by the WTO secretariat on meetings of the negotiating group regarding border enforcement measures wherein the view was that such measures should exempt parallel import goods.[341] The EU took a position supporting international exhaustion for trademarks where it stated,

> Limited exceptions to the exclusive rights conferred by a trademark, which take account of the legitimate interests of the proprietor of the trademark and of third parties, may be made, such as fair use of descriptive terms and exhaustion of rights.[342]

On the contrary, the US presented a proposal in support of national exhaustion of trademarks.[343] This was opposed by the developing countries including India. They had proposed international exhaustion for both patents and trademarks.[344]

The expression of some members against restricting parallel imports was clear in the recorded notes of the Secretariat that stated,

---

340 Trade in Counterfeit Goods: Compilation of Written Submissions and Oral Statements, Prepared by the Secretariat, Doc. No. MTN.GNG/NG11/W/23, 26th April, 1998. Reproduced in UNCTAD – ICTSD, "Resource Book on TRIPS and Development", Cambridge University Press, pg. 98, 2005.

341 Secretariat note dated 16th August 1989 of the Negotiating Group Meetings dated 3–4 July 1989, Doc. No. GNG/NG11/13 at para D7; Secretariat Note dated 12th September, 1989 of the Negotiating Group Meetings dated 12–14 July 1989, Doc. No. MTN.GNG/NG11/14 at paragraph 26.

342 Guidelines and objectives proposed by the European Community, Negotiating Group on TRIPS, including Trade in Counterfeit Goods, Guidelines and Objectives Proposed by the European Community for the Negotiations on Trade-Related Aspects of Substantive Standards of Intellectual Property Rights, dated 7th July 1988, Doc No. MTN.GNG/NG11/W/26, paragraph III.D.3.b(I).

343 Doc. No. MTN.GNG/NG11/W/71 at paragraph 45.

344 Communication from Argentina, Brazil, Chile, China, Colombia, Cuba, Egypt, India, Nigeria, Peru, Tanzania and Uruguay, dated 14th May 1990, Doc No. MTN.GNG/NG11/14 at paragraph (1)(I) for patents and 7(2) for trademarks.

> [Patents] *Article 24: Rights Conferred.* A participant expressed the view that the proposed provisions on rights conferred were not in line with the principles of intellectual property protection, for example because they tried to invalidate parallel imports and the doctrine of exhaustion of rights.[345]

The chairman of the TRIPS negotiating group Lars Anell, ambassador of Sweden presented a draft in July 1990, known as Anell draft. It had reference of allowing exhaustion in goods and services with trademarks, but it did not mention anything about patents.[346] The draft mentioned,

> unless expressly provided to the contrary in this agreement, nothing in this agreement shall limit the freedom of PARTIES to provide that any intellectual property rights conferred in respect of the use, sale, importation and other distribution of goods are exhausted once those goods have been put on the market by or with the consent of the right holder.[347]

The Anell Draft was duly revised to include specific provision on exhaustion separate from the issue of counterfeit goods but there was no modification of the exhaustion clause.[348] This was the first time that the issue of '*exhaustion*' appeared in the issues for negotiations in somewhat direct manner.[349] However due to stiff resistance from the United States which wanted to install a '*national exhaustion*' mode, it was still not clear whether international exhaustion can be introduced universally.[350] The US proposed provisions of national exhaustion was termed as '*international non-exhaustion*' rule where

345 Secretariat note dated 24th April, 1990 of the Negotiating Group Meetings dated 2nd, 4th and 5th April 1990, Doc. No. MTN.GNG/NG11/20. Reproduced in UNCTAD – ICTSD, "Resource Book on TRIPS and Development", Cambridge University Press, pg. 99, 2005.

346 Chairman's report to the group negotiating on goods dated 23rd July 1990, Doc. No. MTN.GNG/NG11/W/76.

347 See, Status of Work in the Negotiating Group, Chairman's Report to the GNG, GATT Doc. No. MTN.GNG/NG11/W76, July 18, 1990 reprinted.

348 UNCTAD – ICTSD, "Resource Book on TRIPS and Development", Cambridge University Press, pg. 101, 2005.

349 Status of Work in the Negotiating Group, Doc. Ref. No. 2341 (Oct. 1, 1990), See Amy S. Dwyer, "The GATT Uruguay Round: A Negotiating History (1986–1994), Trade Related aspects of Intellectual Property Rights, Volume IV: The End Game", Terence P. Stewart (ed.) Kluwer Law International pgs. 30, 31, 1993.

350 Draft Agreement on the Trade Related aspects of Intellectual Property Rights: Communication from the United States, GATT Doc. MTN.GNG/NG11/W/70, May 11, 1990.

the IPRs in one jurisdiction would not exhaust with the first sale in any other WTO member country jurisdiction. The exhaustion issues witnessed North-South cooperation with some of the commonwealth countries like Hong Kong, Australia and New Zealand taking the lead to exclude parallel trade from dispute settlement with number of developing countries following. The industries lobbied extensively with their governments and even when a number of countries preferred international exhaustion, the interest of increased profits restrained the members any consensus position on exhaustion.[351]

The '*Draft Final Act Embodying the Results of the Uruguay Round of Multilateral Trade Negotiation*' was submitted to Ministers in Brussels on 3rd December 1990 and is commonly known as the Brussels Draft. This draft had already formed the foundation of *Article 6* which later stayed on. *Article 6* stated,

> Subject to the provisions of Article 3 and 4 above, nothing in this Agreement impose any obligation on, or limits the freedom of, PARTIES with respect to the determination of their respective regimes regarding the exhaustion of any intellectual property rights conferred in respect of the use, sale, importation or other distribution of goods once those goods have been put on the market by or with the consent of the right holder.[352]

The modification of the earlier draft to change the language content, clearly shows that the drift from the mode of international exhaustion was not focused on any principle of removal of trade barriers but rather to cater to the demand of some influential negotiating members. Further the lack of progress in the negotiations on Agriculture, Services and Market Access also had a negative effect on the TRIPS negotiation. Further study of the negotiations shows that instead of moving towards a consensus the negotiations on determining exhaustion was about to become standstill. There was confusion as to how the right holder would exhaust the right and a deep divide was noticed between

351 Ibid at 322. Also see, Cottier Thomas, "Parallel Trade and Exhaustion of Intellectual Property in WTO Law Revisited", in Ruse Khan Grosse Henning & Metzger Axel (eds.), "Intellectual Property Ordering Beyond Borders", Cambridge University Press, pgs. 193, 194 (189–232), 2022.

352 Brussels Draft, GATT Doc. No. MTN.TNC/W/35/Rev.1 (Dec. 3, 1990); also see Neff & Smallson, "NAFTA: Protecting and Enforcing Intellectual Property Rights in North America 25 (1994)" – A comparison might be drawn here between TRIPS and NAFTA negotiations to note that in both the US vehemently tried to install the mode of national exhaustion.

developing and industrialised members that restricted any consensus on the issue.[353]

Here it is important to note that in 1990 a WIPO Committee of experts on the harmonisation of patent laws had discussed the issue of exhaustion of patent law in its 8th session wherein *Article 19* had opted for national or regional exhaustion. It stated,

> [Products] Where the subject matter of the patent concerns a product, the owner of the patent shall have the right to prevent third parties from performing, without his authorisation, at least the following acts:
>
> the making of the product,
>
> the offering or the putting on the market of the product, the using of the product, or the importing or stocking of the product for such offering or putting on the market or for such use.
>
> [Processes] ...
>
> Exceptions to Paragraphs (1) and (2) (a) Notwithstanding paragraphs (1) and (2), any Contracting Party shall be free to provide that the owner of a patent has no right to prevent third parties from performing, without his authorisation, the acts referred to in paragraphs (1) and (2) in the following circumstances:
>
> Where the act concerns a product which has been put on the market by the owner of the patent, or with his express consent, insofar as such an act is performed after that product has been put on the market in the territory of that Contracting Party, or in the case of a regional market, in the territory of one of the members States of such group.[354]

Finally, a compromise was reached, thus allowing different members to follow different exhaustion modes as was practised in their respective jurisdictions as a compromise.

> There appears to be no dissent from the view that under the existing international regimes, countries are already free to practice whatever system of exhaustion they wish, and it has proved to be impossible to negotiate any modification or restriction on this freedom whatsoever. This is to

353 Reproduced in the UNCTAD – ICTSD, "Resource Book on TRIPS and Development", Cambridge University Press, pg. 102, 2005.

354 Reproduced in the UNCTAD – ICTSD, "Resource Book on TRIPS and Development", Cambridge University Press, pgs. 102–103, 2005.

> a large extent due to the absence of any kind of consensus internationally on what should or what should not be permissible.[355]

The Final Draft Agreement that was presented by Arthur Dunkel, the Director General of the GATT (the draft was referred to as the '*Dunkel Draft*') on 20th December 1991, contained a compromise statement that read,

> for the purposes of dispute settlement and subject to Article 3 and 4, nothing in this Agreement shall be used to address the issue of the exhaustion of intellectual property rights.[356]

It is understood that the US, European and Japanese Pharmaceutical industry representatives that grouped together under the name '*INTERPAT*' exerted influence on their countries' negotiators to take a very strict IPRS stand. In their joint views that they had released after the presentation of the Dunkel Draft, they pressed for complete deletion of the text on exhaustion in *Article 6* and preferred a clear adoption of '*National exhaustion*'.[357] Further they also wanted the related footnote in *Article 28 (1)* to be removed. However, there was strong opposition by developing countries when the industrialised members tried to establish a national exhaustion regime and fearing a total failure on the issue, the matter was dropped. As a result, a compromise took shape in the form of *Article 6* of the TRIPS text (which is an unaltered version of that in the Dunkel Draft). Although it is true that national mode of exhaustion was not introduced, a mode of international exhaustion was also not installed *per se*. However, the compromise resulted in removal of exhaustion related disputes from the purview of the DSB.

One can argue that both national and international exhaustions have their drawbacks. National exhaustion allows market segmentation and differential pricing, so obviously less expensive parallel imports can be blocked. This means that this type of exhaustion is not favourable for the consumer since who would have to pay more for a product that is available at a cheaper price in the international market. International exhaustion is said to be deficient from

---

355 Reinbothe Jörge & Howard Anthony, "The State of Play in the Negotiations on TRIPS (GATT/Uruguay Round)", 5 EIPR, pgs. 159–160, 1991.

356 Draft Final Act Embodying the Results of the Uruguay Round of Multilateral Trade Negotiations, GATT Doc. MTN.TNC/W/FA, Dec. 20, 1991.

357 Pugatch Meir, "The International Political Economy of Intellectual Property Rights: the TRIPS Agreement and the Advanced Pharmaceutical Induarty in Europe", Proquest LLC., pgs. 150, 2014.

the perspective of the IPRs owner who could have reaped higher profits based on the territorial royalty consideration.[358] It is ironical that from the beginning of the negotiations, while members discussed ways and means to remove barriers to trade with immense enthusiasm for globalisation, things changed outright the moment discussion started on exhaustion of IPRs. The negotiations were said to have broken down completely on this issue and although there was a lot of deliberation on how national IPRs were to work at the international level, there was only signs of disagreement as far as the vital issue of exhaustion of IPRs was concerned. As a result of this, TRIPS in its apparent interpretation and without any decision of the DSB of the WTO on the issue of exhaustion of patents, not only remained a dissatisfactory agreement but allowed IPRs to become a barrier to international trade.[359]

6.3 Exhaustion under TRIPS / WTO: Analysis from the Multilateral Trade Perspective

The fundamental principle on which the WTO as a multilateral system is built is the concept of elimination of illegitimate barriers to trade. It advocates removal of barriers that can restrict free movement of goods and services within different geographical boundaries. This is further based on the economic concept of comparative advantage that encourages specialisation to bring in efficiency in the market and thus enhance production. The main reason for bringing IPRs within full purview of GATT 1994 was to remove illegitimate barriers to trade in IP goods through proper enforce mechanisms that got initiated to restrain trade in counterfeits and pirated goods.

Issues like exhaustion of IPRs can be considered core, given that its treatment would ascertain treatment of parallel importation. Once limited to restraining trade through legitimate exceptions, IPRs became an integral part of the WTO multilateral trade regime. It is rather astonishing that even when the aim of GATT is to remove rent-seeking measures, the negotiating members could not determine on the mode of exhaustion and ideally install the type of

358 Cottier Thomas, "The Value and Effects of Protecting Intellectual Property Rights within the World Trade Organization", presentation to the Association Littéraire et Artistique Internationale (ALAI), Journée d'études, 27th & 28th June, 1984.

359 Chiapetta Vincent, "The desirability of Agreeing to disagree: The WTO, TRIPS, International IPR Exhaustion and a few other things", in Introduction, 21 Michigan Journal of International Law pgs. 333, Spring 2000.

exhaustion that would be based on the fundamental principles of the GATT 1994 regulations.[360]

The issue of exhaustion was one of the most difficult issues during the TRIPS negotiations since some, adamantly favoured adopting national exhaustion while others were equally bent on installing international exhaustion. Finally, it was rested by the decision to exclude the issue of exhaustion from the purview of the WTO as a compromise.[361] The cause for the confusion in determining a particular mode of exhaustion is because countries were not sure whether IP law should supersede trade law. In case of national exhaustion, it can be argued that because it restricts entry of competing goods from licensed producers of other countries, the goods might not be available at the lowest price. In addition, it causes hindrance to competition in the market and thus negatively affecting international trade. But at the same time, it enforces a stricter IP regime and allows enhanced exclusivity through stricter enforcement of IPRs. Whereas in the case of international exhaustion, it also allows manufacturers of parallel goods from licensed producers to make use of the comparative advantage and thus manufacture and market their products at a lower price. International exhaustion would enable not only open market competition but also in the process result in more efficient allocation of resources.[362] Such practice is supported by the principles of multilateral trade law in line with the WTO rules. Moreover, one needs to ascertain the level of monopoly that the IPRs should provide.

On the other hand, if international exhaustion is followed then, it is stated by its critics that the economic benefits of a legal monopoly accorded to the owner of an IP might not be exploited to its fullest capacity. Hence according to some critics, it will undermine the purpose of having IPRs. Although one cannot ignore the fact that the essential functions of IPRs are not to artificially partition a market (as it is done when national exhaustion is followed). It is further argued that if the IP owners sold products in one country and exhausted the rights internationally, then the owner would most likely try to charge a higher price to cover the less profit that would result due to exhaustion. Thus, the monetary interest behind having the IP right would be at stake. Further, it

360 Taubman Antony, "A practical guide to working with TRIPS", Oxford University Press 2011, page 85. Also see, Cottier Thomas, "Parallel Trade and Exhaustion of Intellectual Property in WTO Law Revisited", in Ruse Khan Grosse Henning & Metzger Axel (eds.), "Intellectual Property Ordering Beyond Borders", Cambridge University Press, pg. 197 (189–232), 2022.

361 Gervais Daniel, "Exhaustion" in "The TRIPS Agreement: Drafting History and Analysis", Sweet & Maxwell, South Asian Edition, pg. 64, 2011.

362 Ibid at 5, pg. 100.

could also be possible that the IP owner would avoid differential pricing, which in the long run would go against the argument that international exhaustion would encourage more competition and low prices.

There was considerable confusion amongst TRIPS negotiators to commit on a single mode of exhaustion of the IPRS and hence it became a backburner.[363] Before moving into a debate over the confirmation of the most preferred mode of exhaustion from multilateral trade perspective, a detailed analysis of the different Articles of the TRIPS Agreement as well as the GATT and any other covered Agreement of the WTO is essential.

6.3.1 *Patent Exhaustion under the TRIPS Agreement*

6.3.1.1 Preamble to the TRIPS Agreement

An analytical reading of the Preamble to the TRIPS Agreement would raise the question as to whether a mode of national exhaustion would reduce distortions and barriers to international trade as the Preamble aims to do,

> to reduce distortions and impediments to international trade, and taking into account the need to promote effective and adequate protection of intellectual property rights, and to ensure that measures and procedures to enforce intellectual property rights do not themselves become barriers to legitimate trade;[364]

Among the limited number of TRIPS cases that have been addressed by WTO Panels and the AB, in India – Pharmaceutical Patents Case[365] the AB legitimizes the importance of the Preamble of the TRIPS Agreement while referring to it in terms of consistency with the '*Objects and purpose of the TRIPS Agreement*'. Contrary to the aims of the Preamble, the mode of national exhaustion restricts free movement of goods protected by IPRS since it disallows legally licensed products from competing with the patented products. Further, national exhaustion is discriminatory in terms of international trade because although it allows the patent holder to reap monetary benefit through licensing, the patent holder can still restrict importation of the product he first marketed in that country. Thus, in the case of imported products, the titleholder would be allowed to exercise his rights multiple times, i.e. in

363 Gervais Daniel, "Exhaustion" in "The TRIPS Agreement: Drafting History and Analysis", Sweet & Maxwell, South Asian Edition, pg. 64, 2011.

364 Preamble / Foreword to the Agreement on Trade Related Aspects of Intellectual Property Rights (TRIPS).

365 WT/DS50/AB/R, 1997 para 57.

the country where the product was first marketed as well as in the countries of importation, whereas in the domestic market the title-holder is allowed to exercise his rights only once.[366]

If the Preamble to the TRIPS Agreement is followed in letter and spirit, then a member cannot support the mode of national exhaustion since it is not conducive to international trade in a multilateral set up governed by the WTO. On the other hand, a mode of international exhaustion would allow the licensee to market its product simultaneously with the products of the patent holder and hence promote higher competition and encourage removal of barriers to legitimate trade. Thus, it is argued that international exhaustion is the most appropriate mode that reduces distortion and barriers to trade and is in line with the Preamble to the TRIPS Agreement, while at the same time patent enforcement is possible, it does not sacrifice the interest of the patent holder.

6.3.1.2 Article 6: Exhaustion of Intellectual Property Rights

Considering that the MFN principle applies to the TRIPS agreement, where one WTO member's trade preferences or concessions to another, needs to be extended to other members, exhaustion principal is conceptually accepted by the WTO regulatory mechanism without doubt.[367] Along with other relevant Articles, *Article 4* will be discussed to bring out the non-discrimination element in greater detail later in this chapter. In such scenario, it is impossible for any member to avoid exhaustion of patents, it is the intricacies of application of exhaustion with relation to parallel trade that needs to be assessed carefully considering various factors. Here, *Article 6* is discussed before other Articles of TRIPS, since this is the only Article that specifically mentions exhaustion of patents. It states,

> for the purposes of dispute settlement under this Agreement, subject to the provisions of Article 3 & 4 above, nothing in this Agreement shall be used to address the issue of exhaustion of intellectual property rights.

It has been already mentioned (while discussing the negotiating history of TRIPS) that the members of the WTO could not agree to a common mode of exhaustion of IPRS for all members. As a result, apparently *Article 6* was

---

366 Yusuf Abdulqawi and Monacayo Andrés Hase, "Intellectual Property Protection and International Trade", 16 World Competition, pg. 128, 1992.

367 *Article 4* TRIPS, "With regard to the protection of intellectual property, any advantage, favour, privilege or immunity granted by *a Member to the nationals of any other country shall be accorded immediately and unconditionally to the nationals of all other Members.*"

introduced which provides the flexibility to a member to adopt the exhaustion mode that it prefers. However, it is important to note that *Article 6* actually does not give such liberty given that adoption of a particular exhaustion mode is subject to the specific obligations both within this Article and other WTO Agreements.[368]

However, one needs to carefully examine the notion that, *prima-facie Article 6* allows members to follow any mode of exhaustion and further prevents members from referring the disputes to the DSB of the WTO over an issue of exhaustion. Considering the trade enhancing characteristics of international exhaustion and the intention of TRIPS as reflected in the Preamble to the TRIPS, international exhaustion is most appropriate within the WTO system. It is also sometimes argued that the language of *Article 6,* precludes exhaustion of patents being brought as a violation complaint before the WTO DSB.[369] In fact, although apparently it might seem *Article 6* restricts members from bringing exhaustion related disputes to the DSB, there is a qualification wherein disputes can still be brought under *Article 3* (*NT*) and *Article 4* (*MFN, i.e. MFN*). Further, practice of *Article 6* needs to qualify under GATT *Article XX* (*d*) as well as the necessity test as well as is not exempt from assessment of necessity under *Article 31*(*3*)(*c*) of the VCLT.[370] In such scenario a question arises as to how decisions of domestic courts would be treated under NT and MFN. The same is discussed at length later while addressing NT and MFN specifically under GATT and TRIPS. This means, although *Article 6* tends to be neutral in supporting any specific mode of exhaustion, it makes the exhaustion mode subject to *Article 3 and 4*, which are to be applied uniformly.

Further, one can argue that a member does not have the liberty to establish any mode of exhaustion since that could be inconsistent with *Article 28* of the TRIPS, hence exhaustion issue could still be a bilateral dispute issue.[371] This

368 Dutfield Graham and Sutherland Uma, "The international law and political economy of intellectual property", in "Global Intellectual Property", Edward Elgar Publishing Ltd. pgs. 34, 35, 2008. Also see, Cottier Thomas, "Parallel Trade and Exhaustion of Intellectual Property in WTO Law Revisited", in Ruse Khan Grosse Henning & Metzger Axel (eds.), "Intellectual Property Ordering Beyond Borders", Cambridge University Press, pg. 200 (189–232), 2022.

369 Ibid 309, pgs. 172, 173.

370 Yamane Hiroko, "The TRIPS Agreement de Lege Lata: The Outline", in "Interpreting TRIPS Globalisation of Intellectual Property Rights and Access to Medicines" Hart Publishing Ltd., pgs. 155, 156, (148–189), 2011. Also see, Cottier Thomas, "Parallel Trade and Exhaustion of Intellectual Property in WTO Law Revisited", in Ruse Khan Grosse Henning & Metzger Axel (eds.), "Intellectual Property Ordering Beyond Borders", Cambridge University Press, pg. 217 (189–232), 2022.

371 Ibid at 122, pgs. 312, 313, (304–342).

can be of considerable concern from the perspective of the necessary policy space that a WTO member might want to exercise in deciding an exhaustion regime that it finds most appropriate, hence not positively contributing to a solution. It is noticed that even after lobbying attempts by industry groups like the International Trademark Association (INTA), the exhaustion issue is limited to its interpretation in terms of *Article 6*.[372] Thus, if a member invokes an exhaustion mode which violates *Article 3* and *4*, then the matter might be taken up before the DSB. An in-depth study will show that if any mode other than the mode of international exhaustion is followed, '*like products*' would be treated differently. Here it must be noted that exhaustion rules cannot and should not vary depending on the origin of the product.[373]

Albeit this should not apply if the patents in the products does not naturally exhaust, in other words, if they are impacted by market manipulations like government regulatory interventions, price caps, etc. then such products need to be exempted from international exhaustion. The logic being, allowing international exhaustion in such cases will bring an effect of export subsidies not only distorting multilateral trade but also violating the Agreement on Subsidies and Countervailing Measures of the WTO.[374] A case in point is the Swiss Patent law of 2009 that allows regional exhaustion but excludes cases where the patented products have been subjected to price control or similar other measures. However, this would not include general regulatory approvals or those covered under *Article XX* GATT. Considering that the fundamental reasoning of the GATT and TRIPS is to effect equal treatment to like products, such exclusions would be considered compatible of *Article 6* of the TRIPS Agreement.[375]

Some critics refuse to read *Article 6* in conjunction with other Articles of TRIPS and other WTO Agreements and are of the opinion that this Article should be interpreted literally, i.e. exclusively on the basis of its content. These critics thus prefer to take a neutral stand and support the view that Members

372 Blakeney Michael, "Trade Related Aspects of Intellectual Property Rights: A Concise Guide to the TRIPS Agreement", Sweet & Maxwell, pg. 42, 1996.

373 Cottier Thomas, "The WTO System and the Exhaustion of Intellectual Property Rights", May 2000, Draft paper based on previous work presented to the conference on the Exhaustion of Intellectual Property Rights, ILA Trade Law Committee, Geneva 6th & 7th November, 1998.

374 Bonadio Bonadio Enrico, "Parallel Imports in a Global Market: Should a Generalised International Exhaustion be the Next Step?", 33 European Intellectual Property Review (3), pgs. 8, (153–161), 2011.

375 *Article 9a*: Federal Acts of Patents for Invention (Patents Act PatA) as on 1st April 2019. Available at, www.admin.ch/opc/en/classified-compilation/19540108/201904010000/232.14.pdf. Please also see, Ibid. at 5, pgs. 261, 262.

should be allowed to follow any exhaustion mode that they prefer.[376] Here it is important to note that the final wording of *Article 6* resulted after long negotiations and are after careful consideration to maintain a status quo. Given the present circumstances when there are multiple interpretations of the Article specifically dealing with exhaustion, Members need to avoid any reading of *Article 6* in isolation from the other Articles of the TRIPS Agreement or in exclusion of the other WTO Agreements. It is important to give not only due consideration to the other Articles of the TRIPS, but also analyse GATT 1994 and other relevant WTO Agreements to assess their impact on exhaustion. The exhaustion of patents under GATT MFN and NT are dealt with in detail in the next chapter including how in the erstwhile GATT 1947 regime Dispute Settlement panel in 1989 held US Patent Act *Section 337* in violation of NT.[377] The fundamental premise being, there is no material difference of substantial nature in the approach towards the GATT/WTO rules on goods and those on IPRS. Both seek to bring in positive effects for the betterment of international trade.

Further, while *Article 6* of TRIPS does not specifically restrain a member from adopting national or regional exhaustion of IPRS, the application of different relevant Articles of the GATT is implicit. GATT applies independently of TRIPS hence non-violation of TRIPS would not preclude compliance with GATT in any manner.[378] The relevance of GATT is founded in the fact that parallel trade, triggered by international exhaustion of IPRS including patents, refer to the geographical origin of the product and not the nationality of the right holders. Moreover, *Article 6* of TRIPS does not in any way exclude the purview of the GATT 1994. It has also been argued that TRIPS is '*lex specialis*' or '*sui generis*' hence it supersedes in governance of IPRS and the GATT would not be relevant.[379]

> As a general principle of (international) law, the notion of lex specialis derogate generali applies between provisions of a single treaty, between provisions within two or more treaties, between a treaty and a non-treaty standard, as well as between two non-treaty standards. It suggests that whenever two or more norms deal with the same subject matter, priority

376 Bronckers Marco, "The Exhaustion of Patent Rights under WTO Law", 5 Journal of World Trade, pg. 142, 1998.

377 Ibid at 5, pg. 937.

378 Grigoriadis Lazaros, "Trademarks and Free Trade: A Global Analysis", Springer, pg. 105, 2014.

379 Ibid at 376, pg. 143.

> should be given to the norm that is more specific since it often takes better account of the particular context addressed or creates a more equitable result. Confirming the relative nature of inter-legality, the lex specialis principle only applies in relation to those states which are bound by both norms – such as between two international IP treaties for those states bound by both.[380]

Considering that TRIPS Agreement imposes different obligations on WTO members than under GATT and does not regulate discrimination based on origin of goods, it is doubtful if the doctrine of *lex specialis derogat generali* can be applied unchallenged.[381] The impact of different Articles of the GATT on exhaustion of patents and as a result in its treatment of parallel imports have been discussed at length more specifically in the next chapter.

6.3.1.3 Article 3: National Treatment

The NT requirement in TRIPS Agreement require IP applicants and holders including patent holders from outside the WTO member's country the same treatment as that of domestic patent IP holders.[382] Some proponents of national and regional exhaustion, although agree that *Article 3 and 4* of the TRIPS lay down conditions that WTO members are required to accord NT and MFN status to all members, still hold the opinion that national and regional exhaustion does not violate these Articles. According to them, these modes of exhaustion do not discriminate on the basis of the

> origin of the imported goods but on the nationality of the patent right holder, a good case could be made that such exception would not violate the non-discrimination principles of the GATT.[383]

This also shows that even these proponents of national and regional exhaustion admit that goods are discriminated and differentiated on the basis of

380 Ruse-Khan Henning Grosse, "The Protection of Intellectual Property in International Law", Oxford University Press, pg. 2359, 2016.

381 Reichman Jerome, Okediji Ruth, Lianos Ioannis, Jacob Robin and Stothers Christopher, "The WTO Compatibility of a Differentiated International Exhaustion Regime", International Laboratory for Law and Development Research Paper Series, dated, pg. 20. Available at, http://www.eurasiancommission.org/ru/act/finpol/dobd/intelsobs/Documents/WTO%20Compartibility%20of%20Exhaustion%20Regimes_EEC_SkHSEreport.pdf.

382 Ibid at 5, pg. 27.

383 Ibid at 378, pg. 146.

nationality of the patent holders of the different WTO members hence it is important to analyse these two Articles in greater depth.

Here it is important to note the difference between '*Same Treatment*' under the Paris Convention and '*Treatment no less favourable*' in the TRIPS Agreement. Under *Article 2 (1)* & (2) of the Paris Convention, each member country is mandated to grant the same protection to nationals of other member countries that it grants its own nationals and nationals of the non-member countries are also entitled to the same treatment if they are domiciled in the country or have '*real and effective or commercial establishment*' in the member country.[384] It is interesting to note that *Article 3*, of the TRIPS Agreement is not just restricted to same treatment but much beyond and reads similar to *Article III:4* of the GATT Agreement on NT. A study of the negotiating history shows that NT always had been an important principle in international IP laws and was the fundamental principle in the GATT 1947 Agreement as far as trade in goods is concerned. The question that arises is whether NT would also apply to TRIPS in respect of IPRS the same way as it applies in GATT.

NT being specifically incorporated in *Article 3* of the TRIPS Agreement, it reads,

> 1. Each Member shall accord to the nationals of other Members treatment no less favourable than that it accords to its own nationals with regard to the protection (here there is a footnote which states – For the purposes of Article 3 & 4, "protection" shall include matters affecting the availability, acquisition, scope, maintenance and enforcement of intellectual property rights as well as those matters affecting the use of intellectual property rights specifically addressed in this Agreement.) of intellectual property, subject to the exceptions already provided in, respectively, the Paris Convention (1967), the Berne Convention (1971), the Rome Convention or the Treaty on Intellectual Property in respect of Integrated Circuits.

As mentioned, considering that TRIPS Agreement incorporates the provisions of the Paris Convention, it is important to note that 'NT' was included in it in the first category itself as a basic right.

Article 2 (1) of the Paris Convention states,

> Nationals of any country of the Union shall, as regards the protection of industrial property, enjoy in all the other countries of the Union the

384 Article 2, See https://wipolex.wipo.int/en/text/287556.

> advantages that their respective laws now grant, or may hereafter grant, to nationals; all without prejudice to the rights specially provided for by this Convention. Consequently, they shall have the same protection as the latter, and the same legal remedy against any infringement of their rights, provided that the conditions and formalities imposed upon nationals are complied with.

Article 3 further states,

> Nationals of countries outside the Union who are domiciled or who have a real and effective industrial or commercial establishments in the territory of one of the countries of the Union shall be treated in the same manner as nationals of the countries of the Union.[385]

From this it's clear that a country which is a member of the Paris Convention shall have to grant the same level of protection to other member countries' subjects as provided to its own. Interestingly, although both the Paris Convention and TRIPS mandates NT, there is distinction. While Paris Convention mandates same treatment, TRIPS require treatment that is no less favourable.

In GATT there is the notion of de facto non-discrimination that was applied in the *European Communities – Protection of Trademarks and Geographical Indications for Agricultural Products and Foodstuffs* (*EC – GI*) case. In this case, apart from violation of *Article 3* of TRIPS and *Article III (4)* of GATT, the Panel decided in favour of US and Australia that the EC's GI Regulation did not provide NT to other WTO members' right holders and their products. Protection to other members' GI was made contingent upon the government of that country adopting GI protection mechanism equivalent to that of the EC and in the process, provide reciprocal protection to EC GIs. The Panel found that the EC's regulations pertaining to GI themselves being in breach of GATT were as such inconsistent under *Article XX (d)* GATT. Further, the Regulations that was to be introduced by the other WTO members also needed to have a product examination mechanism for cases where applications and objections were raised by other WTO members. In other words, foreign nationals would have access to the EC GI protection only if the EC granted it on examination through the mechanism like that of the EC, hence no guaranteed access. Hence, the

385 Paris Convention for the protection of Industrial Property, see, https://www.unido.org/sites/default/files/2014-04/Paris_Convention_0.pdf.

additional GI protection being challenged as mentioned above failed the consistency test and could not be justified under *Article XX (d)*.[386]

Here it raises the argument that if both are like products as is the case for patented products, whether this will be a valid differentiation based on the origin of the goods. In case of trademark for different products, the test of NT under GATT is whether the marked products originate from the same source.[387] Here reference may be made to the two decisions of the AB of the WTO, *Japan – Taxes on Alcoholic Beverages* (*Japan – Alcoholic Beverages*) *and Korea – Taxes on Alcoholic Beverages* (*Korea – Alcoholic Beverages*) cases.[388] These two orders of the AB emphasised that in case of directly competitive or substitutable products which are in competition with each other, if the imported goods are taxed higher than the locally produced goods, then the dissimilar taxation of the directly competitive or substitutable imported domestic products would be considered as protection accorded to domestic product and this would result in violation of *Article III: 2* of the GATT Agreement.

The question as to whether *Article 3* of the TRIPS Agreement treats exhaustion of IPRS in the same manner as GATT, would ascertain the eligibility of the '*national*' or '*regional*' exhaustion modes under this Article. *Article 3* clearly states that members should accord no less favourable treatment to products from other members as it does to products from its own country. One might argue that if a country follows national exhaustion, it restricts parallel import of products from other members through injunctive relief, damages, etc. on ground that the imported product has infringed the IPRS of the products.[389] On the other hand, no such effect exists for domestic products moving from one part of the country to another or within the markets under FTA. The imported products are manufactured legally under licence from the original producer while being marketed through their own channels instead of the distributors

386 Ruse-Khan Henning Grosse, "The Protection of Intellectual Property in International Law", Oxford University Press, pg. 308, 313–315, 2016. See, *European Communities – Protection of Trademarks and Geographical Indications for Agricultural Products and Foodstuffs* case, See, https://docs.wto.org/dol2fe/Pages/SS/directdoc.aspx?filename=Q:/WT/DS/290R.pdf &Open=True.

387 The HAG case in EU presents the established practice in trademarks long back. See, *Case C10/89, SA CNL – SUCAL NV v HAG GF AG*, (http://curia.europa.eu/juris/showPdf.jsf?docid =96580&doclang=en).

388 *Japan – Taxes on Alcoholic Beverages* case, WT/DS8/AB/R, WT/DS10/AB/R and WT/DS11 /AB/R, of 4th October 1996 and *Korea – Taxes on Alcoholic Beverages case*, WT/DS75/AB/R, WT/DS84/AB/R of 18th January 1999.

389 Verma Surinder, "Exhaustion of Intellectual Property Rights and Free Trade – Article 6 of the TRIPS Agreement", 5 IIC, pgs. 553, 554, 1998.

chosen by the patent holder. However, that is not actually the test for NT in case of TRIPS since the test is whether there is discrimination is between the local patent holder and the foreign right holder.

Under national exhaustion too, the foreign patent holder can stop the entry of parallel imports exactly in the same way as the original patent holder if the same is registered in the country. Hence there is no discrimination from the perspective of NT under *Article 3* TRIPS either for national, or regional or international exhaustion. Hence on comparison with similar provision under GATT, there is a distinct difference. While in case of the former, NT relates to the nationality of the right holder, in case of GATT, it relates to the origin of the product. In the latter there is discrimination between the free movement of goods within the country in modes of exhaustion other than international exhaustion and restrictions imposed on imported like products. The significant difference being the right and title being on the good and not on the right holder.

6.3.1.4 Article 4: Most Favoured Nation Treatment

Article 4 of the TRIPS Agreement discusses the principle of MFN and states,

> With regard to the protection of IP, any advantage, favour, privilege or immunity granted by a Member to the nationals of any other country shall be accorded immediately and unconditionally to the nationals of all other Members.

It must be noted that the MFN principle in TRIPS, is not adopted from the previous IP conventions since it was absent in these conventions. However, it was very much present in the GATT 1947 Agreement although restricted only to its applications to goods. With the extension of the MFN principle to TRIPS, the principle has been extended not just to IPRS but also to persons, i.e. nationals who would hold IPRS in different member countries. Given that it is now concerning right holder, the question related to exhaustion of patent rights any mode other than the '*international exhaustion*' would be in violation of the well-established MFN principle.

In the case of '*national exhaustion*', there is no specific discrimination of the MFN since the principle is not affected by this mode, but the question is whether there is any violation of MFN in case of '*regional exhaustion*'. The GATT & TRIPS negotiators representing the EU managed to include an exception clause to legitimise regional exhaustion even when it was against MFN under GATT. The argument that the EU being a CU, should be treated as a single entity and further the Union was excluded under exemptions provided for regional agreement. Accordingly, necessary provision for the same was made in the TRIPS Agreement. *Article 1* of TRIPS while elaborating the *'Nature and Scope of Obligations',* provides an explanation of *'nationals'* in *footnote 1.* It states,

> When "nationals" are referred to in this Agreement, they shall be deemed, in the case of a separate customs territory Member of the WTO, to mean persons, natural or legal, who are domiciled or who have a real and effective industrial or commercial establishment in that customs territory.

However, given that the other regional blocs like the NAFTA, ASEAN and others do not practice regional exhaustion of IPRs, it is not very clear if such a qualification is restricted only to CU or would apply to FTAs in general.

Another case in point is the Unitary Patent system in EU, considering that it is expected to provide a mechanism for a single patent right for participating members along with a unified patent court, question arises as to whether and if so, why regional exhaustion would still be legitimate.[390] The contrary argument is that, such unitary patent mechanism does not replace the national patents in each member States but exist at parallel with the separate adjudicating mechanisms, hence the question on regional exhaustion within EU is still questionable. Given the fact that the patent right exists in the member State independent of the European patent, considering the entire EU as a single entity for exhaustion is more a decision of market integration enforced through the ECJ, rather than based on legal reasoning.

On the issue of exhaustion, one must note that by allowing exhaustion of IPRs for goods imported from a particular country, a member of the Union while refusing to do the same if the products were from another country a member of the WTO but not of the Union, would seem to outright violate the MFN principle in the GATT. Such discrimination of the MFN principle was however curved in, under a special exemption for regional agreements as provided by *Article XXIV* of the GATT Agreement. It is questionable whether

390 The 'Unitary Patent' system which is expected to come into effect from mid-2020 would enable patent protection to up to 26 EU Members through a single application. The Unified Patent Court expected to be set up as an international court would address the problem of parallel litigation. For more details please see, https://www.epo.org/law-practice/unitary/unitary-patent/start.html. However, it should also be noted that the unitary patent mechanism needs to be ratified in minimum of 13 countries of the EU and at present it has been challenged before the German Constitutional court. The fate of wide adoption of the unitary patent would be influenced by the German court in mid-2020.

such exemption which is against free trade principles, should be accorded to regional agreements at the cost of multilateral trade. Pre-negotiation view of the effect of MFN on IPRs had exposed some problems since there was a view that it was better not to apply MFN to IPRs since then it would have to be extended to persons (which would in turn affect many bilateral and regional agreements).[391] The issue of MFN in GATT 1994 with relation to the exhaustion principle will be discussed in greater details in the analysis of the GATT 1994 Agreement in the next chapter.

It is indeed an irony that multilateral trade agreements like the GATT Agreement and it is covered agreements, including the TRIPS Agreement which aims at reduction of distortions in international trade, does not consider restrictions imposed by way of such exemption null and void. Had it not been that NT relating to the nationality of the right holder or specific exclusions curved in at the formative stage itself, such exemptions would not have qualified in the '*necessity*' test since international exhaustion, which facilitates in the removal of trade barriers also allow protection of IPRs. Given that the TRIPS Agreement being within the larger framework of GATT 1994 Agreement, one might question whether the necessity test as reflected in *Article 8* of TRIPS Agreement needs to be read within the context of GATT 1994.[392] However, based on the above study on NT and MFN, the issue of national and regional exhaustion discriminating over international exhaustion needs to be assessed under relevant provisions of the GATT Agreement rather than the TRIPS.

6.3.1.5 Article 7: Objectives of TRIPS Agreement

Article 7 of the TRIPS Agreement, ties dissemination of knowledge with patent protection through technology transfer. Remedies to patent infringement through injunctive relief, damages, etc. are awarded so that the society is benefited from the invention while the patent holder enjoys government assured market exclusivity for a certain predetermined period. More specifically, *Article 7* aims at promotion of technological innovation and transfer of technology in a manner that is *'conducive to social and economic welfare'* and at the same time brings *'a balance of rights and obligations'*.[393] While interpreting *Article*

---

391 Dhanjee Rajan and Chazournes Laurence de Boisson "Trade Related Aspects of Intellectual Property Rights (TRIPS): Objectives, Approaches and Basic Principles of the GATT and of Intellectual Property Conventions", 24 Journal of World Trade, pg. 12, 1990.

392 Rodrigues Edson Beas Jr., "The general exception clauses of the TRIPS Agreement Promoting Sustainable Development" Cambridge University Press, pgs. 62, 63 (46–64), 2012.

393 *Article 7* states: The protection and enforcement of intellectual property rights should contribute to the promotion of technological innovation and to the transfer and

7 in the background of the exhaustion issue, it will be noticed that international exhaustion enables the licensee to come in to direct competition with the licensor. Hence it enhances more opportunities of technology transfer, enabling increased dissemination of technology through market competition which is most conducive to economic welfare. The other modes do not enable possibilities of any such technology transfer and are far more restrictive, thus would fail to meet the aims of *Article 7*.

6.3.1.6 Article 8: Underlying Principles of TRIPS Agreement

Article 8 (2) states,

> Appropriate measures, provided that they are consistent with the provisions of this Agreement, may be needed to prevent the abuse of IPRs by right holders or the resort to practices which unreasonably restrain trade or adversely affect the international transfer of technology.

It has been mentioned earlier and decided by the ECJ (discussed in detail later) that the mode of national exhaustion restrains trade and it is for this reason, the EC (including countries of the EEA) follows the mode of international exhaustion within the region. It is important to read *Article 8* with Article *XX*(*d*) *GATT*, applying the necessity test, reflecting suitability, necessity and proportionality. There is absolute clarity that, restraining parallel imports by opting out of international exhaustion of patents is untenable.[394] It would be impossible to establish that to protect patents, parallel imports of products need to be restricted.

A careful study of clause (2) of the Article mentioned above will show that it requires appropriate measures (consistent with the provisions of the Agreement) to be taken to prevent practices which unreasonably restrain trade. In such circumstances any mode of exhaustion other than international

---

dissemination of technology, to the mutual advantage of producers and users of technological knowledge and in a manner conducive to social and economic welfare, and to balance of rights and obligations.

394 *Article XX* (*d*) states, "Subject to the requirement that such measures are not applied in a manner which would constitute a means of arbitrary or unjustifiable discrimination between countries where the same conditions prevail, or a disguised restriction on international trade, nothing in this Agreement shall be construed to prevent the adoption or enforcement by any contracting party of measures: … (d) necessary to secure compliance with laws or regulations which are not inconsistent with the provisions of this Agreement, including those relating to … the protection of patents, trademarks and copyrights." Explained in details in the next chapter.

exhaustion calls for outright rejection since it restrains trade. Further, since national exhaustion mode allows the patent holder to benefit from charging royalty more than once, it can be interpreted as an abuse of the monopoly right accorded to the patent holder. Given that often doubts have been raised as to whether strong IPRs regime can exclusively bring in technological change and economic growth, it is logical to install a strong patent regime while at the same time allowing enhanced market competition.[395] If international exhaustion is adopted, parallel trade will be allowed and the industries in the developing countries will be interested in technology transfer as they would gain from comparative advantage.

One might argue that *Article 8* of the TRIPS Agreement, allows discrimination on NT to protect IPRs in the same way as the preamble to the TBT Agreement. More specifically, the preamble to TBT Agreement states,

> Recognizing that no country should be prevented from taking measures necessary to ensure the quality of its exports, or for the protection of human, animal or plant life or health, of the environment, or for the prevention of deceptive practices, at the levels it considers appropriate, subject to the requirement that they are not applied in a manner which would constitute a means of arbitrary or unjustifiable discrimination between countries where the same conditions prevail or a disguised restriction on international trade, and are otherwise in accordance with the provisions of this Agreement.

Here exemption from NT triggers only for specific purposes as mentioned and needs to be justified. It cannot be arbitrary action or disguised restriction on international trade. Similarly, the exemption provided for protection of IPR in *Article 8* of TRIPS, enables patent holders to take specific enforcement measures if the rights are infringed but restricting parallel importation by following the mode of national or regional exhaustion for protecting patents, cannot qualify as justified restriction on NT.

6.3.1.7 Article 28: Patent Rights Conferred

Proponents of national and regional exhaustion usually cite *Article 28* of TRIPS Agreement and state that under this Article, the mode of international exhaustion is not allowed. Before starting a discussion on this Article, the historical

395 Mattoo Aaditya and English Philip (eds.), "Benefiting from Intellectual Property Protection" in, "Development, Trade, and the WTO – A Handbook", The World Bank, Washington D.C., pg. 369, 2002.

developments in IP law in the pre-TRIPS era should be noted when IPRS were governed mainly by the international IP conventions. These conventions acknowledged the principle of territoriality in IP law.[396] It is for this reason many supporters of strong IPRS regimes prefer the mode of national exhaustion and fail to accept the fact that TRIPS has changed the scenario and no longer can one look at IPRS exclusively as a territorial issue without considering its effect on multilateral trade in a global setting.

It is an irony that some critics fail to acknowledge that the main reason to include TRIPS is to promote multilateral trade along with effective protection of IPRS. Often it is overlooked that in line with the overall aim of the WTO Agreements, TRIPS Agreement aims to promote barrier-free trade in addition to its aim of providing a harmonized minimum level of IPR protection. *Article 28* does not restrict the possibility of following international exhaustion in any manner since following international exhaustion cannot lead to infringement of the patent.[397] *Article 28* does not in any manner present even a hypothetical situation of restraining international exhaustion of patents, it only excludes exhaustion issues from being taken up before the DSB of the WTO.

Article 28 states,

> 1. A patent shall confer on its owner the following exclusive rights:
>   (a) where the subject matter of a patent is a product, to prevent third parties not having the owner's consent from the acts of: making, using, offering for sale, selling, or importing (*Here the footnote 6 with reference to 'importing' states that, this right, like all other rights conferred under this Agreement in respect of the use, sale, importation or other distribution of goods, is subject to the provisions of Article 6*) for these purposes that product;
>   (b) where the subject matter of a patent is a process, to prevent third parties not having the owner's consent from the act of using the process, and from the acts of: using, offering for sale, selling, or importing for these purposes at least the product obtained directly by that process (*Emphasis added*).

---

396 Here *Article 4bis* of the Paris Convention might be referred to, which clearly lays down the principle of territoriality but it must be carefully noted that it does not deal in the exhaustion of rights.

397 Demaret Paul & Govaere Inge, "Parallel Imports, Free Movement and Competition Rules! The European Experience and Perspective", in Cottier Thomas and Mavroidis Petros (eds.), "Intellectual Property: Trade, Competition, and Sustainable Development", The University of Michigan Press, pg. 158, 2003.

A careful study of this Article will show that the contradiction in views on the issue of exhaustion occurs because of the mention of '*importing without the owner's consent*' and its treatment.

The critics who support the mode of national exhaustion, often state that this Article allows patent holders to restrict others from, '*making, using, offering for sale, selling or importing* (*emphasis added*)' products that are covered by the patents, hence restrict items of parallel trade since they are marketed without the prior consent of the patent holders. According to them the exclusive right granted by this Article would not allow third parties to import a patented product or a direct product made from a patented process.[398] Further, they are of the opinion that if a WTO member follows international exhaustion, another member that does not follow international exhaustion can retaliate through trade policy sanctions against the member that follows international exhaustion. Such arguments are based on the interpretation that the footnote to *Article 28* (*1*) (*a*) (with reference to *Article 6* of TRIPS), does not change the substantive patent law under TRIPS.[399]

Proponents of national exhaustion often fail to analyse the issue of exhaustion from the perspective of multilateral trade in the setting of global trade rules of the WTO including the TRIPS Agreement the very purpose of having an elaborate agreement on IPRs. They try to interpret the issue from a very narrow (pre-TRIPS) perspective, thus over-ruling international exhaustion. One might argue that under the Paris Convention international exhaustion could be restricted under *Article 4bis* (*1*) *and* (*2*) of the Paris Convention. Under the Paris Union, members are required to treat patent applications in different member countries independent of patents obtained for the same invention in other member countries. Although there is no specific mention of the exhaustion issue, there is no express mention of excluding it either, hence one can argue that it would apparently apply for exhaustion too. Based on such an interpretation, it is sometimes advocated that *Article 4bis* (*2*) mentions the independence of patents. As such if a patent is nullified in one country, it would not necessarily be nullified in the other country or if it lapses in one country would not mean that it would also lapse in another country. Similarly, according to

398 Straus Joseph, "Implications of TRIPS Agreement in the field of Patent Law", in Beier and Shricker edited, "From GATT to TRIPS – The Agreement on Trade – Related Aspects of Intellectual Property Rights", 18 Studies International Review of Industrial Property and Copyright Law (IIC), Max Planck Institute, Munich, pgs. 191, 192, 1996.

399 Footnote to *Article 28* (*1*) (*a*), "This right, like all other rights conferred under this Agreement in respect of the use, sale, importation or other distribution of goods, is subject to the provisions of *Article 6*.

this interpretation, if the patent rights are exhausted in one country it should not necessarily mean that it would exhaust in the other country.

Some critics of international exhaustion further comment that there is no obligation on the part of WTO members to comply with *Article 6* of the TRIPS Agreement since it is placed in Part 1 of the Agreement. According to such interpretation, under *Article 2.1* of TRIPS, Members are obliged to comply with the principles of independence in respect of Parts 2, 3, and 4 of the TRIPS Agreement. Hence, it's argued that even if Article 6 of the TRIPS might allow international exhaustion, it is against the Paris Convention since it is against the principle of independence of patents.[400] Critics also argue that *Article 6* does not affect Part 2 of the TRIPS Agreement and Part 2 which elaborates on the standards concerning the availability, scope and use of IPRS, makes parallel imports illegal based on the principle of territoriality.[401] Such view does not hold ground since the principle of territoriality as established by the Paris Convention, applies to the existence and not the exercise of the patent right.

Under the Convention, the main aim was to emphasise that a right to allow a patent in another country under a priority right was independent or territorial in nature and not dependent on the priority country.[402] We need to read this provision of the Paris Convention along with *Article 1.1* of TRIPS which states,

> Members shall give effect to the provisions of this Agreement. Members may, but shall not be obliged to, implement in their law more extensive protection than is required by this Agreement, provided that such protection does not contravene the provisions of this Agreement. Members shall be free to determine the appropriate method of implementing the provisions of this Agreement within their own legal system and practice.

Here it must also be pointed out that the Paris Convention does not state that due to the territorial and independent nature of the patents, developments outside the country where it is patented would not affect or influence it in any manner. Even when patents follow territoriality principle, it is a standard practice to follow absolute novelty instead of relative novelty. If this is the case, then the novelty will consider '*state of the art*' globally and not nationally.

400 Pires de Carvalho Nuno, "The TRIPS Regime of Patent Rights", Kluwer Law International, pg. 104–105, 2002.

401 Gallus Nick, "The Mystery of Pharmaceutical Parallel Trade and Developing Countries", 7 (2) The Journal of World Intellectual Property, pgs. 170, 169–182, 2004.

402 Osterrieth, "Die Hager Konferenz" 1925, Leipzig 1926, 37: S. Ladas, Patents, Trademarks and Related Rights, Cambridge (Mass.) 11975, 505, cited in Heath Christopher.

Under same logic exhaustion of patent laws should also be international. Here it must be considered carefully that there is nothing contradictory between *Article 4 bis* of the Paris Convention and the doctrine of exhaustion since while the former deals with domestic patent right the latter deals with the economic exploitation of the patented product.[403]

Further, nothing impairs the law of territory to consider effects of facts and events that take place outside the territory. In fact, since the footnote to *Article 28* clearly refers to the exhaustion issue, the right of '*making, using, selling and importing*' cannot escape exhaustion. The footnote makes it clear that the right of importation does not affect exhaustion in any way. It should also be noted that if it is accepted that exhaustion is allowed because of the footnote to *Article 28*, then in true sense there cannot be discrimination between national and international exhaustion. Moreover, one cannot interpret exhaustion based on territoriality principle and at the same time overlook the basic intention of patent law.

Some others who support national and regional exhaustion modes, opine that a mode of international exhaustion is against *Article 1* of the TRIPS Agreement which requires all parties to abide by the TRIPS rules. They confer that *Article 28* requires members to follow the mode of national exhaustion and hence they feel that if a member does not follow such mode of exhaustion, it would be against the member's obligation under *Article 1*.[404] However again these proponents of national and regional exhaustion tend to overlook the fact that the WTO Agreement clearly states that the other covered agreements (which includes the TRIPS Agreement), are governed by the WTO Agreement which aims at removal of trade barriers. Restraining international exhaustion of patent, converts IPRS into non-tariff barriers to trade hence are counterproductive to the aims of the WTO multilateral system.

The critics also argue that since the rights of the patent holder under the TRIPS Agreement are subject to the patent owner's consent, exhaustion is also tied to the consent. Such arguments are flawed given the fact that it undermines the exceptions to such consent which are already embedded in domestic law and TRIPS defines such exceptions, albeit limiting them.[405] Moreover, these interpretations totally fail to acknowledge the fact that the aims and

403 Ibid at 190, pg. 628, (623–632).

404 Harvey Bale James, "The conflicts between parallel trade and product access and innovation: The case of pharmaceuticals", Journal of International Economic Law, pg. 638, 1998.

405 Abbott Frederick, "Parallel trade in pharmaceuticals: trade therapy for market distortions", in Calboli Irene and Lee Edward (eds.), "Research handbook on Intellectual Property Exhaustion and Parallel Imports", Edward Elgar Publishing Ltd., pg. 159 (145–165), 2016.

objectives of the TRIPS is not identical to the IP conventions. *Article 4bis* of the Paris Convention never declared that national exhaustion is to be adopted by members. With the establishment of WTO and with the TRIPS coming into force, protection of IPRS have moved beyond the principle of territoriality to IPRS as crucial component of free trade which cannot enjoy the fruits of IPRS enforcement without honouring foundation of free trade.

In the present scenario under the GATT/WTO regime, the TRIPS Agreement not only makes the IPRS regime strict and effective, it also has a role to promote global trade. International exhaustion of patents aims at promoting a balanced approach towards rights and obligations of producers so that technical knowledge can be used in a way conducive to social and economic welfare. Further, international exhaustion also acts as checks and balance measure to restrain the patent holder from profiteering from the exercise of the patent. It receives its due incentive through the returns on placing the patented product or the product manufactured under a patented process on the market the first time. International exhaustion mandates the patent owner to compete in the global market on principles of free trade and pass on the benefits of consumer benefits by way of access to the patented products at the lowest possible market driven price.[406] The, national exhaustion on the contrary, limits competition only among exclusive licences and distributors operating in restrictive geographical areas.

6.3.1.8 Article 30: Exceptions to the Patent Rights Conferred

Article 30 deals with the exceptions to the patent rights conferred in *Article 27* of TRIPS for any invention in all fields of technology, including processes and products. It states,

> Members may provide limited exceptions to the exclusive rights conferred by a patent, provided that such exceptions do not unreasonably conflict with a normal exploitation of the patent and do not unreasonably prejudice the legitimate interests of the patent owner, taking account of the legitimate interests of third parties.

This can be considered a limited exemption that, on one hand serves the purpose of the exemption, while on the other, does not hinder the legitimate interests of the patent owner. Given its nature, WTO members have used the

406 Soltysinski Stanislaw, "International Exhaustion of Intellectual Property Rights under the TRIPS, the EC Law and the European Agreements", 4 GRUR Int., pg. 317, 1996.

provision to draft laws to allow research exemptions for patents that are similar to '*fair use*' in copyrights.[407] Popular in some jurisdictions as '*Bolar Exceptions*', in the pharmaceutical industry such exceptions are used for applying to regulatory bodies by generic manufacturers before expiry of the patent to enable quick marketing of a generic drug on expiry of the patent.[408]

The legality of use of *Article 30* exception by pharmaceutical manufacturers was challenged before the WTO DSB in the '*Canada – Patent Protection for Pharmaceutical Products*' case (*Canada – Pharmaceuticals*) and found to be permissible. The practice of filing for regulatory compliance of generic versions of patented pharmaceutical drugs before the national drug authority before expiry of the relevant patent and stockpiling of generic drugs in anticipation of the patent expiry were upheld to be within the exemptions provided under *Article 30*. The Panel considered the public policy requirements that a WTO member may need to address while adjudicating the case and decided that this exception claimed by Canada under *Article 30* of the TRIPS Agreement would result in a balanced intellectual property regime. The Panel Report also provided guidance to how the three-step test is to be interpreted as well laid down that the words '*limited*' and '*exceptions*' to be interpreted in combination as a narrow exception. Through the three-step test the Panel decided that the exception curtails the patent owner's right in only a small diminution.[409] The findings in *Canada Pharmaceutical* case confirmed that the TRIPS Agreement allowed WTO members necessary flexibilities in framing and enforcing their municipal legislation to provide certain restricted exemptions to patent protection for a balanced patent regime. Further, as per the Doha Declaration (discussed in details in Chapter 10), WTO members may also authorise exportation and importation of pharmaceutical drugs to address national health emergencies as an exception provided under *Article 30*.[410]

The provisions under *Article 30* have been lauded to bring a balanced patent regime in a WTO member country through limited exceptions to the patent

---

407 Gitter M. Donna, "International conflicts over patenting human DNA sequences in the United States and the European Union: An argument for compulsory licensing and a fair use exception", 76, New York University Law Review 6, pg. 1690, 2001. Available at, https://www.nyulawreview.org/wp-content/uploads/2018/08/NYULawReview-76-6-Gitter.pdf.

408 https://www.wto.org/english/tratop_e/trips_e/factsheet_pharm02_e.htm#art30.

409 *Canada – Patent Protection for Pharmaceutical Products*, WT/DS114/R (2000). See, https://www.wto.org/english/tratop_e/dispu_e/7428d.pdf.

410 Daya Shankar, "Access to medicines, Article 30 of TRIPS in the Doha Declaration and an Anthropological Critique of International Treaty Negotiations", Deakin University – Bowater School of Management and Marketing, 2003. Available at, https://papers.ssrn.com/sol3/papers.cfm?abstract_id=391540.

rights wherein the patent owner would not be able to allege infringement and enforce its rights. However, there would be considerable conditions too as such exceptions would be only applicable under certain conditions. In a hypothetical case, if a generic pharmaceutical company decides to manufacture a patented pharmaceutical drug under *Article 30* exception exclusively for exporting to a WTO member country without capacity to produce the drug, it cannot be considered an infringement. In such a case, the importing country would need to grant CL for such importation exactly in a manner it would have needed to grant for locally producing the patented pharmaceutical product.

Article 30 as interpreted by the Panel in *Canada Pharmaceutical* case, clearly does not impact exhaustion. However if a comparison is to be drawn between the patent exemption regime under *Article 30* and patent exhaustion regime of a WTO member, specifically in case of exportation under the exceptions, international exhaustion would be more seamless and use of *Article 30* could be more restrictive.[411] It has already been found that although patent rights are territorial in nature, legitimate extraterritorial sales outside the authorised dealership via parallel trade is not barred.[412] It must also be noted that the use of *Article 30* exception in an exporting country needs to be in sync with a compulsory licensing for importation under *Article 31* in the importation country would work. Hence, such exportation would be a violation in absence of CL under *Article 31* in the importing country. In other words, if a country evokes *Article 30* and allows a company to produce generic version of a patented product for permitted exceptions but instead exports them to some other WTO member's markets which has not notified importation under *Article 31*, the patent being unenforceable, cannot be considered to have exhausted. Hence, when a patent is temporarily withdrawn or suspended or made un-enforceable under *Article 30*, products covered under such patent shall not exhaust on exportation.

6.3.1.9 Article 31: Use of the Patent without Authorisation of the Right Holder

With the TRIPS Agreement defining patentability and elaborating number of procedural issues, it had expanded beyond the existing international treaties on IPRs. However, concerns of anti-competitive practices through IPRs were raised by developing countries and competition policy checks and balance

---

411 This position has been widely been propagated as a policy option by Medicines sans Frontier. See, https://msfaccess.org/why-article-30-will-work-why-article-31-will-not.

412 Correa Carlos, "Intellectual Property Rights, the WTO and Developing Countries – The TRIPS Agreement and Policy Options", Zed Books Ltd., pg. 84, 2000.

measures were debated.[413] At the end it trickled down to *Article 31* in the form of limitations to the patent rights conferred. *Article 31* of the TRIPS Agreement covers use of patented products without the authorization of the right holder and does not specifically refer to it as CL, a term that later has become well-known and was initially used in the Paris Convention. In *Article 5 (A) (2)* of the Paris Convention it states,

> Each country of the Union shall have the right to take legislative measures providing for the grant of compulsory licenses to prevent the abuses which might result from the exercise of the exclusive rights conferred by the patent, for example, failure to work.[414]

Slightly differing from the provision in the Paris Convention where the aim had been solely to address market abuses, in the TRIPS Agreement, *Article 31* adds on to the exceptions to patent rights that has already been provided in *Article 30*, hence the reason might not necessarily be to address IPR-centric abuses but to address other situations too. Further, subsequently in the Doha Declaration (discussed in details in Chapter 10), the CL provisions under *Article 31* address situations of national calamities or exigencies are vividly dealt with.

There are also specific provisions for Competition law remedies as in *Article 31(c)* with regards to semi-conductor technology where it states,

> The scope and duration of such use shall be limited to the purpose for which it was authorized, and in the case of semi-conductor technology shall only be for public non-commercial use or to *remedy a practice determined after judicial or administrative process to be anti-competitive.* (*Emphasis added*).

Competition law objective can also be noticed in *Article 31(k)* which states,

> Members are not obliged to apply the conditions set forth in subparagraphs (b) and (f)[415] where such use is permitted *to remedy a practice*

413 Schovsbo Jens, "Fire and water make steam – redefining the role of competition law in TRIPS", in Kur Annette and Levin Marianne (eds.), "Intellectual Property Rights in a fair world trading system", pgs. 326, 327, (308–358), 2011.

414 See, https://wipolex.wipo.int/en/text/287556.

415 *Article 30 (b)* states, "such use may only be permitted if, prior to such use, the proposed user has made efforts to obtain authorization from the right holder on reasonable commercial terms and conditions and that such efforts have not been successful within a reasonable period of time. This requirement may be waived by a Member in the case of a

> *determined after judicial or administrative process to be anti-competitive.* The need to correct anti-competitive practices may be taken into account in determining the amount of remuneration in such cases. Competent authorities shall have the authority to refuse termination of authorization if and when the conditions which led to such authorization are likely to recur. (*Emphasis added*).

It is clear that there is no direct relation between *Article 31*, *Article 31bis* and exhaustion of patents hence it is not analysed in further details. However, it is important to note that if *Article 31* or *Article 31bis* is evoked, the patent rights would be curtailed. E.g. in case of issuance of CL the right holder would be restricted from monetising the patent under free market conditions. In such scenario, as earlier discussed in case of evoking *Article 30*, the patents should not be allowed to exhaust since its existence itself is controlled. As such if a patented product is manufactured under CL at restrictive licensing conditions, any import of such products cannot be considered for parallel importation. Exhaustion is and should be adopted independent of *Article 31* and *Article 31bis* and the two should not be linked in any manner.

6.3.1.10 Article 40: Controlling Anti-competitive Practices in Licensing

Article 40 of the TRIPS Agreement provides with measures to control anti-competitive practices that might occur through IP licence contracts. However, most of the measures are guidelines for domestic action by national adjudicators and regulatory authorities hence to be applied in the relevant market and not at the multilateral level. Further, in absence of any definition of '*relevant market*', or clear indication as to what might constitute '*abuse*' of IP, it completely depends on the competent national adjudicators or regulatory authorities to address it on a case-by-case basis. Some guidance is provided by the

---

national emergency or other circumstances of extreme urgency or in cases of public non-commercial use. In situations of national emergency or other circumstances of extreme urgency, the right holder shall, nevertheless, be notified as soon as reasonably practicable. In the case of public non-commercial use, where the government or contractor, without making a patent search, knows or has demonstrable grounds to know that a valid patent is or will be used by or for the government, the right holder shall be informed promptly;" and *Article 30* (*f*) states, "any such use shall be authorized predominantly for the supply of the domestic market of the Member authorizing such use."

United Nations Set of Multilaterally Agreed Equitable Principles and Rules for the Control of Restrictive Business Practices.[416]

It has already been discussed that there are no definite competition/anti-trust laws in the WTO or the TRIPS Agreement to control anti-competitive trade practices. In such circumstance, owners of IPRs might try to supersede their legitimate exclusivity to the extent of abusive monopoly not only directly through IPRs but also through their license contracts. Very often the licensee is unable to negotiate a balanced deal due to the stronger market power of the licensor, resulting in anti-competitive license contracts. Hypothetically, the licensor might contractually bind the licensee not to sale its products beyond a certain market if it receives the patent holder's technology, even when the country's laws on IPRs allow such trade, i.e. allows international exhaustion. This is in essence, a reflection of the Preamble of the TRIPS Agreement wherein, it aims to put in place an effective system of checks and balance so that protection of IPRs does not become an impediment to dissemination of knowledge and technology.

In the first instance, *Article 40* acknowledges the fact that licensing agreements can restrict free and fair competition and at the same time allows countries to take necessary legal measures to restrain owners of IPRs from abusing the monopoly that might have been created through the exclusivity.[417] However the problem lies in the fact that although the aim is to provide sufficient checks against possible abuse of IPRs, there is a proviso that makes any such measure compliant to the protection of IPRs. As such it becomes a matter of interpretation as to whether the protection of IPRs provided is necessary or an excess that constitutes an abuse. Moreover, the action against any anti-competitive contract is also voluntary and not obligatory. This means that member countries can put in place legal measures in their national laws to check

---

416 Roffe Pedro and Spennemann Christoph, "Control of Anti-competitive Practices in Contractual Licenses under the TRIPS Agreement", Kluwer Law, pgs., 322, 323, 324 (293–329), 2008.

417 *Article 40*, "1. Members agree that some licensing practices or conditions pertaining to intellectual property rights which restrain competition may have adverse effects on trade and may impede the transfer and dissemination of technology. 2. Nothing in this Agreement shall prevent Members from specifying in their legislation licensing practices or conditions that may in particular cases constitute an abuse of intellectual property rights having an adverse effect on competition in the relevant market. As provided above, a Member may adopt, consistently with the other provisions of this Agreement, appropriate measures to prevent or control such practices, which may include for example exclusive grant-back conditions, conditions preventing challenges to validity and coercive package licensing, in the light of the relevant laws and regulations of that Member."

any anti-competitive practice but that is not mandatory under TRIPS *Article 40*. Hence, if a country does not have any such laws to check anti-competitive practice, the country cannot be brought before the DSB of the WTO.

It must also be noted that *Article 40* also provides guidance on problems related to cross-border restraints wherein it requires WTO members to solve the problems through consultations. But here too there is no specific right or norm set by TRIPS, hence such clauses are mere guidance which can never contribute effectively in providing any remedy.[418] It has been discussed in Chapter 3.2.3 how in the EU, competition law principles were adopted by the ECJ and international exhaustion within the EU was established by the *Grundig-Consten* case which became a landmark in being known as regional exhaustion. Here the free movement of goods within the EU member countries was considered from the perspective of intra-brand trade. However, the most crucial arguments in the case that superseded trademark laws were that of anti-cartel aspect of European Competition law.[419] Although a country might not be mandated under *Article 40* to remedy an anti-competitive practice through adjudication before the DSB of the WTO, hypothetically not following international exhaustion under *Article 6* might be brought before the DSB in conjunction with *Article 40*.

418 *Article 40*, "3. Each Member shall enter, upon request, into consultations with any other Member which has cause to believe that an intellectual property right owner that is a national or domiciliary of the Member to which the request for consultations has been addressed is undertaking practices in violation of the requesting Member's laws and regulations on the subject matter of this Section, and which wishes to secure compliance with such legislation, without prejudice to any action under the law and to the full freedom of an ultimate decision of either Member. The Member addressed shall accord full and sympathetic consideration to, and shall afford adequate opportunity for, consultations with the requesting Member, and shall cooperate through supply of publicly available non-confidential information of relevance to the matter in question and of other information available to the Member, subject to domestic law and to the conclusion of mutually satisfactory agreements concerning the safeguarding of its confidentiality by the requesting Member. 4. A Member whose nationals or domiciliaries are subject to proceedings in another Member concerning alleged violation of that other Member's laws and regulations on the subject matter of this Section shall, upon request, be granted an opportunity for consultations by the other Member under the same conditions as those foreseen in paragraph 3."

419 Ibid at 107.

CHAPTER 7

GATT 1994 and Exhaustion

The WTO was established after the success of the GATT 1994 negotiations and is an heir to the GATT 1947 Agreement. As far as its relation with IPRs is concerned, it succeeded in creating a link between trade regulations under GATT and the other existing international conventions on IP like the Paris Convention, Berne Convention, Rome Convention for the Protection of Performers, Producers of Phonograms and Broadcasting Organisations, and the '*Washington Treaty on Intellectual Property in Respect of Integrated Circuits*'.[420] The question was on the issue of whether GATT 1994 should draw its standard on IPRs from the existing GATT 1947 and enforce them or build a completely new IP code based on a system that would eliminate trade distortions. The result was the formation of TRIPS, which was based on a system which would remove trade distortions but at the same time acknowledge the existing IP conventions.

Moreover, with the integration of IPRs into the multilateral trading system through the TRIPS Agreement, it directly got linked with the GATT rules on trade in goods and services. Further, the WTO dispute settlement mechanism interpreted and applied IPR standards, reading with the VCLT along with the MFN and NT treatments. Thus, with such integration of IPRs with public international trade law, this legal discipline has moved beyond exclusivity of specialised lawyers and economists as '*fully recognised part of public international law*.'[421]

In the words of Prof. Thomas Cottier, leading expert in WTO regulations and Chief TRIPS negotiator for Switzerland during the Uruguay Round,

> To some extent, building the TRIPS Agreement was an effort to bring these prior agreements and disciplines into the realm of the GATT and trade law and to further refine and expand them to global law, yet without seeking full harmonization.[422]

420 Cottier Thomas, "The Prospects for Intellectual Property in GATT", 28 Common Market Law Review, Kluwer Academic Publishers, pg. 395, 1991.

421 Cottier Thomas, "Embedding Intellectual Property in International Law", in Roffe Pedro and Seuba Xavier (eds.), "Current Alliances in International Intellectual Property Law making: The Emergence and Impact of Mega-Regionals", Issue Number 4 ICTSD and CEIPI, pg. 18, (15–43), September 2017.

422 Cottier Thomas, "Working together towards TRIPS" in Watal Jayashree and Taubman Antony edited, "The Making of the TRIPS Agreement Personal Insights From The Uruguay

 | DOI:10.1163/9789004542815_009

However as discussed earlier, there is also other contemporary views that state that with the TRIPS Agreement coming into existence, the GATT Agreement is no longer relevant for IPRS. According to such view, given that TRIPS was introduced as '*lex specialis*' or '*sui generis*' specifically for IPRS, it takes precedence over the GATT.[423] However, this view has not been universally accepted since TRIPS imposes obligations that are different and additional to that of GATT and fundamentally does not regulate discrimination based on the origin of goods.[424] Moreover, considering that GATT 1994 is accepted as a single independent WTO Agreement, it includes all WTO provisions that members should comply in total, simultaneously and in harmonious interpretation irrespective of TRIPS or any other covered Agreements.[425]

This has recently been asserted in the *Australia – Certain Measures Concerning Trademarks, Geographical Indications and other Plain Packaging Requirements Applicable to Tobacco Products and Packaging* (*Australia – Plain Packaging*) case which involved the Agreement on Technical Barriers to Trade (TBT), considered lex specialis.[426] The panel examined the Australian government's laws to mandate plain packaging of cigarettes to reduce tobacco consumption, which allegedly was in a manner that the trademarks distinguishing one brand with the other, became minimal. The question was whether the trademark right is a negative right solely for restricting unauthorised trademarks from being used on products with authorised trademarks, or was it also an affirmative right for use of the trademark. The panel interpreted trademarks under TRIPS as exclusively negative rights. Further it also examined another *lex specialis* legislation, the Agreement on TBT, as to whether the plain packaging was a TBT resulting reduced consumption of the cigarette products thus its trade, in a legitimate manner. The panel examined whether the Australian government's measure was necessary to protect and promote public health, not

---

Round Negotiations" WTO, pg. 79, 2015. Also available at, https://www.wto.org/english/res_e/booksp_e/trips_agree_e/chapter_4_e.pdf.

423 Bronckers Marco, "The Exhaustion of Patent Rights under WTO Law", 5 Journal of World Trade, pg. 143, 1998.

424 Ibid at 381.

425 *Korea – Definitive Safeguard Measures on Imports of Some Dairy products*, WT/DS98/AB/R, paragraph 24, 2000. Available at, https://www.wto.org/english/tratop_e/dispu_e/98abr.pdf.

426 *Australia – Certain Measures Concerning Trademarks, Geographical Indications and other Plain Packaging Requirements Applicable to Tobacco Products and Packaging*, WT/DS435/R, WT/DS441/R, WT/DS458/R, WT/DS467/R, https://www.wto.org/english/tratop_e/dispu_e/435_441_458_467r_e.pdf.

just under these two agreements but under *Article XX* of GATT as interpreted under *Articles 31 & 32* of the rules of interpretation of the VCLT.[427]

In the earlier GATT 1947 Agreement, reference to IPRS was limited since it was considered distinctly separate from international trade. Further, US was not that adamant in linking international trade and IPRS at the time when GATT 1947 was negotiated, as less than 10% of its exports had IP content.[428] At that time when multilateral trade was regulated under GATT 1947, territoriality of IPRS prevailed and given that independent IPR enforcement mechanisms of contracting parties to the GATT found it sufficient, IPRS were not covered extensively.[429] With the passage of time, multilateral trade not only increased manifold but also became more complex and IPR content in traded goods increased substantially. As a result, there was an increasing demand from IPR owners of industrial countries to have extra-territorial control over their IPRS, especially in developing countries. The effective way to address this was to introduce IPR laws of the industrialised countries to these emerging developing country economies.[430]

The GATT Agreement covered IP issues in *Articles III, IV, IX, X, XI, XII, XVIII and XX*.[431] Of these the two main provisions were *Article IX*, relating to marks of origin and the most significant being *Article XX(d)*, which deals with the general exception in favour of IPRS, both of which were retained in the GATT 1994 Agreement. Hence, the exhaustion of patents and its effect on parallel trade in a broader perspective of multilateral trade needs to be assessed not just under the TRIPS Agreement but also the GATT 1994. The Preamble and *Articles I, III, XX, XI:1, XXIV and XXIII:1*, have been especially analysed in this chapter to relate to the relationship between GATT and exhaustion of IPRS and determine the most appropriate exhaustion regime. The most crucial being *Article XX(d)* in terms of determining whether national and regional exhaustion would pass the necessity test and qualify for exemptions.

427 Frankel Suzy, Gervais Daniel, "Plain Packaging and the Interpretation of the TRIPS Agreement", 5 Vanderbilt Journal of Transnational Law, Volume 46, pgs. 1153, 1155, 1156, (1149–1214), November 2013.

428 Gadbow Michael, "Intellectual Property and International Trade: Merger or Marriage of Convenience?" in Brown Lonnie and Szweda Eric (eds.), "Trade Related Aspects of Intellectual Property", William S. Hein & Co. Inc. pgs. 226 & 230, 1990.

429 Hoekman Bernard and Kostecki Michel, "The Political Economy of the World Trading System: The WTO and Beyond", 2nd Edition Oxford University Press, pg. 282, 2001.

430 See https://www.wto.org/english/res_e/booksp_e/trips_agree_e/chapter_4_e.pdf.

431 Botoy Ituku Elangi, "From the Paris Convention to the TRIPS Agreement, A One-Hundred-and-Twelve-Year Transitional Period for the Industrialized Countries", 7 (1) The Journal of World Intellectual Property, pgs. 115–130, 2004.

7.1 Preamble to the GATT 1994

The Preamble to GATT 1994 provides the intent of the Agreement and states that the aim to establish the WTO regime with multiple agreements was to enhance international trade. The underlying principle of GATT 1994 was to expand production and trade in goods and services through removal of trade barriers. It states,

> Being desirous of contributing to these objectives by entering into reciprocal and mutually advantageous arrangements directed to the substantial reduction of tariffs and other barriers to trade and to the elimination of discriminatory treatment in international trade relations.
>
> Resolved, therefore, to develop an integrated, more viable and durable multilateral trading system encompassing the GATT, the results of past trade liberalisation efforts, and all of the results of the Uruguay Round of Multilateral Trade Negotiations.[432]

Fundamentally, IPRS are not just an enforcement tool in isolation, it should be carefully treated in comprehensive terms of multilateral trade so that it does not become a barrier to trade.[433] The question arises as to whether implied restrictions to NT against the spirit of the preamble can result in a violation. It is also a legitimate argument that conceptually, from the perspective of the GATT and TRIPS, protection of IPRS come along with the goal of enhancing trade.[434] On analysing it from the perspective of the exhaustion issue, it would obviously seem that in a setting where TRIPS was established to facilitate multilateral trade, the mode of exhaustion should be in line removing trade barriers.[435] As such, considering the trade-enhancing nature of international

---

432 "Marrakesh Agreement Establishing the World Trade Organisation" – Objectives / Preamble, paragraphs 1, 3 and 4.

433 Daya Shankar, "Brazil, the Pharmaceutical Industry and the WTO" 5 (1) The Journal of World Intellectual Property Law pg. 74, (53–104) 2002. "Other areas of U.S. intellectual Property law are unaffected by the Agreement on TRIPS. For example, the Agreement does not require any change in current U.S. law or practice with respect to parallel importation of goods that are the subject of intellectual property rights".

434 Sindico Domenico, "On Parallel Importation, TRIPS and European Court of Justice Decisions", 4 Journal of World Intellectual Property, pg. 515, 2002.

435 Frankel Suzy and Gervais Daniel, "International intellectual property rules and parallel imports", in Irene Calboli and Edward Lee edited, "Research handbook on Intellectual Property Exhaustion and Parallel Imports", Edward Elgar Publishing Ltd., pg. 86 (85–105), 2016.

exhaustion, it would be the most appropriate mode of exhaustion in line with the Preamble to the GATT 1994. We now move to the next part of the chapter to find a more detailed analysis of *Article 1* of GATT 1994 to understand the relationship between GATT and patent exhaustion.

7.2 Article I – Most Favoured Nation

The MFN treatment covered in *Article 1* of GATT is one of the foundations of the WTO regulations. Under *Article 1*, a WTO Member is required to accord the MFN given by it for '*like products*' to one country, unconditionally to all other WTO Members at any given time, in terms of trade tariffs and other regulatory treatment including internal taxes, charges and regulations.[436] The MFN treatment would thus require a WTO Member to provide same trade concession that it provides any other nation.[437] Thus, in case of any discriminatory treatment to imports of like products from a WTO Member country vis-à-vis imports from another country, it will be a clear violation. Here it is important to note that '*like product*' does not necessarily mean same product, hence it might be identical or of different variety, but still could qualify as like product. In absence of a clear definition of like product, it is to be considered products that show identical or similar characteristics as was held by the AB in *European Communities – Measures affecting asbestos and asbestos-containing products* (*EC Asbestos*).[438]

In GATT 1947, *Article 1* was interpreted in a broad manner to cover not just tariffs, but any measure that may affect trade between GATT members and include both positive and negative discrimination. A reference may be drawn to the *US – Denial of Most-Favoured-Nation Treatment as to Non-Rubber Footwear from Brazil* (*US – MFN Footwear*) case.[439] MFN is based on equal treatment of all WTO members. Principally to promote non-discrimination in international trade between sovereign equals drawing from *Article 2(1)* of the United Nations

436 https://www.wto.org/english/res_e/booksp_e/gatt_ai_e/art1_e.pdf.

437 Ibid at 5, pg. 27.

438 *European Communities – Measures affecting asbestos and asbestos-containing products*, WT/DS135/AB/R, adopted 5 April 2001, paragraph 91. Also see, Cottier Thomas, "Parallel Trade and Exhaustion of Intellectual Property in WTO Law Revisited", in Ruse Khan Grosse Henning & Metzger Axel (eds.), "Intellectual Property Ordering Beyond Borders", Cambridge University Press, pg. 206–207 (189–232), 2022.

439 *US – Denial of Most-Favoured-Nation Treatment as to Non-Rubber Footwear from Brazil*, DS18/R, adopted 19 June 1992, paragraph 6.8. B.I.S.D. 39S/128, Available at, https://www.wto.org/english/tratop_e/dispu_e/91nruber.pdf.

Charter.[440] But, the fundamental reason behind MFN treatment in trade agreements is comparative advantage. So that the most efficient producer can produce and engage in trade to supply the product while the other members benefit from welfare-enhancing trade.

MFN enforced through the multilateral agreement enables ex-ante removal of trade distortions since it restricts giving trade concessions to one over another trade partner.[441] As such any measure that might be trade-distorting would be considered a violation of *Article I*, including non-fiscal border measures. Here it will be relevant to refer to the *European Communities – Regime for the Importation, Sale and Distribution of Bananas* (*EC Bananas III*) case.[442] In *EC Bananas III* the AB held that if any party has less onerous import requirements, it is an advantageous administrative treatment over the others. In this case, it was found that discrimination was in licensing procedure, where some operators from particular origin were enjoying less complicated licensing procedures along with other in-quota discrimination in tariffs for bananas originating from certain other countries, thus violating *Article I*.[443]

The importance of MFN as one of the foundational pillars of the WTO trading regime is well established and remains largely unchallenged especially in its treatment of like products. In *European Communities – Measures Prohibiting the Importation and Marketing of Seal Products* (*EC – Seals*) case, Canada and Norway challenged EU regulations that used TBT to ban importation and marketing of seal products from their countries while EU raised the issue of morality in killing of seals. It is interesting to note that there were certain seal products that were exempted from the ban. The AB confirmed the panel finding that there was violation of *Article I* and stressed on equal opportunity among all WTO Members for all like products imported.[444] In *EC – Seals* earlier the panel had found that while certain seal products originating from

440 https://www.un.org/en/about-us/un-charter/full-text.

441 Schwartz F. Warren and Sykes O. Alan, "The Positive Economics of Most-Favoured Nation Obligation and its Exceptions in the WTO/GATT System", in Bhandari J. and Sykes Alan, eds., "Economic Dimensions in International Law", 43, Cambridge University Press, pgs. 43–75, 1998.

442 *European Communities – Regime for the Importation, Sale and Distribution of Bananas*, WT/DS27/AB/R, 1997, paragraph 207. Available at, https://docs.wto.org/dol2fe/Pages/SS/directdoc.aspx?filename=Q:/WT/DS/27ABR.PDF&Open=True.

443 Matshushita Mitsuo, Schoenbaum J. Thomas, Mavroidis C. Petros and Hahn Michael, "The World Trade Organization Law, Practice and Policy", The Oxford International Law Library, 3rd Edition, pgs. 158, 159, 161, 162, 2015.

444 *European Communities – Measures Prohibiting the Importation and Marketing of Seal Products*, WT/DS400 & 401/AB/R, paragraph 5.87, 18 June 2014. Available at, https://www.wto.org/english/tratop_e/dispu_e/400_401abr_e.pdf.

Greenland would qualify for the EU market under the allowed exceptions, a large majority from Canada and Norway would not have met such exceptions. Hence although the issue of likeness seemed apparently origin-neutral, it was discriminatory, establishing *de-facto* discrimination which was held as a violation of *Article I*.[445] The decisive question that identified the discrimination as highlighted by the panel and confirmed by the AB was, if it was immoral to allow products from seal hunt, how can such immorality be exempted for like products from certain geographical region.[446]

Let us now apply the above AB findings on '*like products*' to determine whether a patent exhaustion mode can be held in compliance or violative of *Article I*. Hypothetically, let us consider certain patented product that has been manufactured under the same technology, exhibiting same features in two different countries. One, manufactured in the country and another imported from another, thus two originating in two WTO Member countries. Following national or regional exhaustion while treating the import of the patented product and restricting it through enforcement of patent would mean that like products would be discriminated against and thus a violation of *Article I* of GATT.

In such scenario, if international exhaustion is applied on the imported patented products irrespective of where it is originating, there would not be any discrimination. One might argue that the discrimination is not against another member country, but the patented product licensed to be manufactured in another country. Here the author would draw reference to *EC – Seals* case and argue that irrespective of the restraint being imposed on the licensed product, given that manufacturing under license had been opted due to comparative advantage, exports from the WTO member where the licensed product originated, in effect has been discriminated. Following international exhaustion and enabling parallel imports on the other hand would be in true essence, adhering to MFN where IPRS are not used as regulatory measures to discriminate like products.

445 Bossche Peter Van den and Werner Zdouc, "The Law and Policy of the World Trade Organization, Text, Cases and Materials", Cambridge University Press, 4th Edition, pgs. 308–310, 2017.

446 Levy I. Philip and Regan H. Donald, "EC Seal Products: Seals and Sensibilities (TBT Aspects of the Panel and Appellate Body Reports)", EUI Working Paper RSCAS 2014/138, pg. 9, 2014.

7.3 Article III – National Treatment

'*National Treatment*' is the other fundamental requirement existing since GATT 1947 that forms the foundational pillar of the WTO trading system. In essence, under NT, all imported good, service, a service provider, an investor, an IP, a person (both juridical and natural) owning IP or any other property rights should be treated same as their national or domestic equivalent.[447] In other words, it prohibits all types of discrimination between imports and domestic products and thus triggered *lex lata* i.e. by the jurisdiction of the importing WTO Member.[448]

While different Agreements under the WTO regulatory system addresses different aspects, GATT addresses imports of goods and like MFN this too is based on the principle of non-discrimination and takes effect when the import enters the market of the importing country. The history of NT dates to the foundation of Bretton Woods system where in the proposed International Trade Organisation, Article 18 of the Havana Charter covered, '*National Treatment on Internal Taxation and Regulation*' which laid the way to a more revised version in the form of *Article III* of GATT 1947.[449]

NT in case of IPRs under the TRIPS Agreement has been elaborated in previous chapter, the intention here is to analyse NT under GATT 1994 to draw a possible interpretation of how that might affect patent exhaustion. As such, NT in the other Agreements covered by the WTO regulatory system is not addressed in this book. Considering the regulatory span of *Article III,* we consider exclusively imports of legitimate products and not illicit imports. Hence in terms of patent protected products, imports of counterfeits or unauthorised copies of the patented products are not considered. Only those which have been manufactured legally outside a WTO member country are considered. Hence, this would apply to the border measures that impact the products on crossing the importing country's border in a discriminatory manner based on its origin.

Historically, it is important to consider how decisions of national adjudicatory bodies would be considered under GATT, given that WTO dispute settlement mechanism does not consider orders of domestic courts passed in national jurisdictions of WTO members. A reference may be made to the GATT 1947 regulations where certain elements of *Section 337* of the US Patent Act at that time were held inconsistent with GATT NT mandate by a dispute settlement panel in 1989. In this case certain provisions of *Section 337* of the US

447 See, https://www.wto.org/english/res_e/booksp_e/gatt_ai_e/art3_e.pdf.
448 Ibid at 443, pg. 179, 2015.
449 See Havana Charter, https://www.wto.org/english/docs_e/legal_e/havana_e.pdf.

Patent Act operative at that time, did not allow imported products the benefit of patent invalidity defence in an infringement while the same was available for domestically manufactured products. The GATT panel found *Section 337* to be clearly violating US commitment to NT and subsequently the decision *Section 337* was appropriately amended.[450] NT requirements under the GATT has not changed, hence it must be assessed how it is applicable now while drawing an inference as to its applicability and treatment of patent exhaustion.

Further, under the NT requirements in GATT 1994, '*like products*' and its '*non-discriminatory treatment*' are core but *Article III:2* does not define it, instead it is referred in an indirect manner. It states,

> The products of the territory of any contracting party imported into the territory of any contracting party shall not be subject, directly or indirectly, to internal taxes or other internal charges of any kind in excess of those applied, directly or indirectly, to like domestic products. Moreover, no contracting party shall otherwise apply internal taxes or other internal charges to imported or domestic products in a manner contrary to the principles set forth in paragraph 1.[451]

Assessment of whether the imported product is a like product is crucial hence in absence of clear definition, WTO jurisprudence laid down by different panels and the AB becomes important.[452]

NT under *Article III* of GATT mandates WTO Members to treat goods imported from other Members as domestically produced goods the same way by providing equal conditions for imported products vis-à-vis domestic products.[453] This issue of non-discrimination has been lucidly elaborated by AB in one of its initial decisions, *Japan – Alcoholic Beverages*.[454] In *Japan – Alcoholic Beverages* case AB confirmed the findings of the panel that physical characteristics, consumer uses and tariff classification would determine '*likeness*' of the imported products with that produced domestically, dumping the '*Aim and effects test*' propounded in the GATT 1947 era, *United States – Measures affecting*

450 Ibid at 5, pg. 27.

451 See, https://www.wto.org/english/res_e/booksp_e/gatt_ai_e/art3_e.pdf.

452 Ibid at 445, pg. 354.

453 Ibid at 5, pgs. 26, 27.

454 *Japan – Taxes on Alcoholic Beverages*, WT/DS8/AB/R; WT/DS10/AB/R; WT/DS11/AB/R, paragraph 17–17, 4 October 1996. Available at, https://docs.wto.org/dol2fe/Pages/SS/directdoc.aspx?filename=Q:/WT/DS/8ABR.pdf&Open=True.

Alcoholic and Malt Beverages (*US – Beverages*),[455] as baseless and erroneous. However, the rejection of the aims and effect approach without even the slightest consideration in any condition, perhaps to avoid any '*intrusive inquiries into the inner workings of the decision-making procedures in the heterogenous membership*', has raised concerns too.[456]

The crucial issue of like products was dealt with by the AB in *EC – Asbestos*.[457] The assessment of whether the imported products and the domestic products are like products in the true sense of *Article III:4* has been considered from their competitiveness. In other words, whether they directly competed in the market and whether regulatory measures were taken to restrain such competition. If it was established that in direct competition and the measures adopted by the importing member state resulted in the imported like product facing less favourable treatment than that of the domestic product, there was violation of *Article III*. Hence, *Article III* applies to the measures and not just inherently limited to imports. In *EC – Asbestos*, the AB interpreted *Article III* to determine likeness and treatment accorded to the imports by the determination of the nature and extent of the competitive relationship of the two like products.[458] The AB held that if the regulations in the importing WTO Member are typically adopted to distinguish the imports by according it less favourable treatment because the market would not make such distinction, violation is established.[459]

Similarly in *India – Measures affecting the Automotive Sector* (*India – Autos*) case, which was initiated during a period when India had severe balance of payment (BOP) problems, *Article III* applied to the measures although they were not inherent to imports.[460] To address its BOP problems, India adopted broad import licensing regime for '*completely knocked down*' (CKD) and '*semi-knocked down*' (SKD) automobiles and components through indirect measures.

---

455 *United States – Measures affecting Alcoholic and Malt Beverages*, DS23/R, adopted 19 June 1992, B.I.S.D. 39S/206. Available at, https://www.wto.org/english/tratop_e/dispu_e/gatt_e/91alcohm.pdf.

456 Ibid at 443, pgs. 186, 187.

457 Ibid at 438.

458 Lydgate Emily, "Sorting out mixed messages under the WTO National Treatment Principle: A Proposed Approach", Vol 15, World Trade Review, Issue 3, pg. 427, (423–450), 2016.

459 Roessler Frieder, "The Scope of Regulatory Autonomy of WTO Members under Article III:4 of the GATT: A Critical Analysis of the Jurisprudence of the WTO Appellate Body", RSCAS Policy Paper 2015/04, pgs. 1–3, 2015.

460 *India – Measures affecting the Automotive Sector*, WT/DS146/AB/R; WT/DS175/AB/R, 19 March 2002. Avialable at, https://docs.wto.org/dol2fe/Pages/SS/directdoc.aspx?filename=Q:/WT/DS/175ABR.pdf&Open=True.

Passenger car manufacturers in India could obtain an import license for importing CKD and SKD units conditional to them joining in a Memorandum of Understanding that had mandatory local manufacturing requirement as well as local content sourcing and time-bound minimum investment requirements, etc. This was challenged by EC and the US and the measures were held to be discriminatory and protectionist although imports as such were not discriminated.[461]

Even in more recent decisions like, *India – Certain Measures Relating to Solar Cells and Solar Modules* (*India Solar Cells*),[462] the AB persistently held that the NT obligation applied to discriminatory measures, although the product discriminated against was not directly competing with the products purchased. In this case under National Solar Mission of the Government of India, guaranteed price contracts were offered to government agencies conditional to local content mandate, i.e. used Indian made solar cells and modules.[463] Hence *Article III* applied to the measures although they were not inherent to imports if the relationship between the two could be established.

From the series of GATT jurisprudence right from pre-WTO to recent times, analysed above, it has been clearly established that *Article III* mandates non-discrimination between imports of like products that are competitive with their domestic alternates. Further it is not just the imports but also applied to the measures that intend to discriminate between the two. There cannot be any doubt as to the likeness of products manufactured under the same patented technology whether it is manufactured in one country or two or more. In such scenario if a WTO Member follows national or regional exhaustion of patents it will violate its NT obligation. This is because it uses domestic patent enforcement measures on parallel imports of products manufactured under the same patent to restrain direct competition with the products manufactured domestically, clearly violating *Article III*. Whereas in case the importing country adopts international exhaustion, patent infringement measures cannot be used either as border measure at the time of imports nor after the imports reach the market hence would be in right spirit of *Article III*.

---

461 Bagwell Kyle and Sykes O. Alan, "India Measures affecting the automotive sector", Volume 4, World Trade Review Special Issue S1, pgs. 160, 161, (158–178), 2005.

462 *India – Certain Measures Relating to Solar Cells and Solar Modules*, WT/DS456/AB/R, 16 September 2016. Available at, https://www.wto.org/english/tratop_e/dispu_e/456abr_e.pdf.

463 Ibid at 445n, pgs. 348, 349.

7.4 Article XX – General Exceptions

There are number of exceptions that might apply to MFN and NT obligations of which, *Article XX* of GATT specifically provides for exceptions for measures that would otherwise be inconsistent with GATT obligations of a WTO Member. IP rights while would likely be interpreted as justified trade barriers, it would only be so if they are consistent and qualifies in the necessity test under *Article XX (d)* and the non-discrimination requirement under the chapeau to *Article XX* GATT. Further, while interpreting exhaustion under this exceptions clause, one would need to assess the complexity involved assessing different factors.[464] Different cases decided by different panels and AB decisions interpret whether an exception would apply to MFN and NT obligations. GATT *Article XX* the '*General Exception*' and *Article XXIV* the exception for FTAs layout the circumstances where such exceptions would or would not apply.

> As always, the analysis of whether a state acts in a WTO-incompatible manner only starts with the question whether it was incompatible with the pertinent obligations under a WTO agreement. As a second step, justifications for the prima facie illegal act have to be explored.[465]

The intention in this chapter is to analyse how the general exceptions have been applied by parties and interpreted by different panels and the AB to draw an inference as to how that might apply hypothetically in case of patent exhaustion driven restriction on parallel importation came before the WTO DSB.

As mentioned, GATT *Article XX* allows exemptions to the WTO members from their obligations under certain circumstances and its over-arching application on varied provisions. The provision under *Article XX* is actually grandfathered from GATT 1947 and the main intention of retaining it was to provide

464 Condon J. Bradley, "GATT Article XX and Proximity of Interest: Determining the Subject Matter of Paragraphs b and g", Vol 9, UCLA Journal of International Law and Foreign Affairs, No. 2, Fall/Winter, pgs. 137–162, 2004. Also see, Ruse-Khan Henning Grosse, "The Protection of Intellectual Property in International Law", Oxford University Press, pg. 274, 2016. Also see, Cottier Thomas, "Parallel Trade and Exhaustion of Intellectual Property in WTO Law Revisited", in Ruse Khan Grosse Henning & Metzger Axel (eds.), "Intellectual Property Ordering Beyond Borders", Cambridge University Press, pg. 208–209 (189–232), 2022.

465 Ibid at 443, pg. 173.

necessary policy space to the members in way of defence in case of violation complaints by other members.[466] It states,

> Subject to the requirement that such measures are not applied in a manner which would constitute a means of arbitrary or unjustifiable discrimination between countries where the same conditions prevail, or a disguised restriction on international trade, nothing in this Agreement shall be construed to prevent the adoption or enforcement by any contracting party of measures:
> (a) necessary to protect public morals;
> (b) necessary to protect human, animal or plant life or health;

One would observe that *Article XX* exemption is allowed as a defence to adopting measures inconsistent with GATT on assessment of three factors; I) the objective or value of the challenged measure, II) how the measure is expected to meet the objective and III) the impact of such measure on trade between the WTO Members. Based on this, assessment is to be made whether such measure was necessary and if so, whether possible alternatives that are less trade restrictive could have been adopted.[467] As we elaborate further in this section of the chapter it will be discussed how the *Article XX* defence has been allowed or denied through interpretation of different panels and the AB in different cases.

Article XX (a) exempts measures taken by a WTO Member that would otherwise be considered trade restrictive and discriminatory, if it was established to be taken to protect public morals. For a member to argue in favour of some trade restrictive measure to protect public morals, the member must establish that it is designed to protect public morals and such measure is necessary to accord such protection.[468] Now the question arises as to what should be considered as '*public moral*', given that neither GATT or the other WTO Agreements define it. The issue of public morals came up both under GATT and GATS in the *United States – Measures Affection the Cross-Border Supply of Gambling and*

466 Ruse-Khan Henning Grosse, "Assessing the need for a general public interest exception in the TRIPS Agreement", in Kur Annette and Levin Marianne (eds.), "Intellectual Property Rights in a fair world trading system", pgs. 184, 185, (167–207), 2011.

467 Dawar Kamala and Ronen Eyal, "How Necessary? A Comparison of Legal and Economic Assessments GATT Dispute Settlements Under: Article XX (B), TBT 2.2 and SPS 5.6", Vol 8 Trade Law and Development 1, pg. 6, 2016.

468 Ibid at 445, pg. 625.

Betting Services (*US – Gambling*) case decided by the AB.[469] Public morals was '*standards of right and wrong conduct maintained by or on behalf of a community or nation.*' It was also accepted that WTO Members should be able to define and apply it considering their cultural, religious, ethical values.

In *US – Gambling* case, Antigua and Barbuda complained before the WTO DSB against the US that certain US federal laws banned cross-border internet gambling while US evoked GATT *Article XX* (*a*) exception along with the same provisions in *Article XIV* GATS. *US – Gambling* raised two significant questions; first, as to how should the WTO DSB assess legitimacy of a member country's claim of public morals given that it may be subjective to factors that are local and would differ from one member country to another. Secondly, even if such measure was considered legitimate on grounds of public morality, why should another member's otherwise legitimate right to trade with that country, be restrained. In other words, how would the WTO DSB balance between public morals and liberalised multilateral trade.[470]

Both the Panel and AB had found that the measures were genuinely designed to protect public morals but then the AB considered whether the measure was '*necessary*' to protect public morals and whether reasonable alternative was provided. It was stated that the necessity can be established if the alternative is not '*reasonably available*' in technical and economic terms. In other words, if such alternate measure incurs excessive costs or imposes technical inabilities, such alternative could not be considered as reasonably available. Finally on appeal, the US measure did not meet the chapeau requirement on *Article XX* since it was applied in a discriminatory manner only to foreign service suppliers and not to domestic service suppliers. Here it must be noted that the chapeau triggers only after the necessity test is complied.[471]

In another case on the same subject matter, *China – Measures Affecting Trading Rights and Distribution Services for Certain Publications and Audiovisual Entertainment Products* (*China – Audiovisual Services*),[472] China had invoked

---

469 *United States – Measures Affecting the Cross-border Supply of Gambling and Betting Services*, WTO, WT/DS285/AB/R, Appellate Body Report, paragraph 308.

470 Marwell C. Jeremy, "Trade and Morality: The WTO Public Morals Exception After Gambling", New York University Law Review, Vol 81, pgs. 802–805, 2006.

471 'Chapeau' or cap, in literal sense is actual conditions provided for the exceptions to apply. The chapeau clarifies legitimacy of the measures. Also see, Cottier Thomas, "Parallel Trade and Exhaustion of Intellectual Property in WTO Law Revisited", in Ruse Khan Grosse Henning & Metzger Axel (eds.), "Intellectual Property Ordering Beyond Borders", Cambridge University Press, pg. 224 (189–232), 2022.

472 *China – Measures Affecting Trading Rights and Distribution Services for Certain Publications and Audiovisual Entertainment Products*, WT/DS363/AB/R, 21 December 2009, Available at, https://www.wto.org/english/tratop_e/dispu_e/363abr_e.pdf.

Article XX(a) to defend a series of measures regulating importation and distribution of reading materials, audio-visual home entertainment products and sound recordings and films for theatrical release which were challenged by US as non-compliant with China's GATT commitments. The AB found that China could invoke *Article XX (a)* based on its Accession Protocol however on assessing whether such measure was necessary, the AB confirmed the finding of the Panel that China had not demonstrated that the series of measures were necessary to protect public morals. After that the AB however did not go ahead further to assess whether the chapeau to *Article XX* was met. Similarly in *EC – Seals*[473] too, the AB concluded that the EU Seal trade was within the scope of *Article XX (a)* and the measures are relevant and then moved to the '*necessity*' test and found that the alternative measure available was not less trade restrictive. Finally moving on to the chapeau to *Article XX*, the AB found that although the same conditions prevailed in the Seal hunting Inuit communities in Greenland and Canada, there was unjustifiable discriminatory treatment between them.[474]

Article XX(b) exempts from GATT obligations if the measures are to protect human, animal or plant life or health. Similar provision is found in some other WTO Agreements including TRIPS where Article 27.2 which states, '*Members may exclude from patentability inventions, the prevention within their territory of their exploitation of which is necessary to protect human, animal or plant life or health or to avoid serious prejudice to the environment.*' From the wording of the article the policy objective of the measure is clear. Especially environment vs international trade has been a matter of discussion and debate in global circles, however it is important to note that blaming international trade for failing to internalise environmental costs is erroneous. Whether it is public health or environment, WTO panels and the AB had always assessed that the measure adopted by the WTO Member is not intended to trade barriers.[475]

This case of utmost relevance from the perspective of *Article XX (b)* defence is, *EC – Asbestos*.[476] In *EC Asbestos* Canada alleged that certain ban imposed by France on asbestos and asbestos products including their importation was violation of *Articles 2, 3* and *5* of SPS Agreement, *Article 2* of TBT Agreement and *Articles III, XI* and *XIII* of GATT 1994 resulting in nullification and impairment of benefits accruing under these agreements. EC invoked *Article XX(b)* as defence and alleged that such ban was necessary to protect human life or

473 Ibid at 444.
474 Ibid at 443, pgs. 728, 729.
475 Ibid at 443, pg. 173.
476 Ibid at 438.

health. The AB for the first time not only elaborated the '*necessity*' aspect of *Article XX(b)* and applying the test, but also refined it in broad perspective of *Article XX*. Logically without the ban asbestos elimination would not be possible hence there was no way protection could be accorded. However, at the same time the AB assessed through different levels of scrutiny.[477]

The AB formulated four conditions to implement such scrutiny. The first condition to determine whether the measure was necessary, the societal value of the measure at issue and how the measure contributes to the protection or promotion of this value needs to be identified. In this case it was by removing or reducing asbestos fibres that have the life-threatening health risks. The AB then moved to the second condition to assess whether a less trade-restrictive alternative measure was '*reasonably available*'. Canada had alleged that '*controlled use*' of asbestos and asbestos products could not be considered as a reasonable alternative since its implementation was impossible. The AB considered different factors, a pertinent being whether the alternative measure could meet the objective of the original measure and in this case, it held that it was not possible for France to allow '*controlled use*' to meet its health objective i.e. to restrain health risks imposed by use of asbestos and its products. The third condition provided the WTO members policy space to determine health or environment standards that they consider necessary and that was not open for challenge by other WTO members. However, the members could challenge the necessity of such measure for meeting the aimed level of protection. Finally, the fourth condition was that a WTO member may in good faith consider a measure based on qualified scientific and respected sources as appropriate and this may be different from majority scientific opinion. Hence the panel may not consider legitimacy of a measure based on majority scientific evidence available.[478]

Another case in point is *European Communities – Conditions for the Granting of Tariff Preferences to Developing Countries* (*EC – Tariff Preferences*). In this case the measure was an EC generalised tariff preferences (GSP) scheme for combating drug production and trafficking in 12 developing countries and transition economies. India complained that the treatment received by the 12 countries were preferential and argued that the nature of the measure was such that there was no relationship between the stated objectives of the

477 Howse L. Robert and Tuerk Elisabeth, "The Impact on Internal Regulations – A Case Study of the Canada – EC Asbestos Dispute", in Burca d Grainne and Scott Joanne eds., "The EU and the WTO: Legal and Constitutional Issues", Hart Publishing, pg. 325, (283–328), 2002.

478 Ibid at 445, pgs. 560–562.

measures and the drug arrangements.[479] The panel assessed the '*design, structure and architecture*' of the measure and agreed with India that there was no relationship between the objectives stated and the drug arrangements. Further the EC failed to show how such measure was necessary to protect human life or health also it did not pass the test of chapeau to *Article XX* establishing that there was preferential treatment.[480]

In another prominent case, *Brazil – Measures affecting imports of retreaded tyres* (*Brazil – Tyres*), the tests of whether the exception is applicable was clearly laid down by the panel and the AB.[481] In this case, Brazil banned imports of retreaded tyres for environmental and health reasons. One can argue that Brazil's ban was to meet its obligation upholding human rights. However, any such human rights measure cannot circumvent the need to comply with a WTO member's commitment under relevant WTO agreements.[482] EC had complained of GATT *Article XI* violation while Brazil invoked exemption under *Article XX(b)* as defence.

In the *Brazil – Tyres* case the panel and the AB first applied a two-tier test to assess whether the measure was provisionally justified in its objective to protect human, animal or plant life or health: (I) the design threshold of the measure to meet the objective; (II) the '*necessity*' test as to whether such measure was necessary. To assess the second test, the panel and AB assessed to what extent the measure met its legitimate policy objective both general and specific i.e. in this case human health and human life. On being satisfied that the measure was necessary the panel then moved on to assess less trade-restrictive possible alternatives wherein the panel found that Brazil did not meet this requirement. Here the panel observed that the capacity of a country to implement the remedial measure should also consider its cost and use of technologies. Further, moving on to the chapeau of *Article XX*, the AB found that Brazil did not meet the '*Laws and regulations consistency*' test, although the discriminatory measure met its objective, the exemption of Mercosur Members was

479 A case in point is *European Communities – Conditions for the Granting of Tariff Preferences to Developing Countries*, WT/DS246/AB/R, 7 April 2004. Available at, https://docs.wto.org/dol2fe/Pages/SS/directdoc.aspx?filename=Q:/WT/DS/246ABR.pdf&Open=True.

480 Pratap Ravindra, "WTO and Tariff Preferences: India Wins the Case, EC the Law" Vol. 39, Economic and Political Weekly, No. 18, pg. 1788, (1788–1790), May 1–7, 2004.

481 *Brazil – Measures Affecting Imports of Retreaded Tyres*, WTO, WT/DS332/AB/R, 3 December 2007, para 207.

482 Harris Rachel and Moon Gilian, "GATT Article XX and Human Rights: What do we know from the first 20 years? GATT Article XX and Human Rights", Volume 16 Melbourne Journal of International Law 2, 2015, pgs. 4,5,6. Available at, https://law.unimelb.edu.au/__data/assets/pdf_file/0007/1687786/Harris-and-Moon.pdf.

not justified. Hence not only the measure itself is to be non-discriminatory but also the way it was applied.[483]

In the above reference to cases based on *Article XX(a)* one would not expect a party to invoke public morals in defending national or regional exhaustion although the legal requirement of any measure being '*necessary*', reasonably available alternates, as decided by AB decisions in *US – Gambling* and *China – Audiovisuals* are broadly to be considered. However, there has been tendencies of treating parallel imports as counterfeits and invoking border enforcement measures based on national and regional exhaustion of patents. Given that there has never been a WTO dispute decided by any panel or the AB on parallel imports, hypothetically if the products are pharmaceutical drugs and a member applies national or regional exhaustion and restricts entry of parallel imports on the ground that such measure is needed to protect human life and health, it needed to be tested on applicability of *Article XX(b)* exemption.

It has been observed that while *Article XX* creates a regime of exceptions to a WTO member's trade liberalisation commitments, the implementation of the exemptions needs to be in a non-protectionist manner. In interpretation of *Article XX (a)* and *(b)* exemptions, different panels and the AB has tried to meticulously assess that the exemptions allowed are legitimate, necessary, the measures are objective, reasonable alternatives are possible and non-discriminatory. *Article XX(d)* is particularly significant among all the exceptions in this study since it specifically addresses IPRs. It states,

> necessary to secure compliance with laws or regulations which are not inconsistent with provisions of this Agreement, including those operated under paragraph 4 of Article II and Article XVII, the protection of patents, trade marks and copyrights, and the prevention of deceptive practices.

From a reading of this Article, it may be argued that from the perspective of IPRs, the exemptions have been introduced to address IPRs, although independently, but in consonance with the TRIPS Agreement. The aim was to enable certain flexibilities that can help a WTO member address its domestic policy obligations without compromising on the interests of liberalised multilateral trade.[484] The precise nature of the exceptions provided under this Article, if considered in relation to IPRs, would show that the main intention was to

---

483 Ibid at 445, pgs. 557–559.

484 Du Ming Michael, "Autonomy in setting appropriate level of protection under WTO law: Rhetoric or Reality?", Vol 13 Journal of International Economic Law, Volume 13, Issue 4, pg. 1101, (1077–1102), December 2010.

address the issue of IPRs from the perspective of multilateral trade. Further, under *Article XX (d)*, it is important to establish that the GATT-inconsistent measure was necessary individually for each element of such breaches, to protect the patent and there was no other alternative that would have been less trade restrictive.[485] It is important to analyse how the provisions of *Article XX(d)* have evolved through the interpretations by different panels and the AB, also how the chapeau to *Article XX* have been applied.

One of the initial cases in which a party claimed *Article XX(d)* defence *Korea –Measures Affecting Imports of Fresh, Chilled and Frozen Beef* (*Korea – Beef*). The US alleged that various measures of Korea on beef importation and sale in the Korean market was discriminatory and violation of NT apart from other violations. The measure at issue was Korea's regulation affecting importation, distribution and sale of beef. Further its '*dual retail system*' and agricultural domestic support programmes exceeding its aggregate measure of support as per its schedule of commitments.[486] Korea had defended its measures on the ground that it was necessary to restrict fraudulent misrepresentation of the origin of beef hence violation of Korea's Unfair Competition Act.[487]

Article XX(d) while stating '*... secure compliance with laws or regulations which are not inconsistent with provisions of this Agreement. ...*', covers laws and regulations which would impact irrespective of whether they are listed. Having considered the measures in a holistic manner, the AB upheld the panel's finding that the dual retail system was not justified as a measure to comply with Korea's Unfair Competition Act as it did not pass the necessity test of *Article XX(d)*. In other words, it was not necessary to meet the policy objective. To come to such decision, the AB introduced a two-tier legal standard to test Korea's justification of its measures: I) the design requirement needed to comply with laws and regulations like customs laws and IP laws which are themselves not inconsistent with GATT and II) the necessity threshold, i.e. the measure must be necessary.[488]

485 Reichman Jerome, "Intellectual Property in International Trade: Opportunities and Risks of a GATT Connections", 22 Vanderbilt Journal of Transnational Law, pg. 829, 1989. Also see, Ruse-Khan Henning Grosse, "The Protection of Intellectual Property in International Law", Oxford University Press, pg. 284, 2016.

486 *Korea – Measures Affecting Imports of Fresh, Chilled and Frozen Beef*, WT/DS161/AB/R, 11 December 2000, para 164; WT/DS169/AB/R, 12 March 2001, para 172.

487 Andersen Henrik, "India – Solar Cells and Mexico – Taxes on Soft Drinks: Multilevel Rule of Law Challenges in the Interpretation of Art. XX (d) of GATT 1994 in WTO Case Law", Indian Journal of International Economic Law, Vol. X, pg. 80, (60–103), 2019. Available at, https://img1.wsimg.com/blobby/go/05156989-4612-4459-967b-0b66817b7a32/downloads/04_henrik_andersen.pdf?ver=1557336870890.

488 Ibid at 445, pgs. 564–566.

The AB further elaborated that necessity of such measure also needed to weigh in the contribution of the measure to achieve its policy goal and to societal value while balancing it with the impact of the measure on international trade by possible use of alternative less trade restrictive measures.[489] The AB agreed with the panel that Korea failed to demonstrate that it could not achieve its desired level of enforcement using alternative measures that was available. One needs to note that the interpretation in *Korea – Beef* was clear that many types of laws and regulations can be included while assessing the measure if it was necessary to secure compliance under *Article XX(d)*. Hence the assessment of the objective is not only relevant but important.[490] The WTO Secretariat elaborated in its note, different provisions in GATT and cover Agreements that call for necessity tests. '*the necessity tests confirm the right of Members to regulate and to pursue their policy objectives.*'[491]

As elaborated earlier, *Article XX (d)* have been interpreted by different Panels and the AB, through the necessity test, when applied to IPRs, functions as checks-and-balance measure to make sure substantive IP protection is not applied in a manner that it becomes a trade barrier. Now let us apply the AB's interpretation of necessity test as propounded in *Korea – Beef* case in a situation where a country adopts national or regional exhaustion of patents. As has been discussed earlier, country following national or regional exhaustion restricts entry of parallel imports into the country, treating them as an infringement of the patent.

To elaborate this further, let us study the effect of the three modes of exhaustion from the perspective of multilateral trade under the purview of *Article XX(d)*. In case of national exhaustion, given that the patents exhaust only within the national boundary, patent rights are being enforced by the local right holder to restrict entry of identical products that are also protected by parallel patents, on grounds that they are violating the holder's patent rights. Similarly, in case of regional exhaustion, the regional bloc in the form of CU is restricting exhaustion within the bloc. While identical products protected by parallel patents are not restricted into the common market of the regional bloc, they are restricted when they are entering from outside the bloc.

489 Ibid at 486.

490 Alcaraz C.S. Isabel, "The Concept of necessity under the GATT and National Regulatory Autonomy", Vol 10, Universidad Santo Tomas, Bogota, D.C., pg. 80, (77-99), July – December 2015.

491 WTO Secretariat note titled, "Necessity Tests in the WTO" S/WPDR/W/27 of 2nd December 2003.

It is reiterated that such restriction on imports of identical products with legitimate valid patents and distinguished only by way of different national origin, shall not pass the necessity test under *Article XX(d)* as these imports are manufactured outside the importing country under valid patents in legitimate manner. In a hypothetical case, if a WTO Member complains that such measure wherein legitimate products made under identical patented technology is a violation of the countries NT obligation, the defending country would not be able to pass the necessity test propounded in *Korea – Beef* and other cases discussed in this section of the chapter. Here it is important to note that a WTO Member need not restrict parallel imports to protect '*... patent, trade marks and copyrights, and the prevention of deceptive practices;*' since parallel imports are not counterfeits but are also protected under legitimate parallel patents. Hence if the WTO member practices international exhaustion of patents, given that the patent rights exhaust with the products placed under any market without in the world, authorised dealers of the patented product would not be able to restrain its entry into the importing country using patent enforcement mechanisms thus not violating NT or MFN provisions and would not even attract the necessity test under *Article XX (d)*.

Few years later in *Mexico – Tax Measures on Soft Drinks and Other Beverages* (*Mexico Soft Drinks*), where *Article III(d)* defence was invoked, the US complained before the DSB that Mexico has violated its NT obligations. The measures involved were certain tax measures imposed by Mexico on soft drinks and other beverages that use any sweetener other than cane sugar.[492] It is important to understand the backdrop of the case. Mexico claimed that it had the right to impose measures which were not compliant with the GATT NT obligation as a retaliation against US' non-cooperation in another dispute related to another measure under another agreement. Both were members of the erstwhile NAFTA but instead of suspending its obligations under NAFTA to products originating in the US, Mexico adopted measures that was applied to imports from all origins, hence impacting all WTO Members. On the other hand, under the NAFTA dispute settlement mechanisms, US could deny access to third-party adjudication but it preferred to take it to the WTO dispute settlement. It is important to note that under WTO law, a member aggrieved with

492 *Mexico – Tax Measures on Soft Drinks and Other Beverages*, WT/DS308/AB/R, 6 March 2006. https://docs.wto.org/dol2fe/Pages/SS/directdoc.aspx?filename=Q:/WT/DS/308ABR.pdf&Open=True.

discriminatory measures of one other member does not have the right to suspend its obligations of GATT compliance towards all WTO members.[493]

The AB agreed with the panel that Mexico's measures did not comply with its obligations under NAFTA hence did not qualify under *Article XX(d)* requirement of '*to secure compliance with laws or regulations*'. The AB also specified that '*laws and regulations*' refer to that of the WTO Member invoking *Article XX(d)* defence and not another member. Further, the AB held it was important that the measure is designed '*to secure compliance*' even if there was no guarantee that it would achieve its intended result. It also observed that the use of coercion is not a necessary component of a measure designed '*to secure compliance*'.[494]

Later in *China – Measures Affecting Imports of Automobile Parts* (*China – Automobiles*) case, where the dispute involved certain regulatory measures including imposing a 25% charge on automobile parts imported into the country for the purpose of manufacturing vehicles in China. It was alleged that such border charge was in violation of *Article II* and *III* of GATT and further, it was beyond China's tariff concessions that bound it to 10% and hence were. China had argued that there was no violation since the charge was necessary to stop circumvention of avoidance of payment of 25% duties on import of complete vehicles by importers, hence justified under *Article XX (d)*.[495] After examination of the language of the measure at large, '*Policy Order 8*', the Panel found that it did not meet the requirements of the necessity test under *Article XX(d)*. China appealed before the Appellate Body which upheld the Panel's decision, except that there was no inconsistency with China's accession commitments.[496]

Here it is also important to refer to *Brazil – Tyres case*, which was discussed earlier under *Article XX(b)* since it too claimed defence under *Article XX(d)*. The AB not only applied the necessity test both under *Article XX(b)* and *Article XX(d)*, but also addressed the chapeau on *Article III*. The panel decision was

---

493 Roessler Frieder, "Mexico – Tax Measures on Soft Drinks and Other Beverages (DS308) Prepared for the ALI Project on the Case Law of the WTO", Vol 8 World Trade Review, No. 1, pgs. 25, 26, (25–30), 2009.

494 *Mexico – Tax Measures on Soft Drinks and Other Beverages*, WT/DS308/AB/R, 6 March 2006. https://docs.wto.org/dol2fe/Pages/SS/directdoc.aspx?filename=Q:/WT/DS/308ABR.pdf&Open=True.

495 *China – Measures Affecting Imports of Automobile Parts* (WT/DS342/AB/R) 15 December 2008. Available at, https://docs.wto.org/dol2fe/Pages/SS/directdoc.aspx?filename=Q:/WT/DS/342ABR.pdf&Open=True.

496 Wauters Jasper and Vandenbussche Hylke, "China – Measures Affecting Imports of Automobile Parts", 9 World Trade Review, pgs. 201, 205–209, 2012, 2013, 201–238, 2010.

confirmed by the AB on appeal and was held that the measures executing the import ban did not fall within the scope of measures that were designed to secure compliance with the *'laws or regulations that are not themselves inconsistent with'* provision of the GATT.[497] As was discussed earlier in this chapter, the AB found that Brazil was not compliant with the chapeau to *Article XX* as its exemptions of Mercosur Members were discriminatory vis-à-vis the complainant.

It must be noted that while assessing general exceptions defence, it is not considered in isolation but in conjunction with the proviso to *Article XX*, usually referred to as the chapeau to *Article XX*, that forms an additional test. The application of the chapeau to *Article XX* had been established in the early years of GATT 1994 dispute resolution through two landmark cases – *United States – Standards for Reformulated and Conventional Gasoline* (*US – Gasoline*) in 1996 and later in the *United States – Import Prohibition of Certain Shrimp and Shrimp Products* decided in 1998.[498] In the former case it was held by the AB that in applying the exceptions provided under *Article XX*, first it needs to be ascertained if such exception falls under those that are provided in paragraphs (a) to (j) of the Article and if it does, then it is required to ascertain if such exception complies with the terms of the *chapeau.*

In the *Shrimp/Turtle* case the AB corrected the Panel's decision and held that the applicability of the *chapeau* is important.[499] In the *Shrimps/Turtle* case the AB mentioned that in one category of measures, an action of a member might be considered as '*arbitrary discrimination*' or '*unjustifiable discrimination*' or '*disguised restriction on international trade*', but at the same time it might not be considered so, in another type of measure. In fact, in this case the AB made it very clear that although a member could avail the exceptions in *Article XX*, the *chapeau* restricts abuse of the Article and thus balances the rights of the other members.[500]

497 Ibid at 481.

498 *United States – Standards for Reformulated and Conventional Gasoline*, WT/DS2/AB/R, 29 April 1996 and *United States – Import Prohibition of Certain Shrimp and Shrimp Products*, WT/DS58/AB/R, 12 October 1998.

499 McRae Donald, "GATT Article XX and the WTO Appellate Body" in Bronckers Marco and Quick Reinhard (eds.), "New Directions in International Economic Law – Essays in Honour of John H. Jackson", Kluwer Law International, 2000.

500 Johnston G Michael, "Meaning of the terms "Arbitrary or Unjustifiable Discrimination", in the Chapeau of GATT Article XX", Vol.6 Global Journal of Politics and Law Research, No.5, pgs., 7–10, July 2018. Available at, https://www.eajournals.org/wp-content/uploads/Meaning-Of-the-Terms-%E2%80%9CArbitrary-or-Unjustifiable-Discrimination%E2%80%9D-In-the-Chapeau-of-Gatt-Article-XX.pdf.

In *India – Solar Cells case*, the US had challenged India's domestic content measures in the initial phases of its Jawaharlal Nehru National Solar Mission on solar power developers selling electricity to the government.[501] India argued that under different articles including exemption under *Article XX(d)* arguing it was necessary to ensure ecologically sustainable growth. On appeal, the AB agreed with the Panel that India's DCR measures were not justified under *Article XX(d)* and that for any specific national '*laws or regulations*' to qualify for *Article XX(d)* exception, it is important to examine how the domestic legislation was operating and its effect.[502] The AB held that India neither demonstrated that the domestic instruments being challenged set out a rule to ensure ecologically sustainable growth, nor did it prove that the international instruments identified fell within the scope of *Art. XX(d)*.

From the above cases interpreting *Article XX(d)*, the intent is to make sure there is balance between the WTO members' need to comply with domestic laws and regulations, while also ensuring its liberalised trade commitments under the WTO. Hence it is crucial to restrain WTO members from using *Article XX(d)* defence for protectionist purposes.[503] *Article XX(d)* may be compared with *Article 8.1* which states,

> Members may, in formulating or amending their laws and regulations, adopt measures necessary to protect public health and nutrition, and to promote the public interest in sectors of vital importance to their socio-economic and technological development, provided that such measures are consistent with the provisions of the Agreement.

Now on applying it to the interface between IP protection, its enforcement and multilateral trade under the GATT regime is concerned, *Article XX (d)* acts as a balance between possible conflicts of laws. Further, the law and regulations need to be considered as a whole and not in isolation, hence IP laws are to be applied within the broader gamut of economic law and the exhaustion doctrine fits in balancing diverse interests of different stakeholders.[504] One might

---

501 Ibid at 462.

502 Ibid at 445, pgs. 566.

503 Ibid at 487, pgs. 95, 96 (60–103).

504 Ruse-Khan Henning Grosse, "The Protection of Intellectual Property in International Law", Oxford University Press, pg. 306, 2016. Also see, Cottier Thomas, "Parallel Trade and Exhaustion of Intellectual Property in WTO Law Revisited", in Ruse Khan Grosse Henning & Metzger Axel (eds.), "Intellectual Property Ordering Beyond Borders", Cambridge University Press, pg. 211 (189–232), 2022.

lead to believe that TRIPS already covers the same subject matter, however on deeper scrutiny it will be noticed that there are differences. Often it is argued that TRIPS *Article 6* allows a member country to adopt any mode of patent exhaustion but on analysis of a mode of patent exhaustion of a country in terms of its treatment of NT and MFN, a clear violation of national and regional exhaustion can be noticed. Further, TRIPS Agreement does not have anything similar like the chapeau on *Article XX*.

The analysis of how NT and MFN in relation to what exceptions would apply and which would not and the conditions that would apply, determines the trade in patented products. Hence as we have noticed with regards to different cases that have been interpreted by different panels and the AB, if a WTO member adopts national or regional exhaustion instead of international exhaustion, it applies border measures to restrict entry of like products into the market. In the first instance such measure would not pass the necessity test since measures restricting the import is not necessary as the imports legitimate patented products. Further, on the test of how the measure meets the policy objective of restraining parallel imports, it cannot be argued that the restraint is on counterfeit since the patent is owned by the same entity, just that the origin of the patented product is in a different WTO member. Now let us apply the chapeau on parallel imports, those members allowing import based on regional exhaustion would clearly discriminate between members of the regional bloc / CU and those which are not thus failing to pass the chapeau on *Article XX*.

Now let us consider a hypothetical case of a WTO member which did not stop parallel imports through border measures but once it reaches the market, the authorised distributor initiates infringement proceedings against it and obtains an interim prohibitory injunction from selling the products in the market subject to confirmation of permanent injunction through trial. While obviously the municipal adjudicatory body would consider domestic laws based on the country's patent law and determine the exhaustion mode but if injunction is granted, it will be in violation of *Article III*, NT obligation of the WTO member. It will be an outright discrimination between the patented products which are produced and marketed in the country and the parallel imports that are like products which are treated differently. It has been elaborated earlier that during GATT 1947 period there has been such an instant where certain elements of *Section 337* of the US Patent Act at that time were held inconsistent with GATT NT mandate by a dispute settlement panel in 1989.[505] Also based

505 Ibid at 5, pg. 27.

on the analysis of different decisions of the panel earlier in the chapter, it can be confirmed that a preferential treatment over imported products would be inconsistent with GATT 1994.

7.5 Article XI: 1 – General Elimination of Quantitative Restrictions

Article XI:1 prohibits all forms of import and export prohibitions which can become non-tariff barriers to trade, hence aims at removal of all types of quantitative restrictions. It is crucial to understand what could be interpreted as a quantitative non-tariff measure. The Article states,

> No prohibitions or restrictions other than duties, taxes or other charges, whether made effective through quotas, import and export licences or other measure (Emphasis added), shall be instituted or maintained by any contracting party on the importation of any product of the territory of any other contracting party or on the exportation or sale for export of any product destined for the territory of any contracting party.[506]

This makes it clear that there should be no quantitative restrictions or prohibitions of any *'form'* that can hinder the free movement of goods between WTO members.

The language of the Article no doubt provides necessary clarity by being all inclusive and to add on, there has been very clear confirmation of the same through panel decisions. This was established as early as 1988 in the *Japan – Trade in Semi-Conductors* (*Japan – Semi-Conductors*) case in which the panel found that *Article XI:1* covered measures and not laws or regulations hence was encompassing any form of restriction maintained by the trader. In fact, the mere existence of a measure is sufficient to trigger violation and nullification or impairment of trade through that measure may not be established.[507] This was further reinforced in *India – Quantitative Restrictions on Imports of Agricultural, Textile and Industrial Products* (*India – Quantitative Restrictions*) case where the panel again attributed broader scope to the word *'restrictions'*,

506 *Article XI:1*, see, https://www.wto.org/english/res_e/publications_e/ai17_e/gatt1994_art11_gatt47.pdf.

507 *Japan – Trade in Semi-Conductors*, BISD 35/116; paragraphs 104, 106–109, 117. Available at, https://www.wto.org/english/tratop_e/dispu_e/87semcdr.pdf.

> [T]he text of Article XI:1 is very broad in scope, providing for a general ban on import or export restrictions or prohibitions 'other than duties, taxes or other charges'. As was noted by the panel in Japan – Trade in Semi-conductors, the wording of Article XI:1 is comprehensive: It applies to all measures instituted or maintained by a [Member] prohibiting or restricting the importation, exportation, or sale for export of products other than measures that take the form of duties, taxes or other charges. The scope of the term 'restriction' is also broad, as seen in its ordinary meaning, which is a limitation on action, a limiting condition or regulation.[508]

Ultimately it is a test of the limiting effect of the restrictions or prohibition on imports as to whether it would be held violating *Article XI:1*. *Brazil – Tyres* case, established the interpretation of '*prohibition*' as that restricted importation of any products of any other WTO Member into its national market.[509] Further, *Colombia – Indicative Prices and Restrictions on Ports of Entry* (*Colombia – Ports of Entry*) case provided clarity by elaborating that prohibition or restriction in *Article XI:1* covers measures that restrict market access or create uncertainty in investments or makes importation very costly.[510]

Now when one addresses patent rights in relation to *Article XI:1* of GATT, it will be noticed that if the patent holder can exclude imported like products by enforcing the patents or such imports are treated less favourably, then the patent rights would act as quantitative restrictions in breach of NT and MFN rules. If we drew parallel with the interpretation of '*prohibition*' and/or '*restrictions*' referred to in *Article XI:1* with relation to exhaustion of patents, any mode of exhaustion that restrains parallel importation would be in violation of the Article. This is because the exercise of patent rights over parallel imports from another WTO member country would restrict market access constituting a measure equivalent to quantitative restriction.[511] Moreover, market

508 *India – Quantitative Restrictions on Imports of Agricultural, Textile and Industrial Products, WT/DS90/R, paragraphs 5.128 and 5.129, 1999*. Available at, https://www.wto.org/english/tratop_e/dispu_e/90abr.pdf.

509 Ibid at 481.

510 *Colombia – Indicative Prices and Restrictions on Ports of Entry*, WT/DS366/R, paragraph 7.256, 2009. Available at, https://files.pca-cpa.org/pcadocs/bi-c/1.%20Investors/4.%20Legal%20Authorities/CA172.pdf.

511 Ruse-Khan Henning Grosse, "The Protection of Intellectual Property in International Law", Oxford University Press, pg. 273, 2016. Also see, Reichman Jerome, Okediji Ruth, LianosIoannis, Jacob Robin and Stothers Christopher, "The WTO Compatibility of a Differentiated International Exhaustion Regime", International Laboratory for Law and Development Research Paper Series, dated, pg. 20. Available at,

access restrictions by invoking national or regional exhaustion is not maintainable. As far as *Article XI: 2* is concerned, it provides exceptions for several products like foodstuffs and essential products but does not provide any such specific exception for parallel imports hence this Article is not applicable in any manner.

7.6 Article XXIV – In Light of the Most Favoured Nation Principle

The MFN principle is one of the fundamental requirements of the WTO system and is applicable to GATT 1994 as also to TRIPS Agreement. It had already been discussed earlier that all WTO members are expected to provide MFN status to every other member. Given that such requirement is obligatory, apparently the practice of regional exhaustion would not be in line with the GATT. For example, in each case if a member follows regional exhaustion, it would allow international exhaustion when trading with members within the region and national exhaustion when dealing with countries outside the region. This means that the regional exhaustion mode will discriminate between members of the WTO who are in the regional bloc and those who are outside.

This would obviously result in regional exhaustion violate the MFN principle. However, an in-depth analysis will show that due to certain exemptions under *Article XXIV* of GATT 1994, regional agreements, free trade areas and CU, would be exempted.[512] It needs to be analysed in depth as to whether patent exhaustion would qualify under the exemptions for regional agreements under *Article XXIV*. A mutual recognition agreement among members of a regional bloc could allow imports of licensed patent products from the regional bloc while similar licensed patent products from outside the regional bloc could be excluded even when substantive conditions were similar.[513] It is questionable

http://www.eurasiancommission.org/ru/act/finpol/dobd/intelsobs/Documents/WTO%20Compartibility%20of%20Exhaustion%20Regimes_EEC_SkHSEreport.pdf.

512 *Article XXIV (4)* states, "The contracting parties recognize the desirability of increasing freedom of trade by the development, through voluntary agreements, of closer integration between the economies of the countries parties to such agreements. They also recognize that the purpose of a customs union or of a free-trade area should be to facilitate trade between the constituent territories and not to raise barriers to the trade of other contracting parties with such territories."

513 Trachtman Joel, "Toward open recognition? Integration under Article XXIV of GATT", 6 (2) Journal of International Economic Law, Oxford University Press, pg. 470, (452–492) 2003.

as to how much it would promote positive integration while undermining multilateral trade within the WTO.

Further *Article XXIV (4) and (5)* of GATT 1994 are noteworthy. *XXIV (4)* states,

> The contracting parties recognize the desirability of increasing freedom of trade by the development, through voluntary agreements, of closer integration between the economies of the countries parties to such agreements. They also recognize that the purpose of a customs union or of a free-trade area should be to facilitate trade between the constituent territories and not to raise barriers to the trade of other contracting parties within such territories"; and Article XXIV (5) of GATT 1994 states, "Accordingly, the provisions of this Agreement shall not prevent, as between the territories of contracting parties, the formation of a CU or of a free-trade area or the adoption of an interim agreement necessary for the formation of a CU or of a free-trade area; Provided that: (a) with respect to a customs union, or an interim agreement leading to a formation of a customs union, the duties and other regulations of commerce imposed at the institution of any such union or interim agreement in respect of trade with contracting parties not parties to such union or agreement shall not on the whole be higher or more restrictive than the general incidence of the duties and regulations of commerce applicable in the constituent territories prior to the formation of such union or the adoption of such interim agreement, as the case may be.

This means that under the requirements of this Article, WTO members' entry to regional agreements or CU are conditional.[514] One needs to consider the proviso to the Article which states, '*Subject to the requirement that such measures are not unjustifiable discrimination between countries where the same conditions prevail, or a disguised restriction on international trade*' with seriousness. Based on this requirement, regional exhaustion cannot pass the necessity test.

In the *Turkey – Restrictions on Imports of Textile and Clothing Products* (*Turkey – Textiles case*),[515] the AB examined whether *Article XXIV* applies only to the MFN principle or it provides an exception to other requirements of GATT and the relationship between this Article and the other provisions of the GATT.

---

514 Marceau Gabrielle and Reiman Cornelis, "When and how is a Regional Trade Agreement Compatible with the WTO", 3 Leg Issues Econ Integration 297, 2001.

515 *Turkey – Restrictions on Imports of Textile and Clothing Products*, AB decision WT/DS34/AB/R, 1999.

In this case when Turkey finalised its requirements for joining the CU with the EC on 1st January 1996, it harmonised its tariffs and quantitative restrictions on clothing and textiles. By this it introduced new quantitative restrictions instead of what Turkey imposed earlier. At this juncture India claimed that these quantitative restrictions imposed by Turkey on clothing and textiles violated *Article XI, XIII* of GATT and Article 2.4 of the Agreement on Textiles and Clothing. According to India, these restrictions were not justified exceptions provided under *Article XXIV*.

Contrary to the Panel's findings, the AB opined that the *chapeau* of *Article XXIV: 5* was crucial in determining exceptions and held that the exceptions allow certain measures that might be otherwise be held inconsistent with other GATT provisions. But at the same time in its interpretation of the *chapeau* of *Article XXIV:5*, the AB also specified that there must be a balance between the benefits gained from forming the CU and the negative trade effects that are imposed on WTO members who are not members of the CU. The AB clearly stated in its decision that the member that uses the exception (under *Article XXIV*) as a defence, need to establish that requirements under Article *XXIV (5) & (8)* and the necessity test is met. This means that the party claiming such defence need to prove that without these exceptions the CU would not be formed.[516]

Similarly, we have noticed that in the *India – Quantitative* Restrictions case India had imposed quantitative restrictions (QR) on importation of agricultural textile and industrial products on grounds of balance-of-payment (BoP) problem, a justification in line with *Article XVIII (B)* of GATT 1994. On consultation with the BoP Committee of WTO in maintaining the QR and gradually phasing out in 7 years, other members excluding US agreed to it. The US wanted quicker phase out of the QR and on failing to come to an agreement, they requested for a panel and the matter was taken up. The panel concluded that India erred in imposing the QR, this was later upheld by the AB.[517]

Going back to *Turkey – Textiles,* the AB held that the exception in *Article XXIV* sets an over-riding and pervasive purpose of the exception to facilitate trade between territories.[518] The AB, while interpreting *Article XXIV (5)* emphasised the necessity of the exception under *Article XX*. The defence that the exception is necessary can only be accepted if without the exceptions the Preferential Trade Agreement (PTA) would not form or come into existence. Ironically the EU which negotiated its exception, did not have any specific mode of patent

516 Ibid 515.

517 Ibid at 508.

518 Ibid at 515.

exhaustion or that of any IPRs in general. Each member of the PTA had separate modes of exhaustion. The hybrid model of regional exhaustion was only introduced later through judicial pronouncements.

In such scenario it is impossible for the PTA to qualify in the necessity test. Later in *China – Measures related to the Exportation of various Raw Materials* (*China – Raw Materials*) case that was also decided on appeal by the AB, it was held that '*prohibition*' and '*restriction*' under *Article XI* of GATT 1994 would mean that those prohibition measures that had a limiting effect on the quantity of the imports, both *Articles XI:1 and XI:2* of the GATT 1994 refer to prohibitions or restrictions.

> The term "prohibition" is defined as "a legal ban on the trade or importation of a specified commodity." The second component of the phrase, "[e]xport prohibitions or restrictions" is the noun "restriction", which is defined as "[a] thing which restricts someone or something, a limitation on action, a limiting condition or regulation", and thus refers generally to something that has a limiting effect.[519]

If similar reasoning is applied in a hypothetical case where a country that initially followed international exhaustion, is forced to change to regional or national exhaustion as a condition to join a CU, it might become an issue of complaint by a WTO member outside the CU. A third-party WTO member which was a supplier (parallel exporter) country benefiting from international exhaustion would now lose the market of this CU member that needs to restrict parallel trade in order to join the CU. Such an action imposes an additional non-tariff barrier to trade vis-à-vis third countries. In such circumstances, the exemption provided under *Article XXIV* (5) allowing regional exemption would not hold ground. It is well known that PTA creates trade diversion in order to accommodate enhanced post-PTA competition from a member of the PTA. In most cases this occurs by raising barriers against efficient non-members of the PTA rather than by reducing high cost of production at home.[520] *Article XXIV (8) states,*

519 *China – Measures related to the Exportation of various Raw Materials* – WT/DS394/AB/R, *paragraph 319, 2012.*

520 Bhagwati Jagadish, "Free Trade Today", Princeton University Press, pg. 110, 2002.

For the purposes of this Agreement:

(a) A customs union shall be understood to mean the substitution of a single customs territory for two or more customs territories, so that

(I) duties and other restrictive regulations of commerce (except, where necessary, those permitted under Articles XI, XII, XIII, XIV, XIV, XV and XX) are eliminated with respect to substantially all the trade between the constituent territories of the union or at least with respect to substantially all the trade in products originating in such territories, and

(II) subject to the provisions of paragraph 9, substantially the same duties and other regulations of commerce are applied by each of the members of the union to the trade of territories not included in the union;

(b) A free-trade area shall be understood to mean a group of two or more customs territories in which the duties and other restrictive regulations of commerce (except, where necessary, those permitted under Articles XI, XII, XIII, XIV, XV and XX) are eliminated on substantially all the trade between the constituent territories in products originating in such territories.

It will be noticed that '*duties and other regulations of commerce*' under *Article XXIV (8)* is like that in *Article XXIV (5a) and (5b)* and reads consistently with it. The provisions allow the PTA to eliminate other restrictive regulations of commerce to maintain substantial trade between the members of the PTA. However, the caveat to such preferential treatment is in *XXIV (8) (a) (II)* itself, where it makes clear that the '*same duties and other regulations of commerce are applied by each of the members of the union to the trade of territories not included in the union*' (*emphasis added*). This means that the PTA is not authorised to adopt any such measure higher or more trade restrictive for the WTO members outside the PTA. The necessity test has been established as a fundamental requirement within the WTO through decisions of different panels and the AB and across agreements. No party can claim exemption citing TRIPS would not require to meet the necessity test. On application of the AB decision in *Turkey – Textiles*, there would be additional burden of proving the necessity to change from international exhaustion to regional exhaustion mode would be on the PTA members.[521]

Although the exhaustion issue has not been interpreted by any panel, but given the similarity of the exhaustion issue in the interpretation illustrated in

521 Ibid at 515.

Article XXIV (5a) and (5b), a parallel can be drawn with the Panel's interpretation of *Turkey – Textiles* (which was not rejected by the AB). It must be noted that in he ordinary meaning of the terms, *'other regulations of commerce'* may include any regulation having an impact on trade (such as measures in the fields covered by WTO rules, e.g. sanitary and phytosanitary, customs valuation, anti-dumping, technical barriers to trade; as well as other trade related domestic regulation, e.g. environmental standards, export credit schemes). Restriction on international exhaustion to restrain parallel trade by way of enforcement of IPRs, including patents can be interpreted as other regulations of commerce.

Hence any discrimination against patented products due to practice of regional exhaustion of patents should not be tenable. Especially with the formation of the PTA, changing patent exhaustion from international exhaustion to regional exhaustion would restrict parallel imports and would have an impact on trade between the members of the PTA with those non-members within the WTO membership. Here it must be mentioned that once the Unitary patent system is fully adopted in the European Union, the situation would change, however as discussed earlier in this book, such adoption is sub-judice in Germany.[522]

7.7 Article XXIII: 1 – Non-discrimination of Quantitative Restrictions

Article XXIII (1) highlights,

> If any contracting party should consider that any benefit accruing to it directly or indirectly under this Agreement is being nullified or impaired or that the attainment of any objective of the Agreement is being impeded as the result of (a) the failure of another contracting party to carry out its obligations under this Agreement, *or (b) the application by*

522 The *'Unitary Patent'* system which is expected to come into effect from mid-2020 would enable patent protection to up to 26 EU Members through a single application. The Unified Patent Court expected to be set up as an international court would address the problem of parallel litigation. For more details please see, https://www.epo.org/law-practice/unitary/unitary-patent/start.html. However, it should also be noted that the unitary patent mechanism needs to be ratified in minimum of 13 countries of the EU and at present it has been challenged before the German Constitutional court. The fate of wide adoption of the unitary patent would be influenced by the German court in mid-2020.

> *another contracting party of any measure, whether or not it conflicts with the provisions of this Agreement,* or (c) the existence of any situation (*Emphasis added*).

It establishes that even if there might not be a violation of GATT *per se,* if a GATT member opts for a trade distorting measures that causes '*nullification and impairment*' of the trade benefits to the other members that could be brought in before the DSB as a non-violation complaint. A careful study of the modes of national or regional exhaustion might be deemed fit for a non-violation complaint. It might be argued that an aggrieved member might consider such mode of exhaustion a cause of nullification and impairment of the benefits that the member would otherwise have received if its parallel trade imports were not restricted by way of imposing restrictions on IPRS and thus retaliate.[523] However one can also argue that if a country introduced international exhaustion and lost its rights to restrict entry of parallel imports to the country, there could be nullification and impairment caused due to inability to exercise the IPRS.

It is important to note that *Article 64* (2) and (3) of TRIPS Agreement provides a moratorium on non-violation complaints for five years extendable by consensus.[524] The moratorium persists at the time of writing this book.[525] Fundamentally a member is bound by its commitments to allow market access and restricting international exhaustion would restrict market access to parallel imports. Hypothetically, if a member followed international exhaustion but was forced to change it to any other mode to cater to the demands of the

523 "Nullification" is explained in the GATT 1994 glossary as "Damage to a country's benefits and expectations from its WTO membership through another country's change in its trade regime or failure to carry out its WTO obligations".

524 TRIPS *Article 64* (2) states, *"Subparagraphs 1(b) and 1(c) of Article XXIII of GATT 1994 shall not apply to the settlement of disputes under this Agreement for a period of five years from the date of entry into force of the WTO Agreement."* And *Article 64* (3) states, *"During the time period referred to in paragraph 2, the Council for TRIPS shall examine the scope and modalities for complaints of the type provided for under subparagraphs 1(b) and 1(c) of Article XXIII of GATT 1994 made pursuant to this Agreement, and submit its recommendations to the Ministerial Conference for approval. Any decision of the Ministerial Conference to approve such recommendations or to extend the period in paragraph 2 shall be made only by consensus, and approved recommendations shall be effective for all Members without further formal acceptance process."*

525 Moratorium on non-violation complaints under TRIPS 64.2 was extended until December 2019 WTO Ministerial. See, https://www.wto.org/english/tratop_e/trips_e/nonviolation_background_e.htm. However, given that the next ministerial has been postponed to June 2020, the members would need to need to address the moratorium.

trading partner, it would be subject to nullification or impairment in trade benefits due to deviation from such commitments.

It must be noted that the '*nullification and impairment*' clause is foundational in the WTO system. It was developed right at the time when the International Trade Organisation (ITO) was planned and aimed at dealing with government measures that are not covered by the agreement but affected the benefits of tariff concessions negatively. Astonishingly, it never appeared in the '*Suggested Charter*' of the ITO. It was a separate clause that was part of one (Chapter on Commercial Policy) of the five substantive chapters of the Suggested Charter submitted by the United States and was supposed to be applicable only to this chapter.[526]

Here, due consideration should be given to the meaning of '*nullification and impairment*' since it is one of the most important features determining Rules and Procedures governing the dispute settlement system in the WTO. According to the Rules and Procedures governing the dispute settlement if a member claims that another member failed to fulfil its GATT obligations, then the complaining country needs to establish (under *Article XXIII:1*) that such act nullified and impaired the benefit accruing to the Member.[527] It should also be noted that the nullification and impairment is not restricted to the GATT Agreement but also covers the other covered agreements of the WTO.[528]

Let us consider a hypothetical case from nullification and impairment angle, a member lodges complaint that patented products manufactured in its country under patent licensee is restricted from entering another member country through enforcement measures hence it nullifies its ability to trade in that market and impairs from making financial gain. It is indeed an exhaustion issue, but the impact is that of nullification and impairment. If there is an '*impairment*' under TRIPS, although the member might not be able to take unilateral decision to renegotiate the impaired obligation, it might refuse to accept compensation, thus threatening retaliatory actions like those available in the case of a violation of the TRIPS Agreement. However, given the ongoing temporary moratorium on the non-violation complaints, it is not known how any panel would decide this type of complaint if it comes up for adjudication.

526 Hudec Robert, "The ITO Legal System: Nullification and Impairment", in "The GATT Legal System and World Trade Diplomacy", 2nd Edition Butterworths, pgs. 37, 38, 1990.

527 Roessler Frieder, "The Concept of Nullification and Impairment in the Legal System of the World Trade Organisation" in Ulrich Petersmann Ernst (ed.), "Studies in Transnational Economic Law", International Trade Law and the GATT/WTO Dispute Settlement System, Vol. 11, Kluwer Law International, pg. 125, 1997.

528 Ibid 515.

CHAPTER 8

General Agreement on Trade in Services and Its Interface with Patent Exhaustion

8.1 GATS and Patent Exhaustion

The GATS Agreement lays down multilateral rules under the WTO system to govern trade in services. The main aim of this agreement being removal of barriers to trade in services like the removal of trade barriers in trade in goods. Here the difference is that unlike trade in goods where the item traded has a physical definition, services are, '*non-visible, non-storable exchanges of activities requiring simultaneous presence of buyer and seller*'.[529] In general the GATS is the only agreement that deals with different types of issues related to trade in services but it does not cover inter-disciplinary issues within the WTO system, e.g. Service and IPRS. Trade in services is classically addressed distinct from trade in goods and the value-added contribution of services that often come with the goods are not accounted for. In case of technology products that are patent protected, after-sales service although does not establish any direct interface between TRIPS and GATS, the latter's relevance for patents cannot be undermined. E.g. In cases of patented products, they might come with exclusive service attached to the product and raise question as to whether the service would need to be considered separately and severally. Further, in some products like aircraft engines, the patented products are leased under service agreements hence the link between the products and adjoined services cannot be separated.

Protection accorded to IP (e.g. an invention) is in respect of the concerned goods, whereby the goods are protected as per requirements provided by the TRIPS Agreement. In a hypothetical case where a patent holder provides after sales services, if national exhaustion is followed, it is usually argued that since the service is tied to the patented product, no person other than the authorised person can undertake such repairs. It might be argued that a manufacturing process could be qualified as a service and as a result protected by the patent. However, this is not the case since under the TRIPS Agreement, an

529 Dunkley Graham, "At whose service? Services and intellectual property in the Uruguay Round", in "The Free Trade Adventure", pgs. 176, 177, 1997.

infringement of the process patent will extend the effect of the infringement to the products and not to the process on its own, thus not to the service. As such an argument that the service is tied to the patent hence protected, would not hold ground.

A point of reference is a Scottish case, *United Wire Ltd. v Screen Repair Services (Scotland) and others*[530] where the House of Lords in the UK decided that a patent holder could not restrict a third party to conduct repair on a patented product. In this case the court however provided some restrictions too, it stated that if such repair increases the life of the patented product in a manner that the product becomes equivalent to a new product (like the initial patented product), such repair service would result in infringement of the patent. Thus, such a case would fall more under the purview of TRIPS rather than GATS Agreement. If we consider a case where the service is protected by trade mark or service mark, parallel trade in such services would be addressed under TRIPS and/or GATT instead of GATS since the latter does not provide any guidelines related to IPRs. In such circumstances, if international exhaustion is followed, there is no confusion as to rendering of such service and its protection, since any third party would be eligible to undertake such repairs.

In fact, there is a wide range of possibility of parallel trade in services since very often services provided by one organisation is franchised in another country by way of license agreement. In such a case, the licensor might raise the same issue as in patented products. There might be a possibility of competition from its own licensee, which should likely be considered as a problem by the licensor but that is not the case. Often patent owners claim that parallel trade should not be promoted since the products are tied with services and the parallel trader would not be able to provide such service (in other words, only authorised dealers would be able to provide such after sales service). However, in cases where the patented products are sold in the market without a guarantee of after sales services, it should not be possible for the patent holder to impose such restrictions. For example, in the growing trade through electronic media where the product is mailed to the customer, sometimes international service is not included. Further in countries where patents are provided for business methods and computer programmes which are transported from one country to another via internet, servicing of the products could be interpreted an infringement if national exhaustion is followed.

530 Ibid at 140.

8.2 Article II and Article XVII in GATS and Its Impact on Patent Exhaustion

The MFN and NT not only play an important role in GATT but also in GATS. As we have already noticed, GATS aim at liberalising cross-border services and as such the MFN obligation covers not only those who have scheduled market commitments but also those that are not covered. On the other hand, NT in GATS is similar to that of GATT in its treatment of national and foreign service providers but applies to those who have made market access commitments.

In today's global value chain, it is increasingly difficult to de-link goods and services interfaced with IPRs. With an obvious intent to reduce cost and enhance profit, firms are trying to maximise efficiencies by dispersing production to different countries. For example, handheld mobile computing devices in which the design and hardware of the chip (where the significant IP value reside) may be done in one country while the chip manufactured by them in fabless manner in some other country where cost of production is low.[531] Further this chip will go into the device where the battery may be manufactured in another third country while the casing in another and screen in another country and finally sold and serviced under completely a different brand name.

In such scenario where production has become in a way '*factoryless*', given that a single factory in a single country cannot be attributed to the manufacture of a particular product, restricting after sales service exclusively to authorised distributers could attract scrutiny under GATS. Parallel imports manufactured under same patent held in different jurisdiction is automatically getting linked to the related service attached to the product and with restrictions imposed would undermine rights accrued under the WTO member's GATS schedules.

Historically, the GATS had not been included in the 1947 GATT however with increasing trade in services it was needed to be included. Hence a negotiating item making lateral entry had other issues, it had to balance between liberalisation of services at the multilateral platform and at the same time accommodate the existing discriminatory trade practices resulting in certain dissimilarity with GATT.[532] For this reason although the GATS MFN follows the

---

531 See, Fabless manufacturing ... https://www.investopedia.com/ask/answers/050615/what-are-fabless-chip-makers-and-why-are-they-important-semiconductor-market.asp.

532 Mattoo Aaditya, "MFN and the GATS", in Cottier Thomas, Mavroidis Petros (eds.), "Regulatory Barriers and the Principle of Non-Discrimination", in World Trade Law, Ann Arbor 2000, The University of Michigen Press. Based on the paper presented at the World Trade Conference on "Most-Favoured Nation (MFN): Past and Present", at Neuchatel,

GATT MFN in its drafting language, it curves out not only general exceptions but specific ones for RTAs. *Article II* prohibits discrimination between like services and service providers from different WTO members.

It states,

1. With respect to any measures covered by this Agreement, each Member shall accord immediately and unconditionally to services and service suppliers of any other Member treatment no less favourable than that it accords to like services and service suppliers of any other country.
2. A Member may maintain a measure in consistent with paragraph 1 provided that such a measure is listed in, and meets the conditions of, the Annex on Article II Exemptions.
3. The provisions of this Agreement shall not be so construed as to prevent any Member from conferring or according advantages to adjacent countries in order to facilitate exchanges limited to contiguous frontier zones of services that are both locally produced and consumed.

A careful study of this Article enumerated above will show that the MFN requirements are set through a three-prone test as to whether, I) the concerned measure is a '*covered measure*' under GATS; II) the services or service suppliers qualify as '*like services*' and/or '*like service suppliers*'; and III) the member accords '*less favourable treatment*' to the services and service suppliers of another member. Hence, WTO members are mandated to treat all like services and service suppliers of the members without discrimination. This means the Article prohibits a WTO member to discriminate services and service suppliers based on nationality, national origin, or destination of a product.[533]

Unlike in GATT where there is only '*like products*', in GATS the concept of '*like services*' and '*like service suppliers*' need to be considered and hence to determine '*likeness*', it is important to distinguish modes from methods. This is important since services may be supplied by different methods while the GATS commitment might be restricted to only certain modes of supply. The two questions pertinent to determining '*likeness*' is whether it can exist

28–29 August, 1998. Available at, https://www.iatp.org/sites/default/files/MFN_and_the_GATS.htm.

533 Milhem Moawiah, "Most-Favoured-Nations (MFN) and National Treatment (NT) principles under GATT and GATS", Brunel University Law School London, 2013. Available at, https://www.academia.edu/5518155/Most-Favoured-Nations_MFN_and_National_Treatment_NT_principles_under_GATT_and_GATS.

across *modes of service supply* and across *methods of service supply* (*emphasis added*). Now if we address '*likeness*' and relate it to NT, we will need to compare between foreign service that is restricted under the four modes as per GATS *Article I:2* and the service provided domestically.[534]

If the exhaustion of patents is seen through the prism of GATS *Article II*, one would need to examine whether national and regional examination would pass the test of '*covered measure*' or MFN treatment was accorded to '*like services or service suppliers*'. Given that any government '*measure*' is considered as '*covered measure*', a hypothetical question arises as to whether the after-sales service of a patented product restricted only to products sold through authorised distributors can be considered a covered measure. Similarly, whether refusal to provide after-sales service to parallel imports by the manufacturer or authorised distributors of patented products would violate MFN. It is also to be seen when a member discriminates between patented products and their parallel imports restriction on after-sales services, whether the parallel imports that are refused service by the manufacturer or authorised distributors be considered '*less favourable treatment*'.

It is interesting to note that the NT requirement in GATS is subject to the member's market access commitments made in the '*Schedules of Commitment*'. In other words, there are three elements in these commitments, i.e. I) the general principles that affect the services at the time its applied; II) specific schedule of commitments; III) sector-specific annexes as to application of NT. Considering the fact that the GATS is focused on services, it does not specifically address tariffs and quantitative measures.

> *Article XVII* elaborates NT,
>
> 1. In the sectors inscribed in its Schedule, and subject to any conditions and qualifications set out therein, each Member shall accord to services and service suppliers of any other Member, in respect of all measures affecting the supply of services, treatment no less favourable than that it accords to its own like services and service suppliers.
> 2. A Member may meet the requirement of paragraph 1 by according to services and service suppliers of any other Member, either formally identical treatment or formally different treatment to that it accords to its own like services and service suppliers.

534 Diebold F. Nicholas, "Non-Discrimination in International Trade in Services 'Likeness' in WTO/GATS", Cambridge University Press, pgs. 186–219, 2010.

3. Formally identical or formally different treatment shall be considered to be less favourable if it modifies the conditions of competition in favour of services or service suppliers of the Member compared to like services or service suppliers of any other Member.

Interpretation of MFN and NT in context of the GATS can be read in the *EC – Bananas III* case decided by the AB after it went on appeal from the Panel.[535] This is one of the initial GATS cases that addressed both MFN and NT while examining the measure affecting trade in services. The core issue under GATS was whether EC license allocation procedures for the importation of bananas in the EC. Ecuador, Guatemala, Honduras, Mexico and United States complained that EC Regulation 404/93 for importation, distribution and sale of bananas accorded de-facto preferential treatment to those of EC origin. It can be noticed that although EC licensing regulations did not discriminate between banana distributors of EC-origin and non-EC origin, the fact that they had separate operator categories for different service suppliers raised an issue.[536]

On examination of the design, architecture and revealing structure of the measure at issue, the panel found that the EC's schedule of commitments assured favourable treatment under GATS *Article II and XVII* to different '*wholesale trade services*' (both direct and subordinate). It was found that the rules were drafted in a manner that it altered the conditions against the complainants who were foreign-owned or controlled entities. As a result, the complainant's suppliers of wholesale services were de-facto granted less favourable treatment than the EC and ACP[537] suppliers. Further, the '*newcomer*' licenses with '*single-pot*' license rules were also de-facto discriminatory and in violation of *Article XVII*.[538] The AB upheld the Panel's finding that the EC's measures were not consistent with *Articles II* and *XVII*, i.e. they were in violation of MFN and NT.

From the *EC – Bananas III* case even when the license allocation rules of the EC were not directly based on nationality, ownership, or control of the distributor, apparently not discriminatory, it was found otherwise. The AB concurred with the Panel decision that complainant's suppliers of wholesale services

535 Ibid at 442.

536 Ortino Frederico, "The principle of non-discrimination and its exception in GATS: Selected legal issues", paper presented at the conference, "Conflict and Crises – The WTO after Hong Kong", Vienna, pg. 6, 8, 18, (3–20), 24–25 April 2006. Available at, SSRN electronic journal, https://papers.ssrn.com/sol3/papers.cfm?abstract_id=979481.

537 ACP – African Caribbean and Pacific group of countries.

538 See Panel Reports at, https://www.wto.org/english/tratop_e/dispu_e/cases_e/ds27_e.htm.

were de-facto granted less favourable treatment. In a hypothetical case of international exhaustion, if the same reasoning is applied, parallel imports could be deemed to have been meted with less favourable treatment vis-à-vis services for the patented product. In case of patented products manufactured in the country, after-sales service under warranty is provided while the parallel imports manufactured by the patent licensee outside the country is denied warranty and after-sales service. Like the *EC – Bananas III* case, although there is no direct discrimination based on nationalities, less favourable treatment is accorded to the imported from outside the nation.

8.3 Exceptions to Most Favoured Nation and National Treatment and Its Impact on Patent Exhaustion under Article V and Article XIV

The general exceptions provided in *Article XIV* GATS serve similar purpose like that of *Article XX* GATT 1994 where WTO members can justify non-adherence to GATS compliance on certain grounds. In absence of *Article XIV*, some of the actions taken by the members on number of non-trade policy issues would have been clearly considered trade distortive and inconsistent with the WTO regulations at large. In essence the objective to include such exceptions is to maintain a balance between trade liberalisation on one hand and important policy goals of the member state on the other.

It is in such background that *Article XIV* states,

> subject to the requirement that such measures are not applied in a manner which would constitute a means of arbitrary or unjustifiable discrimination between countries where like conditions prevail, or a disguised restriction on trade in services, nothing in this Agreement shall be construed to prevent the adoption or enforcement by any Member or measures:
> (a) necessary to protect public morals or to maintain public order;[539]
> (b) necessary to protect human, animal or plant life or health;
> (c) necessary to secure compliance with laws or regulations which are not inconsistent with the provisions of this Agreement including those relating to:

539 Footnote 5 to *Article XIV* (c) states, "*The public order exception may be invoked only where a genuine and sufficiently serious threat is posed to one of the fundamentals interests of society*".

(i) the prevention of deceptive and fraudulent practices or to deal with the effects of a default on services contracts;
(ii) the protection of the privacy of individuals in relation to the processing and dissemination of personal data and the protection of confidentiality of individual records and accounts;
(iii) safety;

(d) inconsistent with Article XVII, provided that the difference in treatment is aimed at ensuring the equitable or effective imposition or collection of direct taxes in respect of services or service suppliers of other Members;[540]

(e) inconsistent with Article II, provided that the difference in treatment is the result of an agreement on the avoidance of double taxation or provisions on the avoidance of double taxation in any other international agreement or arrangement by which the Member is bound.

From the language of the text in *Article XIV*, it is understood that the exceptions are broad hence their applications are not meant to be uniform, instead it would vary from one member's requirement to the other. This is interesting since WTO regulations seek to introduce uniformity in trade regulations of member countries through a common framework with an intent to remove trade barriers. However, GATS exhibit relatively more flexibility than GATT and

540 Footnote 6 to *Article XIV (d)* states, "*Measures that are aimed at ensuring the equitable or effective imposition or collection of direct taxes include measures taken by a Member under its taxation system which: (i) apply to non-resident service suppliers in recognition of the fact that the tax obligation of non-residents is determined with respect to taxable items sourced or located in the Member's territory; or (ii) apply to non-residents in order to ensure the imposition or collection of taxes in the Member's territory; or (iii) apply to non-residents or residents in order to prevent the avoidance or evasion of taxes, including compliance measures; or (iv) apply to consumers of services supplied in or from the territory of another Member in order to ensure the imposition or collection of taxes on such consumers derived from sources in the Member's territory; or (v) distinguish service suppliers subject to tax on worldwide taxable items from other service suppliers, in recognition of the difference in the nature of the tax base between them; or (vi) determine, allocate or apportion income, profit, gain, loss, deduction or credit of resident persons or branches, or between related persons or branches of the same person, in order to safeguard the Member's tax base. Tax terms or concepts in paragraph (d) of Article XIV and in this footnote are determined according to tax definitions and concepts, or equivalent or similar definitions and concepts, under the domestic law of the Member taking the measure.*"

TRIPS in this respect, hence both market access under MFN and NT obligations are comparatively less stringent.[541]

The '*Security exceptions*' in *Article XIV bis*, by nature of exceptions is like the general exceptions but can be evoked essentially to justify security situations that the WTO members may face. This, although similar in nature, makes it qualitatively different to the general exceptions in two distinctive manner a) the exception does not have any '*chapeau*' that means it is not subject to any arbitrary or unjustifiable discrimination; and b) members need to assess their security and consider that the measure engages their essential security interests. Hence, this would enable a member to evoke security exception if the circumstances fell into any of the general scenarios mentioned in *Article XIV bis*.[542]

> *Article XIV bis* states,
> 1. Nothing in this Agreement shall be construed:
>   (a) to require any Member to furnish any information, the disclosure of which it considers contrary to its essential security interests; or
>   (b) to prevent any Member from taking any action which it considers necessary for the protection of its essential security interests:
>   (I) relating to the supply of services as carried out directly or indirectly for the purpose of provisioning a military establishment;
>   (II) relating to fissionable and fusionable materials or the materials from which they are derived;
>   (III) taken in time of war or other emergency in international relations, or
>   (c) to prevent any Member from taking any action in pursuance of its obligations under the United Nations Charter for the maintenance of international peace and security.

541 Cottier Thomas, Delimatsis Panagiotis and Diebold Nicolas, "Article XIV GATS: General Exceptions", in Wolfrum Ruediger, Stoll Peter-Tobias and Feinaugle Clemens (eds.) "Max Planck Commentaries on World Trade Law, WTO – Trade in Services", Vol 6, Martinus Nijhoff Publishers, pgs. 287–328, 2008. Available at, https://papers.ssrn.com/sol3/papers.cfm?abstract_id=1280215.

542 Ayres Glyn and Mitchell Andrew, "General and Security Exceptions under the GATT 1994 and the GATS", in Carr Indira, Bhuiyan Jahid and Alam Shawkat (eds.), "International Trade Law and WTO", Federation Press, pg. 266, 2012. Available at, https://papers.ssrn.com/sol3/papers.cfm?abstract_id=1951549.

2. The Council for Trade in Services shall be informed to the fullest extent possible of measures taken under paragraphs 1(b) and (c) and of their termination.

The security exceptions as provided in *Article XIV bis*, clearly pans very widely and although have sparsely invoked, might attract WTO members given the increasing security concerns globally, including cyber espionage threats of varied nature. At the same time given its breadth, possibilities of protectionism disguised under security exception cannot be ruled out. In such scenario countries have already started opting for regulatory requirements in their local legislation like mandatory data localisation, etc. that, outside the security exception would have clearly violated the MFN and or NT obligations.

The recent *Russia – Measures Concerning Traffic in Transit* (*Russia –Transit Measures*) case under *Article XXI(b)* GATT security exception, decided by the Panel although deliberates on GATT, is worth noting given that the ramifications on similar situation under GATS cannot be ruled out. In this case dealing with Ukraine's complaint against Russia's transit restrictions, interpretation of '*essential security threat*' is important. In this specific case, Russian measures mandated certain travel routes from Ukraine to Kazakhstan and Kyrgyzstan only through the Belarus-Russia border, subject to certain conditions and imposed certain transit bans directly and indirectly. Ukraine alleged violation of *Articles V* and *X* of GATT[543] and Russia's related commitment to its WTO Accession Protocol but Russia claimed, '*essential security interest*' defence under *Article XXI(b)* GATT.[544] The Panel opined that the invocation of the exception is not '*self-judging*' and justiciable, hence to be scrutinized by the WTO DSB. It then let down the two-prong legal test under GATT

Article XXI (b):

I. objective determination whether the requirements under Article XXI(b) under the concerned sub-paragraphs are met;
II. once the requirements are met, were they genuinely taken for the member's essential security interest in good faith or for some other unrelated reason. It must be noted that the Panel distinguished between 'security interests' as broad and 'essential security interests'

543 GATT *Article V*: https://www.wto.org/english/res_e/publications_e/ai17_e/gatt1994_art5_gatt47.pdf; GATT *Article X*: https://www.wto.org/english/res_e/publications_e/ai17_e/gatt1994_art10_gatt47.pdf.

544 *Russia – Measures Concerning Traffic in Transit*, Panel Report WT/DS512/R, 5 April 2019. Available at, https://www.wto.org/english/tratop_e/dispu_e/512r_e.pdf.

> as narrow and more specific, e.g. to protect the people, internal law and order and any external threats. However, the Panel opined that the member would be free to define its 'essential security interests' although would still be required to demonstrate the essential security interests and how the measure would enable protection as well as whether this was necessary.

Considering that Ukraine and Russia were close to '*hard core*' armed conflict at that time with an emergency-like situation in 2014, the travel transit restrictions were not unrelated and conformed to Russia declaring them as '*essential security interests*', hence the measures qualified under GATT *Article XXI(b)* scrutiny.

The case has no direct relation with IPRs and it is difficult to construe how the general exceptions under *GATS Article XIV* can apply in case of parallel imports of patented goods tied with after-sales service. Drawing an analogy with the *Russia – Transit Measures* case, let us consider a hypothetical case – A WTO member which follows international exhaustion restricts parallel imports of telecommunication equipment from a particular country discriminating with similar parallel imports from other WTO countries, apparently violation of both NT and MFN obligations. The importing country claims security exceptions under *Article XIV bis and GATT Article XXI(b)* and establishes that the parallel imports of the telecom equipment which enables voice and data telephony services, had been embedded with malware and spyware for cyber espionage. After *Russia – Transit Measures* case it is difficult how the '*essential security interests*' would not meet in this case.

CHAPTER 9

Free Trade Agreements and Exhaustion: Different Regional Trade Agreements

9.1

9.1.1 *Regionalism and Its Relationship with Multilateralism*

The issue of patent exhaustion under a regional or preferential trade agreement in relation to the broader gamut of the multilateral trade governed by the WTO becomes crucial. It is important to understand how the relationship between the two are defined and interpreted to ascertain the exhaustion mode that should be adopted. In this chapter the aim has been to understand the dynamics of regionalism within the framework of multilateral trade rules as applied to patent exhaustion. Subsequently the chapter presents the mode of exhaustion practiced in some of the CU. Given the uniqueness of EU where the regional exhaustion was introduced, attempt has been to elaborate how the practice evolved through jurisprudence.

Efforts to update international rules on multilateral trade to bring it up to speed with time became successful under the GATT regime moving towards formation of the WTO. Despite their support for multilateral trade that prompted the parties to establish the WTO, some of the negotiating countries tried to curve out gaps for regionalism to accommodate RTA and PTA at parallel. The advocates of regional trade within these countries lobbied with their respective governments to continue with the regional trade arrangements on the ground that this enhances free trade in the region since it allows reciprocal removal of trade barriers. They negotiated provisions into the GATT 1947 that they believed could assist maintaining membership within the regional bloc and GATT simultaneously. Thus, *Article XXIV* pertaining to RTA, PTA and FTA would also include CU and considered valid under GATT 1994 Agreement although it was not beyond criticism due to lack of clarity.[545]

This move towards parallelism did not become the problem in the path towards multilateralism since countries also brought in the old (1979) '*Enabling Clause*' as a '*Special and Differential Treatment*' (S & DT) for countries that met

545 Bhagwati Jagdish, "Regionalism and Multilateralism: An Overview", in de Melo Jaime and Panagriya Arvind (eds.), "New Dimensions in Regional Integration", Cambridge University Press, pg. 44, 1993.

certain criteria, e.g. LDCs. Such non-reciprocal tariff preferences and different other such preferences were provided as an exception to the well-established MFN requirement and members did not oppose this parallelism through creation of regional exclusivity. However certain checks and balance measures were put in place to make sure the regionalism that was introduced, was a parallel effort in enhancing trade liberalisation and was not counter-productive.

PTA are still opted by different WTO members and it was not a practice of the past. In fact, in today's multipolar world, new power structures are constantly evolving moving from erstwhile transatlantic leadership. Inter-regionalism is providing new dimension, especially with the entry of China within the WTO fold. With the multilateral trade negotiations stalled or moving in a snail's pace, countries are seeking alternates. One sometimes tends to focus on WTO and GATT only as a trade negotiating forum, hence criticising it for being unproductive due to the state of negotiations and reasoning for the tilt towards regionalism and PTA. It must be noted that irrespective of stalled negotiations, multilateral trade has been increasing all the while with more people depending on it for livelihood. With the administration of various trade agreements, technical cooperation for members and the crucial dispute settlement mechanisms, WTO has been far more than just a platform for trade negotiations.[546]

Considering that free trade is welfare enhancing, the philosophical basis of the PTA is not alien to WTO since both are founded on the principles of market access, non-discrimination and transparency. The aim of the PTA is to enhance free trade among its members, but often these agreements contain additional explicit requirements than those under WTO agreements. On careful analysis as to the tendency for such enhanced or stricter requirements, one would have to consider the socio-economic developments. Disparities in income both domestically within the WTO members as well as inter-State within the WTO membership has caused and causing mass migration into more prosperous geographies. This has increased protectionist tendencies in the prosperous members reflecting in the agricultural market or in services, as well as there is substantial increase in cases of local content requirements in domestic legislation. In such a scenario, new groupings and re-groupings of countries enable to have revised market access negotiations based on new trade regulations.[547] This forum shifting obviously is not globally trade enhancing with many developing and least developed countries (LDC) left out as well as detrimental to WTO decision making since it influences negotiating position of members.

546 Cottier Thomas, "The Common Law of International Trade and the Future of the World Trade Organization", 18 Journal of International Economic Law, pgs. 3, 4, 6, (3–20), 2015.

547 Ibid at 536, pgs. 6, 8, 18, 24, 25.

Before one gets into the debate on multilateralism versus regionalism, one needs to understand the concept of '*regionalism*'. Regionalism is often referred to as institutionalised co-operation among countries forming a bloc that provide certain trade or other benefits, exclusively to members in the regional bloc.[548] It is founded on the formation of a CU or based on RTA or FTA. While exploring the reasons that might have prompted such move by some of the negotiating parties of the WTO, one would find that in a multi-polar world, different countries pursue different interests. In such circumstances, to supplement the efforts towards integration on a global scale, there would be synergy in enhanced integration on the domestic and regional front so that global challenges can be addressed as a bloc if not individually while continuing to engage multilaterally.[549]

The relationship between the TRIPS Agreement and the FTAs, leads to the question as to what or how should IPRs be treated between the two, whether the FTAs executed after the TRIPS should follow the TRIPS or go beyond. Considering the possibilities of conflict of laws, one needs to address this under *Article 41* VCLT to read the constitutional elements of the TRIPS that is the common goals of IP protection and enforcement. Thus, conditions regarding IPRs laid down in any FTA cannot derogate from the TRIPS Agreement.[550]

Further, considering the benefits of enhanced integration, even when multilateralism was being established, regionalism was never abandoned. There might be different motives for opting for regionalism, but some common ones are:

- It is believed that since there is relocation of factors of production and specialisation, there will be subsequent price cuts. Thus, there will be rise in productivity resulting in higher competition, more investment flow and higher income. This will have immediate effect in boosting national economic welfare as well be good in the long run.
- It is usually argued that regionalism brings in trade diversion with suppressing effects, it is better than trade cutting since there is enhanced market access.

548 Donald Barry and Ronald Keith, "Introduction: Changing Perspectives on Regionalism and Multilateralism" in Barry and Keith edited, "Regionalism, Multilateralism, and the Politics of Global Trade", UBC Press Vancouver, Toronto, pg. 3, 1999.

549 "Regional Perspectives on the WTO Agenda: Concerns and Common Interests", paper presented at the "ESCAP/UNCTAD High-level Meeting of ESCAP Developing Countries in Preparation for the Fourth WTO Ministerial Conference" and at the "Doha and Beyond: Expert Group Meeting on the Future WTO Agenda" Bangkok, pgs. 1, 2, (24–26), September 2001.

550 Ibid at 380, pgs. 5122, 5123.

- It reduces transaction costs since it reduces communication, transportation and information dissemination costs considerably.
- It cannot be ignored that political interests in forming and/or maintaining RTA, PTA, FTA regionally is often significant. Sometimes political stability in the region is aimed through RTA on the notion that if neighbouring countries invest in each other's markets, going against each other would negatively affect one's own economy hence conflicts would be avoided.
- Often when multilateral trade negotiations fail or become slow due to lack of consensus, countries that are interested in trade liberalisation try to move towards RTA.[551]

Recent trends will show that there has been a shift on IP issues from the multilateral arena under WTO/TRIPS to PTA with an intention to introduce protection of IPRs far beyond the TRIPS (commonly termed as TRIPS-plus requirements).[552] The growing tendency of getting countries to agree to TRIPS-plus IP protection and enforcement through these international agreements create a '*spaghetti bowl*' of PTAs and RTAs of standards different from that of TRIPS.[553] This trend in moving TRIPS-plus in FTAs is not new it has been a growing for quite some time as noticed in the US FTA with Chile, Singapore, CUFTA and is worrisome.[554] The trend of moving from one forum to another by way of changing venues to get single decision in favour of the shifter is well known as '*Forum shopping*' and has its own problems. The trend in moving from multilateral trade agreement to a PTA or from one PTA to another is more complex given its international political dynamics. In these scenarios, States as well as non-state actors (e.g. private conglomerates) relocate the entire rule-making processes and not just the venues to favour their financial and other interests and their own mandates. This is a complete '*Regime Shifting*' that is initiated with a long-term strategy that may not only change the laws and entire rulemaking processes but also involves a complete change even in the policy space of the concerned countries and its entire decision-making.[555]

Hence whether one prefers or not, apart from promoting regional trade interests, RTA, PTA and FTA would continue being used as foreign policy

---

551 Schultz Siegerid, "Regionalisation of World Trade: Dead End or Way Out?" in Dijk Pieter van and Sideri Sandro (eds.), "Multilateralism versus Regionalism: Trade Issues after the Uruguay Round", EADI, pg. 22, 1996.

552 See pg. 80, https://www.wto.org/english/res_e/booksp_e/trips_agree_e/chapter_4_e.pdf.

553 Ibid at 380, pg. 9548.

554 Mayne Ruth, "Regionalism, Bilateralism, and "TRIPS PLUS" Agreements: The Threat to Developing Countries" UNDP, pg. 14–16 2005.

555 Helfer Lawrence, "Regime Shifting in the International Intellectual Property System", No.1, Symposium: International Regime Complexity, Vol. 7, pg. 39, 40, (39–43), March 2009.

tool to exert influence over members.[556] In such negotiations like Regional Comprehensive Economic Partnership (RCEP), the recently closed PTA/RTA negotiations, a number of trade issues are involved that have cross-effect. Hence maintaining coherence with already agreed standards of trade liberalisation under the WTO is even more important.[557] Considering that regime shifting is happening and will continue to happen, WTO members engaging in PTAs need to prepare in advance to restrain TRIPS-plus provisions being adopted. To be able to effectively nullify any such effect of regime shifting, the affecting countries (often developing countries and LDC) need to integrate counter-regime norms so that TRIPS-plus provisions are not injected into the WTO system and its dispute settlement mechanism through back door. It is only by adopting such multi-step strategies that members can enhance their negotiating power.[558]

9.1.2 *Development of Regionalism in Different Parts of the World*

It has been already mentioned that the exclusions favourable to regional trade was not newly incorporated in the GATT 1994 Agreement but was even there in the original GATT 1947 Agreement. Here it must be noted that under this clause, both CU and FTA were permitted, allowing regionalism within multilateralism. As a result of this, different regional groups grew up historically with the creation of the European Coal and Steel Community (ECSC), with Belgium, France, Germany, Italy, Luxembourg and the Netherlands as members. When this model succeeded in its goals, it encouraged the formation of the EC (here it must be noted that these ECSC countries signed the Treaty of Rome in 1957 which took shape of the first European Community). This was followed up by the formation of number of other regional groups in Europe, of which, the European Free Trade Association (EFTA) formed in 1960 is worth a mention. However, it must also be mentioned that it was not the aim of the proponents of the multilateral trading system to set up a hundred percent CU and FTA within it although regionalism within multilateralism was allowed.[559]

---

556 Cattaneo Olivier, "The Political Economy of PTAs", in Simon Lester and Brian Mercurio edited, "Bilateral and Regional Trade Agreements: Commentary and Analysis", Cambridge University Press, pgs. 28, 77, 2009.

557 The ASEAN web page provides a good overview of the RCEP. Available at, http://asean.org/?static_post=rcep-regional-comprehensive-economic-partnership.

558 Ibid at 555, pgs. 41, 42.

559 Bhagwati Jagdish, "Regionalism and Multilateralism: An Overview", in Bhagwati, Krishna & Panagriya edited, "Alternative Approaches to Analyzing Preferential Trade Agreements", The MIT Press, pg. 9, 1999.

Multilateralism and regionalism started existing at parallel now more than fifty years without clashing with each other.

This trend of regionalism was initially not followed in other parts of the world, even when there were many such proposals (e.g. North American Free Trade Agreement – NAFTA, Pacific Free Trade Area – PAFTA, Latin American Free Trade Area – LAFTA, which was later modified into Latin American Integration Agreement – LAIA). It was only in the 1980s that the trend in regionalism expanded to countries outside the European Community (EC) and finally with NAFTA coming into existence in 1994, regionalism became a transatlantic phenomenon. Initially the US (which became a party to the NAFTA) did not support regionalism but the change in their trade policy came mainly to counter the trade protectionism tendencies of the EU. Interesting to note that although multilateralism gained a big boost with the formation of the WTO, it was never able to supersede regionalism. One can clearly notice that although the multilateral rules of trade are usually followed and lapses leading to disputes are settled under the WTO, whenever there was no agreement between WTO members on going forward with trade rules, PTA gained prominence.

The failure of the WTO's Cancún Ministerial meet in 2003 that practically halted the movement of Doha development round, '*galvanised*' efforts to push regionalism along with bilateral trade deals.[560] After 19 years since then, although negotiations have not been called off, there has been very slow progress, more of an adhoc nature specific to some issues rather than a closure of the Doha round. In 2008, the '*July package*' was expected to help conclude the Doha Round with consultations on a range of subjects including revised draft modalities for agriculture and non-agricultural products but to no avail.[561] Later, the '*Bali package*' in 2013 witnessed addressing the '*Food security*' issues that were of crucial importance to developing countries and on the other hand the coming into existence of the Trade Facilitation Agreement.[562] The '*Nairobi package*' of 2017 has been marked as historic for Africa and particularly significant for many LDC. It includes six Ministerial Decisions on agriculture, especially on cotton and issues specific to LDC.[563] Finally it is only as late as in the

560 Jonquieres Guy de and Mallet Victor, "Failure at Cancún spurs trade deals in Asia – With the Doha round at a halt, more bilateral and regional accords are being negotiated", Financial Times, 16th October, 2003.

561 July Package, see, https://www.wto.org/english/tratop_e/dda_e/meet08_e.htm.

562 Bali Package, see, https://www.wto.org/english/news_e/news13_e/mc9sum_07dec13_e.htm.

563 Nairobi Package, see, https://www.wto.org/english/news_e/news15_e/mc10_19dec15_e.htm.

12th Ministerial Conference in 2022 at Geneva after 7 years that there were some directional outcomes based on consensus.

9.1.3 *Relation between Regionalism and Multilateralism with Reference to Articles XIV and XXIV of the GATT / WTO Agreement*

The founding members of the GATT[564] clearly based the multilateral trade agreement on the practice of non-discrimination made effective through the principle of MFN, one of the founding pillars of GATT. But specific exceptions were made to allow CU and FTA under *Article XXIV*. Efforts were made to enable co-existence of regionalism and multilateralism curving out exceptions with checks and balance measures but there has always been a doubt as to whether both can function effectively while in co-existence. A preferential trade liberalisation model is fundamentally different from a model based on non-discriminatory trade liberalisation. In fact, FTA are two-faced, they support free trade by removing tariffs for member countries while imposing additional burden on non-members by initiating external tariffs against them.

Very often PTA takes the form of regional agreements because of certain common regional trade interests. It is noticed that the growth and development of regional organisations have increased to a great extent in the last few years as result of which there have been requests for GATT to examine their eligibility criteria. Earlier many developing countries availed the possibility to form regional agreements and be exempted under the S & DT that is allowed to LDC. But now such chances are less, even if they are permitted it is under *Article XXIV* like any industrialised country i.e. only if it is reciprocal and not one-way.[565] Apart from *Article XXIV*, one needs to consider *Article XIV* of the GATT 1947 while analysing the clauses dealing with exceptions to non-discrimination since it is incorporated in the GATT 1994 Agreement.

More precisely these exceptions elaborate:

1. A contracting party which applies restrictions under Article XII or under Section B of Article XVIII may, in the application of such restrictions, deviate from the provisions of Article XIII in a manner having equivalent effect to restrictions on payments and transfers for current international transactions which that contracting party

564 At the time of signing of first GATT Agreement on there were 23 members, 30th October 1947.

565 Page Sheila, "The Integration of Regional Groups into Multi-Country Organisations", in Pieter van Dijk Meine and Sideri Sandro (eds.) "Multilateralism versus Regipnalism", EADI, pg. 86, 1986.

may at that time apply under Article VIII or XIV of the Articles of Agreement of the International Monetary Fund (IMF), or under analogous provisions of a special exchange agreement entered into pursuant to paragraph 6 of Article XV.

2. A contracting party which is applying import restrictions under Article XII or under Section B of Article XVIII may, with the consent of the contracting parties, temporarily deviate from the provisions of Article XIII in respect of a small part of its external trade where the benefits to the contracting party or contracting parties concerned substantially outweigh any injury which may result to the trade of other contracting parties.
3. The provisions of Article XIII shall not preclude a group of territories having a common quota in the IMF from applying against imports from other countries, but not among themselves, restrictions in accordance with the provisions of Article XII or of Section B of Article XVIII on condition that such restrictions are in all other respects consistent with the provisions of Article XIII.
4. A contracting party applying import restrictions under Article XII or under Section B of Article XVIII shall not be precluded by Articles XI to XV or Section B of Article XVIII of this Agreement from applying measures to direct its exports in such a manner as to increase its earnings of currencies which it can use without deviation from the provisions of Article XIII.
5. A contracting party shall not be precluded by Articles XI to XV, inclusive, or by Section B of Article XVIII, of this Agreement from applying quantitative restrictions:
   (a) having equivalent effect to exchange restrictions authorized under Section 3 (b) of Article VII of the Articles of Agreement of IMF, or
   (b) under the preferential arrangements provided for in Annex A of this Agreement, pending the outcome of the negotiations referred to therein.

From the above it can be clearly stated that CU, RTA and/or FTA were encouraged on the grounds that there would be increased integration of free trade by removal of barriers to trade and as such would be supplementary to multilateral trade. An important requirement is that trade barriers against non-members of the FTA/RTA/CU are not raised in a manner to make trade more restrictive than before. Hence the moment existing members establish a regional group and impose a different level of tariff against non-members, if there is no effort to impose an average tariff, non-members can claim compensation because of the raised tariff.[566]

If one carefully studies the relationship between regionalism and multilateralism in the light of the WTO Agreement, one question would invariably arise as to whether the RTA follow the rules set in by the WTO and to what extent the WTO rules themselves get adjusted to the RTA that are established. Joining the FTA might involve switching over from one country's existing laws to other partner member's laws, which is often an expensive process. In such scenario, countries prefer to have their own standards accepted by other countries rather than address the positive externalities. Obviously, the members with lesser negotiating power often succumb to the conditions laid down by the powerful members and accept conditions that they would not have accepted otherwise.[567]

For these reasons it is often argued that there should be additional criteria for members to churn out PTA and RTA to avoid it becoming a regional channel to protectionism. Here it must be noted that regionalism often creates inefficient trade diversions instead of reducing inefficient costs with tendencies to favour new trade partners within the bloc while raising trade barriers against non-members.[568] To address such anomalies, generally it is accepted that these CU should be open-ended, allowing others to join. Further, they should be limited to specific geographical areas and established by parties that already have considerable economic integration and existing trade ties so that there is minimum trade diversion, if any. Finally, there should be not only cross-border trade but also sufficient flow of capital and technology.[569] Technically CU, RTA and FTA may decide not to address exhaustion of IPRs and leave it to each member to decide which might seem compatible with the TRIPS agreement. However, if they practice regional exhaustion, as is the case with EC, there would be an inherent discrimination against parallel imports based on the country of origin as has been elaborated in earlier chapters.

566 Frankel Jeffrey with Stein Ernesto and Shang-Jin Wie, "Introduction to Regional Trading Arrangements" in "Regional Trading Blocs in the World Economic System", Institute for International Economics, Washington DC, pg. 3, October 1997.

567 Sideri Sandro, "GATT and the Theory of Intellectual Property", in Pieter van Dijk Meine and Sideri Sandro (eds.) "Multilateralism versus Regionalism" EADI, pg. 144, 1986.

568 Bhagwati Jagdish, "Getting to Free Trade: Alternative approaches and their theoretical rationale", Free Trade Today, Princeton University Press, pg. 110, 2002.

569 Hart Michael, "A Matter of Synergy: The Role of Regional Agreements", in Donald Barry and Ronald Keith (eds.) "Regionalism, Multilateralism and the Politics of Global Trade", pgs. 48–49, UBC Press Vancouver, Toronto, 1999.

9.2 The European Union, European Free Trade Association, European Economic Area and Patent Exhaustion

Patents granted by the European Patent Office (EPO) are rights in different countries in Europe, hence governed by the patent laws in those countries. Automatically the assessments of the validity of these patents are made under the substantive patent law in the relevant countries. In such situation often there are differences in assessment in one country and another leading to disputes based on validity resulting in conflicting litigation and fragmented decisions.[570] The European regulation on '*Unitary Patent*' will not only harmonise the different patent laws of the member states but moved from the dependency on case laws to codified regulation. The establishment of the Unified Patent Court, once functional, would further help in consistency and predictability of patent litigation especially in the area of validity issues and infringement.[571] At present, given the different national patent systems existing at parallel and applicants having the ability to file separately in a country or at the EPO, the system is all but harmonised.

Undoubtedly there have been significant efforts to harmonize patent protection both including prosecution and adjudication. Uniformity in patent exhaustion in EU has been spelled out in clear terms in *Article 6* that deals in '*Exhaustion of the rights conferred by a European patent with unitary effect*[572]' and further states,

> The rights conferred by a European patent with unitary effect shall not extend to acts concerning a product covered by that patent which are carried out within the participating Member States in which that patent has unitary effect after that product has been placed on the market in the Union by, or with the consent of, the patent proprietor, unless there are legitimate grounds for the patent proprietor to oppose further commercialisation of the product.

However even with such definitive harmonisation, the European patent exercised through the EPO is still burdened with high transaction costs due to

570 Coyle Patrick, "Uniform Patent Litigation in the European Union: An Analysis of the viability of recent proposals aimed at unifying the European Patent Litigation System", Washington University Global Studies Law Review, Volume 11 issue 1, pg. 180, (171–192), January 2012.

571 Yarsky Joseph Kenneth, "Hastening harmonization in European Union Patent law through a preliminary reference power", Boston College International and Comparative Law Review, Volume 40, Issue 1, pg. 168 (167–193), 2017.

572 Regulation (EU) No. 1257/2012 of the European Parliament and of the Council. Available at, https://eur-lex.europa.eu/LexUriServ/LexUriServ.do?uri=OJ:L:2012:361:0001:0008:en:PDF.

multiple fees, translation costs among others. In the absence of a total seamless harmonisation of IPRS in the EU, exhaustion of IPRS is the single issue that has managed a uniform common EU position that got established as a result of harmonisation of the internal market. Now that the Protocol on Provisional Application of the UPC Agreement has been ratified on 19th January 2022, it is to be seen how harmonisation proceeds henceforth.

The intention to provide free movement of goods originating in the EU member States has been paramount right from its existence through *Article 28 to 37* of the Treaty on Functioning of the EU (TFEU). While *Article 28(1)* TFEU prohibits charges like customs duties and quantitative restrictions like quotas, *Article 34 and 35* TFEU imposes prohibition on measures that can have effect of quantitative restrictions. As a result, products legally manufactured in any of the EU Member State should not be restricted from any of the EU member's markets.[573] However this was not the case in addressing exhaustion of patents to allow parallel imports. Due to lack of harmonised patent law in the EU, there were differences in members' treatment of exhaustion of IPRS too, but this was streamlined and harmonised by the ECJ.[574] The court assessed whether there was need to restrict parallel imports to uphold patent rights of the owners and decided against such move. If parallel imports within the EU were restricted, the patents would act as non-tariff barriers to trade and become quantitative restrictions. To maintain balance between patent rights and movement of goods within the EC, community-wide exhaustion of patents was adopted.[575] The reason in support of introduction of this hybrid exhaustion that blended international exhaustion within the CU while maintaining national exhaustion with outside the region has been explained in Chapter 3. In this section of the book the focus is on the evolution of this regional exhaustion mode through case laws as it stands today.

As elaborated in Chapter 4.3, Exhaustion of IPRS was first introduced in EU through trademark exhaustion in *Consten and Grundig v Commission*, where the Court emphasised on the distinction between '*existence*' and '*exercise*' of intellectual and industrial property rights and referred to *Article 81 and 82* of the EC Treaty that adhered to the creation of a common market.[576] We have

573 Free movement of goods, Fact Sheets on the European Union – 2018. Available at, http://www.europarl.europa.eu/ftu/pdf/en/FTU_2.1.2.pdf.

574 Burnside Michael, "The Community Patent Convention: Is it Obsolete in its Present Form", 8 EIPR, pgs. 285–289, 1992.

575 Bentley Lionell and Shaw Brad, "Intellectual Property Law", Oxford, pg. 616, 617, 2014.

576 Joined cases Nos. 56/54 and 58/64, *Establishments Consten S.à.R.L. snd Grundig-Verkaufs-GmbH v. Commission of the European Community (1966)* ECR 299; Available at, https://eur-lex.europa.eu/legal-content/EN/TXT/HTML/?uri=CELEX:61964CJ0056&from=EN. See

noted earlier that the same reasoning of the common internal market superseding the possibility of enforcing IPRs to restrict parallel imports within the EU was extended to exhaustion of trademarks and copyrights in *Deutsche Grammophon* case.[577] In this case too, the ECJ held that the trademarks and copyright owner exhausted its right to enforce further sale of the product with the sanctioned use of it and hinder free movement of the copyright product within the internal market.[578]

The first case related to patent exhaustion was *Centrafarm BV v Sterling Drug* related to the drug '*Negram*', patented both in the UK and Netherlands by Sterling Drug.[579] The same drug was 50% more expensive in Netherlands than in UK and Centrafarm bought it in the UK and then resold it in the Netherlands. Sterling Drug tried to stop the parallel import of the medicine by invoking its patent right. However, the Court relied on the mode of regional exhaustion and stated that the patent owner would not be able to restrict free movement of the concerned goods by invoking patent rights since he has exhausted these rights once he has put the product in the community market. The statement of the Court expressed the mode of regional exhaustion very clearly,

> As far as the patent was concerned, the court stated:
>
> 4 This question requires the court to state whether, under the conditions postulated, the rules in the EEC Treaty concerning the free movement of goods prevent the patent holder from ensuring that the product protected by the patent is not marketed by others.
>
> 5 As a result of the provisions in the Treaty relating to the free movement of goods and in particular of Article 30, quantitative restrictions on imports and all measures having equivalent effect are prohibited between Member States.
>
> 6 By Article 36 these provisions shall nevertheless not include prohibitions or restrictions on imports justified on grounds of the protection of industrial or commercial property.

---

for detailed discussion, Renato Nazzini, "Parallel Trade in the Pharmaceutical Market – Current Trends and Future Solution", 26 (1) World Competition, pg. 60, (53–74), 2003.

577 Case No. 78/70, *Deutsche Grammophon Geselischaft mbH v Metro-SB Grossmarkte GmbH & Co. KG*, 1971 ECR 487, 1971 CMLR 631.

578 Gold Michael, "European Patent Law and the Exhaustion Principle", University of Chicago Legal Forum, Volume 1992, Issue 1, pg. 442, 443, (441–456), 1992.

579 Case No. 15/74, *Centrafarm BV v. Sterling Drug Inc.*, 31st October 1974 [1974] 2 CMLR 480, [1974] ECR 1147, 6 IIC 102 (1975). Available at, https://eur-lex.europa.eu/legal-content/EN/TXT/HTML/?uri=CELEX:61974CJ0015&from=EN.

7 Nevertheless, it is clear from this same Article, in particular its second sentence, as well as from the context, that whilst the treaty does not affect the existence of rights recognised by the legislation of a Member State in matters of industrial and commercial property, yet the exercise of these rights may nevertheless, depending on the circumstances, be affected by the prohibitions in the treaty.

8 In as much as it provides an exception to one of the fundamental principles of the Common Market, Article 36 in fact only admits of derogations from the free movement of goods where such derogations are justified for the purpose of safeguarding rights which constitute the specific subject-matter of this property.

9 In relation to patents, the specific subject-matter of the industrial property is the guarantee that the patentee, to reward the creative effort of the inventor, has the exclusive right to use an invention with a view to manufacturing industrial products and putting them into circulation for the first time, either directly or by the grant of licences to third parties, as well as the right to oppose infringements.

10 An obstacle to the free movement of goods may arise out of the existence, within a national legislation concerning industrial and commercial property, of provisions laying down that a patentee's right is not exhausted when the product protected by the patent is marketed in another Member State, with the result that the patentee can prevent importation of the product into his own Member State when it has been marketed in another State.

11 Whereas an obstacle to the free movement of goods of this kind may be justified on the ground of protection of industrial property where such protection is invoked against a product coming from a Member State where it is not patentable and has been manufactured by third parties without the consent of the patentee and in cases where there exist patents, the original proprietors of which are legally and economically independent, a derogation from the principle of the free movement of goods is not, however, justified where the product has been put onto the market in a legal manner, by the patentee himself or with his consent, in the Member State from which it has been imported, in particular in the case of a proprietor of parallel patents.

12 In fact, if a patentee could prevent the import of protected products marketed by him or with his consent in another Member State, he would be able to partition off national markets and thereby restrict trade between Member States, in a situation where no such

restriction was necessary to guarantee the essence of the exclusive rights flowing from the parallel patents.

13 The plaintiff in the main action claims, in this connection, that by reason of divergences between national legislations and practice, truly identical or parallel patents can hardly be said to exist.

14 It should be noted here that, in spite of the divergences which remain in the absence of any unification of national rules concerning industrial property, the identity of the protected invention is clearly the essential element of the concept of parallel patents which it is for the courts to assess.

15 The question referred should therefore be answered to the effect that the exercise, by a patentee, of the right which he enjoys under the legislation of a Member State to prohibit the sale, in that State, of a product protected by the patent which has been marketed in another Member State by the patentee or with his consent is incompatible with the rules of the EEC Treaty concerning the free movement of goods within the Common Market.[580]

Initially there was scepticism on the *Centrafarm* judgment on the differentiation between '*existence of rights*' and '*exercise of these rights*' and free movement of goods superseding the need for protection of industrial property but there was no turning back. One issue that came up was that of the parallel patent rights in different member countries and how the individual courts would interpret them. To be more precise, the proviso in *Article 36* refers to the existing laws on the subject in the members ('*Bestandsgarantie*' or guarantee of existence). Their application and implementation by concerned governments and courts as well as by private individuals and industry were a matter of concern although there was no doubt that it would not interfere in the legislative powers of the members to frame laws on the subject.[581] Distinctly being judge-made law, with time the regional exhaustion mode got accepted and well established through a series of ECJ decisions.[582]

To highlight the process of evolution of the regional exhaustion mode, the next important case decided by the ECJ on patent exhaustion was *Merck-I*

580 Case No. 15/74, *Centrafarm BV v Sterling Drug Inc.*, 31st October, 1974 [1974] 2 CMLR 480, [1974] ECR 1147, 6 IIC 102 (1975).

581 Beier Friedrich-Karl, "Industrial Property and the Free Movement of Goods in the Internal European Market", 21 (2) IIC, pg. 147–148, 1990.

582 Ibid at 166, 282.

case.[583] In this judgement, the court went ahead a step further to state that the patent owner will exhaust his/her rights with the first sale irrespective of whether such first sale had occurred under a parallel patent or not. Hence, even when the Dutch patent holder was not in a monopoly position which restricted his activity to make usual profit from the patent, the exhaustion principle was allowed because the Dutch patent holder had consented to the marketing of the medicine in Italy.[584] However the court did not follow any stereotype in the issue of exhaustion and was careful enough not to allow the real issue of infringement of patents being allowed in disguise of exhaustion.

Here it is important to note that while regional exhaustion was promoted, the court did not in any manner exempt unauthorised manufacture of patented products, hence the protection of patents was never compromised. A case in point is *Park Davis and Co. v Probel* in which, the drug was patented in the Netherlands but was manufactured without the consent of the patent holder in Italy.[585] The Dutch patent holder was able to restrict importation of the product from Italy since the patent exhaustion was not established. In this case the patent holder did not have the marketing consent from the patent holder hence the marketing of the source product was itself unauthorised.[586] Later in *Pharmon v Hoechst* the ECJ made it clear that the doctrine of exhaustion would not apply in extra-ordinary market conditions like in cases when a compulsory licence was in operation. In this case it was emphasised that exhaustion doctrine would be applicable within the EC only in cases where the patent holder freely consents to the sale of the patented product and not when he is forced to do so.[587]

Later in another landmark case the ECJ stated that patents would exhaust once the patent owner puts the patented product in the market with his consent, even if the product was not patented in the country of marketing.[588] In

583 Case No. 187/80, Merck & Co. Inc. v Stephar BV and Petrus Stephanus Exier, July 14, 1981, [1981] ECR 2063, 13 IIC 70 (1982). Available at, https://eur-lex.europa.eu/legal-content/EN/TXT/HTML/?uri=CELEX:61980CJ0187&from=EN.

584 Alexander Willy, "Exhaustion of Trade Mark Rights in the European Economic Area", 24 E.L.R., pg. 7, Sweet, Maxwell and Contributors, 1999.

585 Case No. 24/67, *Parke Davis and Co. v Probel, Reese, Beintema-Interpharm and Centrafarm*, Gerechtshof's-Gravenhage-Netherlands, 1968, Beintema-Interpharm and Centrafarm (Policy of the EEC) [1968] EUECJ R-24/67 (29 February 1968). Available at, https://eur-lex.europa.eu/legal-content/EN/TXT/HTML/?uri=CELEX:61967CJ0024&from=LT.

586 Brainbridge David, "Intellectual Property", Longman, 5th edition, pg. 427, 2002.

587 Case No. 19/84, Pharmon BV v Hoechst AG, ECR 2281 (1985). Available at, https://eur-lex.europa.eu/legal-content/EN/TXT/HTML/?uri=CELEX:61984CJ0019&from=EN.

588 Joined cases, C 267/95 and C 268/95, *Merck & Co. Inc., Merck Sharp & Dohme Ltd. and Merck Sharp & Dohme International Services BV v Primecrown Ltd., Ketan Himatlal Mehta, Bharat Himatlal Mehta and Necessity Supplies Ltd. and Beecham Groupp PLC v Europharm*

this case, the pharmaceutical product was patented in the UK whereas there was no patent production available for pharmaceutical products in Spain and Portugal at that time (Spain and Portugal were not member of the EC at that time). The medicine was cheaper in Spain and Portugal than in England prompting a parallel trader to import the cheaper pharmaceutical product to England for re-sale in Portugal and Spain. Since these two countries were in the process of joining the EU, under the Acts of Accession to the EC, they were allowed to introduce pharmaceutical patents within three years, hence the concerned pharmaceutical products were patentable in three years.[589] There was confusion among the parties as to the calculation of three years of the patent to determine the effective date of exhaustion. Whether the three years was to be calculated once such product became patentable, or the three years were to be calculated from the end of the calendar year.[590] The patent holder challenged the applicability of the principle of free movement in this case since there was no patent in these two countries from where the pharmaceutical product was imported. The patent holder argued that the case was like that in *Merck v Stephar* where the patent was not functional due to issuance of CL.[591] The parallel trader tried to defend international exhaustion based on the fact that the patent owner had put the product in the Portuguese and Spanish market under free market conditions and was not forced to put it on the market unlike in *Merck v Stephar*.[592]

The ECJ held that the three years period would be considered from the specific time when the drugs became patentable and not from the end of the calendar year. Further, the Court emphasised on its earlier judgement in *Merck v Stephar* on the free movement of goods within the common market and stated that the patent holder had freely sold the product in Portugal and Spain so the exhaustion principle should be applicable, thus allowing re-importation.[593] Irrespective of whether the product was patented in the country of import the rights existed in UK hence once the UK owner marketed it, it was considered

---

of Worthing Ltd., ECRI 6285 (1996). Available at, https://eur-lex.europa.eu/legal-content/EN/TXT/HTML/?uri=CELEX:61995CJ0267&from=EN.

589 Ibid at 584.

590 Glynn Dermot, "Article 82 and Price Discrimination in Patented Pharmaceuticals: the Economics", 3 European Competition Law Review, pg. 134 (134–142) 2005.

591 *Merck v Stephar*, Case No. 187/80, dated July 14, 1981, [1981] ECR 2063, 13 IIC 70 (1982).

592 Campolini Manuel, "Parallel Import of Pharmaceutical Products within the European Union: Could Adalat be a Bacon in the Dark for the Innovative Industry?", 1 International Trade Law Review, pg. 31, 2002.

593 Case No. 19/84, Pharmon BV v Hoechst AG, ECR 2281 (1985). Available at, https://eur-lex.europa.eu/legal-content/EN/TXT/HTML/?uri=CELEX:61984CJ0019&from=EN.

as exhausted. If the patented medicines were manufactured in Portugal and Spain given the absence of patents in these countries, those products would have been barred from re-importation to UK as they would have been considered counterfeits.

Although exhaustion of IPRS in the EU was established through judicial pronouncements and subsequently there were no statutory changes made, there were efforts to change the practices through policy interventions. The European Parallel Importers' Coalition (EPIC) tried to influence the European countries to introduce international exhaustion in trademark law. They solicited international exhaustion of trademarks on grounds that previous to 1989, it was possible to import original IP protected products from low-price markets and sell them in the common market at low price benefiting consumers.[594] The efforts to introduce/re-introduce international exhaustion and allow parallel imports in the area of trademarks continued but the industrial lobby of IP holders managed to successfully influence the European Parliament (EP) not to accept any such request and such attempt was aborted.[595]

Another early case reflecting tension between *Article 28* and *Article 30* is *Generics v Smith Kline & French Laboratories*.[596] In this case, Smith Kline & French Laboratories Ltd. (SKF) held the patent for the pharmaceutical drug '*Cimetidine*' in Netherlands while a third party applied for marketing authorisation for Cimetidine with the Dutch Assessment Board for Medicinal Products (DABMP). Authorisation was granted after the submitted samples of the drug were checked. The authorisation was assigned to Generics BV shortly before the expiry of the patent. SKF moved a motion for injunctive relief before the Court and was granted an ad-interim injunction effective for 14 months from the expiry of the patent in order to restrict Generics BV from selling or distributing the drug in any manner. In this decision of the Dutch Court, the patent holder could restrict others from selling the drug Cimetidine after the expiry of the patent. It is interesting to note that even when the medicine was already in the other EU markets and neither the *Dutch Patent Act of 1977* nor the EPC treated the issue of obtaining authorisation as an infringement, the medicine could not be imported to Netherlands for sale. One could consider that such

594 Position Paper of The European Parallel Importers Coalition (EPIC), "The Case for re-introducing Global Trademark Exhaustion in EU legislation", dated January 2001.

595 Ibid at 593.

596 *Generics BV v Smith Kline & French Laboratories Ltd.*, RPC 801 (1997). Available at, http://curia.europa.eu/juris/showPdf.jsf;jsessionid=9ea7d2dc30dbc81efbb3c3ea4e3e9551d7ffed674088.e34KaxiLc3qMb40RchoSaxqTbNno?text=&docid=100690&pageIndex=0&doclang=en&mode=req&dir=&occ=first&part=1&cid=18338.

restriction would violate *Article 28* of the EC Treaty and act as quantitative restriction on importation. However, the ECJ allowed this restriction and held that it was justified to restrict the use of samples to obtain authorisation under *Article 30* of the EC Treaty, since it was to be treated as '*specific subject matter*' of the patent.

In another case, *Karate,* Der Bundesgerichtshof (the German Federal Court of Justice) considered the issue of exhaustion in the light of the EC Treaty. In this case the concerned product was a pesticide named '*Karate*' which enjoyed German and European patent for the process of manufacturing its ingredient '*lambda-cyhalothrin*' by the plaintiff. The defendant bought the pesticide containing '*lambda-cyhalothrin*' from a French company 'S' and sold it under the name '*Orefa Lambda-Cyhalothrin 5 EC*'. The plaintiff alleged infringement of its patent and initiated an action against the defendant. In defence, the defendant pleaded exhaustion of rights on grounds that one of the three shareholders of the French company that supplied the patented product was one of the plaintiff's authorised dealers for the product in France. While interpreting the exhaustion issue as it applied to the EEA, the court acknowledged that under *Article 30* (previously *Article 36*) of the EC Treaty all quantitative restrictions on imports and all measures having same effect were also prohibited.

The court further acknowledged that if the patent holder could restrict parallel import of the patented product from another member, the patent holder would be able to partition national markets with EEA and thus be able to restrict trade between members even when such restriction of parallel imports would not be necessary to protect the patent rights.[597] In this case, the court opined,

I. the defendant failed to establish that the pesticide sold by the defendant was the same product that had been placed in the EEA market by the plaintiff or its licensee,
II. The fact that the defendant bought the patented product from a supplier based in France did not prove that the supplier had sourced the product from the plaintiff and not from outside the EEA (if it was from outside the EEA then defence of exhaustion would not stand ground).
III. The defendant did not prove that the concerned product came from the same stock that the plaintiff sold in France through its subsidiary.

597 Decision on '*Karate*' of the German Federal Supreme Court (Bundesgerichtshof) dated 14th December, 1999, Case No. X ZR 61/98. See detailed discussion of the case in English in 32 (6) IIC, pg. 687 (685–693), 2001.

The court examined the defendant's contention that at least one of the three shareholders of the French company 'S' (which supplied the patented product) was one of the plaintiff's authorised dealers for the product in France and could not find it reasonable. The court relied on the simple logic that it was obviously economical to buy goods directly from the supplier instead of paying extra commission to an agent. In this case instead of buying the product directly from the authorised supplier, the defendant bought it from 'S' which would be more expensive unless the product was sourced from outside the EEA at a cheaper price. Here the court also highlighted the fact that the plaintiff had already been taking legal action against two enterprises affiliated to the defendant's suppliers for placing its patented product in the community market without its consent. Since the defendant failed to prove these fundamental requirements, the appeal brought in by the defendant was rejected, although this did not invalidate regional exhaustion.

In another case of Bayer AG, parallel imports of the medicine '*Adalat*' were reported from Spain and France and to control and limit the supply of the medicine, Bayer AG stopped the supply of the medicines to their wholesalers in these two countries.[598] The wholesalers complained to the Commission that through the wholesaler agreement in Spain and France, Bayer AG had imposed on them an export ban hence restricted free movement of products. The Commission found Bayer AG in violation of *Art 101(1) TFEU* and based on the earlier case of *Merck and Beecham*, opined that protection of parallel imports is important in all circumstances irrespective of the rights of even the members to regulate the price of the products (e.g. through CL, price caps, etc.). On appeal initially before the General Court and later before the ECJ the Commission's decision was overturned. It was held that it could not be presumed that Bayer AG did anything to stop free movement of goods. Its decision to stop supplying of the patented products to its authorised distributors was not in any arrangement with the distributors but unilateral, hence within its legitimate right to decide where it would market and where it would not.[599]

GlaxoSmithKline (GSK), another important case few years later, was also contested right up to the ECJ. In this, GSK had notified the Commission a dual-pricing scheme for wholesalers determining whether the medicine was

598 Joined Cases Nos. C-2/01P C-3/01P, Bayer AG v Commission of the European Communities (T-41/96) [2000] E.C.R. II-3383; [2001] 4 C.M.L.R. Available at, https://eur-lex.europa.eu/legal-content/EN/TXT/HTML/?uri=CELEX:62001CJ0002&from=EN.

599 Tsouloufas Georgios, "Limiting Pharmaceutical Parallel Trade in the European Union: Regulatory and Economic Justifications", 36 E.L. Review, pg. 398 (385–404), June 2011.

reimbursable under the Spanish regulators. However, it was devised to restrain possibilities of parallel trade and was assessed by the Commission as to whether it had anti-competitive effect and also whether it restrained free movement. The Commission held that GSK's dual-pricing scheme was intended to restrain free movement of the products and impede competition in the market that was challenged before the Court of First Instance (CFI).[600] In an interesting note like the Bayer AG case, the CFI held that the actions of the IP holder is not just to be assessed as to whether there was attempt to limit pharmaceutical parallel trade and partition the common market but beyond. It is important to establish that there were efforts to restrain competition in the market in any manner that the end consumers would be negatively affected. Based on its assessment that given the medicines were subjected to prevalent price regulation mechanisms, it could not be taken for granted that parallel imports would reduce price of the medicines in the hands of the customers, the CFI rejected the Commission's findings.[601] The decision of the CFI was challenged before the ECJ where it held that the dual-pricing agreement had specific anti-competitive element that would have restrained the end consumers from benefiting from parallel importation. The agreement was clear that the restrain on parallel imports and the market segregation was intentional and was not done to promote technical or economic progress in any manner.[602]

One of the recent cases on exhaustion dealing with used software has been of significant interest both to the software programmers as well as traders in software programmes. Although it is based on copyright exhaustion, its ramifications on patent exhaustion could be similar. In the matter of *Usedsoft v Oracle*, the globally known software developer Oracle was granted an injunction by the '*Landgericht München*' (Munich Regional Court) restraining Usedsoft, a reseller of used software from reselling Oracle software in Germany. On failing to obtain a hearing on appeal by the '*Oberlandgericht München*' (High Court of the Region), Usedsoft appealed before the '*Bundesgerichtshof*' and managed to obtain a stay order over the proceedings until three questions posed before the ECJ were answered for preliminary ruling.[603] In essence the main query

600 Ibid at 592.

601 Case No. T-168/01, *GlaxoSmithKline Services Unlimited v Commission of the European Communities*, [2006] E.C.R. II-2969; [2006] 5 C.M.L.R. Available at, https://eur-lex.europa.eu/legal-content/EN/TXT/PDF/?uri=CELEX:62001TJ0168&from=EN.

602 Joined Case Nos. C-501/06 P, C-513/06 P, C-515/06 P, *GlaxoSmithKline Services Unlimited v Commission of the European Communities*, E.C.R. I-9291, 2009.

603 Case No. C 128/11, Usedsoft GmbH v Oracle International Corp, 3 C.M.L.R. 44, 2012. Available at, http://curia.europa.eu/juris/document/document.jsf?docid=124564&doclang=EN.

was whether software distribution through the online mode came under the purview of exhaustion considering the strict norms of distribution usually placed in the distribution contract. It was also asked whether the first authorised acquirer could further distribute the programme based on the doctrine of exhaustion and if so, whether the acquirer of the used software was also its lawful acquirer with authority to distribute it further.

The case also touched upon the exhaustion of rights as elaborated in *Article 4(2)* of the Software Directive that clearly allows exhaustion of software programmes.[604] Given the digital nature of the products, the ECJ assessed whether online distribution or sale would be considered equivalent to offline sales in terms of availability of the product offline. Considering the fact that the license is granted after payment of due remuneration and it is tied with the downloading of the software, the licensing was considered to exhaust the right.[605] In other words, even if the software developer downloaded the programme online from the website and did not buy it in hard form e.g. CD-ROM, etc., it would trigger exhaustion within the region. The relevancy of the case in this book is whether such exhaustion as applied in case of copyright products read with *Article 4(2)* of directive on computer programme for patented products. The question is, if these software programmes qualified for patents on computer implemented inventions (CII), would they have exhausted too. Here one needs to understand that the software directive is specific to copyrights hence there is absolute clarity but in case of patents, the exhaustion issue would need to be ascertained independent of the software code and that would not necessarily foreclose exhaustion. In case of patent exhaustion in case of CII, it is important to note that as usually the case, they are method and device patents hence in absence of any instance of exhaustion of method patents the jurisprudence in this area is yet to evolve.

The most important factor in relation to exhaustion of IPRs in the EC is clearly established as regional exhaustion where it will exhaust if the IP product is within the CU and would not exhaust if it is from outside the CU. However, it also raises questions on how it follows such exhaustion based on

604 Article 4(2) of Directive 2009/24 on the legal protection of computer programs state, *"The first sale in the Community of a copy of a program by the right-holder or with his consent shall exhaust the distribution right within the Community of that copy, with the exception of the right to control further rental of the program or a copy thereof."*

605 Savic Masa, "The Legality of Resale of Digital Content after UsedSoft in Subsequent German and CJEU Case Law", 37 European Intellectual Property Issue 7, pgs. 414, 415, (414–429), 2015.

the principles of free trade while it does not follow international exhaustion, which is based on same principles of free trade and market integration.[606]

9.3 North American Free Trade Area (NAFTA), United States Mexico Canada Agreement (USMCA) and Patent Exhaustion

9.3.1 *NAFTA: Historical Perspective and Evolution*

The development of NAFTA was not based on independent aim of regional integration but practically to counter the European trade bloc. In 1982 USTR Mr. William Brock met with strong opposition from the Europeans, which stalled any possibility of having a new round of trade ministerial under the GATT. The USTR wanted to show that US was not dependent on the outcome of multilateral trade talks and as a result of the failure in Geneva, the US-Israel FTA and the Caribbean Basin initiative were negotiated at bi-lateral and regional level. Subsequently the idea of NAFTA also gained importance as a tri-lateral agreement.[607]

The idea of having a trilateral economic arrangement was first mooted by Mr. Ronald Reagan, Presidential contender from the Republican party in 1979 in the US but Canada and Mexico initially rejected the idea. However, after the global economic recession in 1981–82 there was pressure from the business communities in both the countries and finally the idea was given serious consideration by the Mulroney government in Canada in 1985. After two years of negotiations the two countries formed the Canada-US Free Trade Agreement (CUSFTA) with the intention of removing tariffs and within ten years, trade in agriculture and financial services were liberalised.

On the other side, Mexico joined the GATT in 1986 and gradually opened up towards multilateral trade with the US. This was the key to NAFTA since negotiations began in June 1991. As a result, after August 1992 the provisions of the CUSFTA were extended to Mexico thus covering three countries – US, Canada and Mexico.[608] President George Bush (I) tried to move on with the formal

606 Rognstad Old-Andreas, "The exhaustion/competition interface in EC la – is there room for a holistic approach?", in Drexel Josef edited, "Research handbook on Intellectual Property and Competition law", Edward Elgar Publishing Ltd., pg. 3, 429, 430, (427–450), 2008.

607 Mckinney Joseph, "NAFTA's effects of North American Economic Development: A United States Perspective" at the conference on, "NAFTA and the Future of North America: Trilateral Perspectives on Governance, Economic Development and Labour", University of Toronto, 7th February 2015.

608 Ibid at 548, pgs. 12, 13.

formation of NAFTA but was not very successful and only later in 1993 President Bill Clinton with the aid of proactive USTR Carla Hills, was able to close the negotiations resulting in the formal functioning of NAFTA in January 1994. The Agreement established rules governing agriculture, energy, goods and services, IP, government procurement, etc. and a binding dispute-settlement process.

9.3.2 *NAFTA: Legal Rules on Intellectual Property Rights and Patent Exhaustion*

Issue of IPRS and its laws are covered under Chapter 17 of the NAFTA where the clauses of the Agreement on IPRS reflect the principal of NT in *Article 1708*, similar to that of the TRIPS. Further, like the TRIPS, NAFTA incorporates and applies pre-existing international treaties and conventions on IPRS like the Geneva Convention, Bern Convention, Paris Convention and others. It cannot be ignored that rules on IPRS in the NAFTA were negotiated specifically based on the Dunkel Draft that was later largely adopted as text of the TRIPS Agreement. Hence it can be said that TRIPS had direct influence in shaping the IPR provisions of NAFTA.[609] As far as the rules on IPRS in the NAFTA are concerned, Mexico had already changed its laws in line with that of USA, Canada needed to modify its IP laws.[610] Although both Canada and US still needed to change their laws on IPRS in compliance with the TRIPS Agreement.

It is worth noting that Mexico, confident about its strengths of comparative advantage in production and aware of market segmentation issues, preferred regional exhaustion of IPRS but due to US resistance succeed in thwarting efforts to establish regional exhaustion. It was very clear that the US did not intend to establish a regional agreement that would result in a common market like the EU.[611] The interest was to benefit from the low cost of production in Mexico and the markets of all the three countries without making it a boundary-less common market.

As far as the issue of exhaustion of IPRS is concerned, although the practice of international exhaustion in trademarks was very much prevalent in the three member countries of NAFTA, no mode of exhaustion in any field of IPRS was adopted. Canada continued following international exhaustion in all its

---

609 Villarreal Angeles and Fergusson Ian, "NAFTA Renegotiation and Modernization", Congressional Research Service, pg. 21, 27th February 2018.

610 Condon Bradly, "NAFTA, WTO and Global Business Strategy – How AIDS, Trade and Terrorism Affect Our Economic Future", Quorum Books, pg. 116, 2002.

611 Calboli Irene, "Trademark Exhaustion and Free Movement of Goods: A Comparative Analysis of the EU/EEA, NAFTA and ASEAN", Pg. 29, No. 25 Transatlantic Technology Law Forum, 2016.

IPRs. E.g. patents, trademarks, copyrights, designs, plant breeder's rights etc. but that was not installed in NAFTA similarly the other two continued with their own practices of exhaustion. One might argue that there is an express provision in case of Copyrights that may read as restricting international exhaustion in case of copyrights in Canada.[612] However the Canadian courts have interpreted it based on the doctrine of international exhaustion in a manner supportive of free movement of goods into Canada.[613] In Canada, based on the provisions of statutory abuse in *Section 70,* international exhaustion would apply even to patents that are subject to CL.[614]

Considering that NAFTA and TRIPS were negotiated nearly at parallel, the harmonised bottom line of high level of protection of IPRs was already established through TRIPS hence NAFTA already had high standards of IPR protection. On the issue of exhaustion of IPRs, we see the similarity between TRIPS and NAFTA since both remained silent on it. We find Mexico preferring regional exhaustion and Canada practicing international exhaustion nationally, while US courts followed implied license and its government preferred national exhaustion. With the large number of IP-centric multinationals in US interested in NAFTA markets, US preferred IPRs with either national exhaustion or without any specific exhaustion regime. We will notice that with time when new technologies evolved and demands of even higher protection started reverberating, US tried to push more for national exhaustion.

Catering to such demands, the negotiating pattern of US witnessed increasing influence of TRIPS-Plus provisions in FTA negotiations.[615] As a result US has pushed for far more extensive standards than TRIPS for protection and administration of IPRs irrespective of the fact that its own courts, including

612 *Section 27.1 (1)* of the Canadian Copyright Act expressly prohibits the importation of books without the consent of the copyright owner even where the books were produced in another country with the consent of the copyright owner, where the importer knew or should have known would infringe copyright if made in Canada.

613 The Canadian Federal Court of Appeal in trademark case, Smith & Nephew Inc. v Glen Oak Inc., (1996) 68 C.P.R. (3d) 153, before the Supreme Court of Canada in patent case, *Eli Lilly and Co. v Novopharm Ltd.* (1998), 80 C.P.R. (3d) 321 at 352.

614 *Sections 65–71* provides the statutory abuse provisions and Section 70 treats a compulsory license exactly in the same way as a voluntary license and thus subject to all patent doctrines that would be normally be applicable to patents in general.

615 Bryan Mercurio, "TRIPS-Plus Provisions in FTAs: Recent Trends", The Chinese University of Hong Kong, pg. 220, November 2006. Available at Researchgate, https://www.researchgate.net/publication/228154939_TRIPS-Plus_Provisions_in_FTAs_Recent_Trends.

the apex court has repeatedly decided in favour of international exhaustion or cases of implied license.[616]

9.3.3 *USMCA: Background and Evolution*

The USMCA or the United States-Mexico-Canada Agreement replaced the NAFTA in 2020 with an intent of better regional integration between the three countries.[617] It is interesting to note that although the NAFTA was created to facilitate inter-country trade in the region, it was not aimed at regional integration like the European common market. However gradually since its inception in 1994, in more than two decades, there has been impressive regional integration that helped the three countries' trade interests.[618] At the same time there has been significant changes in different factors that influence multilateral trade whether in terms of technological advancement, sustainability issues like environment or security issues as trade over the air has increased.[619] The NAFTA however did not have any sunset clause based on achievement of its goals or any provision for its structural update which made many of its regulation either redundant or obsolete. While the integration between the three countries had witnessed positive gains, there were many areas that needed significant updates.

With an aim to address the updates the countries started re-negotiating NAFTA from May 2017 until 2018 when it was signed and finally came into effect on 1st July 2020. The USMCA came into effect at a time when the COVID 19 pandemic had already shrunk global trade.[620] The USMCA is actually an update of NAFTA hence it is based without changing some of the core components. However, considering developments in number of areas, it has made considerable changes in IPRs and contemporary issues like digital trade and cross-border data flows apart from a completely new chapter on agriculture.

---

616 Drahos Peter, Lokuge Buddhima, Faunce Tom, Goddard Martyn and Henry David, "Pharmaceuticals, Intellectual Property and Free Trade: The Case of the US-Australia Free Trade Agreement", 22 Prometheus, pg. 243, 249, 250, (243–257), September 2004. Available at, https://law.anu.edu.au/sites/all/files/users/u9705219/236-artprometheusfta.pdf.

617 https://www.trade.gov/usmca.

618 Robertson Raymond, "Why we need the USMCA? (The Agreement formerly known as NAFTA)", Vol. 9, Mosbacher Institute, Issue 5, November 2018. Available at, https://oaktrust.library.tamu.edu/bitstream/handle/1969.1/172747/V9-5%20Why%20We%20Need%20USMCA%20NAFTA.pdf?sequence=1&isAllowed=y.

619 Gagne Gilbert and Rioux Michele, "Digital Trade", Springer, pgs., 103, 104, (99–106), 2022. Available at, https://www.academia.edu/73049957/Digital_Trade.

620 See, https://ustr.gov/trade-agreements/free-trade-agreements/united-states-mexico-canada-agreement.

It also addresses tariff issues in another crucial area – raw and refined oil and gas products where it maintains a tariff-free treatment within the parties.[621] As mentioned, the USMCA changed number of rules and that included the rules on IPRS.

9.3.3.1 USMCA: Legal Rules on Intellectual Property Rights and Patent Exhaustion

Protection of IPRS have been revamped on many fronts keeping pace with the technological developments and said to be TRIPS compliant, most of the new or updated provisions are TRIPS plus in nature. For example, the minimum protection of for industrial designs under USMCA is 15 years while in TRIPS it is 10 years. For Copyrights it is life of author plus 50 years or 50 years from the date of publication wherein it is for life of author plus 70 years or date of publication plus 75 years. Interesting to note that the copyright protection in Canada is for life of author plus 50 years and Mexico it is 100 years, both after life of author or from date of publication while USMCA accords national treatment on copyrights.

Extension of patent term to accommodate regulatory delays or delays in patent office a demand by the pharmaceutical industry since a very long time has been accommodated. Similarly Trade Secrets which have not been elaborated much in the TRIPS have been made stringent under the USMCA. However, amidst many new inclusions and modifications some in a TRIPS plus manner, there has been no change in the mode of exhaustion practiced under NAFTA and now under USMCA. *Article 20.11* states,

> Nothing in this Agreement prevents a Party from determining whether or under what conditions the exhaustion of intellectual property rights applies under its legal system. (It adds a footnote: "For greater certainty, this Article is without prejudice to any provisions addressing the exhaustion of intellectual property rights in international agreements to which a Party is a party.)[622]

621 Anderson, Bakst, Burton, Griffith, Gatsuo, Grezler, Haislmaier, Katz, Loris, O'Quinn and Roberts, "An Analysis of the United States-Mexico-Canada Agreement", Whiting K. Tory and Beaumont-Smith Gabriella eds., Backgrounder No. 3379, The Heritage Foundation, pgs. 4–6, 28 January 2019. Available at, https://www.heritage.org/sites/default/files/2019-01/BG3379_0.pdf.

622 USCMA Chapter 20: Intellectual Property Rights, https://ustr.gov/sites/default/files/files/agreements/FTA/USMCA/Text/20%20Intellectual%20Property%20Rights.pdf.

9.4 Association of Southeast Asian Nations (ASEAN) and Patent Exhaustion

Many of the East Asian countries forming the regional bloc ASEAN have witnessed impressive industrial achievement.[623] There has been employment creation and development to the extent that many Asian countries came to be known as the Asian tiger economies. However, a careful analysis will show that even when there has been some considerable industrial progress in these nations, the input of these countries towards indigenous research and development-based inventions and innovations is insignificant.[624]

Creation of IP assets have been weak in the region and thus patents have not gained the importance that many industrialised nations of the west have witnessed. It is only in the recent past that some ASEAN countries like Singapore and Malaysia have been able to contribute towards the total patent statistics largely because of their microelectronics industry.[625] This has contributed towards an increasing trend in patent-based innovation in the region since investment in production and trade of patented products have increased.[626]

Traditionally most of these ASEAN countries followed patent law that was established by their colonial rulers but with the advancement of science and technology in the ASEAN countries and global investments from industrialised countries, independent patent regimes were established. Their involvement in multilateral trade also increased their need to ascertain a definite policy on IPRs catering to their development. Moreover, there have been efforts to harmonise the IP laws of the ASEAN countries through compliance to different international agreements (e.g. TRIPS). In addition, the internal harmonisation of IP laws under the ASEAN Framework Agreement on IP Cooperation started in 1994 and the Hanoi Plan of Action of the ASEAN Summit was put in place in 1998.[627] Issues that were taken up were mainly enforcement related rather

623 There are ten member countries forming ASEAN. Prominent among them are six countries namely, Indonesia, Malaysia, the Philippines, Singapore, Thailand and Vietnam. The other four members are, Brunei Darussalam, Cambodia, Laos and Myanmar.

624 Lam N.V., "A perspective on Entrepreneurship, Intellectual Property Creation, Enterprise development and Competitiveness in ASEAN" Socio-economic Analysis Section, Poverty and Development Division, UNESCAP, pg. 78 (75–91) 2005.

625 During the period 1997–2001, 872 patents were registered at the United States Patent Office to Singapore Residents and 151 to Malaysian residents.

626 Ibid at 242, pgs. 54, 55.

627 Weeraworawit Weerawit, "The Harmonisation of Intellectual Property Rights in ASEAN", in C. Antons, M. Blakeney and C. Heath (eds.), "Intellectual Property Harmonisation Within ASEAN and APEC", Kluwer Law International, pgs. 113–114, 2004.

than those related to multilateral or regional trade, hence exhaustion never found a place. The ASEAN countries established their own exhaustion policy independent of the countries' membership in the association.

After significant efforts, finally in 2015 the ASEAN Economic Community (AEC) was established mainly to fructify the region as a single market.[628] The main aim was to remove trade barriers and facilitate free movement of goods within the member countries' markets. However, given the fact that the members address the exhaustion issue nationally, there is lack of uniformity among the member countries on it.

9.5 Gulf Cooperation Council (GCC) and Patent Exhaustion

The Gulf Co-operation Council (GCC) was formed on 25th May 1981 and they introduced the model patent law in December 1992, which was later revised in December 1999 and adopted by the CGC member countries.[629] Membership of GCC includes United Arab Emirates, Kingdom of Bahrain, Kingdom of Saudi Arabia, Sultanate of Oman, States of Qatar and Kuwait, all predominantly Arab States.[630] The Middle Eastern region, although majorly influenced by Islamic laws, it also has pockets of exception as Jewish religion exists at parallel. Further, Jews, Arabs, Persians, Turks forming varied cultural background have influenced rights over creativity with variation. Amidst such a mosaic, the efforts of creating an internal common market is witnessed among Arab States hence subject of this study.

Historically one may draw parallels of IP protection with the administration of authorship rights and moral rights under Sharia (Islamic) law in the Arab States. Arguably there are two schools of thoughts among Islamic scholars, one is of the opinion that Sharia covers only tangible objects and nothing intangible and the other argues that nothing in the Sharia is against protection of IPRs. The former highlights that there is nothing elaborated in the Quran, Sunnah or interpretations of Islamic jurists that accorded any sort of protection to intangible object.[631] In fact like other oriental belief, they claim that

628 See http://asean.org/asean-economic-community/.

629 Abu–Ghazaleh (Intellectual Property Law firm), "Intellectual Property Laws of the ARAB countries", Kluwer Law International, pg. XI, 2000.

630 Gulf Cooperation Council membership details are available at, http://www.gcc-sg.org/en-us/AboutGCC/Memberstates/pages/Home.aspx.

631 Quran is the holy book for Muslims and Sunna are the traditions based on the hadith or sayings of the prophet. Elaborated further in, Bashar H. Malkawi, "Intellectual Property Protection from a Sharia perspective", 16 Southern Cross University Law Review, pg. 89,

since knowledge is not considered property, individual exclusive rights in the form of IPRS cannot be accorded. While the other school weighs in with majority that nothing in Sharia restrains protection of one's right, including IPRS and honouring contracts have always been Islamic, hence protection of IPRS cannot be said to be against Sharia.[632] The latter view is further established in the fact that material compensation for intangible property was relevant practice under Sharia. e.g. Califs bought important books and made copies of them after adequately compensating the authors.[633]

In the light of this historical perspective we will find that structured development of IPRS in the Arab region was witnessed only when international developments started with Tunisia being the first to join the Paris Convention in 1884 and Bern Convention in 1887 with Morocco, Lebanon and Egypt following.[634] However the Arab States still did not join any of the international conventions on IPRS until as recent as 2000 and the revamping of their laws on IPRS and streamlining them mainly started with US pushing them towards WTO membership.[635]

The GCC members joined the Bern and Paris Conventions only post-2000.[636] Aiming at establishing a common market and a monetary union within the GCC, in the area of IPRS too there have been efforts to harmonise laws. One of the distinct developments in the area of protection of IPRS was the adoption of unitary patent right covering all GCC countries. Considering the uniqueness of the influence of the Sharia and historical difference between experts some considering IPRS as legitimate while others as un-Islamic, there is an additional criterion for an invention to qualify for grant of patent other than

(87–121), 2013. Available at, http://www.austlii.edu.au/au/journals/SCULawRw/2013/4.pdf.

632 Raslan Heba, "Shari'a and the Protection of Intellectual Property – The Example of Egypt", 7(4) IDEA – The Intellectual Property Law Review, pg. 501, 502, (497–559), 2001. Available at, https://ipmall.law.unh.edu/sites/default/files/hosted_resources/IDEA/idea-vol47-no4-raslan.pdf.

633 Milani Alireza, "The Legitimacy of Intellectual Property Rights in the Light of Islamic Law (Sunni and Shia Fiqh)", 7(3) World Journal of Islamic History and Civilization, pg. 37, (37–46), 2017. Available at, https://idosi.org/wjihc/wjihc7(3)17/1.pdf.

634 Ibid at 630.

635 Caroll John, "Intellectual Property Rights in the Middle East: A Cultural Perspective", 11(3) Fordham Intellectual Property, Media and Entertainment Law Journal, pg. 568, (555–600), 2001.

636 Details of Berne and Paris Convention memberships of CGC States are available at, http://www.wipo.int/treaties/en/ShowResults.jsp?country_id=ALL&start_year=ANY&end_year=ANY&search_what=C&treaty_id=15&treaty_id=2.

'Novelty', *'Inventive Step'* and *'Industrial Applicability'*, i.e. the invention needs to be in compliance with Sharia.[637]

Article 12 states,

> 2. Where the Patent subject is a product, the Patent owner shall have the right to prevent others from manufacturing, use, sale, offering for sale, or import of the product for such purposes, without his prior consent. However, where the patent subject is industrial process, he shall have the right to prevent others from actual use of the process. He shall also have the right to prevent others from use, and offering for sale, sale or import of at least the products directly obtained by using such process, for such purposes, without his prior consent.

The law does not provide any exception for import of patented products from outside GCC where it has been placed with prior consent of the patent holder. The language in Article 12/2 mandates *'prior consent'* of the patent holder confirming national exhaustion and restricting parallel imports. With a significant development the GCC abandoned the unitary patent right covering all GCC countries on 26th January 2021 and the amended patent law is functional from this date. After the amendment the filing of the patent can be through GCC Patent Office but the grant would need to be through each of the member states separately.[638]

9.6 Common Market of the South (MERCOSUR) and Patent Exhaustion

Established by the Common Market of the South (MERCOSUR) Agreement in 1991 by the Treaty of Asuncion, it is the largest internal of South America.[639] Initially Argentina, Brazil, Paraguay and Uruguay became members and were later joined by Venezuela in 2012 (but suspended in 2016) while Bolivia, Chile, Colombia, Ecuador, Guyana, Peru, and Suriname are Associate Members.[640] With the intention of creating a regionally integrated market for free movement

637 Holder Sara, "Gulf Co-operation Council Countries – Patent Landscape", Rouse The Magazine, 16th January 2018. Available at, https://www.rouse.com/magazine/news/gulf-co-operation-council-countries-patent-landscape/.

638 Information about the amendment of the Unitary Patent Regulation of GCC is available at, https://www.gccpo.org/ and an English commentary in English at http://www.kadasa.com.sa/news/181?type=END_TO_UNITARY_PATENT_SYSTEM_IN_THE_GCC.

639 The Common Market of the South (MERCOSUR) Agreement is available at, https://wits.worldbank.org/GPTAD/PDF/archive/MERCOSUR.pdf.

640 Details of MERCOSUR is available at, https://www.mercosur.int/en/.

of goods and services among members their attempt has been to remove customs duties and non-tariff barriers to trade. At a macro level it aimed to coordinate sectoral and macro-economic policies to synergise foreign trade, agriculture, industry and other factors. With such broad aim, harmonisation of IPRs within the region was attempted but even the '*Harmonization of Intellectual Property Provisions in MERCOSUR on Trademarks, Indications of Source and Appellations of Origin*' was ratified only by Paraguay and Uruguay. The members of MERCOSUR are allowed to opt for any mode of exhaustion which has resulted in a mixed practice of exhaustion. At present Brazil and Venezuela follows national exhaustion while Argentina, Bolivia, Paraguay and Uruguay follow international exhaustion of patents allowing parallel imports from anywhere in the world.[641]

9.7 Comprehensive and Progressive Agreement for Trans-Pacific Partnership (CPTPP), IPRs and Patent Exhaustion

The Comprehensive and Progressive Agreement for Trans-Pacific Partnership (CPTPP) was initially ratified between six countries Australia, Canada, Japan, Mexico, New Zealand and Singapore on 30th December 2018.[642] Later Brunei Darussalam, Chile, Malaysia, Peru and Vietnam joined with total members reaching 11 and most recently received request for accession from the United Kingdom. Covering nearly all sectors of trade, it is a FTAs allowed under the WTO regulatory regime, its intention is to eliminate or reduce barriers to trade in a transparent and consistent manner.[643] IP in CPTPP has been elaborated in *Article 18*, a lot borrowed from the previous Trans-Pacific Partnership (TPP) which collapsed after US withdrew from it in 2017. *Article 18* links protection and enforcement of IPRs with technological innovation with transfer and dissemination of technology and accords NT to its members.

As far as exhaustion of IPRs are concerned, it allows its members to decide any mode that they consider fit.

641 Correa Carlos and Correa Juan, "Parallel imports and the principle of exhaustion of rights in Latin America", in Calboli Irene and Lee Edward (eds)., "Research handbook on Intellectual Property Exhaustion and Parallel Imports", Edward Elgar Publishing Ltd., pages 199, 200 (198–225), 2016.

642 See, https://www.mfat.govt.nz/assets/Trade-agreements/CPTPP/Comprehensive-and-Progressive-Agreement-for-Trans-Pacific-Partnership-CPTPP-English.pdf.

643 See, https://www.international.gc.ca/trade-commerce/trade-agreements-accords-commerciaux/agr-acc/cptpp-ptpgp/index.aspx?lang=eng; https://www.dfat.gov.au/trade/agreements/in-force/cptpp/comprehensive-and-progressive-agreement-for-trans-pacific-partnership.

Article 18.11: Exhaustion of Intellectual Property Rights – Nothing in this Agreement prevents a Party from determining whether or under what conditions the exhaustion of intellectual property rights applies under its legal system. The footnote to it states, "For greater certainty, this Article is without prejudice to any provisions addressing the exhaustion of intellectual property rights in international agreements to which a Party is a party." [644]

9.8 Comprehensive Economic and Trade Agreement (CETA) and Patent Exhaustion

The Comprehensive Economic and Trade Agreement (CETA) is an FTA between the European Union and Canada which was signed by Canada on 30th October 2016 and approved by the European Parliament approved it on 15th February 2017. Considering that ratification is expected to be slow due to the large number of member countries of the European Union, CETA is provisionally applied since 21st September 2017.[645] Interesting to note that even before it was ratified, Belgium challenged the legitimacy of its dispute settlement mechanism under EU law but was held valid by the ECJ.[646] The agreement is far-reaching with very ambitious commitments both on goods and services. It covers issues like protection of environment, mitigation of climate change and labour rights, on which there has not been significant difference between the parties in the WTO. Binding on all the parties, the agreement has thirty Articles (also referred to as chapters) providing the edifice on which sensitive issues like rights of workers, food safety, etc. will depend.[647]

IP is covered under Article 20 elaborately in 50 sub-Articles and like some other FTAs, the intent is to develop regulations and standards that are consistent to EU and Canada to protect and enforce IP. *Article 20: 2* in defining the '*Nature and Scope*' clearly mentions it to complement the TRIPS Agreement and that it does not create any obligation on distribution of resources between IP enforcement and enforcement of law in general. In *Article 20: 4* on '*Exhaustion*', it states, '*This chapter does not affect the freedom of the Parties*

644 See https://www.international.gc.ca/trade-commerce/trade-agreements-accords-commerciaux/agr-acc/tpp-ptp/text-texte/18.aspx?lang=eng.

645 See https://ec.europa.eu/trade/policy/in-focus/ceta/ceta-explained/.

646 See https://www.lawsocieties.eu/viewpoint/the-ceta-opinion-of-the-cjeu-right-of-access-to-an-independent-tribunal-by-emily-hay/5067617.article.

647 See https://ec.europa.eu/trade/policy/in-focus/ceta/ceta-chapter-by-chapter/.

to determine whether and under what conditions the exhaustion of intellectual property rights applies.'[648]

648 See https://ec.europa.eu/trade/policy/in-focus/ceta/ceta-chapter-by-chapter/.

PART 3

Policy Dimensions of Patent Exhaustion

CHAPTER 10

Patents and Public Health: Patents and Access to Medicines – The Exhaustion Dimension

10.1 Historical Perspective of Patents, Public Health Concerns and Access to Medicines: The Indian Experience

In this book it has been discussed how patent laws existing in industrialised nations since centuries, were introduced to their colonies forming the patent laws in most of today's developing countries and LDCs. The colonial governments' policies were regressive and promoted exclusively their monopolistic interests. The Indian experience is shared in this chapter given its path to becoming the largest global supplier of generic pharmaceutical drugs and seen as a model for other developing countries. India's experience with trade under the colonial rulers had a serious impact on accessibility of medicines at reasonable price,

> India was forced to absorb Britain's surplus of increasingly obsolescent and non-competitive industrial exports. By 1910 this included two-fifths of the UK's finished cotton goods and three-fifths of its exports of electrical products, railway equipment, books and *pharmaceuticals* (*Emphasis added*).[649]

This is not an isolated example that one might think the local industry in India and other developing countries of today were unable to produce enough at that period. On the contrary, colonies like India did not just cater to the local market, but also contributed generously to global markets. But unfortunately, systematically this eroded during colonial rule. The table below reflects the statistics on share of world manufacturing and the dramatic difference between the years 1750 and 1900, hence presents a clear picture of the global manufacturing in this period.[650] The influence of industrial revolution can be

---

649 Davis Mike, "Late Victorian Holocausts El Niño Famines and the Making of the Third World", Verso New York, pg. 298,Table 9.3, 2001. Reproduced from Tomlinson B. R., "Economics: The Periphery", in Porter Andrew edited, "The Oxford History of the British Empire: The Nineteenth Century", Oxford pg. 69, 1990.

650 Ibid at 649.

DOI:10.1163/9789004542815_012

TABLE 1 Shares of World Manufacturing Output (in %), 1750–1900

Countries	1750	1800	1830	1860	1880	1900
Tropics	*76.8*	71.2	63.3	39.2	23.3	*13.4*
China	*32.8*	33.3	29.8	19.7	12.5	*6.2*
India	*24.5*	19.7	17.6	8.6	2.8	*1.7*
Europe	*23.1*	28.0	34.1	53.6	62.0	*63.0*
UK	*1.9*	4.3	9.5	19.9	22.9	*18.5*

seen in the numbers of Europe from 1860 onwards but until then the statistics favoured the developing countries of today, the erstwhile colonies.

In such backdrop where colonial rulers had choked local industrial development and where indigenous production was destroyed, patent law made its entry into some of these countries. The patent law aimed to protect the rights of the colonial rulers who mainly used it to import among other things, bulk drugs, active ingredients and formulations for pharmaceutical drugs to sell them in the captive colony markets at exorbitant prices. In India it was noticed that 90% of the patents were never worked locally creating constant shortage and high medicine prices.[651] Interesting to note that while colonies had no choice but to follow their rulers' laws, at the same time some other countries like France, Germany, and Switzerland adopted weak patent laws enabling legitimate reverse engineering and growth of local pharmaceutical industry.[652] In fact the Swiss legislature initially rejected proposals for enacting patent law until 1887 when it finally passed it. Similarly, Netherlands had repealed their patent law in 1869 and re-enacted it only after the home industry was ready, after more than 40 years in 1910.[653]

The example of India is important since its patent law was the main pillar behind the growth of the country's generic pharmaceutical industry and it

651 Barnes Stephen, "Pharmaceutical Patents and TRIPS: A Comparison of India and South Africa", 91 Kentucky Law Journal, pg. 911, 2003.

652 Balasubhramaniam K., "Access to Medicines and Public Policy Safeguards under TRIPS", in Bellmann Christopher, Dutfield Graham and Meléndez-Ortiz Ricardo (eds.), "Trading in Knowledge – Development Perspectives on TRIPS, Trade and Sustainability", pg. 139 (135–142) Earthscan 2003.

653 Scherer F.M., "The Political Economy of Patent Policy Reform in the United States", Volume 7 Journal on Telecomm & High Tech. Law, pg. 168, 169 (167–216), 2009.

became an example for other developing countries. After gaining independence, prices of medicines in India were still exorbitant, leading to serious problems related to access to medicines, hindering a meaningful solution to the plethora of diseases and epidemics.[654] The government commissioned a detailed study under the leadership of retired Lahore High Court judge Dr. T.B. Chand in 1948 and later another study was commissioned in 1957 under the leadership of Justice N. Rajagopala Ayyangar. These two studies analysed patent laws of different countries of the world as they had evolved as well as industrial policies related to pharmaceutical production and recommended sweeping changes. The '*Tek Chand Committee Report*' and the '*Ayyangar Committee Report*' formed the foundation of the Indian Patent Act 1970.[655] India was one of the first developing countries to assess the patent law as one of the main reasons for high price and lack of access to pharmaceutical medicines and subsequently change their patent law.

With the new patent law in effect from 1971, India transformed from a medicine-starved country to not only self-sufficiency, but also became the global supplier of high quality low-priced generic pharmaceutical drugs. Gradually following this example other developing nations also excluded pharmaceutical products from product-patents so that their local industries could reverse engineer and manufacture its generic equivalents locally or be able to legally import generics into their countries.[656] This undoubtedly had a global welfare enhancing effect, enabling the low-income nations access pharmaceutical drugs at reasonable prices in absence of patents.[657] However the divide between the industrialised countries as introducers of these drugs globally and the developing countries manufacturing high quality legitimate copies and marketing globally, became a matter of serious contention.

While most of the developing countries were at a very nascent stage of industrialisation during the 1980–1990s, the industrialised countries had moved well ahead. With countries increasingly moving towards laissez faire economy, government support in pharmaceutical production kept reducing

654 Ibid at 2.

655 History of Indian Patent system available at, http://www.ipindia.nic.in/history-of-indian-patent-system.htm.

656 Sterckx Sigrid, "Patents and access to drugs in developing countries: An ethical analysis", 4 Developing World Bioethics, Blackwell Publishing, pg. 61 (58–75) November 2004.

657 Scherer Sigrid and Watal Jayashree, "Post-TRIPS Options for Access to Patented Medicines in Developing Nations", 5 Journal of International Economic Law, (913–940) 2002; Scherer F. M., "Global Welfare in Pharmaceutical Patenting", Presentation made at the conference on "Markets for Pharmaceuticals and the Health of Developing Nations" in Toulose, France, 5th–6th December, 2003. Available at, www.idei.fr/doc/conf/pha/scherer.pdf.

while private sector investments in pharmaceutical industry kept increasing. The multinational pharmaceutical giants operating in the global market are some of the lead spenders in R&D across industry with a rapidly expanding investment throughout the years.[658] While it is true that unlike government backed research, profit motive runs the private pharmaceutical companies and one cannot negate their contribution to new drug discoveries. In such scenario their demand for lead-time over their competitors through patents, were legitimate and the possibility of reverse engineering through weaker patent laws obviously would free-ride on their costs. While the pharmaceutical companies needed sufficiently strong patent laws to recuperate their R&D investments, the patents often lead to a monopoly-pricing situation that increased the drug prices leading to an access problem.[659] The TRIPS Agreement was introduced within the new WTO regime at this juncture in 1994, coming into effect in 1995, with developing countries getting 10 more years with certain conditions and the LDCs are still under extended transition period.

10.2 Post-TRIPS Scenario: Patents, Public Health Concerns and Access to Medicines

It has already been discussed while elaborating on the negotiating history of TRIPS that TRIPS was introduced at this juncture bringing sweeping changes including patent protection for all technologies and minimum 20 years patent term upon filing.[660] This had an adverse impact on the HIV/AIDS related drugs since most of them were patented except the basic conventional ones on the WHO list. This gave considerable leverage to the research-based pharmaceutical companies to negotiate pricing favourable to them while affected countries had already lost the possibility to procure cheaper generic versions post-2005

658 The pharmaceutical industry spending in R&D is one of the top among different sectors and the graph shows how the spending is increasing. Data available at, https://www.statista.com/statistics/265645/ranking-of-the-20-companies-with-the-highest-spending-on-research-and-development/.

659 Nielsen Jane and Nicol Dianne, "Pharmaceutical Patents and Developing Countries: The Conundrum of Access and Incentive", 13 Australian Intellectual Property Journal, pg. 21 (21–40) February 2002.

660 *Article 27* of the TRIPS Agreement obligated all members to introduce both product and process patent protection for all inventions from 2005 and a pipeline protection for the transition period of 1995 to 2000 for industrialised countries and 1995 to 2005 for developing countries under *Articles 70(8)* and *70 (9)* of TRIPS.

after the transition period for developing countries lapsed.[661] Historically, CL had been extensively used by the US not as a provision in its patent law (since it does not exist in patent law) but as measure to remedy anti-competitive practices. Brazil, Canada, France and Israel had also used it to a considerable extent.[662] Hence using CL should not have been a problem hence developing countries facing public health crisis, tried to use the TRIPS provisions of using CL as well as allowing parallel imports to access pharmaceutical drugs at reasonable prices during their national emergencies.

One also needs to understand that CL provisions in the TRIPS *Article 31* are extra-ordinary measures to address extra-ordinary circumstances, hence there are elaborate conditions to be met for such grant. Meanwhile when countries were gradually coping with the new compliance requirements introduced by TRIPS, HIV/AIDS had become a serious health crisis in Brazil and South Africa with most of the African continent affected. It was found that although 95% of the existing essential drugs were not under patents,[663] they did not work while the more modern anti-retroviral drugs were under patents and EMR and were too expensive. At the same time on the other hand, it was also argued that patents were not responsible for the high price of medicines there were other factors[664] and it would be wrong to deduce that patent was the only reason since in some of the LDCs patents were not even filed.[665]

10.3 Public Policy Implications of Public Health Crisis Leading to TRIPS Amendment

As mentioned earlier, the HIV/AIDS problem had already reached a pandemic stage and was posing a worldwide threat particularly in Africa, Asia and

661 Cottier Thomas, "The Doha Waiver and Its Effects on the Nature of the TRIPS System and on Competition Law. The Impact of Human Rights"' in Govaere Inge and Ullrich Hanns (eds.), "Intellectual Property, Public Policy and International Trade", "College of Europe Studies No.6", P.I.E. Peter Lang, pgs. 176, 177, (73–199), 2007.

662 Correa Carlos, "Integrating Public Health Concerns into Patent Legislation in Developing Countries", South Centre, pg. 93, 94, 2000.

663 Beall F. Reed, "Patents and the WHO Model List of Essential Medicines (18th Edition): Clarifying the debate on IP and access", WIPO Global Challenges Brief, 2016. Available at, https://www.wipo.int/edocs/mdocs/mdocs/en/wipo_gc_ip_ge_16/wipo_gc_ip_ge_16_brief.pdf.

664 Reinhardt Eric, "Intellectual Property Protection and Public Health in the Developing World" 17 Emory International Law Review, pg. 485 (475–489) 2003.

665 Thorpe Phil, "Study on the implementation of the TRIPS Agreement by developing countries" Study Paper No. 7 of the Commission on Intellectual Property Rights, UK, 2002.

Latin America.[666] Brazil raised the problem at multiple international forums. It moved a resolution before the United Nations Commission on Human Rights claiming that access to medicines for diseases like HIV/AIDS was a basic human right that needed protection. It also moved a resolution in the Economic and Social Council where it was passed by 52 out of 53 voting members (the US abstained from voting) with the UN General Assembly adopting the Declaration of Commitment on HIV/AIDS in 2000.[667] The United Nations General Assembly also held a Special Session on HIV/AIDS next year from 25th through 27th June 2001, pledging for "Global Crisis – Global Action".[668] The resolution emphasised the need to reduce cost of pharmaceutical drugs and related technologies in close collaboration with the private pharmaceutical sector to promote innovation and development of domestic industries in the developing nations.[669]

Brazil and South Africa also initiated domestic measures to make the medicines available at the cheapest possible price by using available TRIPS flexibilities. Hence while Brazil tried to negotiate with the multinational pharmaceutical companies to lower the price of HIV/AIDS drugs through the threat of issuance of CL, South Africa brought legislation to allow both parallel importation and CL. However, this resulted massive retaliation from the powerful pharmaceutical industry, 41 companies organised under the Pharmaceutical Manufacturer's Association (PMA), moved locally in South Africa. The PMA brought a suit before the Pretoria High Court in 1998 alleging that the CL and parallel imports were in violation of the South African patent law and were not in compliance with the TRIPS Agreement.[670] On the other hand the pharmaceutical companies convinced the US government to bring a complaint against

666 UNAIDS, "Aids Epidemic Update: December 2000", pg. 5 UNAIDS Report, Geneva 2000. It points out that among the 36.1 million people who were infected with AIDS at that time, 25.3 million lived in Sub-Saharan Africa, 5.8 million in South Asia and South-East Asia and 1.4 million in Latin America.

667 The U.N. High Level Meeting Polictical Declarations can be found at, https://www.hrw.org/legacy/backgrounder/hivaids/ungass0806/3.htm.

668 The Resolution "Global Crisis – Global Action". Details available at, http://www.unaids.org/sites/default/files/sub_landing/files/aidsdeclaration_en_0.pdf.

669 UNAIDS press release of 11 December 2001 available at, www.unaids.org.

670 Case No. 4138/98. For more details see, Colvin Christopher and Heywood Mark, "Negotiating ARV Prices with Pharmaceutical Companies and the South African Government: A Civil Society / Legal Approach", in "Negotiating and Navigating Global Health – Case Studies in Global Health Diplomacy", World Scientific Publishing CO. Pte. Ltd., pgs. 355 and 356, 2012.

Brazil at the WTO DSB on 30 May 2000, alleging that Brazil's IP law relating to CL was in violation of TRIPS.[671]

Given that TRIPS Agreement was not only a legal document but also a political one, inability to use TRIPS flexibilities by sovereign members due to existing power asymmetries between manufacturers and users of medicine, raised international concern.[672] At the WTO this time there was already growing discontentment amongst developing nations on multiple GATT issues like trade in agricultural goods, non-agricultural market access (NAMA). The TRIPS enforcement issue in the background of the health crisis heightened the conflict between developing and industrialised countries. As a result, the Seattle Ministerial meeting of WTO failed leading the path to a development round[673] in the next ministerial meeting in Doha Qatar from 14th–19th November 2001. The Director General of the WTO, Mr. Mike Moore acknowledged the pitiful state of public health in many developing countries and assured that the TRIPS was balanced enough to provide necessary flexibilities on public health.[674]

The Doha ministerial meeting saw distinct division among members not just on CL but also parallel importation through international exhaustion which the developing countries preferred. The paper submitted by the developing countries to the TRIPS Council Special Discussion on '*Intellectual Property and Access to medicines*' made it clear,

> adoption of the principle of international exhaustion of rights [allowing parallel trade] can be a useful tool for health policies. Where the prices of pharmaceutical products are lower in a foreign market, for instance, a government may allow importation of such products into the national market, so as to allow offers of drugs at more affordable prices.[675]

671 Brazil – Measures Affecting Patent Protection. See, https://www.wto.org/english/tratop_e/dispu_e/cases_e/ds199_e.htm.

672 Sell Susan, "Legal Movements in Trade & Intellectual Property – Trade Issues & HIV/AIDS", 17 Emory International Law Review, pg. 591 (591–601) 2003.

673 McManis Charles and Contreras Jorge, "Compulsory Licensing of intellectual property: A viable policy lever for promoting access to critical technologies?" In, Ghidini Gustavo, Peritz Rudolph and Ricolfi Marco (eds.), "TRIPS and Developing Countries Towards a New IP World Order?", Edward Elgar Publishing Ltd. 2014, pages 109, 110 (109–131).

674 Moore Mike, DG WTO Secretariat in regular Press Statement "IP and Access to Medicines" dated 20th June 2001.

675 See, paper submitted by the Africa group, Barbados, Bolivia, Brazil, Dominican Republic, Equador, Honduras, India, Indonesia, Jamaica, Pakistan, Paraguay, the Philippines, Peru, Sri Lanka, Thailand, and Venezuela to the TRIPS Council for the special discussion on intellectual Property and access to medicines, 20th June 2001, WTO Geneva. See,

The US vehemently opposed both allowing any inclusion of parallel imports and CL, even in case of serious public health problems. Although ironically it did not hesitate considering CL itself when there was a threat of public health crisis.[676]

Following the 9/11 terrorist attacks in USA, there were a series of bio-terrorism scare through use of anthrax-embedded postal mails resulting death of some postal employees. '*Ciproflaxin*' was the only drug effective in treating anthrax and Bayer held the patent over it. US government tried to negotiate a cheaper price for the drug in US, failing which, after some time joined Canada threatening to issue CL to enable generic production of the drug. This double standard of the US could not help it sustain its negotiating stand at the TRIPS negotiations and it had to accept the developing countries demand. At the same time, there was finally a breakthrough and both Canada and US could negotiate an agreeable royalty rate without using CL. While the CL threat proved credible, the entire episode also exposed the gap in arguments de-linking patents and access to pharmaceuticals drugs.[677]

The intent of the framers of the TRIPS Agreement enabling a WTO Member to use necessary flexibilities to take policy decisions in the wake of any public health crisis was confirmed when the Doha Declaration on the TRIPS and public health was adopted on 14th November 2001 affirming *Article 8.1* of TRIPS.[678] The Doha Declaration acknowledged the seriousness and magnitude of the health problems in many developing countries and LDCs with diseases like HIV/AIDS, tuberculosis, malaria and others and reaffirmed the flexibility available under the TRIPS Agreement.[679] The declaration brought to the front

---

Developing countries' group paper IP/C/W/296, available at https://www.wto.org/english/tratop_e/trips_e/paper_develop_w296_e.htm.

676 Raghavan Srividhya, "Patent and Trade Disparities in Developing Countries", in "The international trade regime in perspective", Oxford University Press, pg. 184, 185 (168–199), 2012.

677 Sell Susan, "Life after TRIPS – Aggression and Opposition", in Maskus Keith (ed.), "The WTO, Itellectual Property Rights and the Knowledge Economy", Edward Elgar Publishing Ltd., pgs. 110,111 (72–119), 2004.

678 Cottier Thomas, "TRIPS, the Doha Declaration and Public Health", pgs. 386, 385–388, Vol. 6, No. 2 The Journal of World Intellectual Property, 2003. Based on the remarks made by the author at the 9th Geneva Global Arbitration Forum held on 4th–5th December, 2002 in Geneva, Switzerland; Also see paragraph 4 of the Doha Declaration on the TRIPS Agreement and Public Health, Doha WTO Ministerial 2001: TRIPS, WT/MIN(01)/DEC/2, available at, https://www.wto.org/english/thewto_e/minist_e/min01_e/mindecl_trips_e.htm.

679 Matthews Duncan, "Lessons from negotiating an amendment to the TRIPS Agreement: Compulsory Licensing and access to medicines" in Westkamp Guido (ed.), "Emerging Issues in Intellectual Property", Edward Elgar Publishing Ltd. 2007, pgs. 225, 226, (222–249).

much-debated issues like CL and exhaustion of rights and in paragraph 5.d stated, '*The effect of the provisions in the TRIPS Agreement that are relevant to the exhaustion of IPR is to leave each member free to establish its own regime for such exhaustion without challenge, subject to the MFN and NT provisions of Article 3 and 4*' (*Emphasis added*).[680]

The confirmation of a member to adopt international exhaustion provided clarity amidst different emerging opinions on the contrary.[681] Explained lucidly by Prof. Frederick Abbott, '*further argument from the US, Switzerland, and the pharmaceutical sector that while Article 6 of the TRIPS Agreement precludes TRIPS dispute settlement on the issue of exhaustion, Article 28 nonetheless prevents parallel importation of patented drugs.*' was proven wrong.[682] The Doha Declaration thus reaffirmed that the member countries can set up any exhaustion mode and adopt international exhaustion allowing parallel importation.[683] Amidst unnecessary clutter of contradicting views, the Doha Declaration reiterated what was already provided for in the TRIPS Agreement.[684] Often raised doubts about its eligibility being a political document, the Doha Declaration even being a political document, helped to move the discussions on IPRs from bilateral levels in FTA negotiations back to the multilateral level in an effective manner.[685] It also provided much needed

680 Declaration on the TRIPS Agreement and Public Health, Doha WTO Ministerial 2001: TRIPS, WT/MIN(01)/DEC/2, available at, https://www.wto.org/english/thewto_e/minist_e/min01_e/mindecl_trips_e.htm.

681 The Road to Doha and Beyond – A Road Map for Successfully Concluding The Doha Development Agenda, WTO 2001. Available at, https://www.wto.org/english/res_e/booksp_e/roadtodoha_e.pdf.

682 Abbot Frederick, "The Doha Declaration on the TRIPS Agreement and Public Health: Lighting a dark corner at the WTO", 5 (2) Journal of International Economic Law, pg. 494 (469–506) 2002.

683 Kongolo Tshimanga, "TRIPS, the Doha Declaration and Public Health", 6 (2) The Journal of World Intellectual Property, pg. 374 (373–378) 2003. Based on the remarks made by the author at the 9th Geneva Global Arbitration Forum held on 4th–5th December, 2002 in Geneva, Switzerland.

684 Noehrenberg Eric, "TRIPS, the Doha Declaration and Public Health", 6 (2) The Journal of World Intellectual Property, pg. 379 (379–383) 2003. Based on the remarks made by the author at the 9th Geneva Global Arbitration Forum held on 4th–5th December, 2002 in Geneva, Switzerland; Also see, Bloche Gregg, "WTO Difference to National Health Policy: Toward an interpretive Principle", 5 (4), Journal of International Economic Law, pg. 839 (825–848) 2002 and Thuo Gathii James, "The Legal Status of the Doha Declaration on TRIPS and Public Health Under the Vienna Convention on the Law of Treaties", 15 Harvard Journal of Law and Technology, pg. 308, 309 (291–317) 2002.

685 United States Trade Representative (USTR) Mr. Robert Zoellick referred to the Doha declaration as a 'political declaration' in the USTR Press Release dated 14th November, 2001.

clarity on the processes for execution of the TRIPS flexibilities without imposing additional legal implications.[686]

In the Cancun Ministerial meeting procedural work to operationalise the Doha Declaration continued at the TRIPS Council. Council chair, Mexican Ambassador Eduardo Pérez Motta presented a solution to the impasse through a self-imposed moratorium on any complaint by members for use of CL until the TRIPS was amended to that effect.[687] The US refused to accept the Chairman's proposed dispute coverage and wanted to restrict the diseases only to HIV/AIDS, Tuberculosis and Malaria. The developing countries were strongly opposed to any dilution of the Doha declaration and were not ready to accept any alteration of the declaration through the footnote since paragraph 1 of the Doha Declaration already stated, '*from HIV/AIDS, tuberculosis, malaria and other epidemics.*' (*emphasis added*). Finally, EU suggested a list of at least 23 other infectious diseases that could be extended on recommendation by the WHO and US agreed with a footnote to their earlier proposal to include other epidemics of comparable gravity and scale. US, EU and Switzerland joined the moratorium as a stop-gap measure until the final decision to implement the Doha declaration was reached by the General Council of the WTO on the 30th August 2003.[688]

Initially there was disagreement on whether production under the CL can be only for the domestic market or in cases of national emergencies or extreme urgencies or for public non-commercial use, could also be for another country.[689] The implementation of the waiver in Doha declaration confirmed that it would not only be for cases of national emergencies or cases of extreme urgencies or for public non-commercial use in domestic market but also for export to another developing country. Subsequently amidst concerns of misuse, elaborate and stringent procedures were introduced for import and export under CL.[690] The decision to implement the Doha Declaration was taken on 30th

686 Schott Jeffrey, "Comment on the Doha Ministerial", 5 (1) Journal of International Economic Law, pg. 195 (191–219) 2002.

687 Draft Proposal presented by the Chairman of the TRIPS Council on 16th December 2002.

688 Decision of the General Council of the WTO taken on 30th August 2003, Document No. WT/L/540, available at, https://www.wto.org/english/tratop_e/trips_e/implem_para6_e.htm.

689 Roffe Pedro, Spennemann Christoph and von Braun Johanna, "From Paris to Doha: The WTO Doha Declaration on the TRIPS Agreement and Public Health", in Roffe Pedro, Tansey Geoff and Vivas-Eugui David (eds), "Negotiating Health – Intellectual Property and Access to Medicines", Earthscan, pg. 19–22, 2006.

690 Fact Sheet: TRIPS and Pharmaceutical Patents, Obligations and Exceptions. See, https://www.wto.org/english/tratop_e/trips_e/factsheet_pharm02_e.htm#importing. Also see, Vandoren Paul and Van Eeckhaute Jean Charles, "The WTO Decision on Paragraph 6 of

August 2003 following which, the first amendment to the TRIPS Agreement was adopted on 6th December 2005 while the temporary waiver continued until countries adopted the decision.[691] The amendment came in to effect on 17th November 2017 with two-third of the WTO members formally accepting it.[692]

It introduces *Article 31bis*, which states,

1. The obligations of an exporting Member under Article 31(f) shall not apply with respect to the grant by it of a compulsory licence to the extent necessary for the purposes of production of a pharmaceutical product(s) and its export to an eligible importing Member(s) in accordance with the terms set out in paragraph 2 of the Annex to this Agreement.
2. Where a compulsory licence is granted by an exporting Member under the system set out in this Article and the Annex to this Agreement, adequate remuneration pursuant to Article 31(h) shall be paid in that Member taking into account the economic value to the importing Member of the use that has been authorized in the exporting Member. Where a compulsory licence is granted for the same products in the eligible importing Member, the obligation of that Member under Article 31(h) shall not apply in respect of those products for which remuneration in accordance with the first sentence of this paragraph is paid in the exporting Member.
3. With a view to harnessing economies of scale for the purposes of enhancing purchasing power for, and facilitating the local production of, pharmaceutical products: where a developing or least developed country WTO Member is a party to a regional trade agreement within the meaning of Article XXIV of the GATT 1994 and the Decision of 28 November 1979 on Differential and More Favourable Treatment Reciprocity and Fuller Participation of Developing Countries (L/4903), at least half of the current membership of which is made up

---

the Doha Declaration on the TRIPS Agreement and Public Health – Making it Work", 6 The Journal of World Intellectual Property, pg. 789, November 2003.

691 Decision of 30th August 2003, to implement the Doha Declaration available at, https://www.wto.org/english/tratop_e/trips_e/implem_para6_e.htm; For further details of countries which have already accepted the decision and other details see: http://www.wto.org/english/tratop_e/trips_e/amendment_e.htm.

692 Out of total 164 members 110 needed to ratify by 31st December 2019 and the amendment took effect on 17.11.2017. See https://www.wto.org/english/tratop_e/trips_e/amendment_e.htm.

of countries presently on the United Nations list of least developed countries, the obligation of that Member under Article 31(f) shall not apply to the extent necessary to enable a pharmaceutical product produced or imported under a compulsory licence in that Member to be exported to the markets of those other developing or least developed country parties to the regional trade agreement that share the health problem in question. It is understood that this will not prejudice the territorial nature of the patent rights in question.

4. Members shall not challenge any measures taken in conformity with the provisions of this Article and the Annex to this Agreement under subparagraphs 1(b) and 1(c) of Article XXIII of GATT 1994.
5. This Article and the Annex to this Agreement are without prejudice to the rights, obligations and flexibilities that Members have under the provisions of this Agreement other than paragraphs (f) and (h) of Article 31, including those reaffirmed by the Declaration on the TRIPS Agreement and Public Health (WT/MIN(01)/DEC/2), and to their interpretation. They are also without prejudice to the extent to which pharmaceutical products produced under a compulsory licence can be exported under the provisions of Article 31(f).

10.4 TRIPS Amendment: Patent Exhaustion Enabling Parallel Trade

A careful study of the global discourse to address the HIV/AIDS public health crisis that led to the amendment of the TRIPS Agreement will show that a balanced relationship between IPRs and human rights is necessary.[693] Developing countries needed to carefully incorporate these flexibilities into their laws to enable them to utilise them in time of need.[694] It has been noticed that the ratification itself and the adoption of *Article 31bis* has been very slow due to cumbersome administrative requirements for implementation.[695] After the amendment, countries without the capacity to manufacture pharmaceutical products domestically under grant of CL, should be able to import the patented products from another country under CL however practically that has

693 Gumbel, Mike, "Is Article 31Bis Enough? The Need to Promote Economies of Scale in the International Compulsory Licensing System", Vol. 22, Temple International & Comparative Law Journal, No. 1, pg. 164, 2008.

694 Global initiatives to create technologies for human development, Human Development Report, released by the United Nations Development Programme (UNDP), pg. 105, 2001.

695 Ibid at 693, pgs. 185–190.

not been the case. If a country facing public health crisis does not have the capacity to manufacture the medicines domestically under CL and needs to import, the conditions under TRIPS *Article 31bis* are even more stringent.[696]

This raises the question as to whether the amendment of the TRIPS Agreement and insertion of *Article 31bis* has provided the much-needed solution of availability of patented medicines at reasonable price in developing countries and developing countries. From its slow and reluctant implementation, the answer would not be difficult to guess however the reasons are many. Multitude of administrative requirements starting from notification to the TRIPS Council, to labelling and listing requirements increase the administrative burden of a resource crunched LDC.[697] There has been an over dependency on access of patented medicines through grant of CL either within the country domestically or through importation when the alternate option of using international exhaustion and allowing parallel trade is being neither cumbersome nor such restrictive is more favourable.

A WTO Member can exercise policy options that it considers most suitable to address access to patented products at low price. Parallel importation is an effective solution, which can be adopted broadly for all products and specifically for making the medicines available at reasonable (lower) price.[698] Earlier chapters have dealt at length how international exhaustion is the most suitable option from either the perspective of international trade due to its trade-enhancing ability or from the perspective of patent law where one would note that the purpose of a grant of patent is to protect the invention from unauthorised usage and not to allocate geographical markets. Parallel trade is possible only if a country adopts international exhaustion of IPRs and the Doha Declaration had clearly reconfirmed that a WTO Member can adopt any mode of exhaustion.

Following international exhaustion, allows parallel importation from markets where the price of the medicine is lowest enabling more patients to access the medicines at the same time not undermining the patent rights.[699] Hence experts often solicit in favour of parallel imports especially for pharmaceutical

---

696 See https://www.wto.org/english/docs_e/legal_e/31bis_trips_annex_e.htm.

697 Vincent Nicholas, "TRIP-ing Up: The Failure of TRIPS Article 31bis", Gonzaga Journal of International Law, pg. 21, 22, 23, 2020.

698 Europe Economics, "Medicines Access and Innovation in developing countries", pg. 23, Chancery House, September 2001.

699 Abbot Frederick, "The TRIPS Agreement, Access to Medicines, and the WTO Doha Ministerial Conference", 1 The Journal of World Intellectual Property, pg. 34, 2002.

products as an appropriate option.[700] The problem occurs when countries have different modes of exhaustion, since parallel trade would likely be considered illegal in the country practicing national exhaustion and infringement proceedings or border measures executed. To add to this problem of uncertainty, there has been an increasing tendency by proponents of national exhaustion to export it to other countries through contractual bindings often under prerequisites of bilateral trade agreements and FTAs.[701] These agreements are executed often conditional that the partner country also follows national exhaustion hence actually removing the country's ability to adopt any mode of exhaustion and engage in parallel trade.

The confusion in allowing or disallowing parallel trade is since some experts see parallel imports as a solution to the public health crisis while others see it as a problem. Those against parallel imports state,

> The problem, however, is most acute in that sector because, directly or indirectly, all the governments of Member States control the price of medicines at levels that vary – some by limiting the price that may legally be charged, others by negotiating with the IP holders to reduce their prices if they want the cost of the medicines to be paid or reimbursed by a national health service, etc.[702]

It is argued that if it is illegal to charge over certain bound rates in one country, the pharmaceutical company should be able to choose to sell it at higher rate in another country where it is possible, without having the profit neutralised by international exhaustion.

It is also often argued that the medicines sold for the developing countries at a relatively low price compared to the global market, would be bifurcated to industrialised-country markets as parallel imports, thus not serving the purpose of supplying the markets they are meant for. However, research by the World Health Organisation (WHO) has shown otherwise. WHO studies show that often pharmaceutical drugs are sold in developing countries at prices

700 The Indian delegation to the WTO TRIPS Council supported this view. See Minutes of the TRIPS Council Special Discussion on Intellectual Property and Access to Medicines, 18th–22nd June 2001. WTO Doc. No. IP/C/M/31, WTO, Geneva.

701 Some examples of it can be found in the FTAs signed by US with Singapore (2003), Australia (2004), Morocco (2004).

702 Korah Valentine, "Intellectual Property Law in the context of Competition Law: 'Consent' in relation to curbs of parallel trade in Europe", Fordham International Law Journal, pg. 973 (972–981) April 2002.

even higher than in industrialised countries hence these arguments do not hold ground.[703] It has also been addressed in earlier chapters that the argument of countries no longer choosing price differentiation hence the price in countries practicing international exhaustion will go up, is erroneous. Markets for pharmaceutical products are highly segmented where companies price same products differently depending on their demands and not necessarily paying capacity, which has been clearly established in the WHO study.[704] The only reason against parallel imports is it hinders their ability to make higher profits through dividing markets based on patent rights, hence banning of parallel imports by adopting national exhaustion. There might be indeed some valid concerns in specific cases that need to be addressed through appropriate checks and balance measures on a case-by-case basis.

Here while adopting international exhaustion, it must only be applicable to products manufactured under valid patent that has not been subjected to CL. Since in case of a CL the patent is effectively kept in abeyance as such the question of exhaustion cannot arise, thus cannot be included in parallel trade.

703 WHO, "More Equitable Pricing for Essential Drugs: What do we mean and what are the issues?", pg. 3, Background Paper prepared by the WHO Secretariat for the WHO – WTO Secretariat Workshop on Differential Pricing and Financing of Essentail Drugs, Hosbjor, Norway from 8th–11th April 2001. The paper states that because pharmaceutical purchases in developing and are mainly financed by individuals where they are negotiated individually prices of medicines are LDC often higher than those in developed countries where the prices are often negotiated by insurance companies or the government.

704 Ibid at 703.

CHAPTER 11

Exhaustion and Competition Policy: Patent Exhaustion and Its Relation with Competition Law and Policy

11.1 Competition Law and Policy in the Multilateral Trading System

Historically, evolution of '*IPR protection*' as a discipline of law and '*Competition law*' as a domain for regulating market competition have been separate and independent of each other.[705] As such their statutory goals have also been different. IPRS are aimed at protecting creativity in different forms of its applications, while the aim of competition law (also referred to as antitrust laws) have been to enable market competition. From their well-differentiated aims, one might be led to believe that these are two conflicting disciplines of laws, however that is not the case. On the contrary, these two disciplines complement one another while often interfacing with each other.[706]

The relationship between competition law and protection of IPRS is like balancing of static and dynamic efficiencies in the market. Competition law protects static efficiency through restraints on collusion, abuse of dominance, promoting entry of more competitors and increasing the benefits in the hands of the consumers. It facilitates reducing costs in the marketplace and helps refine existing products. On the other hand, protection of IPRS through incentivising innovation creates dynamic efficiency through new inventions, improved processes, products, etc. For this reason, both are required for consumer welfare hence there needs to be a balance through existence of both, IPRS and competition laws.[707] If the protection is extended beyond new knowledge or the statutory lead time is breached, then instead of dynamic efficiency there would be distortion of the market. Similarly, if competition law

705 Anderman, Steven, "The Competition law/IP 'interface': an introductory note", in Anderman Steven (eds.), "The interface between IPR and Competition Policy", Cambridge, pg. 1, (1–24), 2007.

706 Kolstad Olaf, "Competition law and intellectual property rights – outline of an economics-based approach" in Drexel Josef (eds), "Research handbook on Intellectual Property and Competition law", Edward Elgar Publishing Ltd., pg. 3, 4, 6 (3–26), 2008.

707 Nguyen Tu Thanh, "Competition Law, Technology Transfer and the TRIPS Agreement Implications for Developing Countries", Edward Elgar Publishing Ltd. pg. 33, 34, 37, 2010.

interventions are frequent or too intrusive, then there would not be sufficient incentives for innovation affecting dynamic efficiency. For such reasons, there exists the possibility of an IP owner acquiring a dominant position and then abusing the market power through its IP. Competition law steps in as checks and balance measure in such situations and market competition is restored.

Competition policy is of broad scope, laying down the guidelines for different stakeholders in a market to operate without any unnecessary restraint. While competition law is more a policy tool along with other tools that rests with the government to regulate the market. It is the government's competition policy that would determine the conditions that are suitable to allow maximum competition between private firms in the country and as such the government's responsibility to set the norms.[708] Multilateral trade regulations and competition laws work in tandem as a balance between protection, free competition and restrictions that are implemented through certain exceptions.[709]

IP or Intellectual assets have economic value hence we designate legal rights to these intellectual assets so that they can be protected, assigned and be used to generate market power. Competition law on the other hand regulates market power, including those generated with the help of these intellectual assets. Hence both the legal disciplines interface at different stages of their interplay in the market.[710] IPRs are guaranteed by law as a time-bound exclusivity for the creator when certain conditions are met. If the time period of such time-bound exclusivity is extended by manipulating the terms and conditions for which it has been accorded, or the terms and conditions are not met, the legitimate exclusivity granted through IPRs would distort the market hence lose its legality.[711]

Consumer welfare is the ultimate goal of competition policy of any country and the role of the competition regulator is to achieve it through effective market competition enabling maximum choice to the consumer at the best price

708 Hoekman Bernard and Holmes Peter, "Competition Policy, Developing Countries and the WTO", World Bank and CEPR No. 2211, pgs. 2, 3, 1999.

709 Schloegl Herwig, "Trade and Competition Policy Aspects of VERs: A Comment" in Petersmann Ernst-Ulrich and Hilf Rheinhard (eds.), "The new GATT Round of Multilateral Trade Negotiations", Kluwer Law, pg. 433, 1991.

710 Regibeau Pierre and Rockett Katharine, "The relationship between intellectual property law and competition law: an economic approach", Cambridge University Press, pg. 25, 2009.

711 Singham Shanker, "Competition Policy and the Stimulation of Innovation: TRIPS and the interface between competition and patent protection in the pharmaceutical industry", Brooklyn Journal of International Law, pg. 371 (363–415) 2000.

point.[712] Countries usually prefer to address consumer welfare through competition policy where consumer protection is either a result of it or addressed separately.[713] If a country has an effective competition policy in place then it would not only help the local consumers in getting the products at the most competitive price, but also help the local industries. For example, a good competition policy backed by effective competition law-enforcement mechanisms can be used to assess mergers and joint ventures so that there is balance between the market power in the hands of an entrepreneur and the availability of consumer choice. Further, technology transfer licence agreements may also be examined to make sure that the domestic industry is not adversely affected due to market aberrations.[714]

With monetisation-centric innovation and large-scale commercialisation of inventions where MNCs spend significant resources in R&D, protection of IPRs become crucial. However, tendencies to extend such IPRs beyond its intent can lead to anti-competitive market situations calling for regulators to step in. Questions like, '*What is free and fair competition?*'; '*What should be considered as profit beyond which it would constitute an abuse?*'; '*What role does IPRs play in creation of such profits?*'; '*When should the regulator step in?*' are often sources of debates and conflicts bringing to the fore the sensitive interplay between IPRs and competition law. Addressing such queries extend the discussion beyond competition law and involves competition policy interventions at large.

With increasing global trade where MNCs, often controlling such trade, governments had mooted the idea of establishing a global regulatory framework on competition law and policy. Subsequently, there were global efforts to introduce international competition law regulations. The main aim was to introduce competition law at the global level and make sure that while enhanced efforts were being made by governments to open markets, they were not prey to closure or capture by private corporate entities. Competition policy and law first reflected in the multilateral trading system when the ITO was planned. The ITO was expected to establish a non-discriminatory economic system

712 UNCTAD, "The benefit of competition policy for consumers", TD/B/C.I/CLP/27, pg. 8, 29th April 2014. Available at, http://unctad.org/meetings/en/SessionalDocuments/ciclpd27_en.pdf.

713 International Competition Network (ICN), "Competition Enforcement and Consumer Welfare Setting the Agenda", pg. 21, 22, 10th Annual Conference at The Hague held on 17th–20th May 2011.

714 Lahouel Mohamed and Maskus Keith, "Competition Policy and Intellectual Property Rights in Developing Countries: Interests in Unilateral Initiatives and a WTO Agreement", presentation at the WTO forum, "Developing Countries' in a Millennium Round, WTO Secretariat, Centre William Rappord", Geneva 20–21, September 1999.

among the members of the UN on a MFN basis.[715] Considering the existence of widespread influence of the international cartels in the 1930s, the ITO aimed at including measures on restrictive business practices.[716] The ITO's specific trade related section dealt with the trade in goods and services under the '*Havana Charter*' which elaborated on the issue of competition.[717] However the Havana Charter never became functional mainly due to the fear among US industries that it could become bigger than the sovereign and pose threat as a super-national (or supranational) authority.[718] Since the ITO did not take off as expected, focus was mainly diverted to the GATT along with being the forum for reducing trade tariffs and other measures to remove barriers to multilateral trade.

If one considers the efforts to bring competition issues in the GATT agreement, one would note that there is a general apprehension that neither the GATT 1947 nor the GATT 1994 provide any specific provision on competition law.[719] However a deeper study will show that not only attempts were made to frame rules on separate competition law and policy at the WTO, but these attempts are still on. Discussions on whether competition issues should be included in the GATT, began as early as 1958 when a group of experts examined whether restrictive business practices could possibly be treated through non-violation complaints.[720] This was perhaps the first time that competition policy issues were considered anywhere at a global platform. At the time when GATT 1994 was being negotiated there was another effort to introduce an international

715 Fikentscher Wolfgang, "Historical Origins and Opportunities for Development of an International Competition Law in the TRIPS Agreement of the World Trade Organization (WTO) and Beyond", in Beier and Shricker "From GATT to TRIPS – The Agreement on Trade – Related Aspects of Intellectual Property Rights", 27 Studies International Review of Industrial Property and Copyright Law (IIC), Max Planck Institute, Munich, pgs. 227–228, 1996.

716 Woolcock Stephen, "International Competition Policy and the World Trade Organisation", Paper presented at the LSE Commonwealth Business Council Trade Forum in South Africa, Content 2.0, Undated.

717 Ibid at 449.

718 Fox Eleanor, "Competition Law and the Millennium Round", Journal of International Economic Law pg. 666 (665–679) 1999.

719 Heinemann Andreas, "Antitrust Law of Intellectual Property in the TRIPS Agreement of the World Trade Organisation", in Beier and Shricker "From GATT to TRIPS – The Agreement on Trade – Related Aspects of Intellectual Property Rights", 27 Studies International Review of Industrial Property and Copyright Law (IIC), Max Planck Institute, Munich, pg. 239, 1996.

720 Roessler Frieder, "Should Principles of Competition Policy be incorporated into WTO Law through non-violation complaints?", Journal of International Economic Law, pg. 413 (413–421) 1999.

competition law under the GATT. This was the *'Draft International Antitrust Code'* (DIAC) negotiated during 1991–1995 and modelled to be a plurilateral agreement within the WTO system that was being established.[721] The DIAC aimed at establishing structured competition law with systematic provisions for implementation, including elaborate provision for IPRS. *Article 6,* of the DIAC provided for, *'Restraints in Connection with Intellectual Property Rights'* where *Section* 2 stated,

> Licensing of Intellectual Property Rights: It is part of the legal content of an intellectual property right to grant, during the life of the right, licenses which may be exclusive and territorially restricted and to impose on a licensee justified obligations and restrictions.[722]

There were other efforts too, by different organisations to harmonise competition issues internationally. The OECD made recommendations in 1976 to stop restrictive business by MNCS.[723] UNCTAD brought out its *'Rules for the Control of Restrictive Business Practices'* in 1980.[724] Discussions are still on in these forums but mainly to the extent of sharing global best practices. Here it must be mentioned that efforts in the US to synergize different competition regimes globally, also included the formation of *'International Competition Network'* (ICN). A brief look into the history will show that it started with the need to address competition / antitrust issues in the new developments in international trade and competition interface.

The International Competition Policy Advisory Committee (IPAC) was formed in 1997 and commissioned to recommend ways to address global competition / antitrust issues in the new dimension of global economic integration, e.g. large-scale mergers, etc. IPAC engaged with academia, governments and private enterprises came out with its first report in February 2000. In the

721 Fikentscher Wolfgang, "The Draft International Antitrust Code ("DIAC") In the Context of International Technological Integration – The Institutional and Jurisdictional Architecture", Volume 72 Issue 2 Chicago Kent Law Review, pg. 535, (533–543), 1996.

722 Gifford Daniel, "The Draft International Antitrust Code Proposed at Munich: Good Intentions Gone Awry", and its Appendix, "The Draft International Antitrust Code as A GATT-MTO-Plurilateral Trade Agreement", Volume 6 Issue 1, Minnesota Journal of Global Trade, pg. 29, (1–30) and Appendix pgs. 38, 39, (32–66), 1996.

723 OECD, "Guidelines for Multinational Enterprises", Declaration by OECD governments on International Investment and Multinational Enterprises, 21st June 1976.

724 UNCTAD, "Restrictive Business Practices Code" of the United Nations Conference on Trade and Development was finalised on 22nd April 1980 and adopted by the UN General Assembly as a consensual resolution on 5th December 1980.

final report, the US was asked to explore possibilities of creating a '*Global Competition Initiative*' platform for different competition law and policy stakeholders to interface globally. The idea of establishing an international competition network to interface competition authorities and other stakeholders on a single platform, gathered impetus. Later at IPAC's Brussels conference in September 2000, it was endorsed by both the US and the EC. And subsequently in February 2001 at the International Bar Association's meeting further endorsements came from more than 40 senior competition officials. Finally, the ICN was formed on 25th October 2001 with senior officials from competition authorities of 14 countries with the meeting in New York city.[725]

The ICN can be credited with the development of competition law regimes in number of countries and streamlining antitrust adjudication by providing a common platform to competition authorities from different jurisdictions. It is important to note that ICN is the only global network that addresses competition law enforcement and engages significantly in sharing best practices within members. Through its working groups, it regularly engages in training and capacity building, shares papers, holds webinars and contributes positively towards the evolution of the global competition law domain.

11.2 Competition Law/Policy and IPRs within the GATT/WTO Regime

Institutional work at the WTO on competition regulation in the formative years of WTO encouraged some of its members to introduce competition issues. Subsequently a WTO Working Group on Trade and Competition Policy (WGTCP) was established at the Singapore Ministerial Conference in 1996 and the WGTCP brought out a number of papers (the Competition law issues along with others raised in the meeting was later often referred to as one of the Singapore issues).[726] It was further taken up after few Ministerial Meetings at the Doha Ministerial in 2001 and was agreed by some members that there was need to get clarity on what would be the core principles to focus, modalities of voluntary cooperation, provisions on hardcore cartels, etc. to determine the scope of the agreement. However, there was strong opposition from the developing countries against introducing competition policy as an agenda item.[727]

725 For the International Competition Advisory Committee and the formation of International Competition Network see, https://www.internationalcompetitionnetwork.org/about/.

726 The first Ministerial Conference of the WTO was held at Singapore from 9th until 13th December 1996. Competition issues was discussed and the WGCTP was set up. Details available at, https://www.wto.org/English/tratop_e/comp_e/history_e.htm.

727 The Hindu, "India warns against Singapore issues at the WTO", June 2003.

Lacking consensus on the modalities for competition policy, it reached a deadlock at the Cancun Ministerial in 2003.[728] Later in the July package of 2004 it was decided that considering the priorities of the Doha Round, Singapore issues, including competition policy shall not be taken up any further and the Working Group was made inactive.[729] However the discussions on competition regulation within the WTO is still on and in 2018 the Economics, Research and Statistics department published a Working Paper on Competition Policy. The paper aimed at collating all the work done so far under the aegis of WTO and includes recent developments in the Competition Law and Policy discipline globally as well as under different regional agreements. In essence it reflects upon the important synergies that link multilateral trade and competition policy considering the ongoing work by other international agencies like the ICN.[730]

Critics of including Competition Regulations within the WTO is of the opinion that the WTO would not have the power to restrain the MNC from forming cartels since these would be under national jurisdiction. To add to this, developing country members argue that such competition regulations could become a constraint in a developing country's economic growth hence necessary transition might be required.[731] One would need to understand the reasons for the strong divide between the industrialised nations on one side and the developing countries and LDCs on the other on the issue of framing competition regulations within the WTO. '*The international conflict can roughly be summarised as one between trade officials in exporting countries trying to force open markets set against officials in poorer importing countries trying to ensure economic development in their nations through industrial policy space.*'[732] The MNCs in these countries have global market power operating in multiple

728 The Cancun Ministerial reached a deadlock on Competition policy (Non acceptance of Singapore issues). Details available at, https://www.wto.org/English/thewto_e/minist_e/min03_e/min03_14sept_e.htm.

729 The Singapore issues dropped in the July package and working group became defunct. Details available at, https://www.wto.org/English/tratop_e/dda_e/draft_text_gc_dg_31july04_e.htm.

730 Anderson D. Robert, Kovacic E. William, Mueller C. Anna and Sporysheva Nadezhda, "Competition Policy, Trade and the Global Economy: Existing WTO Elements, Commitments in Regional Trade Agreements, Current Challenges and Issues for Reflection", Staff Working Paper WTO ERSD-2018-12, 31 October 2018. Available at, https://www.wto.org/english/res_e/reser_e/ersd201812_e.pdf.

731 Singh Ajit, "Competition Policy, Development and Developing Countries", Working Paper No. 50, Indian Council for Research on International Economic Relations, pg. 27, 1999. Available at, http://icrier.org/pdf/wto7.pdf.

732 Sandrey Ron, "WTO and the Singapore Issues", No. 18 TRALAC Working Paper, pg. 19, 2006.

markets in any given time, whereas the size of most of the firms in the developing countries are usually much smaller thus creating worries among these countries. Developing countries fear that while they would open the competition in their market, they would not be able to restrain the hard-core cartels nationally and would have to depend on the global governance of the WTO.[733]

Further, industrialised countries like Switzerland had proposed unconditional and unqualified NT.[734] The developing or LDCs were reluctant to agree to NT obligations since they want to retain necessary policy space to increase the cost of entry for the MNCs to their market. With Competition rules framed under the WTO, any country that would try to protect their domestic market would become actionable before the WTO DSB. In such scenario, there is a fear that considering the asymmetrical powers of the MNC, this would lead to competition complaints against the developing countries and LDCs. Hence the developing countries called for differential treatment for domestic firms subject to size and efficiency of local firms.[735]

It is also stated that the WTO is not structured as a market regulator,

> Because competition law is typically enforced through judicial or quasi-judicial bodies, dispute settlement bodies of the WTO should not be given the ability to review competition decisions (or judgments) taken in specific cases by national competition authorities (or courts). Their task should exclusively be to assess, when if there is a complaint against a country, whether the government of that country has lived up to its commitment to enact a (non-discriminatory and transparent) law, establish a competition authority, and provide for cooperation with the competition authorities of other countries.[736]

---

733 ICTSD, "The Singapore Issues: Investment, Competition Policy, Transparency in Government Procurement and Trade Facilitation", Volume 1 (6) Doha Round Briefing Series, pg. 3, February 2003. EU was the only country agreed to outright ban hardcore cartels while all the other industrialised countries preferred voluntary cooperation. Details in https://www.wto.org/english/forums_e/ngo_e/iisd_singapore_e.pdf.

734 Switzerland stressed rule of law based transparent 'National Treatment'. Details available at, https://docs.wto.org/dol2fe/Pages/FE_Search/FE_S_S009-DP.aspx?language=E&CatalogueIdList=7356,1998,2060,46167,1625,25828,54923,83896,68482,80668&CurrentCatalogueIdIndex=6&FullTextHash=&HasEnglishRecord=True&HasFrenchRecord=True&HasSpanishRecord=True.

735 Communications from India available at https://docs.wto.org/dol2fe/Pages/FE_Search/FE_S_S009-DP.aspx?language=E&CatalogueIdList=6397,35679,25805,42310,44426,74607,63445,71416,34053,14015&CurrentCatalogueIdIndex=5&FullTextHash=&HasEnglishRecord=True&HasFrenchRecord=True&HasSpanishRecord=True, reflects the message.

736 AGCM, "International Trade and Competition Policy: the WTO Experience".

The above argument is on the premise that competition complaints are factual in nature. As such, the DSB would need to identify the problems based on the domestic market conditions of the concerned member and then obtain all confidential documents for investigation completely depending on the member hence completely at the mercy of the member.[737] Irrespective of whether competition regulation is included in the WTO regulatory regime as an independent discipline or otherwise, there is already a trilateral interface between IPRs, International Trade and Competition laws, operating as checks and balance measures within the WTO through the TRIPS Agreement.

11.3 Competition Law/Policy TRIPS and Parallel Imports

The TRIPS Agreement was introduced with the intention to restrain trade in counterfeit and pirated goods. However, by the time the agreement was negotiated and signed, it introduced minimum level of harmonised protection for a wide gamut of IPRs. Further, with the introduction of intricate rules for each type of IPRs – about their acquisition and management as well as enforcement mechanisms, it turned out to be a comprehensive agreement on IPRs which also includes competition law provisions. In case of patents, these provisions cater to cases where, by virtue of the market power gained by the indispensability of patents, competitors could be unduly excluded through anti-competitive means. Such action could be investigated for abuse of dominance by the relevant national adjudicators for breach of market competition. Because there is no competition law provision under the WTO, the TRIPS includes such provisions by which members can take necessary corrective action nationally.[738]

As such, the *Preamble* of the TRIPS, *Articles 8(2), 31 and 40* are some examples where competition law elements step in as checks on IPRs. With the minimum standard of protection of IPRs being established within the larger WTO membership through the TRIPS Agreement, there is enhanced protection of IPRs in the member countries. This also increases the chances of restrictive contractual licence obligations by MNCs controlling multiple markets. As far as the ambit of patent or any other IP licenses, this would be considered empowering the holder of IPRs to contractually control movement of a licensed product,

737 Hoekman Bernard and Mavroidis Petros, "Economic Development, Competition Policy and the WTO", World Bank Research Working Paper 2917, pg. 24, October 2002.

738 Kaur Annette and Levin Marianne, "The IPT Project – proposals to reform the TRIPS Agreement", in Ghidini Gustavo, Peritz Rudolph and Ricolfi Marco (eds.), "TRIPS and Developing Countries", Edward Elgar Publishing Ltd., pgs. 175, 176 (163–215), 2014.

hence determine the mode of exhaustion of IPRs through license agreements. Given that market competition becomes intensive whenever the export price of a commodity is low, this often prompts the authorised distributor in a country to control distribution of rights and restrict legitimate competition in an anti-competitive manner acting as export cartels.

The issue of export cartels can be addressed appropriately by managing the exhaustion of the patent right. As such, a country adopting national exhaustion would result in an unproductive export cartel extending to an anti-competitive level. On the other-hand, international exhaustion would restrict possibilities of such export cartels by enabling parallel trade. Although one might argue in favour of national exhaustion claiming no welfare gain happens through parallel imports since the welfare gain at the end of the consumers is negated by the welfare loss of producers. However, given the fact that the producer already has his/her share of welfare gain by obtaining royalty, parallel imports only enable to transfer the additional gain to the consumers without any loss to the producers, hence such argument is baseless.

There is also the classic argument of free riding on the authorised manufacturer and distributor. The free riding argument as discussed earlier, usually made in case of trademark exhaustion also does not hold ground since the expenses are borne for promoting the IPRs of its owner. It is in the *Grundig, Consten* Case of 1966, that the anticompetitive market power of the IP owner (in this case the trademark owner), exercised through national exhaustion was first exposed. The case, discussed earlier, dealt with parallel importation of German Grundig products into France by its authorised distributor in France named Consten SaRL. Against Grundig and Consten's complained of infringement to the EC, the EC had decided in favour of exhaustion under the Treaty of Rome to support free movement of goods within the EU market. The ECJ, deciding on appeal against the EC decision, addressed the anti-cartel aspect of the European law and confirmed the EC's order.[739]

This was the first time that anti-cartel in European Competition law was applied in terms of regional market integration and international exhaustion was allowed, albeit within the EC, thus propounding what came to be known as regional exhaustion. From then onwards, it has been construed that the effect of restrictions on parallel imports enable market segmentation harming market competition.[740] Competition regulatory framework would not

739 Ibid at 107. Forsyth Miranda and Rothnie Warwick, "Parallel imports", Cambridge University Press, pg. 457, (429–465).

740 Ibid at 739, pg. 457.

only provide corrective measures to rectify abusive monopoly but also restrain abuse of monopoly by preventive measures, e.g. by mandating international exhaustion.[741] Moreover, restricting parallel imports act like government permission in support of vertical restraints raised by the exclusive distributors through patents (and other IPRS) to restrict import competition. The admission of international exhaustion within the European common market have been already tested (of course within EU) successfully.[742] Now extending it to all WTO members should be the most logical conclusion from the multilateral trading platform under the WTO.

In case of patents too, arguments raised in support of curbing parallel imports also state that vertical restraints enhance efficiency in distribution of the patented product by restricting free riding.[743] They argue that, the patent holder would enhance their reach in the market through exclusive territorial dealership rights which would actually help them to monitor the quality of the products and enable marketing better quality.[744] This argument of maintaining quality through exclusive distributor channel is self-defeating since in any case the patent holder would have such control in the jurisdiction from where the product is first sourced through importation. Even in case of licensed manufacturing, the patent holder could allow the licensee to produce the patented product under specified terms and conditions of the licensed agreement. Hence, if interested in maintaining high quality, they can do so by specifying such monitoring requirement in the license agreement itself.

On the contrary it can be argued that in an oligopolistic market, allowing parallel trade would help in controlling collusive tendencies of patent holders to restrict possibilities of patent abuse. In this regard, it is argued that vertical restraints have pro-competitive focus.[745] It is claimed that if vertical restraints are allowed, it would increase the net revenue obtained through the IPRS by way of distributive efficiency and thus it would promote competition.[746] But

---

741 Grey Rodney, "The Conflict Between Trade Policy and Competition Policy: A Comment", in Petersmann Ernst-Ulrich and Hilf Rheinhard (eds.), "The new GATT Round of Multilateral Trade Negotiations", Kluwer Law, pgs. 447, 1991.

742 Ibid at 148, pgs. 79, 80, (78–90).

743 Anderson Robert, "The Interface Between Competition Policy and Intellectual Property in the context of the International Trading System", Journal of International Economic Law, pgs. 659 (655–678) 1998.

744 Chard and Mellor, "Intellectual Property Rights and Parallel Imports", 12 (1) World Economy, pgs. 69–84, 1989.

745 Frankel Suzy and McLay Geoff, "Intellectual Property in New Zealand", LexisNexis Butterworths, pg. 74, 2002.

746 Bork Robert, "The Rule of Reason and the Per Se Concept: Price Fixing and Market Division", Yale Law Journal, pg. 403, 1966.

that is not true in case of restricting parallel imports through such vertical restraints since there is no societal benefit. Such arguments overlook the fact that allowing vertical restraints on distribution would affect output negatively and increase monopoly rents leading to consumers being forced to purchase products that have an artificially raised price. It cannot be overruled that vertical control combined with private exclusive territorial rights through control of parallel imports would likely attract collusive behaviour among dealers of patented products. In such markets that are susceptible to cartels, vertical restraints are bound to reduce competition.[747]

It is also argued that allowing or disallowing parallel imports are not to be considered under IP law as exhaustion issue or under competition law as a ban on vertical restraints but can be controlled contractually.[748] The licence contract can strictly specify the market where the licensee can sell the product, thus allowing or restricting parallel importation. In effect this would be a case of implied licence where in absence of specific restriction of the market, it would imply that there was no restriction on parallel importation. But this means that due to the asymmetrical market power, especially in case of the MNC patent owners, there would always be a possibility of them restricting parallel importation contractually. In US and EU, the two initial jurisdictions where competition law evolved, it can be noticed that pricing has not been regulated by the competition authorities and has been left to the market. The logic being, even excessive pricing would attract substitutes, hence incentives to create and compete should not be hindered. Based on such logic, if there is any restraint on IPRS through competition adjudication, it would negatively affect innovation.[749] Hence competition law can effectively balance excessive IPRS only if it could be applied *ex-ante* where it could be imposed to address any possible market abuse. Applying competition law in an *ex-post* manner to rectify any possible market abuse would be an imperfect solution.[750]

It has already been mentioned that TRIPS has built-in provisions that members can use to take necessary corrective action against anti-competitive

747 Fox Eleanor, "Parallel Imports, The Intra-brand/Interbrand Competition Paradigm, and the Hidden Gap between Intellectual Property Law and Antitrust", Fordham International Law Journal 2002, pg. 983, 982–986.

748 Gallini Nancy and Hollis Adian, "A Contractual approach to the Gray Market", University of Calgary 1999.

749 Ibid at 739, pg. 457.

750 Fox Eleanor, "Can Antitrust Policy Protect Global Commons from the Excesses of IPRS?" in, Maskus Keith and Reichman Jerome (eds.) "International Public Goods and Transfer of Technology under a Globalized Intellectual Property Regime", Cambridge University Press, pg., 758–769, 2005.

practices. However, there are multiple issues that at present restrain TRIPS being used as an effective remedial measure against any such export cartel. First, under *Article 8*, members are free to adopt measures that they deem appropriate to address abuse of IPRs and further *Article 40* enables action under competition laws only within national jurisdictions where there is no harmonisation nor mandate with the article itself. Hence it is completely depending on the domestic legislation of a WTO member as to whether it addresses distribution goals of competition law and take corrective measures. Secondly, one can notice that these provisions are adapted from prevailing US and EU practices that are conceptually focused on innovation-centric competition policy rather than distribution-centric competition policy. This completely changes any possible action based on human-rights aspects of distributive goals that would determine access issues.[751] Hence taking necessary action even under *Article 31 (k)* TRIPS might not be possible.

As mentioned, none of these provisions to address anti-competitive abuses have any specific remedial measures hence the competition policy provisions in the TRIPS Agreement are permissive rather than perspective.[752] Attempts to enforce the competition policy provisions in TRIPS effectively would also face technical challenges since there could be coordination problems in absence of any harmonious global standard as to what should be considered anticompetitive. Different jurisdictions could consider anticompetitive acts differently and further remedies imposed in one jurisdiction based on local market circumstances could impact economic welfare in another jurisdiction in negative manner.[753]

Moreover, the TRIPS Agreement in its present form, is interpreted to let owners of IPRs use their discretion to allow or restrict parallel importation

751 Ibid at 657.

752 Anderson Robert, "Intellectual Property Rights, Competition Policy and International Trade: Reflections on the Work of the WTO Working Group on the Interaction between Trade and Competition Policy (1996–1999)", in Cottier Thomas and Mavroidis Petros (eds.), "Intellectual Property: Trade Competition & Sustainable Development", Michigan University Press, pg. 251 (235–265), 2003; Also, Anderson, Feuer, Rivard & Ronayne, "Intellectual Property Rights and International Market Segmentation", in Anderson Robert and Gallini Nancy (eds.), "Competition Policy and Intellectual Property Rights in the Knowledge-Based Economy", University of Calgary Press, pgs. 424, 425, 1998.

753 Anderson Robert, Kovacic William, Mueller Anna Caroline and Sporysheva Nadezhda, "Competition Policy, Trade and the Global Economy: Existing WTO Elements, Commitments in Regional Trade Agreements, Current Challenges and Issues for Reflection", Staff Working Paper ERSD-2018-12, World Trade Organization, pgs. 16, 17, and 18, 31 October 2018.

exclusively, hence adopt either international, national or regional exhaustion.[754] One needs to consider that with such flexibility on one hand and strengthened laws on IPRs on the other, the possibility of encouraging export cartels through IPRs would increase if parallel imports can be restricted. Hence restricting parallel importation would not be considered anticompetitive by a member's competent national adjudicatory body if the country adopted national or regional exhaustion. A country would intend to introduce competition laws that would necessarily focus exclusively on issues that might affect their economy on short term and hence might not be interested in curbing export cartels.[755] These competition clauses in the TRIPS agreement have so far not proved to be sufficient and hence it has been argued that an international competition regulation is necessary.[756]

In absence of any international agreement on restriction on export cartels, countries with competition laws would choose to restrict export cartels based on whether it harms domestic competition.[757] This would not be sufficient deterrence from the perspective of multilateral trade. E.g. A country might have comparative advantage in producing a patented product locally, more efficiently under license not just for the local market but also for exports. If the country's laws allow parallel imports while being silent on parallel exports, the patent holder could restrict the market of the patent licensee contractually hence restraining possibility of parallel exports. Since this would not harm the domestic market competition, the domestic competition regulator would not intervene, but this would restrict other WTO members to benefit from such trade.

754 Anderson Robert, "Intellectual Property Rights, Competition Policy and International Trade: Reflections on the Work of the WTO Working Group on the Interaction between Trade and Competition Policy (1996–1999)", in Cottier Thomas and Mavroidis Petros (eds.), "Intellectual Property: Trade Competition & Sustainable Development", Michigan University Press, pg. 251 (235–265), 2003; Also, Anderson, Feuer, Rivard & Ronayne, "Intellectual Property Rights and International Market Segmentation", in Anderson Robert and Gallini Nancy (eds.), "Competition Policy and Intellectual Property Rights in the Knowledge-Based Economy", University of Calgary Press, pg. 424, 425, 1998.

755 Molina del Pozo Carlos Fransisco, Martinez Gutierrez Enrique and Pescador Diaz Javier, "International Cooperation in Antitrust Enforcement: The European Perspective", in Alexandre Daniele / Petchsiri Apirat (eds.), "Trade Regulations between the EU and ASEAN", Nomos Verlagsgesellschaft Baden-Baden, pg. 49, 2000.

756 Cottier Thomas and Meitinger Ingo, "The TRIPS Agreement without a Competition Agreement?", at the "Fondazione Eni Enrico Mattei Trade and Competition in the WTO and Beyond", pg. 7, Venice 4th–5th December 1998.

757 Suslow Valerie, "The Changing International Status of Export Cartel Exemptions", Volume 20, Issue 4 American University International Law Review, pg. 815 (785–828), 2005.

Even when international exhaustion is the most suitable mode of exhaustion from competition law perspective, political considerations influenced by influential manufacturers' associations had restrained members from adopting international exhaustion at the WTO. Further, the flexibility of choice of exhaustion has enabled mixing different exhaustion modes for different IPRs in the same country. This has complicated the applicability of exhaustion even more, a country that practices international exhaustion might find their home industry at a disadvantage if their trade partners have a different mode of exhaustion thus they might be compelled not to follow international exhaustion.[758] Even if a country has competition law provisions guiding towards international exhaustion, if it's an importing country with a strong industry lobby which is against international exhaustion, it may chose non-application of competition law.

If we consider its effect on developing countries, given the fact that developing countries are usually net importers of IP, it is often considered as '*IP tax*' on its citizens. Although they would have no other provision to excuse such '*tax*', the international exhaustion allowing parallel imports would balance it. Appropriate market driven returns for the patent being obtained on one hand by first sale of the patented product, '*double-tipping*' through additional patent revenues would be restricted.[759] Hence domestic importers in these countries would be able to source patented products from anywhere in the world where it is cheapest, leading to more efficient allocation of resources and better prices for all consumers. However, just by introducing international exhaustion in developing countries would not suffice, since trade barriers under the multilateral trade regime of WTO would still exist. Hence there is need to introduce international exhaustion regime within the WTO membership in a harmonious manner. Necessary restrictions on application of international exhaustion on certain cases where that would lead to unwanted trade distortions can also be introduced under *Article XX (d)* GATT. E.g. where products are not under

---

758 Conde Gallego Beatriz, "The Principle of Exhaustion of Rights and its Implications for Competition Law", Volume 34 (2) IIC, pg. 491, 492 (473–580), 2003.

759 Anderson Robert, "Intellectual Property Rights, Competition Policy and International Trade: Reflections on the Work of the WTO Working Group on the Interaction between Trade and Competition Policy (1996–1999)", in Cottier Thomas and Mavroidis Petros (eds.), "Intellectual Property: Trade Competition & Sustainable Development", Michigan University Press, pg. 251 (235–265), 2003; Also, Anderson, Feuer, Rivard & Ronayne, "Intellectual Property Rights and International Market Segmentation", in Anderson Robert and Gallini Nancy (eds.), "Competition Policy and Intellectual Property Rights in the Knowledge-Based Economy", University of Calgary Press, pg. 96, 1998.

patent protection or manufactured under government administered license controls, etc.

With '*Trade Facilitation*' one of the '*Singapore Issues*' making its way as agenda item and finally trade facilitation being adopted, new aspirations have been noticed on the competition and investment issues. However, disagreement on independent competition regulations under the WTO and given that the burden of framing competition law measures to check abusive market aberrations will shift back to national jurisdictions of members have been of paramount concern. Hence it did not make its way even to the WTO Ministerial meeting at Buenos Aires in December 2017. The issue of exhaustion is not dependent on a dedicated competition policy/law at the WTO since it can be addressed through an amendment of the TRIPS. Hence while the members consider deciding on introducing competition regulation as an independent discipline within WTO, it is proposed that international exhaustion be introduced through an amendment of the TRIPS Agreement.

Conclusion and Final Remarks

CHAPTER 12

Conclusion and Recommendation: Adoption of International Exhaustion of Patents, Globally

12.1 Purpose of Patent Protection, Ubiquity and Need for Balance

A patent is set of rights granted by the State to the inventor of a novel (new) product or process of making a product, involving an inventive step (which is non-obvious for a person ordinarily skilled in the art) and has industrial applicability (or practically useable). The rights enable the inventor to exclude others from direct competition for a limited period of 20 years from the date of filing of the patent (as per the TRIPS Agreement) against the most important requirement of '*enabling disclosure*'. This requirement of mandatory enabling disclosure is important since it elaborates the invention to the general public and provides the best mode to practice it. As a result, innovation is incentivised by rewarding the inventor with legal protection to exclude any third party from unauthorised use while disclosure helps in dissemination of knowledge. Further, the limited duration of the patent also serves the purpose of balancing private rights and public interest in the invention.

Whether patents incentivise to invent or it just helps in raising investments as has been argued by Fritz Machlup (discussed earlier in this book) is debatable. But there is no doubt that the legal exclusivity enhances costs and in areas of technology where public and social interests are critical, patents can impose significant costs for developing countries.[760] One would also argue that in certain fields of technology where possibility to imitate an invention is equally difficult and expensive as inventing it, the legal exclusivity through patents would only lead to market distortion.[761] In any such scenario, because of the ubiquitous nature of patents (which enables existence of the same patent rights over multiple number of units of a product situated at different places

760 Abbott Frederick, Correa Carlos and Drahos Peter, "Emerging markets and world patent order: The forces of change", in Abbott Frederick, Correa Carlos and Drahos Peter (eds.), "Emerging Markets and the World Patent Order", Edward Elgar Publishing Ltd., pg. 9, 2013.

761 Encaoua David, Guellec Dominique and Martinez Catalina, "Patent systems for encouraging innovation: Lessons from economic analysis", Journal of Economic Law, pg. 1425, (1423–1440), 2006.

DOI:10.1163/9789004542815_014

at the same time), the patent rights become a very powerful tool in controlling different markets at any single time.

Considering the above facts, the patent holder can charge the consumer higher than the competitive price for the product. This power to charge higher price than the marginal cost of the product introduces static inefficiencies where some consumers pay more while others cannot even access the product due to high price. If the patented product does not have any alternative, then there might be a monopolistic situation raising the possibility of abuse of the monopoly. On the other hand even if there are alternatives, they might not be as efficient as the patented technology, hence the exclusivity would further distort the market.[762] In such scenario among other tools to balance the private rights and enhance access to patented technology products or the processes, exhaustion of patents steps in as an appropriate balance.

As it has been discussed in the analysis and arguments put forward in this book, the patent system is not solely transactional but an amalgamation of two goals, private incentives and public good. Given these two contradictory goals of the patent system, we have noticed that along with conferring benefits to the society, it also imposes costs. This makes it essential to put in place different mechanisms to balance the goals so that the patent system can contribute to societal welfare. Exhaustion of patents is one of the most important factors in the IP system as it balances the private nature of IPRS and its consumer benefits aspect.

12.2 Patent Exhaustion in Different Countries: Need for Uniform International Exhaustion

Exhaustion of patents have been one of the ways that countries have tried to address the ubiquitous nature of patents and balance market exclusivity on one hand and access on the other. As has been presented in this book, the UK approach has been more of contractual nature following the doctrine of implied license. As per the doctrine of implied license, the sale of a physical product would also include not only the rights to use the IP but also to part with it (unconditional sale) unless expressly restrained to do so. Hence if there is a sale of a patented product, in absence of any express notice curtailing

762 Rothnie A. Warwick, "Parallel Imports", Sweet & Maxwell, pg. 108, 1993.

further distribution of the product, it is implied that the patent right is also licensed to the purchaser along with the product.[763]

The argument in favour of implied license is based on the laws of contract that provides the patent holder (as seller or licensor) to determine what conditions of sale might be negotiated, i.e. whether markets would be defined, etc. Hence in absence of any such conditions either by intention or by oversight, the patent holder should be able distribute (re-sell and/or import and/or export) the patented product further without infringing the patent. However, the patent holder would still be able to enforce the patent in case of unauthorised manufacture of the patented product or further distribution if the product has been altered or repaired or modified in a manner that the patent has been infringed. It is important to note that although in effect implied license through unconditional sale would enable parallel importation, it is not a case of exhaustion of rights. In this case there is no exhaustion of rights as such but completely based on the contractual terms or their absence.

As we have discussed in this book, Josef Kohler, an eminent German jurist, academic and judge, introduced the doctrine of exhaustion, as a concept in one of his writings. He opined that the common proprietary right of the owner should prevail over the IP right of the product. This opinion was used to interpret the *Duotal* case by the German Imperial Supreme Court of the time in 1902 where the term '*Konsumtion*' was used.[764] The literal English meaning of konsumtion would be '*consumption*' referring to being consumed. In other words, exhausted, where '*exhaustion*' implies that once an IP embedded product is placed in the market by virtue of sale or any other mode of distribution against which the patent holder receives a payment, the patent holder exhausts the right to enforce the patent against further distribution. At the time Kohler introduced the doctrine, the exhaustion referred in terms of the movement of the patented product from one German State to the other. However, there was no indication of whether the exhaustion should be restrained within the boundaries of the State or should it be extended internationally.

From analysis presented in this book it will be noticed that while the foundation of the doctrine of implied license is contracts, in case of exhaustion of patents, it is an interface between patent laws and international trade regulation. Whether the patent owner can restrict movement of the patented

763 Christopher Heath, "Patent Exhaustion rules and self-replacing technologies", in Irene Calboli and Edward Lee edited, "Research handbook on Intellectual Property Exhaustion and Parallel Imports", Edward Elgar Publishing Ltd., pg. 291 (289–307), 2016.

764 Reichgericht in Zivilsachen (RGZ) 50, 362 – "*Duotal*", cited by Christopher Heath, Also see Ibid at 105, pg. 16.

product from one territory to another would depend on '*adopting appropriate legal technique*' to create a State imposed embargo or in other words a non-tariff barrier to trade.[765] This practice of restraining exhaustion within national boundaries developed in the practice of the '*national exhaustion*' mode and when exhaustion triggered by placing the product anywhere in the world, the mode of '*international exhaustion*' came into existence.

It has been presented in this book how national exhaustion imposes constraints in free movement of patented products from one market to the other. It is for this reason the EU as a regional bloc adopted international exhaustion within the regional bloc. However ironically, they also adopted the more trade restrictive national exhaustion while trading with countries outside EU/EFTA. Subsequently this was established as a hybrid mode by consecutive rulings of the ECJ and came to be referred to as '*regional exhaustion*' (which was later codified).[766] If a country allowed international exhaustion of patents, then third parties in a country would be able to buy the patented products anywhere in the world and import it to the country at parallel to the official distribution channel of the patent holder. This is referred to as '*parallel imports*', whereas if the patents exhausted only within national boundaries, then the patent holder could enforce the patents and restrict entry of parallel imports.

Different countries adopted different models in dealing with patents and movement of patented products from one country to the other. Many following the colonial ties in UK followed the practice of implied license while few others followed the French practice of destination rights where the destination of the products follow the rights of the country of origin. Some others followed international exhaustion and some the national exhaustion mode. There have also been efforts to model regional blocs in Latin America in line with the European practice of regional exhaustion but as elaborated in this book, they have not been that successful. The mode of exhaustion that a country prefers to adopt, depends on its market and has been found that countries that are net importers of patented products or broadly other IPR products prefer to follow international exhaustion enabling entry of parallel imports in the country. On the other hand, those who are net exporters of IPR products prefer to restrict parallel imports.

Since each country practices different modes of exhaustion, as trade expanded beyond boundaries, this difference often culminated in legally enabled obstructions to trade. This not only leads to confusion, e.g. a country

765 W.R. Cornish, "Intellectual Property: Patents, Copyrights, Trade Marks And Allied Rights", Sweet & Maxwell London, pg. 23, 1981.

766 Ibid at 62, pgs. 425, 426.

might follow international exhaustion for patents but national exhaustion for copyrights, as in Australia. By enabling WTO Members to follow any mode of exhaustion in a decentralised manner, the ultimate goal of removal of illegitimate barriers to trade is far from achieved. Among WTO members where the patent owners have strong influence, there is a tendency to opt for national exhaustion. It has been presented through elaborate analysis in the different chapters of the book as to how such practice creates market distortion. To balance such distortions, members may be tempted to use CL provisions or other market regulations. A harmonised practice of international exhaustion while exercising strict patent rights, would balance the two differing interests. Moreover, this would also balance the trading interests of the industrialised countries on one hand and the developing countries and LDCs on the other.

Harmonisation of international exhaustion should not just be restricted to patents but across industrial property rights since none can operate in isolation or in other words, they often are embedded in a complete marketable product. In a hypothetical case, where parallel importation of a patented product is allowed, if it needs to be packed with an instruction manual and packaged with writings and diagrams which are copyright protected, following national exhaustion in copyrights would mean that the packaging with leaflets be sourced separately for the parallel imports. Further, in absence of international exhaustion, a country might allow parallel imports but restrict parallel exports contractually, thus hindering open market competitions globally. Moreover, it has been presented in this book that having different exhaustion modes in different countries defeat the purpose of multilateral trade based on comparative advantages of production, calling for harmonising exhaustion into international exhaustion with necessary conditions.

12.3 Patent Exhaustion and Multilateral Trade: Need for Removal of Non-Tariff Barriers

Today's global trade regime has come a long way since the 1930s when '*nationalism*' reached an abusive interpretation in Europe leading to the World War II. After the war when sense prevailed, with US leadership a new liberal economic order was set up in 1947 through the General Agreement on Tariffs and Trade (GATT). The aim was to systematically regulate global trade under a multilateral rule-based trading system focusing on reducing barriers to trade based on reciprocity. By doing so, the intention was to avoid such conflicting positions in trade that could lead to armed conflicts.[767]

The framers of the multilateral rules were careful not to touch the politically sensitive issues like trade in agriculture, services, investments and technology. IP was not included within the GATT regulatory regime at length, since trade in IP goods were not so significant while there were specialised international treaties for their governance. Interesting to note that the newly minted multilateral rules curved out neat grooves to fit in rules of the regional blocs.[768] It is much later in such setting that US introduced The Trade Act 1984 domestically where IPRs were introduced. After introducing IPRs in subsequent bilateral agreements, it first came up in the Tokyo Round in 1978 to restrain commercial counterfeiting.[769] With the initial focus on reducing tariffs and quotas, unfortunately the curve of liberalism gradually turned towards protectionism in the 1970s and the situation was even worse in 1980s with the global recession. Back at the GATT negotiations subjects presented failed to get included in the negotiating agenda.[770]

Finally, with the launch of the Uruguay Round in 1986, IPRs were gradually introduced as a part of the aim to fully integrate the global trading system and bring those issues that were left out earlier, within the realm of GATT. Hence along with the primary negotiations on new sets of rules on trade in agriculture and trade in services, IP was also included.[771] The very ambitious and challenging attempt finally was successful with the tariffs being lowered and phased out in time-bound manner. The most distinct and significant introduction of GATT 1994 was the dispute settlement mechanism, which also had retaliatory provisions thus having the strength of enforcement built-in and including IPRs within its realm.[772]

As has been presented in this book, one might question as to why IPRs were included in the trade negotiations. Trade liberalisation produces positive efficiency however high standards of IPRs harmonised at the minimum level of protection could hinder access to IP products and in such conditions would not necessarily culminate in positive efficiency.[773] On the other hand it was

767 Mckenzie Francine, "Free Trade and Freedom to Trade: The Development Challenge to GATT 1947–1968"' in "International Organizations and Development 1945–1990" by Mckenzie Francine, Springer, pg. 150, 2014.

768 Exceptions for PTA, RTA and FTAs included at the very beginning of the negotiations.

769 Ibid at 303, pg. 386, 387.

770 Ibid at 323.

771 Ibid at 332.

772 Ibid 332.

773 Ibid 314, pg. 43.

noticed that due to rising cost of manufacturing in the industrialised countries, they gradually diverted their R&D to services and IP products. While in other cases they restricted only to creation of IP and the physical production was often outsourced to developing countries. Most of the MNCs engaged in such manufacturing catered to the global market, hence if it was possible to harmonise the laws on IPRs in countries where they operate, it would reduce the MNCs' transaction cost. Further, with increase of such IP-centric trade, there was also increase in counterfeits and piracy. The industrialised country members of GATT wanted to introduce stricter rules on IPR and its enforcement and introduced it as rules restricting trade in counterfeits and pirated goods. But gradually what started as an agreement to restrain such trade in counterfeits, landed up in the far-reaching, elaborate and comprehensive IP regime under the TRIPS Agreement.

Ironically, although the very basis of the new GATT multilateral trading system is global welfare enhancing through removal and reduction of barriers to trade, the members failed to install international exhaustion of IPRs that facilitates reduction of trade barriers. Once patents (and other IPRs) were brought within the mainstream of multilateral trade rules for the purpose of protection against counterfeits, it should not have been allowed for market segmentation through modes of exhaustion. This is essential to avoid patents becoming a non-tariff barrier and going against the fundamental purpose of trade liberalisation.

It has been noted that although *Article 6* of the TRIPS Agreement allows WTO members to choose any mode of exhaustion, it has been presented in this book through elaborate analysis of TRIPS, GATT and GATS that any mode other than international exhaustion would not qualify under the WTO regulatory system. Practice of national and regional exhaustion distorts trade and would not pass the essential tests of exemption from NT and MFN either under TRIPS or GATT hence be actionable before the WTO's DSB. It is also argued that the caveat in *Article 6* which is expected to exempt parties from challenging any exhaustion mode before the DSB would not be the right interpretation since TRIPS cannot be read in isolation, but analysed under different Articles of TRIPS, GATT and GATS.[774] The argument that as patent rights are territorial and allows only national exhaustion under *Article 28 (1)*, no longer holds ground as this Article does not restrain international exhaustion. It restrains exhaustion to be taken up before the DSB.

774 Ibid 370, 155, 156, (148–189), 2011.

The patent rights granted by a WTO member under national laws in compliance of the TRIPS need to be compatible with GATT 1994. Hypothetically, if patented products sold legally in a WTO member country is restricted from being imported to another WTO country on grounds that the patent holder has not permitted importation, it would cause nullification and/or impairment of the trade benefits of the importing country.[775] Given that the patent holder is same, being a case of its licensee's product or the product of parallel patents, such discrimination based on the origin of the patented products causing nullification and/or impairment is actionable by the affecting WTO member under *Articles XXII and XXIII*. The analyses of *Article XX* as to whether general exceptions would trigger and exempt the practice of national or regional exhaustion of patents and thus restrict parallel trade has shown that such exemptions would only be allowed subject to necessity tests, establishing proportionality, especially under *Article XX (d)*.

The argument that *Article XX(d)* allows a WTO member to take necessary measures to protect IPRs, in this case, patents, have also been analysed and not denied. However, through interpretations of different AB and Panel decisions it has been established that restricting parallel imports is neither essential for protecting IPRs, nor the measures allowing only products manufactured domestically under same patent is a reasonable alternative. Further, being blatantly discriminatory, the measure would not qualify the chapeau on *Article XX* too.[776] However as argued, there might be certain conditions in which the patented products are imported, e.g. under grant of CL which would not qualify under the GATT or TRIPS rules and appropriately restricted.

Some experts have opined that the '*TRIPS is a lex specialis or sui generis, which as far as matters related to intellectual property protection are concerned has absolute precedence over the GATT*.'[777] But such views are also contested since the *lex specialis* nature of TRIPS is restricted to protection of IPRs and not beyond, while the issue of exhaustion enabling parallel imports is completely an issue of trade regulation. It is clear from the TRIPS Agreement that it did not aim to go beyond protection of IPRs in the realm of commercial

775 Elaborated in Chapter 7.1.3 of this book.

776 *Article XX (d)* states, "Subject to the requirement that such measures are not applied in a manner which would constitute a means of arbitrary or unjustifiable discrimination between countries where the same conditions prevail, or a disguised restriction on international trade, nothing in this Agreement shall be construed to prevent the adoption or enforcement by any contracting party of measures: ... (d) necessary to secure compliance with laws or regulations which are not inconsistent with the provisions of this Agreement, including those relating to ... the protection of patents, trademarks and copyrights."

777 Ibid at 376, pg. 142.

exploitation of IPRs and market access issues (like that of parallel importation) that accrue under GATT. Hence the argument that TRIPS as a special law supersedes GATT is not sustainable.[778]

The issue of exhaustion being one core issue in free movement of patented products from one country to another has also been addressed within different regional agreements. As argued earlier, apart from the fact that whether separate exhaustion regimes under regional trade pacts are in line with the multilateral rules, there has not been homogeneity in practice even among different trade blocs. Further, there has been increasing efforts by asymmetric power among partners of FTAs to install national exhaustion even when other partners of the FTAs existent practice have been international exhaustion.[779]

From the above it is evident that in absence of a global harmonised rule on exhaustion, attempts are made to remove trade benefits by restraining international exhaustion. Moreover, the various types of exhaustions practiced by the WTO members only add to problems of disharmony in multilateral trade. Automatically, countries facing exigencies like lack of access to patented pharmaceutical drugs would be tempted to opt for more severe options like CL rather than more trade-friendly options like parallel importation. Also, one cannot leave the important issue of allowing parallel imports to contractual decisions of member countries since it would enable restricting exhaustion through express notification.[780]

As mentioned earlier, apart from addressing patent exhaustion under GATT, the issue of exhaustion has also been analysed under GATS in this book. The relationship between liberalisation in trade in services that is related to patented technology and treatment under *Articles II* (*MFN*), *XVII* (*NT*) and *V and XIV* (*Exceptions*) are of utmost importance too. From the analysis of the provisions of different WTO agreements and different regional practices, it is argued that patents cannot be used as non-tariff barriers hence international exhaustion need to be adopted globally. At the same time legitimate concerns of re-imports of patented products, regulatory interventions like CL, price-caps, etc. while adopting international exhaustion, can be restricted through *Article XX* itself through elaborately laid down procedures. Following international exhaustion would also restrain IPRs being used as QRs without compromising their strict enforcement.

778 Ibid at 511.

779 Ibid at 380, pg. 2359.

780 Ibid at 657.

12.4 International Exhaustion of Patents – Balancing IPR Protection and Consumer Welfare through Competition Policy

It has been highlighted that price differentiation by patent holders in different markets based on demand and supply or due to other comparative advantages results in arbitrage. Such arbitrage would encourage legitimate trade outside the channel of the authorised distribution encouraging gain from the arbitrage enabled through parallel importation.[781] Allowing the patent holder to restrain such parallel trade would restrain market competition of legitimate alternates. Further, if there was market fixing through cartelization by the patent holder and its authorised distributors, parallel importation would remedy such cartels.[782]

'*In essence, a rule of international exhaustion is a tool for promoting competition and the efficient allocation of resources.*'[783] As has been argued earlier, IPRs increase the dynamic efficiency through the invention whether as new technology product or process. However, this also increases costs and due to the exclusivity involved in IPRs, there can be monopolisation that can further become abusive. In such scenario, competition policy brings static efficiency promoting enhanced access and lower prices through enhanced market competition resulting in higher consumer welfare. Restricting parallel imports would enable vertical restraints to be raised by exceeding the ambit of patents and increasing the price of the patented products.[784]

The argument that the vertical restraints would benefit the patent holder is true only within the first sale, where the patent holder is able to increase net revenue. After that it exceeds the net revenue from the patent and the revenue collected is only due to market segmentation where additional revenue is collected separately from each market riding on the patent. Restraining such exceeding ambit of a patent through the mode of exhaustion and enabling parallel imports would help increase the distributive efficiency and promote market competition.

It has been elaborated how there has been efforts to introduce exclusive international competition policy at the international level at the GATT/WTO as well as at other international forums without much success. However as

781 Ibid at 98, pg. 377.

782 Hewitt Garry, "Synthesis Report On Parallel Imports", Com/Daffe/Comp/Td (2002)18/Final, Directorate For Financial, Fiscal And Enterprise Affairs Trade Directorate, Joint Group on Trade and Competition OECD 26th June 2002.

783 Ibid at 55, pg. 18.

784 Ibid at 739, pg. 457.

discussed earlier, the TRIPS have competition law elements as checks and balance measures that can be used by national competition law agencies of WTO members to restrain anti-competitive market behaviour. The issue of exhaustion of IPRS need not be addressed under these provisions since it has been addressed exclusively in *Article 6* of the TRIPS Agreement. Instead, *Article 6* can be suitably amended to allow international exhaustion of patents across WTO membership as an *ex-ante* measure from the competition policy perspective subject to essential exceptions.

12.5 Addressing Parallel Imports under State Control and Restraints on Intellectual Property Rights

The above discussions have summarised why international exhaustion of patents is necessary considering different aspects of international trade governed under the WTO regulations. It is now important to elaborate those circumstances where international exhaustion should not apply and hence while recommending adoption of international exhaustion as a global rule, these circumstances should be considered as exceptions. The foremost being that international exhaustion can only trigger-in when the patent exists under market conditions without any market intervention or alteration of the rights, including by the State.[785] Broadly these interventions are categorised in two distinct sections as elaborated below.

12.5.1 *Restraint on Parallel Imports Due to Non-existence of Patents in Country of Export or Patents being Subject to Compulsory Licenses and Other Controls*

Patents are granted as unencumbered market exclusivity to provide lead-time over competitors and incentivise innovation. The aim is to enable the inventor to earn IP revenue as reward for introducing the invention and disclosing it. The inventor is allowed to charge an additional patent value when the patented product is sold or can charge royalty if it is licensed under market driven negotiated terms. The doctrine of international exhaustion triggers-in only after the patented product is first sold and revenue collected. The aim is to restrain repeat collection of patent revenue from different markets. However

785 National Economic Research Associates (NERA), SJ Berwin & Co and IFF Research, "The Economic Consequences of the Choice of a regime of Exhaustion in the area of Trademarks", Final Report for DGXV of the European Commission, London, 8th February 1999.

international exhaustion should not impact those products which are outside the purview of patents or do not enjoy unencumbered market access.

1. In case the patent does not exist because the country does not have a patent law or the invention is outside the realm of patents then such products would not qualify as parallel imports. If the patents do not exist in the first place, there is no possibility of exhaustion of the patent rights. E.g. A pharmaceutical company manufactures a drug under patent in country 'A' and apart from selling it in the country at US$ 100/-, exports and sells in country 'B' at US$ 70/- where the patent holder enjoys patent protection but the country practices international exhaustion of patents. Another pharmaceutical company legally manufactures a generic version of the same drug in country 'C' a LDC, where the law enables such production outside patents due to transitional exemptions under the TRIPS and sells at US$ 20/- in the country.

A trader in country 'B' buys the generic version of the drug in country 'C' and imports it to country 'B' claiming it to be parallel imports since country 'B' follows international exhaustion. The imports would not qualify under international exhaustion since although country 'B' follows international exhaustion, in the source country even when the generic drug was manufactured legally, there was no patent that would have exhausted on placing for distribution the first time. Hence such imports would have the characteristic of unauthorised production and considered to be an infringed product in country 'B' where the drug is protected under patent.

2. In case the patent is subject to and produced under a CL, or subject to price cap or quantity cap, the patent does not enjoy unencumbered market exclusivity. The revenue generated by sale or collection of royalty is not market driven but through government intervention. Patent exhaustion triggers when the patent holder has been able to obtain the patent value through first sale/distribution. In this case due to encumbrances, the patent holder is unable to raise revenue under competitive market conditions. In such scenario, patents should not be considered exhausted and parallel imports should not be allowed. If such parallel imports of patented products subjected to market regulation either by CL or any other means were allowed, it would distort trade.

One may argue that the CL or other State intervention could be to regulate anti-competitive behaviour by the patent holder. While such cases of market intervention by the State regulator through issuance of CL or any other measure might be justified, its appropriateness would depend on specific factors in the case. Any such decision of the regulator might be later subject to judicial intervention and declared unjustified. Allowing parallel imports of such cases of State intervention even if initiated for valid local reason, would create uncertainty, confusion and risk the possibility of distorting the importing market hence should not be allowed.

12.5.2 *Restraint on Parallel Imports due to Inferior Quality of Products*

Patents are often licensed for production in different countries to cater to different markets. Sometimes production under patent license differentiates qualities for different markets as a result the patented product manufactured under license may be of inferior quality. The instances of qualitative difference in the patented product and that produced under a license is like trademarks. The possibility of such inferior quality product manufactured under license being cheaper than that of other market where it is of higher quality cannot be ruled out. Once international exhaustion is applied, such patented products would also be subject to international exhaustion, but allowing parallel imports of such products would be unjustified and distorting the market by entry of poor-quality products. Allowing parallel imports of such inferior quality product in the market would create confusion in the minds of buyers. The customers might consider the quality of the cheaper product same as that of the higher quality, costlier product sold through the authorised distributor.

Necessary measures need to be taken to address such anomalies. Although one might argue that the decision to make the inferior quality product was that of the patent holder and even when the licensee produced it, quality control measures could be contractually implemented. Hence the authorised distributor of the patent holder should not be allowed to restrain entry of such parallel imports. Drawing parallels with cases of price differentiation when a patent holder sells the products cheaper at one market creating the source for parallel imports by way of re-importation, one might argue that parallel imports with different quality should be allowed. However, this is not an issue of restraining parallel imports to benefit the patent holder but a case of material difference between the patented product being sold by the authorised distributor of the patent holder and the parallel importer. In case of price differentiation, the consumer is not subject to any deception or confusion and gains from the distributive efficiency enabled through parallel importation. In the case of parallel importation of cheaper patented goods of inferior quality, the consumer suffers confusion and even deception by the patent holder for no error of judgment of the customer.

Restriction of parallel imports of such products would be logical but on the other hand this might also attract frivolous complaints from the authorised distributor with sole intention of restricting market competition. Even when the quality of the product might be same as that being sold by the authorised distributor, there may be allegations and parallel imports stopped from entering the market. Hence such cases of restricting parallel imports of inferior quality products manufactured under legitimate patent license should be on a case-by-case basis. The most appropriate way to establish a process of restricting trade in such inferior products can be by exercising *Article XX* (*d*) wherein such restriction shall need to pass the necessity test, the principle of proportionality and also qualify under the chapeau of *Article XX*.

For the reasons cited above, based on the international exhaustion of patents through licensing, irrespective of the quality of the parallel imports, they should be allowed. Given that whether a product is a genuine parallel import or a case of counterfeit can still be adjudicated domestically. As such the authorised local distributor or the patent holder's local representative should be allowed to initiate appropriate legal action in the jurisdiction to enjoin the sale of such parallel imports as unauthorised due to material difference of the products being sold. This would enable both the parties to be subjected to natural justice and if the patent holder or the authorised distributor can establish material difference to the extent of inferiority of the parallel imports, they shall be barred. This would also discourage prospective parallel importers from importing inferior quality products.

12.6 Amendment of the TRIPS Agreement: Proposed Draft Amended Text for Article 6, TRIPS

> The blurring of boundaries between disciplines, formalised frameworks for ownership of the developed knowledge and fair benefit sharing between partners to create niche domains are issues that society will have to cope with. The emerging scene in the near future will seek positive linkages between enhancing competition in society on one hand (discourage monopolistic practices) and establishing legal ownership of innovations (with enforcement of acquired rights) on the other. Strongly knitted societal, moral and ethical issues are getting intertwined into technology management, ownership of innovations and business process.[786]

The following text in *Article 6* of the TRIPS titled *'Exhaustion'*, *'For the purposes of dispute settlement under this Agreement, subject to the provisions of Article*

786 Ganguli Prabuddha, "Intellectual Property Rights – Unleashing the Knowledge Economy", Tata McGraw-Hill Publishing Company Ltd., pg. 12, 2001.

3 and 4, nothing in this Agreement shall be used to address of the exhaustion of intellectual property rights.' is proposed to be replaced by the text below:

> For the purpose of identifying the rights of the IP owner as provided in Article 28 and subject to the provisions of Articles 3 and 4 of this Agreement, the holder shall exhaust the IPRs in all forms once the IP protected product has been placed on the market of any WTO Member by the IP holder or with express authorisation of the IP holder. Such exhaustion shall take effect subject to the subsistence of un-encumbered IP rights in the country of first sale.
>
> The IP holder shall not be entitled to restrict importation/exportation of any form of the IP products from market of one WTO member to another either by contract or in any other manner, once the product has been distributed by the IP holder or with express authorisation of the IP holder in any of the WTO member country markets.
>
> Nothing shall restrain the IP holder to restrict importation/exportation of such products that are not IP protected in the country of exportation, either due to absence of necessary IP regulations and/or due to temporary or permanent withdrawal and/or suspension of the IP rights or restrictions on exercise of the IP rights, irrespective of reasons for the same.

As has been analysed in this book, patents increase costs to incentivise innovation but considering the ubiquitous nature of patents the market exclusivity legalised through patents could be extended beyond its ambit creating market distortion. It is argued that there is need to address such ubiquity and balance static and dynamic efficiencies. It has also been presented how different countries tried to address the issue through exhaustion of the patents on first sale of the patented products or products manufactured by the patented process. From the perspective of multilateral trade, restricting international exhaustion enables the patents to act as a non-tariff barrier hence functioning directly opposing to the aims of the multilateral trade regime governed by WTO regulations.

In today's scenario where trading between WTO members have immensely increased, it would be practical to allow international exhaustion with certain conditions rather than opt for other exhaustion modes and consider one's own products as infringed. One might argue as to when WTO members have not been able to come to a consensus on international exhaustion earlier during the TRIPS negotiations, how can it be resolved now. To address such arguments, one need to assess number of issues, the circumstances during the

TRIPS negotiations and at present are completely different. First, at the time TRIPS was negotiated, the exhaustion issue was not broadly tested in member countries. As has been presented, most of the countries national courts have decided in favour of international exhaustion in some form and some of the national governments have also adopted it. The application of regional exhaustion in EU and EEA has shown how international exhaustion has benefited in removal of trade barriers within the region hence it would be a successful model at the WTO. Further, the implementation of Doha Declaration confirmed that countries can adopt international exhaustion beyond doubt.

Finally, it has been proven that following international exhaustion reduces costs and is consumer welfare enhancing. In any country if IPRs become an access issue due to excessive costs, the government would be forced to intervene, whether by imposing CL or introducing price cap or other such measures. While CL measure is expected to be utilised as last resort but without any other effective means, they would increasingly become the easiest way of intervention. If WTO members adopt international exhaustion as standard practice, then the possibility of offsetting the high costs through legitimate cheaper imports would be automatic. The tendency of using CL or other State interventionist measures will be least hence benefitting all. Given that the WTO negotiations are now witnessing new issues like '*E-commerce*', '*Competition Policy*', and '*Trade-Facilitation*' at the contemporary Ministerial Rounds, international exhaustion might be introduced too. In such scenario a global regime of international exhaustion introduced through amendment of the TRIPS Agreement is being proposed in this book.

Bibliography

Abbott Frederick, Cottier Thomas, Gurry Francis, International Intellectual Property in an Integrated World Economy 4th edition, Aspen Case Book Series, Wolter Kluwer, 2019.

Abbott Frederick, “First Report (Final) to the Committee on International Trade Law of the International Law Association on the subject of Parallel Importation”, 1 JIEL 4, 1998.

Abbott Frederick, “WTO TRIPS Agreement and 1st Implications for Access to Medicines in Developing Countries”, Study Paper 2a, Commission on IPR, 2002.

Abbot Frederick, “The Doha Declaration on the TRIPS Agreement and Public Health: Lighting a dark corner at the WTO”, 5 (2) Journal of International Economic Law, 2002.

Abbott Frederick, “Parallel trade in pharmaceuticals: trade therapy for market distortions”, in Calboli Irene and Lee Edward (eds.), “Research handbook on Intellectual Property Exhaustion and Parallel Imports”, Edward Elgar Publishing Ltd., 2016.

Abbott Frederick, Correa Carlos and Drahos Peter, “Emerging markets and world patent order: The forces of change”, in Abbott Frederick, Correa Carlos and Drahos Peter (eds.), “Emerging Markets and the World Patent Order”, Edward Elgar Publishing Ltd. 2013.

Abbot Frederick, “Toward a new era of objective assessment in the field of TRIPS and variable geometry for the preservation of multilateralism”, 8 (1) Journal of International Economic Law, 2005.

Abbot Frederick, “The TRIPS Agreement, Access to Medicines, and the WTO Doha Ministerial Conference”, 1 The Journal of World Intellectual Property, 2002.

Abu–Ghazaleh (Intellectual Property Law firm), “Intellectual Property Laws of the ARAB countries”, Kluwer Law International, 2000.

Agreement on the Common Effective Preferential Tariff (CEPT) Scheme for the ASEAN Free Trade Area (AFTA), Jan. 28, 1992, art. 5, WIPO Lex. No. TRT/AFTA/001.

Alcaraz C.S. Isabel, “The Concept of necessity under the GATT and National Regulatory Autonomy”, Vol 10, Universidad Santo Tomas, Bogota, D.C., July – December 2015.

Alexandre Daniele / Petchsiri Apirat (eds.), “Trade Regulations between the EU and ASEAN”, Nomos Verlagsgesellschaft Baden-Baden, 2000.

Alexander Willy, “Exhaustion of Trade Mark Rights in the European Economic Area”, 24 E.L.R., Sweet, Maxwell and Contributors, 1999.

Amy S. Dwyer, “The GATT Uruguay Round: A Negotiating History (1986–1994), Trade Related aspects of Intellectual Property Rights, Volume IV: The End Game”, Terence P. Stewart (ed.) Kluwer Law International 1993.

Anderman, Steven, "The Competition law/IP 'interface': an introductory note", in Anderman Steven (eds.), "The interface between IPR and Competition Policy", Cambridge, 2007.

Anderson, Feuer, Rivard & Ronayne, "Intellectual Property Rights and International Market Segmentation", in Anderson Robert and Gallini Nancy (eds.), "Competition Policy and Intellectual Property Rights in the Knowledge-Based Economy", University of Calgary Press, 1998.

Andersen Henrik, "India – Solar Cells and Mexico – Taxes on Soft Drinks: Multilevel Rule of Law Challenges in the Interpretation of Art. XX (d) of GATT 1994 in WTO Case Law", Indian Journal of International Economic Law, Vol. X, 2019.

Anderson Robert, "The Interface Between Competition Policy and Intellectual Property in the context of the International Trading System", Journal of International Economic Law, 1998.

Anderson Robert, "Intellectual Property Rights, Competition Policy and International Trade: Reflections on the Work of the WTO Working Group on the Interaction between Trade and Competition Policy (1996–1999)", in Cottier Thomas and Mavroidis Petros (eds.), "Intellectual Property: Trade Competition & Sustainable Development", Michigan University Press, 2003.

Anderson Robert, Kovacic William, Mueller Anna Caroline and Sporysheva Nadezhda, "Competition Policy, Trade and the Global Economy: Existing WTO Elements, Commitments in Regional Trade Agreements, Current Challenges and Issues for Reflection", Staff Working Paper ERSD-2018-12, World Trade Organization, 31 October 2018.

Anderson, Bakst, Burton, Griffith, Gatsuo, Grezler, Haislmaier, Katz, Loris, O'Quinn and Roberts, "An Analysis of the United States-Mexico-Canada Agreement", Whiting K. Tory and Beaumont-Smith Gabriella eds., Backgrounder No. 3379, The Heritage Foundation, 28 January 2019.

Anderson Simon and Ginsburgh Victor, 7 (1) Review of International Economics, 1999.

Anell Lars, "Keynote speech at the TRIPS Symposium 26 February 2015" in Watal Jayashree and Taubman Antony (eds.), "The Making of the TRIPS Agreement Personal Insights from The Uruguay Round Negotiations" WTO, 2015.

Antons Christoph and Priapantja Cita Citrawinda, "Exhaustion and Parallel Imports in Indonesia", Jakarta, 1999.

Ariyanuntaka Vichai, "Exhaustion and Parallel Imports in Thailand", in Heath Christopher (ed.) "Parallel imports in Asia", Kluwer Law International, 2004.

Arrow Kenneth, "Economic Welfare and the Allocation of Resources for Invention", in the "Rate and Direction of Inventive Activity: Economic and Social Factors", Nelson (ed.), 1962.

Ayres Glyn and Mitchell Andrew, "General and Security Exceptions under the GATT 1994 and the GATS", in Carr Indira, Bhuiyan Jahid and Alam Shawkat (eds.), "International Trade Law and WTO", Federation Press, 2012.

Bagwell Kyle and Sykes O. Alan, "India Measures affecting the automotive sector", Volume 4, World Trade Review Special Issue S1, 2005.

Bailey Christopher and Wang Lucy, "Exceptions and Limitation", in Luginbuehl Stefan and Ganea Peter (eds.), "Patent Law in Greater China", Edward Elgar Publishing Ltd., 2014.

Beall F. Reed, "Patents and the WHO Model List of Essential Medicines (18th Edition): Clarifying the debate on IP and access", WIPO Global Challenges Brief, 2016.

Beier Friedrich-Karl, "Industrial Property and the Free Movement of Goods in the Internal European Market", 21 (2) IIC, 1990.

Brainbridge David, "Intellectual Property", Longman, 5th edition, 2002.

Balasubhramaniam K., "Access to Medicines and Public Policy Safeguards under TRIPS", in Bellmann Christopher, Dutfield Graham and Meléndez-Ortiz Ricardo (eds.), "Trading in Knowledge – Development Perspectives on TRIPS, Trade and Sustainability", Earthscan 2003.

Baldia Sonia, "Exhaustion and Parallel Imports in India", Heath Christopher eds., "Parallel imports in Asia", Kluwer Law International, 2004.

Barber Simon, "U.S. Witholds Benefits Over Zuma's Bill", Africa News, July 15, 1998.

Barett Margrett, "Intellectual Property cases and materials", West Group, 2001.

Barfield Claude and Groombridge Mark, "The Economic Case for Copyright Owner Control over Parallel Imports", 1 (6) The Journal of World Intellectual Property, 1998.

Barnes Stephen, "Pharmaceutical Patents and TRIPS: A Comparison of India and South Africa", 91 Kentucky Law Journal, 2003.

Barrett Margreth, "A Fond Farewell to Parallel Imports of Patented Goods: The United States and the Rule of International Exhaustion", Issue 12 E.I.P.R. 2002.

Barzel Yoram, "Economic Analysis of Property Rights", Cambridge University Press 2nd edition, 1989.

Bashar H. Malkawi, "Intellectual Property Protection from a Sharia perspective", 16 Southern Cross University Law Review, 2013.

Basheer Shamnad and Kochupillai Mrilani, "'Exhausting' Patent Rights in India: Parallel Imports and TRIPS Compliance", Journal of Intellectual Property Rights, Vol. 13, September 2008.

Basheer Shamnad, "India's Tryst with TRIPS: The Patents (Amendment) Act, 2005", 1 The Indian Journal of Law and Technology, 2005.

Beier Friedrich-Karl, "Industrial Property and the Free Movement of Goods in the Internal European Market", 21 (2) IIC, 1990.

Beintema-Interpharm and Centrafarm (Policy of the EEC) [1968] EUECJ R-24/67 (29 February 1968).

Bentham Jeremy, "Introduction to the Principles of Morals and Legislation" written in 1780 and published in 1789.

Bentley Lionell and Shaw Brad, "Intellectual Property Law", Oxford, 2014.

Bhagwati Jagdish, "Getting to Free Trade: Alternative approaches and their theoretical rationale", Free Trade Today, Princeton University Press, 2002.

Bhagwati Jagdish, "Regionalism and Multilateralism: An Overview", in de Melo Jaime and Panagriya Arvind (eds.), "New Dimensions in Regional Integration", Cambridge University Press, 1993.

Bhagwati Jagadish, "Free Trade Today", Princeton University Press, 2002.

Bhagwati Jagdish, "Regionalism and Multilateralism: An Overview", in Bhagwati, Krishna & Panagriya edited, "Alternative Approaches to Analyzing Preferential Trade Agreements", The MIT Press, 1999.

Blakeney Michael, "Trade Related Aspects of Intellectual Property Rights: A Concise Guide to the TRIPS Agreement", Sweet & Maxwell, 1996.

Bloche Gregg, "WTO Difference to National Health Policy: Toward an interpretive Principle", 5 (4), Journal of International Economic Law, 2002.

Bonadio Bonadio Enrico, "Parallel Imports in a Global Market: Should a Generalised International Exhaustion be the Next Step?", European Intellectual Property Review, 33(3), 2011.

Bond Patrick, "Globalization, Pharmaceutical Pricing and South African Health Policy: Managing Confrontation with U.S. Firms and Politicians", 29 (4) International Journal of Health Services, 1999.

Bork Robert, "The Rule of Reason and the Per Se Concept: Price Fixing and Market Division", Yale Law Journal, 1966.

Bossche Peter Van den and Werner Zdouc, "The Law and Policy of the World Trade Organization, Text, Cases and Materials", Cambridge University Press, 4th Edition, 2017.

Botoy Ituku Elangi, "From the Paris Convention to the TRIPS Agreement, A One-Hundred-and-Twelve-Year Transitional Period for the Industrialized Countries", 7 (1) The Journal of World Intellectual Property, 2004.

Bradley Jane, "Intellectual Property Rights, Investment and Trade in Services in the Uruguay Round: Laying the Foundations." 23 Stanford Journal of International Law, 1987.

Braga Carlos Primo and Fink Carsten, "The relationship between intellectual property rights and foreign direct investment", Duke Journal of Comparative and International Law, 1998.

Braga Carlos Primo, "The Economics of Intellectual Property Rights and the GATT: A View from the South", Brown Lonnie and Szweda Eric (eds.), "Trade Related Aspects of Intellectual Property", Vanderbilt Journal of Transnational Law, William S. Hein and Co. Inc., 1990.

Braga Carlos Primo, "Trade-related intellectual property issues: the Uruguay Round Agreement and its economic implications", in Maskus Keith (ed.), "The WTO, Intellectual Property Rights and the Knowledge Economy", Edward Elgar Publishing Ltd., 2004.

Bronckers Marco, "The Exhaustion of Patent Rights under WTO Law", 5 Journal of World Trade, 1998.

Brown Jeremy, "International Exhaustion in Europe", Les Nouvelles, September 1997.

Brainbridge David, "Intellectual Property", Longman, 5th edition, 2002.

Bryan Mercurio, "TRIPS-Plus Provisions in FTAS: Recent Trends", The Chinese University of Hong Kong, pg. 220, November 2006.

Burnside Michael, "The Community Patent Convention: Is it Obsolete in its Present Form", 8 EIPR, 1992.

Calboli Irene, "Trademark Exhaustion and Free Movement of Goods: A Comparative Analysis of the EU/EEA, NAFTA and ASEAN", Pg. 29, No. 25 Transatlantic Technology Law Forum, 2016.

Campolini Manuel, "Parallel Import of Pharmaceutical Products within the European Union: Could Adalat be a Bacon in the Dark for the Innovative Industry?", 1 International Trade Law Review, 2002.

Caroll John, "Intellectual Property Rights in the Middle East: A Cultural Perspective", 11(3) Fordham Intellectual Property, Media and Entertainment Law Journal, 2001.

Cattaneo Olivier, "The Political Economy of PTAS", in Simon Lester and Brian Mercurio edited, "Bilateral and Regional Trade Agreements: Commentary and Analysis", Cambridge University Press, 2009.

Chard and Mellor, "Intellectual Property Rights and Parallel Imports", 12 (1) World Economy, 1989.

Charnovitz Steve, "The Legal Status of the Doha Declarations", 5 (1) Journal of International Economic Law, 2002.

Chaudhuri Shubham, Goldberg Pinelopi and Jia Panle, "The effects of extending Intellectual Property Rights Protection to Developing Countries: A case study of the Indian Pharmaceutical Market", National Bureau of Economic Research Working Paper 10159 Cambridge MA 2003.

Chiappetta Vincent, "Working toward international harmony on intellectual property exhaustion (and substantive law)", in Calboli Irene and Lee Edward (eds.), "Research handbook on Intellectual Property Exhaustion and Parallel Imports", Edward Elgar Publishing Ltd., 2016.

Chiapetta Vincent, "The desirability of Agreeing to disagree: The WTO, TRIPS, International IPR Exhaustion and a few other things", in Introduction, 21 Michigan Journal of International Law, Spring 2000.

Chong John, "Exhaustion and Parallel Imports in Malaysia", in Heath Christopher (ed.) "Parallel imports in Asia", Kluwer Law International, 2004.

Christopher May, "A Global Political Economy of Intellectual Property Rights – The New Enclosures?", Routledge, 2000.

Clugston Christopher, "International Exhaustion, Parallel Imports and the Conflict between the Patent and Copyright Laws of the United States", 3 Beijing Law Review, Vol 4, 2013.

Commercial Finance Association (CFA), "Intellectual Property Issues Affecting a Secured Transactions Regime", March 2004.

Conde Gallego Beatriz, "The Principle of Exhaustion of Rights and its Implications for Competition Law", Volume 34 (2) IIC, 2003.

Condon Bradly, "NAFTA, WTO and Global Business Strategy – How AIDS, Trade and Terrorism Affect Our Economic Future", Quorum Books, 2002.

Condon J. Bradley, "GATT Article XX and Proximity of Interest: Determining the Subject Matter of Paragraphs b and g", Vol 9, UCLA Journal of International Law and Foreign Affairs, No. 2, Fall/Winter, 2004.

Cornish William, "Intellectual Property and Monopoly" in "Intellectual Property: Patents, Copyright, Trade Marks and Allied Rights", 4th edition, Sweet & Maxwell, 1999.

Cornish William and Lewelyn David, "Intellectual Property: Patents, Copyright, Trade Marks and Allied Rights", 5th edition Sweet and Maxwell, 2003.

Cornish William and Llewelyn David, "Intellectual Property: Patents, Copyright, Trade Marks and Allied Rights", 7th Edition, Sweet and Maxwell, 2010.

Cornish William, "(c) After manufacture: exhaustion of rights" while discussing the Scope of Monopoly in Patents in Chapter 6 of "Intellectual Property", 3rd edition, Sweet & Maxwell, 1996.

Cornish William, D. Llewelyn and T. Alpine, "Intellectual Property: Patents, Copyrights, Trade Marks and Allied Rights", Sweet & Maxwell, 2010.

Cornish William, "Intellectual Property: Patents, Copyrights, Trade Marks And Allied Rights", Sweet & Maxwell London, 1981.

Correa Carlos, "International Exhaustion of Rights", in "Trade Related Aspects of Intellectual Property Rights A commentary on the TRIPS Agreement", Oxford University Press, 2007.

Correa Carlos, "Intellectual Property Rights, the WTO and Developing Countries – The TRIPS Agreement and Policy Options", Zed Books Ltd., 2000.

Correa Carlos and Correa Juan, "Parallel imports and the principle of exhaustion of rights in Latin America", in Calboli Irene and Lee Edward (eds)., "Research handbook on Intellectual Property Exhaustion and Parallel Imports", Edward Elgar Publishing Ltd., 2016.

Correa Carlos, "Integrating Public Health Concerns into Patent Legislation in Developing Countries", South Centre, 2000.

Cottier Thomas and Oesch Matthias, "International Trade Regulation", Cameron May & Staempfli, Bern & London 2005.

Cottier Thomas, "Current and Future issues related to the TRIPS Agreement: A European Perspective" in "Trade and Intellectual Property Protection in WTO Law Collected Essays", Cameron May, 2008.

Cottier Thomas, "Intellectual Property and Mega-Regionals Trade Agreements: Progress and Opportunities Missed", in S Griller, W Obwexer, Erich Vranes (Eds.), "Mega-Regional Trade Agreements: CETA, TTIP and TiSA", Oxford University Press, 2017.

Cottier Thomas, "The Prospects for Intellectual Property in GATT", 28 Common Market Law Review, Kluwer Academic Publishers 1991.

Cottier Thomas & Schneider Lena, "The philosophy of non-discrimination in international trade regulation", in Sanders Anselm Kamperman edited, "The Principle of National Treatment in International Economic Law Trade, Investment and Intellectual Property" Edward Elgar Publishing Ltd., 2014.

Cottier Thomas, "The WTO System and the Exhaustion of Intellectual Property Rights", May 2000, Draft paper based on previous work presented to the conference on the Exhaustion of Intellectual Property Rights, ILA Trade Law Committee, Geneva 6th& 7th November, 1998.

Cottier Thomas, "The Value and Effects of Protecting Intellectual Property Rights within the World Trade Organization", presentation to the Association Littéraire et Artistique Internationale (ALAI), Journée,'études, 27th& 28th June, 1984.

Cottier Thomas, "The Doha Waiver and Its Effects on the Nature of the TRIPS System and on Competition Law. The Impact of Human Rights"' in Govaere Inge and Ullrich Hanns (eds.), "Intellectual Property, Public Policy and International Trade", "College of Europe Studies No.6", P.I.E. Peter Lang 2007.

Cottier Thomas and Meitinger Ingo, "The TRIPS Agreement without a Competition Agreement?", at the "Fondazione Eni Enrico Mattei Trade and Competition in the WTO and Beyond", Venice 4th–5th December 1998.

Cottier Thomas and Stucki Marc, "Conflit entre importations paralléle et propriéte intellectuelle? Actes du colloque de Lausanne, comparativa no. 60" translated by Meitinger Ingo as, "Parallel Imports in Patents, Copyrights and Industrial Design Law – The Scope of European and International Public Law", and reprinted in The International Intellectual Property System Commentary and Materials – Part 1, Kluwer Law International, 1999.

Cottier Thomas, "TRIPS, the Doha Declaration and Public Health", Vol. 6, No. 2 The Journal of World Intellectual Property, 2003.

Cottier Thomas, "Embedding Intellectual Property in International Law", in Roffe Pedro and Seuba Xavier (eds.), "Current Alliances in International Intellectual Property Law making: The Emergence and Impact of Mega-Regionals", Issue Number 4 ICTSD and CEIPI, September 2017.

Cottier Thomas, "Working together towards TRIPS" in Watal Jayashree and Taubman Antony edited, "The Making of the TRIPS Agreement Personal Insights from The Uruguay Round Negotiations" WTO, 2015.

Cottier Thomas, "The Common Law of International Trade and the Future of the World Trade Organization", 18 Journal of International Economic Law, 2015.

Cottier Thomas, Delimatsis Panagiotis and Diebold Nicolas, "Article XIV GATS: General Exceptions", in Wolfrum Ruediger, Stoll Peter-Tobias and Feinaugle Clemens (eds.) "Max Planck Commentaries on World Trade Law, WTO – Trade in Services", Vol 6, Martinus Nijhoff Publishers, 2008.

Cottier Thomas, "Parallel Trade and Exhaustion of Intellectual Property in WTO Law Revisited", in Ruse Khan Grosse Henning & Metzger Axel (eds.), "Intellectual Property Ordering Beyond Borders", Cambridge University Press, 2022.

Coyle Patrick, "Uniform Patent Litigation in the European Union: An Analysis of the viability of recent proposals aimed at unifying the European Patent Litigation System", Washington University Global Studies Law Review, Volume 11 issue 1, January 2012.

Crampes Claude and Hollander Abraham, "The pricing of pharmaceuticals facing parallel imports", Journal of Economic Law, University of Montreal, 2003.

Daniele Archibugi and Filippetti Andrea, "The Globalisation of Intellectual Property Rights: Four Learned Lessons and Four Theses", Volume 1, Global Policy, London School of Economics and Political Science and John Wiley and Sons Ltd., Issue 2, May 2010.

Danizon Patricia, "Pharmaceutical Price Regulation: National Policies versus Global Interests", The American Enterprise Institute, Washington D.C., 1997.

Danton Patricia, "The Economics of Parallel Trade", in Towse Ruth and Holzhauer Rudi (eds.), "The Economics of Intellectual Property", Edward Elgar Publishing Ltd., 2002.

Dasgupta Partha, "The Economic theory of Technology Policy: An Introduction" in Dasgupta Partha and Stoneman Paul (eds.), "Economic Policy and Technological Performance", Cambridge University Press, 1987.

Davis Mike, "Late Victorian Holocausts El Niño Famines and the Making of the Third World", Verso New York, 2001.

Dawar Kamala and Ronen Eyal, "How Necessary? A Comparison of Legal and Economic Assessments GATT Dispute Settlements Under: Article XX (B), TBT 2.2 and SPS 5.6", Vol 8 Trade Law and Development 1, 2016.

Daya Shanker, "Brazil, the Pharmaceutical Industry and the WTO" 5 (1) The Journal of World Intellectual Property Law 2002.

Daya Shankar, "Access to medicines, Article 30 of TRIPS in the Doha Declaration and an Anthropological Critique of International Treaty Negotiations", Deakin University – Bowater School of Management and Marketing, 2003.

Demaret Paul & Govaere Inge, "Parallel Imports, Free Movement and Competition Rules! The European Experience and Perspective", in Cottier Thomas and Mavroidis Petros (eds.), "Intellectual Property: Trade, Competition, and Sustainable Development, The University of Michigan Press, 2003.

Dhanjee Rajan and Chazournes Laurence Boisson de "Trade Related Aspects of Intellectual Property Rights (TRIPS): Objectives, Approaches and Basic Principles of the GATT and of Intellectual Property Conventions", 24 Journal of World Trade, 1990.

Dhar Biswajit and Rao Niranjan, "Transfer of Technology for Successful Integration into the Global Economy – A case Study of the Pharmaceutical Industry in India" (1–10), Document No. UNCTAD/ITE/IPC/Misc.22, UNCTAD New York and Geneva 2002.

Diebold F. Nicholas, "Non-Discrimination in International Trade in Services 'Likeness' in WTO/GATS", Cambridge University Press, 2010.

Dijk Theon van, "The Economic Theory of Patents: A Survey", MERIT Research Memorandum 2/94–017, Maastricht Economic Research Institute on Innovation and Technology, Netherlands, 1994.

Donald Barry and Ronald Keith, "Introduction: Changing Perspectives on Regionalism and Multilateralism" in Barry and Keith edited, "Regionalism, Multilateralism, and the Politics of Global Trade", UBC Press Vancouver, Toronto, 1999.

Draft Agreement on the Trade Related aspects of Intellectual Property Rights: Communication from the United States, GATT Doc. MTN.GNG/NG11/W/70, May 11, 1990.

Drahos Peter, Lokuge Buddhima, Faunce Tom, Goddard Martyn and Henry David, "Pharmaceuticals, Intellectual Property and Free Trade: The Case of the US-Australia Free Trade Agreement", 22 Prometheus, September 2004.

Drexel Josef, "EU competition law and parallel trade in pharmaceuticals: lessons to be learned for WTO/TRIPS?", in Jan Rosén edited, "Intellectual Property at the Crossroads of Trade", Edward Elgar Publishing Ltd., 2012.

Du Ming Michael, "Autonomy in setting appropriate level of protection under WTO law: Rhetoric or Reality?", Vol 13 Journal of International Economic Law, Volume 13, Issue 4, December 2010.

Dunkley Graham, "At whose service? Services and intellectual property in the Uruguay Round", in "The Free Trade Adventure", 1997.

Dutfield Graham and Sutherland Uma, "The international law and political economy of intellectual property", in "Global Intellectual Property", Edward Elgar Publishing Ltd., 2008.

Dwyer Amy, "Trade-Related Aspects of Intellectual Property Rights" in "The GATT Uruguay Round: A Negotiating History (1986–1994)", Volume IV: "The End Game", Stewart Terence (ed.), Kluwer Law International, 1999.

Dwyer Amy, "The GATT Uruguay Round: A Negotiating History (1986–1994), Trade Related aspects of Intellectual Property Rights, Volume IV: The End Game", Terence P. Stewart (ed.) Kluwer Law International, 1993.

Ebb Lawrence, "The Grundig-Consten Case Revisited: Judicial Harmonisation of National Law and Treaty Law in The Common Market", 6 University of Pennsylvania Law Review, Volume 115, 1967.

Encaoua David, Guellec Dominique and Martinez Catalina, "Patent systems for encouraging innovation: Lessons from economic analysis", Journal of Economic Law, 2006.

Endshaw Assafa, "Intellectual Property in ASEAN: A Survey" in "Intellectual Property in Asian Emerging Economies", Ashgate Publishing Ltd., 2010.

Europe Economics, "Medicines Access and Innovation in developing countries", Chancery House, September 2001.

European Parallel Importers Coalition (EPIC), "The Case for re-introducing Global Trademark Exhaustion in EU legislation", Position Paper, EPIC January 2001.

Fider Alex Ferdinand, "Exhaustion and Parallel Imports in the Philippines", in Heath Christopher (ed.) "Parallel imports in Asia", Kluwer Law International, 2004.

Fikentscher Wolfgang, "The Draft International Antitrust Code ("DIAC") In the Context of International Technological Integration – The Institutional and Jurisdictional Architecture", Volume 72 Issue 2 Chicago Kent Law Review, 1996.

Fikentscher Wolfgang, "Historical Origins and Opportunities for Development of an International Competition Law in the TRIPS Agreement of the World Trade Organization (WTO) and Beyond", in Beier and Shricker, "From GATT to TRIPS – The Agreement on Trade – Related Aspects of Intellectual Property Rights", 27 Studies International Review of Industrial Property and Copyright Law (IIC), Max Planck Institute, Munich, 1996.

Fink Carsten, "Entering the Jungle of Intellectual Property Rights – Exhaustion and Parallel Imports", Department of Economics, University of Heidelberg, Germany, 1999.

Fisher Matt, "Fundamentals of patent law: Interpretation and scope of protection", Bloomsbury, 2007.

Fisher William III and Rigamonti Cyrill, "The South Africa AIDS Controversy A Case Study in Patent Law and Policy", The Law of Business of Patents, Harvard Law School, Feb 2005.

Forsyth Miranda and Rothnie Warwick, "Parallel imports", Cambridge University Press, 2007.

Fox Eleanor, "Competition Law and the Millennium Round", Journal of International Economic Law 1999.

Fox Eleanor, "Parallel Imports, The Intra-brand/Interbrand Competition Paradigm, and the Hidden Gap between Intellectual Property Law and Antitrust", Fordham International Law Journal 2002.

Fox Eleanor, "Can Antitrust Policy Protect Global Commons from the Excesses of IPRs?" in, Maskus Keith and Reichman Jerome (eds.) "International Public Goods and Transfer of Technology under a Globalized Intellectual Property Regime", Cambridge University Press 2005.

Frankel Suzy and Gervais Daniel, "International intellectual property rules and parallel imports", in Irene Calboli and Edward Lee edited, "Research handbook on Intellectual Property Exhaustion and Parallel Imports", Edward Elgar Publishing Ltd., 2016.

Frankel Suzy, Gervais Daniel, "Plain Packaging and the Interpretation of the TRIPS Agreement", 5 Vanderbilt Journal of Transnational Law, Volume 46, November 2013.

Frankel Jeffrey with Stein Ernesto and Shang-Jin Wie, "Introduction to Regional Trading Arrangements" in "Regional Trading Blocs in the World Economic System", Institute for International Economics, Washington DC, October 1997.

Frankel Suzy and McLay Geoff, "Intellectual Property in New Zealand", LexisNexis Butterworths, 2002.

Frederick Abbott, "First Report (Final) to the Committee on International Trade Law of the International Law Association on the subject of Parallel Importation", 1 JIEL 4, 1998.

Freytag Christiane, "Parallelimportenach EG und WTO Recht", Dunckler and Humblot, Berlin 2001.

Friedman David, Landes William and Posner Richard, "Some Economics of Trade Secret Law", Journal of Economic Perspectives, 1991.

Fujino Jinzo, "Parallel Imports of Patented Goods – The Supreme Court Talks about Its Legality".

Gadbaw Michael, "Intellectual Property and International Trade: Merger or Marriage of Convenience?" in Brown Lonnie and Szweda Eric (eds.), "Trade-Related Aspects of Intellectual Property", 1990.

Gadbaw and Michael, Timothy J. Richards, "Intellectual Property Rights in the New GATT Round", Westview Press, 1988.

Gagne Gilbert and Rioux Michele, "Digital Trade", Springer, 2022.

Gallini Nancy and Hollis Adian, "A Contractual approach to the Gray Market", University of Calgary 1999.

Gallus Nick, "The Mystery of Pharmaceutical Parallel Trade and Developing Countries", 7 (2) The Journal of World Intellectual Property, 2004.

Ganea Peter, "A comparative study on parallel imports in patented and trademarked commodities in Japan and in the EU, discussed in the light of economic theory", Institute of Intellectual Property, Japan, March 2001.

Ganguli Prabuddha, Summary Report of the International Association for the Protection of Intellectual Property (AIPPI) released at the AIPPI Congress in Melbourne 2001.

Ganguli Prabuddha, "Intellectual Property Rights – Unleashing the Knowledge Economy", Tata McGraw-Hill Publishing Company Ltd., 2001.

Ganslandt Mattias, Maskus Keith, "Intellectual Property Rights, Parallel Imports and Strategic Behaviour", Journal of Economic Law, 2007.

Gerster Richard, "Patents and Development Lessons Learnt from the Economic History of Switzerland", Intellectual Property Rights Series, Third World Network 2001.

Gervais Daniel, "Exhaustion" in "The TRIPS Agreement: Drafting History and Analysis", Sweet & Maxwell, South Asian Edition, 2011.

Ghosh Shubha, "Incentives, contracts and intellectual property exhaustion" in Calboli Irene and Lee Edward (eds.), "Research handbook on Intellectual Property Exhaustion and Parallel Imports", Edward Elgar Publishing Ltd., 2016.

Gifford Daniel, "The Draft International Antitrust Code Proposed at Munich: Good Intentions Gone Awry", and its Appendix, "The Draft International Antitrust Code as A GATT-MTO-Plurilateral Trade Agreement", Volume 6 Issue 1, Minnesota Journal of Global Trade, 1996.

Gitter M. Donna, "International conflicts over patenting human DNA sequences in the United States and the European Union: An argument for compulsory licensing and a fair use exception", 76, New York University Law Review 6, 2001.

Glanslandt Mattias, Maskus Keith, "Intellectual Property Rights, Parallel Imports and Strategic Behaviour", IFN Research Institute of Industrial Economics, Working Paper No. 704, 2007.

Global initiatives to create technologies for human development, Human Development Report, released by the United Nations Development Programme (UNDP), 2001.

Glynn Dermot, "Article 82 and Price Discrimination in Patented Pharmaceuticals: The Economics", 3 European Competition Law Review, 2005.

Gold Michael, "European Patent Law and the Exhaustion Principle", University of Chicago Legal Forum, Volume 1992, Issue 1, 1992.

Govaere Inge and Demaret Paul, "The TRIPS Agreement: A Response to Global Regulatory Competition or an Exercise in Global Regulatory Coercion?", in Esty Daniel and Damien Geradin (eds.) "Regulatory Competition and Economic Integration", Oxford University Press, 2001.

Graff Garrett, "The Patent Trap" in The Harvard Magazine, July–August 2005.

Grey Rodney, "The Conflict Between Trade Policy and Competition Policy: A Comment", in Petersmann Ernst-Ulrich and Hilf Rheinhard (eds.), "The new GATT Round of Multilateral Trade Negotiations", Kluwer Law, 1991.

Grigoriadis Lazaros, "Trademarks and Free Trade: A Global Analysis", Springer 2014.

Gumbel, Mike, "Is Article 31Bis Enough? The Need to Promote Economies of Scale in the International Compulsory Licensing System", Vol. 22, Temple International & Comparative Law Journal, No. 1, 2008.

Gutterman Alan, "Innovation and Competition Policy", Kluwer Law, 1997.

Haedicke Maximilian and Timman Henrik, "Patent Law: A handbook on European and German Patent law", C.H. Beck, 2014.

Hamilton Merci, "The TRIPS Agreement: Imperialistic, Outdated and Overprotective" in Adam D. Moore (eds.), "Intellectual Property: Moral, Legal, and International Dilemmas", Lanham, MD: Rowman & Littlefield, 1997.

Hammer Peter, "Differential Pricing of Essential AIDS Drugs: Markets, Politics and Public Health", 4 (2) Journal of International Economic Law, Oxford University Press, 2002.

Harris Rachel and Moon Gilian, "GATT Article XX and Human Rights: What do we know from the first 20 years? GATT Article XX and Human Rights", Volume 16 Melbourne Journal of International Law 2, 2015.

Hart Michael, "A Matter of Synergy: The Role of Regional Agreements", in Donald Barry and Ronald Keith (eds.) "Regionalism, Multilateralism and the Politics of Global Trade", UBC Press Vancouver, Toronto, 1999.

Hartridge David and Subramanian Arvind, "Intellectual Property Rights: The Issues in GATT", 22 Vanderbilt Journal of Transnational Law, 1989.

Harvey Bale James, "The conflicts between parallel trade and product access and innovation: The case of pharmaceuticals", Journal of International Economic Law, 1998.

Haugen Hans Morten, "TRIPS and compatible protection", in "The right to food and the TRIPS Agreement", MartinusNijhoff Publishers, Boston, 2007.

Heath Christopher, "Patent Exhaustion rules and self-replacing technologies", in Calboli Irene and Edward Lee (eds.), "Research handbook on Intellectual Property Exhaustion and Parallel Imports", Edward Elgar Publishing Ltd., 2016.

Heath Christopher, "Legal Concepts of Exhaustion and Parallel Imports", in Christopher Heath edited, "Parallel Imports in Asia", Kluwer Law International, 2004.

Heath Christopher, "Parallel Imports and International Trade", 28 (5) IIC, 1997.

Heath Christopher, "From "Parker" to "BBS" – The Treatment of Parallel Imports in Japan", 24 (2) IIC, 1993.

Heinemann Andreas, "Antitrust Law of Intellectual Property in the TRIPS Agreement of the World Trade Organisation", in Beier and Shricker "From GATT to TRIPS – The Agreement on Trade – Related Aspects of Intellectual Property Rights", 27 Studies International Review of Industrial Property and Copyright Law (IIC), Max Planck Institute, Munich, 1996.

Helfer R. Lawrence, "Adjudicating Copyright Claims Under the TRIPS Agreement: The Case for a European Human Rights Analogy", in 39 Harvard International Law Journal, 1998.

Helfer Lawrence, "Regime Shifting in the International Intellectual Property System", No.1, Symposium: International Regime Complexity, Vol. 7, March 2009.

Hewitt Garry, "Synthesis Report On Parallel Imports", Com/Daffe/Comp/Td (2002)18/ Final, Directorate For Financial, Fiscal And Enterprise Affairs Trade Directorate, Joint Group on Trade and Competition OECD 26th June 2002.

Hilke John, "Free Trading or Free-Riding: An Examination of the theories and available empirical evidence on gray market imports", 32 World Competition, 1988.

Hoekman Bernard and Kostecki Michel, "The Political Economy of the World Trading System: The WTO and Beyond", 2nd Edition Oxford University Press, 2001.

Hoekman Bernard and Holmes Peter, "Competition Policy, Developing Countries and the WTO", World Bank and CEPR No. 2211, 1999.

Hoekman Bernard and Mavroidis Petros, "Economic Development, Competition Policy and the WTO", World Bank Research Working Paper 2917, October 2002.

Holder Sara, "Gulf Co-operation Council Countries – Patent Landscape", Rouse The Magazine, 16th January 2018.

Holyoak Jon and Torremans Paul, "Themes in Intellectual Property" in "Intellectual Property Law", Butterworths 1995.

Howse L. Robert and Tuerk Elisabeth, "The Impact on Internal Regulations – A Case Study of the Canada – EC Asbestos Dispute", in Burca d Grainne and Scott Joanne eds., "The EU and the WTO: Legal and Constitutional Issues", Hart Publishing, 2002.

Hudec Robert, "The ITO Legal System: Nullification and Impairment", in "The GATT Legal System and World Trade Diplomacy", 2nd Edition Butterworths, 1990.

ICTSD, "The Singapore Issues: Investment, Competition Policy, Transparency in Government Procurement and Trade Facilitation", Volume 1 (6) Doha Round Briefing Series, pg. 3, February 2003.

International Competition Network (ICN), "Competition Enforcement and Consumer Welfare Setting the Agenda", 10th Annual Conference at The Hague held on 17th–20th May 2011.

Jehoram Herman, "Prohibition of Parallel Imports through Intellectual property Rights", 30 (5) IIC 1999.

Johnston G Michael, "Meaning of the terms "Arbitrary or Unjustifiable Discrimination", in the Chapeau of GATT Article XX", Vol.6 Global Journal of Politics and Law Research, No.5, July 2018.

Jonquieres Guy de and Mallet Victor, "Failure at Cancún spurs trade deals in Asia – With the Doha round at a halt, more bilateral and regional accords are being negotiated", Financial Times, 16th October, 2003.

Katz Ariel, "The economic rationale for exhaustion: distribution and post-sale restraints" in Calboli Irene and Lee Edward (eds.), "Research handbook on Intellectual Property Exhaustion and Parallel Imports", Edward Elgar Publishing Ltd., 2016.

Kaunpoth Jakrit, "Intellectual Property Protection after TRIPS: An Asian experience" in Mallon Justin and Lawson Charles (eds.), "Interpreting and implementing the TRIPS Agreement Is it Fair?" Edward Elgar Publishing Ltd., 2008.

Kaur Annette, "Limitations and exceptions under the three-step test – how much room to walk the middle ground?" in Kur Annette and Levin Marianne (eds.), "Intellectual Property Rights in a Fair World Trade System", Edward Elgar Publishing Ltd., 2011.

Kawaguchi Hiroya, "Exhaustion of Patent right" in "The Essentials of Japanese Patent Law", Kluwer Law International, 2007.

Khan Zarina and Sokoloff Kenneth, "Historical perspectives on Patent Systems in economic development", in Netanel Neil Weinstock (ed.), "The Development Agenda Global Intellectual Property and Developing Countries", Oxford University Press, 2009.

Kieff Scott, "Quanta v LG Electronics: Frustrating Patent Deals by taking Contracting Options off the Table?", John M. Olin Program in Law and Economics, Stanford Law School, Working Paper No. 366, September 2008.

Kitch Edmund, "The Nature and Function of the Patent System", Journal of Law and Economics 20, 1977.

Kolstad Olaf, "Competition law and intellectual property rights – outline of an economics-based approach" in Drexel Josef (eds), "Research handbook on Intellectual Property and Competition law", Edward Elgar Publishing Ltd., 2008.

Kongolo Tshimanga, "TRIPS, the Doha Declaration and Public Health", 6 (2) The Journal of World Intellectual Property, 2003.

Korah Valentine, "Intellectual Property Law in the context of Competition Law: 'Consent' in relation to curbs of parallel trade in Europe", Fordham International Law Journal, April 2002.

Kosolkitiwong Punjaporn, "The legend and practical measures to prevent parallel imports", Special Topic Report to Anti-Counterfeiting Committee of Asian patent Attorneys' Association (APAA), 60th& 61st Council Meetings, 27–31 October 2012.

Krugman Paul and Obstfeld Maurice, "International Economics Theory and Policy", Pearson Education, 2000.

Kur Annette, "Limitations and exceptions under the three-step test – how much room to walk the middle ground?" in Kur Annette and Levin Marianne (eds.), "Intellectual Property Rights in a Fair World Trade System", Edward Elgar Publishing Ltd., 2011.

Kur Annette and Levin Marianne, "The IPT Project – proposals to reform the TRIPS Agreement", in Ghidini Gustavo, Peritz Rudolph and Ricolfi Marco (eds.), "TRIPS and Developing Countries", Edward Elgar Publishing Ltd., 2014.

Lahouel Mohamed and Maskus Keith, "Competition Policy and Intellectual Property Rights in Developing Countries: Interests in Unilateral Initiatives and a WTO Agreement", presentation at the WTO forum, "Developing Countries' in a Millennium Round, WTO Secretariat, Centre William Rappord", Geneva 20–21 September 1999.

Lam Ngo Van, "A perspective on Enterpreneurship, Intellectual Property Creation, Enterprise development and Competitiveness in ASEAN" Socio-economic Analysis Section, Poverty and Development Division, UNESCAP, 2005.

Lam Ngo Van and Wattanapruttipaisan Thitapha, "Intellectual Property Rights and Enterprise Development in ASEAN" 7 (1) The Journal of World Intellectual Property, 2004.

Landes William and Posner Richard, "The Economic Structure of Intellectual Property Law", The Belknap Press of Harvard University Press, 2003.

Land Molly, "Adjudicating TRIPS for development", in TRIPS and Developing Countries Towards a New IP World Order? Edward Elgar Publishing Ltd., 2014.

Langinier Corinne and Moshini Gian Carlo, "The Economics of Patents: An Overview", CARD Working Papers, 2002.

Lau, Laurence J., "The sources of East Asian economic growth" in F. Gerard Adams and Shinichi Ichimura (eds.) "East Asian Development: Will the East Asian Miracle Survive?" Praeger, London, 1998.

Levy I. Philip and Regan H. Donald, "EC Seal Products: Seals and Sensibilities (TBT Aspects of the Panel and Appellate Body Reports)", EUI Working Paper RSCAS 2014/138, 2014.

Lim Hoe, "Trade and Human Rights: What's at Issue?", 2 Journal of World Trade, Volume 35, 2001.

Loon Ng-Loy Wee, "The exhaustion doctrine in Singapore: different strokes for different IP folks", in Calboli Irene and Lee Edward (eds.), "Research Handbook on Intellectual Property Exhaustion and Parallel Imports", Edward Elgar Publishing Ltd., 2004.

Lydgate Emily, "Sorting out mixed messages under the WTO National Treatment Principle: A Proposed Approach", Vol 15, World Trade Review, Issue 3, 2016.

Machlup Fritz, "An Economic Review of the Patent System", Study No. 5, "Study of the Subcommittee on Patents, Trademarks and Copyrights of the Committee on the Judiciary, US Senate", 1958.

Malueg David and Schwartz Marius, "Parallel Imports, Demand Dispersion, and International Price Discrimination", 37 Journal of International Economics, 1994.

Mandich Giulio, "Venetian Patents (1450–1550)", 30 J. Patent & Trademark Off. Society, 1948.

Marceau Gabrielle and Reiman Cornelis, "When and how is a Regional Trade Agreement Compatible with the WTO", 3 Leg Issues Econ Integration 297, 2001.

Marwell C. Jeremy, "Trade and Morality: The WTO Public Morals Exception After Gambling", New York University Law Review, Vol 81, 2006.

Maskus Keith, "Benefiting from Intellectual Property Protection", in Bernard Hoekman, Aaditya Mattoo and Philip English edited, "Development, Trade and the WTO – A Handbook", The World Bank, 2002.

Maskus Keith, "Globalisation and the Economics of Intellectual Property Rights: Dancing the Dual Distortion", in "Intellectual Property Rights in the Global Economy", Institute for International Economics, Washington D.C., August 2000.

Maskus Keith, "Parallel imports in pharmaceuticals: Implications for competition and prices in developing countries", Final Report to World Intellectual Property Organisation, April 2001.

Maskus Keith, "Economic perspectives on exhaustion and parallel imports" in Calboli Irene and Lee Edward (eds.), "Research handbook on Intellectual Property Exhaustion and Parallel Imports", Edward Elgar Publishing Ltd., 2016.

Maskus Keith and Reichman Jerome, "The Globalization of Private Knowledge Goods and the Privatization of Global Public Goods", 7 (2) Journal of International Economic Law, 2004.

Maskus Keith, "Intellectual Property Rights in the Global Economy", Institute for International Economics, Washington D.C., 2000.

Matthews Duncan, "Lessons from negotiating an amendment to the TRIPS Agreement: Compulsory Licensing and access to medicines" in Westkamp Guido (ed.), "Emerging Issues in Intellectual Property", Edward Elgar Publishing Ltd. 2007.

Matsushita Mitsuo, "Issues Regarding Parallel Importation of Trademarked and Patented Products and Competition Policy in Japan", in Cottier Thomas and Mavroidis Petros (eds.), "Intellectual Property: trade, Competition and Sustainable Development", The Michigan University Press, 2003.

Matshushita Mitsuo, Schoenbaum J. Thomas, Mavroidis C. Petros and Hahn Michael, "The World Trade Organization Law, Practice and Policy", The Oxford International Law Library, 3rd Edition, 2015.

Mattoo Aaditya and English Philip (eds.), "Benefiting from Intellectual Property Protection" in, "Development, Trade, and the WTO – A Handbook", The World Bank, Washington D.C., 2002.

Mattoo Aaditya, "MFN and the GATS", in Cottier Thomas, Mavroidis Petros (eds.), "Regulatory Barriers and the Principle of Non-Discrimination in World Trade Law, Ann Arbor, The University of Michigen Press, 2000.

May Christopher and Sell Susan, "Intellectual Property Rights: A Critical History", Lynne Reinner Publishers, 2006.

May Christopher and Sell Susan, "Intellectual Property Rights A Critical History", Viva Books Pvt. Ltd., 2008.

May Christopher, "A Global Political Economy of Intellectual Property Rights – The New Enclosures?", Routledge 2000.

Mayne Ruth, "Regionalism, Bilateralism, and "TRIPS PLUS" Agreements: The Threat to Developing Countries" UNDP, 2005.

McGinnis John & Movsesian Mark, "The World Constitution" 114 Harvard Law Review at 2000.

Mckenzie Francine, "Free Trade and Freedom to Trade: The Development Challenge to GATT 1947–1968" in "International Organizations and Development 1945–1990" by Mckenzie Francine, Springer, 2014.

Mckinney Joseph, "NAFTA's effects of North American Economic Development: A United States Perspective" at the conference on, "NAFTA and the Future of North America: Trilateral Perspectives on Governance, Economic Development and Labour", University of Toronto, 7th February 2015.

McManis Charles and Contreras Jorge, "Compulsory Licensing of intellectual property: A viable policy lever for promoting access to critical technologies?" In, Ghidini Gustavo, Peritz.

McRae Donald, "GATT Article XX and the WTO Appellate Body" in Bronckers Marco and Quick Reinhard (eds.), "New Directions in International Economic Law – Essays in Honour of John H. Jackson", Kluwer Law International, 2000.

Meitinger Ingo, "Parallel Imports in Patents, Copyrights and Industrial Design Law – The Scope of European and International Public Law", The International Intellectual Property System Commentary and Materials – Part 1, Kluwer Law International, 1999.

Meitinger Ingo, "Parallel Imports into Switzerland – A Spot of Global Free Trade amidst Fortress Europe?" in Cottier Thomas and Mavroidis Petros (eds.), "Intellectual Property: Trade, Competition, and Sustainable Development", Michigan University Press, 2003.

Merwe Van der L. A., "The Exhaustion of Rights in Patent Law with specific emphasis on the issue of parallel importation", 3 Intellectual Property Quarterly, 2000.

Michael R. Gadbaw and Timothy J. Richards, "Intellectual Property Rights in the New GATT Round", Westview Press, 1988.

Milani Alireza, "The Legitimacy of Intellectual Property Rights in the Light of Islamic Law (Sunni and Shia Fiqh)", 7(3) World Journal of Islamic History and Civilization, 2017.

Milhem Moawiah, "Most-Favoured-Nations (MFN) and National Treatment (NT) principles under GATT and GATS", Brunel University Law School London, 2013.

Moens Annelis, "IP Rights loosening grip on parallel imports", Les Nouvelles, March 1999.

Moir Hazel, "What are the costs and benefits of patent systems?", in Arup Christopher and Caenegem William van (eds.), "Intellectual Property Policy Reform", Edward Elgar Publishing Ltd., 2009.

Molina del Pozo Carlos Fransisco, Martinez Gutierrez Enrique and Pescador Diaz Javier, "International Cooperation in Antitrust Enforcement: The European Perspective".

Molly Land, "Adjudicating TRIPS for development", in TRIPS and Developing Countries Towards a New IP World Order? Edward Elgar Publishing Ltd., 2014.

Moore Adam, "Intellectual Property: Theory, Privilege, and Pragmatism" 16 Canadian Journal of Law and Jurisprudence, 2003.

Moore Mike, DG WTO Secretariat in regular Press Statement "IP and Access to Medicines" dated 20th June 2001.

Mukherjee Santanu, "The Journey of Indian Patent Law towards TRIPS Compliance", 35 (2) IIC, 2004.

Naoko Nanao, Takahiro Koyama and Hiromi Sudo, "Decisions on Parallel Imports of Patented Goods", The Journal of Law and Technology, 1996.

Naomi Gross, "Trade Mark Exhaustion: The U.K. Perspective", 5 E.I.P.R, Sweet and Maxwell Ltd. 2001.

National Economic Research Associates (NERA), SJ Berwin& Co and IFF Research, "The Economic Consequences of the Choice of a regime of Exhaustion in the area of Trademarks", Final Report for DGXV of the European Commission, 8th February 1999, London.

Nelson Richard, "Introduction to the Rate and Direction of Inventive Activity: Economic and Social Factors" in Nelson Richard (ed.), "The Rate … Factor", Princeton University Press, 1962.

"Negotiating and Navigating Global Health – Case Studies in Global Health Diplomacy", World Scientific Publishing Co. Pte. Ltd. 2012.

Nguyen Tu Thanh, "Competition Law, Technology Transfer and the TRIPS Agreement Implications for Developing Countries", Edward Elgar Publishing Ltd. 2010.

Nielsen Jane and Nicol Dianne, "Pharmaceutical Patents and Developing Countries: The Conundrum of Access and Incentive", 13 Australian Intellectual Property Journal, February 2002.

Norman Helen, "Parallel Imports from Non-EEA Member States: The Vision Remains Unclear", 4 E.I.P.R., Sweet, Maxwell and Contributors, 2000.

Nolff Markus, "The relevance of TRIPS for Patent Law", in "TRIPS, PCT and Global Patent Procurement", Kluwer Law International, 2001.

Noehrenberg Eric, "TRIPS, the Doha Declaration and Public Health", 6 (2) The Journal of World Intellectual Property, 2003.

OECD, "Guidelines for Multinational Enterprises", Declaration by OECD governments on International Investment and Multinational Enterprises, 21st June 1976.

OECD "Overview of recent trends in patent regimes in United States, Japan and Europe" Working Party on Innovation and Technology Policy of the Directorate for Science, Technology and Industry, June 2003.

Ortino Frederico, "The principle of non-discrimination and its exception in GATS: Selected legal issues", paper presented at the conference, "Conflict and Crises – The WTO after Hong Kong", Vienna 24–25 April 2006.

Osterrieth, "Die Hager Konferenz" 1925, Leipzig 1926, 37: S. Ladas, Patents, Trademarks and Related Rights, Cambridge (Mass.) 11975, 505, cited in Heath Christopher.

Ostry Sylvia, "Intellectual Property Protection in the WTO: Major issues in the millennium round", Fraser Institute Conference Santiago, Chile, 19th April 1999.

O'Toole Francis and Treanor Colm, "The European Union's Trade Mark Exhaustion Regime", 25 (3) World Competition, 2002.

Otten Adrian, "Implications of the TRIPS Agreement for Dispute Settlement in Industrial Property" in Cottier Thomas and Widmer Peter (eds.), "Strategic Issues of Industrial Property Management in a globalising Economy", Hart Publishing, 1999.

Painchod Francois and Cebron Claire, "Overview of the implications of the Quanta Computer Inc. v LG Electronics Inc. Decision on the drafting of License Agreements from a Canadian Perspective", les Nouvelles June 2009.

Pai Yogesh, "The hermeneutics of the Patent exhaustion", in Calboli Irene and Lee Edward (eds.), "Research handbook on Intellectual Property Exhaustion and Parallel Imports", Edward Elgar Publishing Ltd., 2016.

Page Sheila, "The Integration of Regional Groups into Multi-Country Organisations", in Pieter van Dijk Meine and Sideri Sandro (eds.) "Multilateralism versus Regionalism", EADI, 1986.

Panagariya Arvind, "TRIPS and the WTO: An uneasy Marriage", in Maskus Keith (ed.), "The WTO, Intellectual Property Rights and the Knowledge Economy", Edward Elgar Publishing Ltd., 2004.

Paul John, Freeman Kia, Gerstenblish Bart and Underwood Jessica, "The U.S. Supreme Court clarifies Patent Exhaustion", Les Nouvelles, September 2008.

Penrose Edith Tilton, "Economics of the International Patent System", Johns Hopkins Press, 1951.

Peter Drahos, "Intellectual Property and Human Rights", Intellectual Property Quarterly, pg. 6, 7, 1999.

Petersmann Ernst-Ulrich, "The WTO Constitution and Human Rights", Journal of International Economic Law, 2000.

Petersmann Ernst-Ulrich, "The WTO Constitution and the Millennium Round", in Bronckers M. and Quick R. eds. "New Directions in International Economic Law", Kluwer, 2000.

Pires de Carvalho Nuno, "The TRIPS Regime of Patent Rights", Kluwer Law International, 2002.

Pham Duy Nghia, "Exhaustion and Parallel Imports in Vietnam", in Heath Christopher (ed.) "Parallel imports in Asia", Kluwer Law International, 2004.

Pigou Arthur Cecil, "The Economics of Welfare", Macmillan and Company Ltd., 4th Edition 1932.

Position Paper of The European Parallel Importers Coalition (EPIC), "The Case for re-introducing Global Trademark Exhaustion in EU legislation", dated January 2001.

Prahl Dennis, "Exhausted and gray, but still going strong: A comparative view of parallel imports from the trademark perspective", 2001.

Pratap Ravindra, "WTO and Tariff Preferences: India Wins the Case, EC the Law" Vol. 39, Economic and Political Weekly, No. 18.

Pugatch Meir, "The International Political Economy of Intellectual Property Rights: the TRIPS Agreement and the Advanced Pharmaceutical Industry in Europe", Proquest LLC., 2014.

Raghavan Srividhya, "Patent and Trade Disparities in Developing Countries", in "The international trade regime in perspective", Oxford University Press, 2012.

Raslan Heba, "Shari'a and the Protection of Intellectual Property – The Example of Egypt", 7(4) IDEA – The Intellectual Property Law Review.

Rawls John, "A Theory of Justice", Library of Congress Cataloging-in-Publication Data 1921, Revised Edition, Harvard University Press, Pg. 10, 1971.

Regibeau Pierre and Rockett Katharine, "The relationship between intellectual property law and competition law: an economic approach".

"Regional Perspectives on the WTO Agenda: Concerns and Common Interests", paper presented at the "ESCAP/UNCTAD High-level Meeting of ESCAP Developing Countries in Preparation for the Fourth WTO Ministerial Conference" and at the "Doha and Beyond: Expert Group Meeting on the Future WTO Agenda" Bangkok, September 2001.

Reichgericht in Zivilsachen (RGZ) 50, 362 – "*Duotal*", cited by Heath Christopher, "Legal Concepts of Exhaustion and Parallel Imports", in Heath Christopher (ed.), "Parallel Imports in Asia", Kluwer Law International, 2004.

Reichman Jerome, "Intellectual Property in International Trade: Opportunities and Risks of a GATT Connections", 22 Vanderbilt Journal of Transnational Law, 1989.

Reichman Jerome, Okediji Ruth, Lianos Ioannis, Jacob Robin and Stothers Christopher, "The WTO Compatibility of a Differentiated International Exhaustion Regime", International Laboratory for Law and Development Research Paper Series, dated.

Reinbothe Jörge & Howard Anthony, "The State of Play in the Negotiations on TRIPS (GATT/Uruguay Round)", 5 EIPR, 1991.

Reinhardt Eric, "Intellectual Property Protection and Public Health in the Developing World" 17 Emory International Law Review, 2003.

Resnik David, "A pluralistic account of intellectual property", 46 Journal of Business Ethics, Kluwer Law, 2003.

Rey Patrick and Stiglitz Joseph, "The Role of Exclusive Territories in Producers' Competition", 26 (3) Rand Journal of Economics, 1995.

Ricardo David, "On The Principles of Political Economy and Taxation", 1817 (third edition 1821), Batoche Boohenerks Kitc, 2001.

Robertson Raymond, "Why we need the USMCA? (The Agreement formerly known as NAFTA)", Vol. 9, Mosbacher Institute, Issue 5, November 2018.

Rodrigues Edson Beas Jr., "The general exception clauses of the TRIPS Agreement Promoting Sustainable Development" Cambridge University Press, 2012.

Roessler Frieder, "The Concept of Nullification and Impairment in the Legal System of the World Trade Organisation" in Ulrich Petersmann Ernst (ed.), "Studies in Transnational Economic Law", International Trade Law and the GATT/WTO Dispute Settlement System, Vol. 11, Kluwer Law International, 1997.

Roessler Frieder, "Should Principles of Competition Policy be incorporated into WTO Law through non-violation complaints?", Journal of International Economic Law, 1999.

Roessler Frieder, "The Scope of Regulatory Autonomy of WTO Members under Article III:4 of the GATT: A Critical Analysis of the Jurisprudence of the WTO Appellate Body", RSCAS Policy Paper 2015/04, 2015.

Roessler Frieder, "Mexico – Tax Measures on Soft Drinks and Other Beverages (DS308) Prepared for the ALI Project on the Case Law of the WTO", Vol 8 World Trade Review, No. 1, 2009.

Roffe Pedro and Spennemann Christoph, "Control of Anti-competitive Practices in Contractual Licenses under the TRIPS Agreement" Kluwer 2008.

Roffe Pedro, Spennemann Christoph and von Braun Johanna, "From Paris to Doha: The WTO Doha Declaration on the TRIPS Agreement and Public Health", in Roffe Pedro, Tansey Geoff and Vivas-Eugui David (eds), "Negotiating Health – Intellectual Property and Access to Medicines", Earthscan, 2006.

Rognstad Old-Andreas, "The exhaustion/competition interface in EC la – is there room for a holistic approach?", in Drexel Josef edited, "Research handbook on Intellectual Property and Competition law", Edward Elgar Publishing Ltd., 2008.

Ross Julie and Wasserman Jessica, "The GATT Uruguay Round: A Negotiating History (1986–1994), Trade Related aspects of Intellectual Property Rights", Volume II: Commentary in Stewart Terence (ed.) Kluwer Law, 1993.

Rothchild John, "Exhaustion of intellectual property rights and the principle of territoriality in the United States", in Calboli Irene and Lee Edward (eds.), "Research handbook on Intellectual Property Exhaustion and Parallel Imports", Edward Elgar Publishing Ltd., 2016.

Rothnie A. Warwick, "Parallel Imports", Sweet & Maxwell, 1993.

Rudolph and Ricolfi Marco (eds.), "TRIPS and Developing Countries Towards a New IP World Order?", Edward Elgar Publishing Ltd. 2014.

Ruse-Khan Henning Grosse, "Assessing the need for a general public interest exception in the TRIPS Agreement", in Kur Annette and Levin Marianne (eds.), "Intellectual Property Rights in a fair world trading system", 2011.

Ruse-Khan Henning Grosse, "The Protection of Intellectual Property in International Law", Oxford University Press, 2016.

Said S., "U.S. Free trade pact to boost S'pore GDP by 0.5 Pct", Malaysia Economic News, May 7 2003.

Sandrey Ron, "WTO and the Singapore Issues", No. 18 TRALAC Working Paper, pg. 19, 2006.

Savic Masa, "The Legality of Resale of Digital Content after UsedSoft in Subsequent German and CJEU Case Law", 37 European Intellectual Property Issue 7, 2015.

Scherer F.M., "The Political Economy of Patent Policy Reform in the United States", Volume 7 Journal on Telecomm & High Tech. Law, 2009.

Scherer Sigrid and Watal Jayashree, "Post-TRIPS Options for Access to Patented Medicines in Developing Nations", 5 Journal of International Economic Law, 2002.

Scherer F. M., "Global Welfare in Pharmaceutical Patenting", Presentation made at the conference on "Markets for Pharmaceuticals and the Health of Developing Nations" in Toulose, France, 5th–6th December, 2003.

Schovsbo Jens, "Fire and water make steam – redefining the role of competition law in TRIPS", in Kur Annette and Levin Marianne (eds.), "Intellectual Property Rights in a fair world trading system", 2011.

Schloegl Herwig, "Trade and Competition Policy Aspects of VERs: A Comment" in Petersmann Ernst-Ulrich and Hilf Rheinhard (eds.), "The new GATT Round of Multilateral Trade Negotiations", Kluwer Law, 1991.

Schott Jeffrey, "Comment on the Doha Ministerial", 5 (1) Journal of International Economic Law, 2002.

Schultz Siegerid, "Regionalisation of World Trade: Dead End or Way Out?" in Dijk Pieter van and Sideri Sandro (eds.), "Multilateralism versus Regionalism: Trade Issues after the Uruguay Round", EADI, 1996.

Schwartz F. Warren and Sykes O. Alan, "The Positive Economics of Most-Favoured Nation Obligation and its Exceptions in the WTO/GATT System", in Bhandari J. and Sykes Alan, eds., "Economic Dimensions in International Law", 43, Cambridge University Press, 1998.

Sell Susan, "Legal Movements in Trade & Intellectual Property – Trade Issues & HIV/AIDS", 17 Emory International Law Review, 2003.

Sell Susan, "Life after TRIPS – Aggression and Opposition", in Maskus Keith (ed.), "The WTO, Itellectual Property Rights and the Knowledge Economy", Edward Elgar Publishing Ltd., 2004.

Shanker Daya, "Brazil, the Pharmaceutical Industry and the WTO" 5 (1) The Journal of World Intellectual Property Law, 2002.

Sideri Sandro, "GATT and the Theory of Intellectual Property", in Pieter van Dijk Meine and Sideri Sandro (eds.) "Multilateralism versus Regionalism" EADI, 1986.

Sindico Domenico, "On Parallel Importation, TRIPS and European Court of Justice Decisions", 4 Journal of World Intellectual Property, 2002.

Singham Shanker, "Competition Policy and the Stimulation of Innovation: TRIPS and the interface between competition and patent protection in the pharmaceutical industry", Brooklyn Journal of International Law, 2000.

Singh Ajit, "Competition Policy, Development and Developing Countries", Working Paper No. 50, Indian Council for Research on International Economic Relations, 1999.

Slotboom Marco, "The Exhaustion of Intellectual Property Rights, Different Approaches in EC and WTO Law", 6 The Journal of World Intellectual Property, 2003.

Soltysinski Stanislaw, "International Exhaustion of Intellectual Property Rights under the TRIPS, the EC Law and the European Agreements", 4 GRUR Int., 1996.

Sothers Christopher, "Patent Exhaustion: the UK Perspective" in "Parallel Trade in Europe: Intellectual Property, Competition and Regulatory Law", Hart, Oxford, 2007.

Sterckx Sigrid, "Patents and access to drugs in developing countries: An ethical analysis", 4 Developing World Bioethics, Blackwell Publishing, November 2004.

Stern Richard, "Intellectual Property" in Finger Michael and Olechowski Andrzej (eds.) "The Uruguay Round – A Handbook for the Multilateral Trade Negotiations", World Bank publication 1987.

Stoll Peter-Tobias, Busche Jan and Arend Katrin, "WTO – Trade-Related Aspects of Intellectual Property Rights", Max Planck Institute for Comparative Public Law and International Law, Martinus Nijhoff Publishers, 2009.

Straus Joseph, "Implications of TRIPS Agreement in the field of Patent Law", in Beier and Shricker edited, "From GATT to TRIPS – The Agreement on Trade – Related Aspects of Intellectual Property Rights", 18 Studies International Review of Industrial Property and Copyright Law (IIC), Max Planck Institute, Munich, 1996.

Supasiripongchai Noppanun, "Parallel Importation of Patented Products in Thailand: The need for the New Patent Exhaustion Regime in the light of ASEAN Economic Community (AEC)", Volume 7 Queen Mary Journal of Intellectual Property, Issue 4, 2017.

Suslow Valerie, "The Changing International Status of Export Cartel Exemptions", Volume 20, Issue 4 American University International Law Review, 2005.

Taubman Antony, "A practical guide to working with TRIPS", Oxford University Press 2011.

The Hindu, "India warns against Singapore issues at the WTO", June 2003.

The Lien Hoang (eds.), "Commentary of the Civil Code", The National Politics Publishing House, Hanoi, 1998.

The Road to Doha and Beyond – A Road Map for Successfully Concluding The Doha Development Agenda, WTO 2001.

Theo Papadopoulos, "The Economic Case against Copyright Owner Control over Parallel Imports – The Market for Sound Recordings", 6 (2) The Journal of World Intellectual Property, 2003.

Thorpe Phil, "Study on the implementation of the TRIPS Agreement by developing countries" Study Paper No. 7 of the Commission on Intellectual Property Rights, UK 2002.

Thuo Gathii James, "The Legal Status of the Doha Declaration on TRIPS and Public Health Under the Vienna Convention on the Law of Treaties", 15 Harvard Journal of Law and Technology, 2002.

Tomlinson B. R., "Economics: The Periphery", in Porter Andrew (ed.), "The Oxford History of the British Empire: The Nineteenth Century", Oxford, 1990.

Trachtman Joel, "Toward open recognition? Integration under *Article XXIV* of GATT", 6 (2) Journal of International Economic Law, Oxford University Press, 2003.

Tsouloufas Georgios, "Limiting Pharmaceutical Parallel Trade in the European Union: Regulatory and Economic Justifications", 36 E.L. Review, June 2011.

Turton Michael and Mills Aleta, "The first sale doctrine and parallel imports in the United States after Jazz photo", Comments 3 E.I.P.R., 2004.

UNAIDS, "AIDS Epidemic Update: December 2000", pg. 5 UNAIDS Report, Geneva 2000.

UNCTAD – ICTSD, "Resource Book on TRIPS and Development", Cambridge University Press pg. 111, 2005.

UNCTAD, "Restrictive Business Practices Code" of the United Nations Conference on Trade and Development was finalised on 22nd April 1980 and adopted by the UN General Assembly as a consensual resolution on 5th December 1980.

UNCTAD, "The benefit of competition policy for consumers", TD/B/C.I/CLP/27, 29th April 2014.

U.S. Trade Representative, National Trade Estimate, Report, 1985.

Vandoren Paul and Van Eeckhaute Jean Charles, "The WTO Decision on Paragraph 6 of the Doha Declaration on the TRIPS Agreement and Public Health – Making it Work", 6 The Journal of World Intellectual Property, November 2003.

Vautier Kerrin, "The Economics of Parallel Imports", in Heath Christopher and Sanders Anselm Kamperman (eds.), "Industrial Property in the Bio-Medical Age – Challenges for Asia", Kluwer Law International, 2003.

Verbraeken Erik, "Recent U.S. and EU developments: The Exhaustion Theory is not yet exhausted", les Nouvelles, September 2009.

Verma Surinder, "Exhaustion of Intellectual Property Rights and Free Trade – Article 6 of the TRIPS Agreement", 5 IIC, 1998.

Villarreal Angeles and Fergusson Ian, "NAFTA Renegotiation and Modernization", Congressional Research Service, 27th February 2018.

Vincent Nicholas, "TRIP-ing Up: The Failure of TRIPS Article 31bis", Gonzaga Journal of International Law, Fall 2020.

Vivekanandan V.C., "The Indian Patent Matrix: issues in patent amendment 2005", in Bird Robert and Jain Subhash (eds.), "The Global Challenge of Intellectual Property Rights", Edward Elgar Publishing Ltd., 2008.

Walterscheid Edward, "The early evolution of the United States Patent Law: Antecedents", 76 J. Patent & Trademark Off. Society, 1996.

Warwick Rothnie, "Parallel Imports", Sweet & Maxwell, 1993.

Watal Jayashree, "Intellectual Property Rights in the WTO and Developing Countries", Oxford University Press, 2002.

Watal Jayashree, "Parallel Imports and IPR-Based Dominant Positions: Where Do India's Interests Lie?" in Cottier Thomas and Mavroidis Petros (eds.), "Intellectual Property: Trade, Competition and Sustainable Development" The Univ. of Michigan Press, 2003.

Watal Jayashree, "From Punta del Este to Doha and Beyond: Lessons from the TRIPS Negotiating Process", SSRN Electronic Journal, 2011.

Wauters Jasper and Vandenbussche Hylke, "China – Measures Affecting Imports of Automobile Parts", 9 World Trade Review 2010.

Weeraworawit Weerawit, "The Harmonisation of Intellectual Property Rights in ASEAN", in C. Antons, M. Blakeney and C. Heath (eds.), "Intellectual Property Harmonisation Within ASEAN and APEC", Kluwer Law International, 2004.

WHO, "More Equitable Pricing for Essential Drugs: What do we mean and what are the issues?", pg. 3, Background Paper prepared by the WHO Secretariat for the WHO – WTO Secretariat Workshop on Differential Pricing and Financing of Essential Drugs, Hosbjor, Norway from 8th–11th April 2001.

WHO, "More Equitable Pricing for Essential Drugs: What do we mean and what are the issues?", Background Paper prepared by the WHO Secretariat for the WHO – WTO Secretariat Workshop on Differential Pricing and Financing of Essentail Drugs, Hosbjor, Norway from 8th–11th April 2001.

WIPO Standing Committee on the Law of Patents, WIPO SCP/21/7 October 6, 2014.

WIPO, "The Concept of Intellectual Property" in WIPO Intellectual Property Handbook: Policy, Law and Use, paragraph 1.1, 2001.

WTO Secretariat note titled, "Necessity Tests in the WTO" S/WPDR/W/27 of 2nd December 2003.

Wolff Alan, "What did Doha do? An initial assessment", 5 (1) Journal of International Economic Law, 2002.

Woolcock Stephen, "International Competition Policy and the World Trade Organisation", Paper presented at the LSE Commonwealth Business Council Trade Forum in South Africa, Content 2.0, Undated.

Xintian Yin, "Parallel Importation as viewed from the Chinese Patent Law", 2 China Patents & Trademarks, 2001.

Yamane Hiroko, "The TRIPS Agreement de Lege Lata: The Outline", in "Interpreting TRIPS Globalisation of Intellectual Property Rights and Access to Medicines" Hart Publishing Ltd., 2011.

Yarsky Joseph Kenneth, "Hastening harmonization in European Union Patent law through a preliminary reference power", Boston College International and Comparative Law Review, Volume 40, Issue 1, 2017.

Young David, Watson Antony, Thorley Simon and Miller Richard, "Terrell on the Law of Patent", 14th Edition, London Sweet and Maxwell 1994.

Yusuf Abdulqawi, "TRIPS: Background, Principles and General Provisions", in Correa Carlos and Yusuf Abdulqawi (eds.), "Intellectual Property and International Trade – The TRIPS Agreement", Walters Kluwer 2nd Edition, 2008.

Yusuf Abdulqawi and Monacayo Andrés Hase, "Intellectual Property Protection and International Trade", 16 World Competition, 1992.

Yu Xiang, "Exhaustion and Parallel Imports in China" (The *Patent Act of 2000*, adopted on 25th August 2000, entered into force on July 2001 reproduced in English); 26 European Intellectual Property Review, 2004.

Zaveri Narendra, "The TRIPS Agreement and generic production of HIV/AIDS Drugs", in Bellmann Christopher, Dutfield Graham and Meléndez-Ortiz Ricardo (eds.) "Trading in Knowledge – Development Perspectives on TRIPS, Trade and Sustainability", Earthscan 2003.

Zhang Hui, Mengling and Yang James, Wolters Kluwer Patent Blog, May 29, 2018.

Legal Texts and WTO Documents

GATT Doc. No. MTN.GNG/NG11/W76, July 18, 1990.
GATT Doc. MTN/FA, 15, December 1993.
GATT Doc. No. MIN(86)/W/19 DEC (20 September 1986).
GATT Doc. No. MTN.GNG/NG11/W76, July 18, 1990.
GATT Doc. L/8417 (31 July 1979).
GATT Doc. MTN.GNG/NG11/W/70, May 11, 1990.
GATT Doc. MTN.TNC/W/FA, Dec. 20, 1991.
UNCTAD Document No. UNCTAD/ITE/IPC/Misc.22, 2002.
WTO Doc. No. WT/MIN(01)/DEC/2.
WTO Doc. No., MTN.GNG/NG11/W/71 (14th May 1990).
WTO Doc. No. MTN.GNG/NG11/W/23, 26th April, 1998.
WTO Doc. No. GNG/NG11/13 at para D7.
WTO Doc. No. MTN.GNG/NG11/14.
WTO Doc No. MTN.GNG/NG11/W/26.
WTO Doc. No. MTN.GNG/NG11/W/71.
WTO Doc No. MTN.GNG/NG11/14.
WTO Doc. No. MTN.GNG/NG11/20.
WTO Doc. No. MTN.GNG/NG11/W/76.
WTO Doc. No., MTN.GNG/NG11/W/71 (14th May 1990).
WTO Doc. No. MTN.GNG/NG11/W/23, 26th April, 1998.
WTO Doc. No. GNG/NG11/13 at para D7.
WTO Doc. No. MTN.GNG/NG11/14.
WTO Doc No. MTN.GNG/NG11/W/26.
WTO Doc. No. MTN.GNG/NG11/W/71.
WTO Doc No. MTN.GNG/NG11/14.
WTO Doc. No. MTN.GNG/NG11/20.
WTO Doc. No. MTN.GNG/NG11/W/76.
WTO Doc. No. IP/C/M/31, WTO, Geneva.
WTO Secretariat note S/WPDR/W/27 of 2nd December 2003.
WTO Doc. No. IP/C/M/31, WTO, Geneva.
WTO Doc. No. WT/L/540.
WTO Doc. No. WT/MIN(01)/DEC/2.
WTO Doc. No. IP/C/W/296.

List of Cases

WTO Cases

Australia – certain measures concerning trademarks, geographical indications and other plain packaging requirements applicable to tobacco products and packaging, WT/DS435/R, WT/DS441/R, WT/DS458/R, WT/DS467/R.
Brazil – Measures affecting Imports of Retreaded Tyres, WTO, WT/DS332/AB/R, 3 December 2007.
Canada – Patent Protection for Pharmaceutical Products, WT/DS114/R (2000).
China – Measures Affecting Imports of Automobile Parts (WT/DS342/AB/R) 15 December 2008.
China – Measures Affecting Trading Rights and Distribution Services for Certain Publications and Audiovisual Entertainment Products, WT/DS363/AB/R, 21 December 2009.
China – Measures related to the Exportation of various Raw Materials – WT/DS394/AB/R, 2012.
Colombia – Indicative Prices and Restrictions on Ports of Entry, WT/DS366/R, 2009.
Dominican Republic – Measures affecting the importation and internal sale of cigarettes, WTO, WT/DS302/AB/R, 25th April 2005.
European Communities – Regime for the Importation, Sale and Distribution of Bananas, WT/DS27/AB/R, 1997.
European Communities – Measures Affecting Asbestos and Asbestos-Containing Products, WT/DS135/AB/R, 12 March 2001.
European Communities – Conditions for the Granting of Tariff Preferences to Developing Countries, WT/DS246/AB/R, 7 April 2004.
European Communities – Protection of Trademarks and Geographical Indications for Agricultural Products and Foodstuffs, WT/DS290/R; 20th April 2005.
European Communities – Measures Prohibiting the Importation and Marketing of Seal Products, WT/DS400 & 401/AB/R, paragraph 5.87, 18 June 2014.
India – Quantitative Restrictions on Imports of Agricultural, Textile and Industrial Products – WT/DS90/R, paragraphs 5.128 and 5.129, 1999.
India – Measures affecting the Automotive Sector, WT/DS146/AB/R; WT/DS175/AB/R, 19 March 2002.
India – Certain Measures Relating to Solar Cells and Solar Modules (WT/DS456/AB/R) 16 September 2016.
Japan – Trade in Semi-Conductors, BISD L/6309–35S/116, 24th March 1988.

Japan – Taxes on Alcoholic Beverages case, WT/DS8/AB/R, WT/DS10/AB/R and WT/DS11/AB/R, of 4th October 1996 and Korea – Taxes on Alcoholic Beverages case, WT/DS75/AB/R, WT/DS84/AB/R of 18th January 1999.

Korea – Definitive Safeguard Measures on Imports of Some Dairy products, WT/DS98/AB/R, 14th December 1999.

Korea – Measures Affecting Imports of Fresh, Chilled and Frozen Beef, WT/DS161/AB/R, 11 December 2000, WT/DS169/AB/R, 12 March 2001.

Mexico – Tax Measures on Soft Drinks and Other Beverages, WT/DS308/AB/R, 6 March 2006.

Russia – Measures Concerning Traffic in Transit, Panel Report WT/DS512/R, 5 April 2019.

Turkey – Restrictions on Imports of Textile and Clothing Products, AB decision WT/DS34/AB/R, 1999.

United States – Denial of Most-Favoured-Nation Treatment as to Non-Rubber Footwear from Brazil, DS18/R, adopted, B.I.S.D. 39S/128, 19 June 1992.

United States – Measures affecting Alcoholic and Malt Beverages, DS23/R, B.I.S.D. 39S/206. adopted 19 June 1992.

United States – Standards for Reformulated and Conventional Gasoline – Report of the Appellate Body (WT/DS2/AB/R), 29th April 1996.

United States – Import Prohibition of Certain Shrimp and Shrimp Products, WT/DS58/AB/R, 12 October 1998.

United States – Measures affecting the cross-border Supply of Gambling and Betting Services, WTO, WT/DS285/AB/R, 7th April 2005.

National and Regional Cases

Betts v. Willimott, [1871] 6 L.R.Ch. 239, 245.

Adam v Burke, 84 U.S. 453 (1873).

Bloomer v. McQuewan, 14 How. 539.

Holiday v. Mattheson, 24 Fed. 185–1866 (C.C.S.D.N.Y. 1885).

Boesch v. Graff 133 US 697 (1890).

E. Bement & Sons v National Harrow Co., 1Boesch86 U.S. 70, 91 (1902).

United States v Univis Lens Co., 316 U.S. 241 (1942).

Sanofi S.A. v. Med-Tech Veterinarian Products Inc. 565 F. Supp. 931 (1983).

Jazz Photo Corp. V. International Trade Commission, 264 F. 3d 1094 (Fed. Cir. 2001), U.S. Supreme Court No. 01–1158, filed February 6, 2002.

Quanta Computer, Inc., et al. v. LG Electronics, Inc. (No. 06–937) 453 F. 3d 1364, reversed (Supreme Court, 9 June, 2008).

Monsanto Co. v. Bowman, 657 F.3d 1341 (Fed. CIRC. 2011) and Bowman v Monsanto Co., 133 S. Ct. 1761, 1766 (2013).

Impression Products Inc. v. Lexmark International Inc., 137 S Ct. 1523 (2017).

Brunswick Corp. v Orian Kogyo Kabushiki Kaisha (1969), 1 Mutai / Saishu 160, Osaka District Court, 9th June, 1969.

Tokyo District Court's decision in BBS Wheels, Wa-No. 16565 of 1992.

Strix decision in BBS Wheels, Ne-No. 3272 of 1994.

Supreme Court of Japan decision in BBS Wheels, Wo-No. 1988 of 1997.

Stauffer Chemical Co. v Agricura Ltd. 1979 BP 168 (CP).

Strix Ltd. v. Maharaja Appliances Ltd. (2008) I.A. No. 7441 of 2008 in C.S. (OS) No. 1206 of 2008 (India).

Kodak v Jumbo-Markt AG, 4C.24/1999/rnd, 7 December 1999.

Generics BV v Smith Kline & French Laboratories Ltd., RPC 801 (1997).

'Karate' of the German Federal Supreme Court (Bundesgerichtshof) dated 14th December, 1999, Case No. X ZR 61/98.

The Canadian Federal Court of Appeal in trademark case, Smith & Nephew Inc. v Glen Oak Inc., (1996) 68 C.P.R. (3d) 153, before the Supreme Court of Canada in patent case, Eli Lilly and Co. v Novopharm Ltd. (1998), 80 C.P.R. (3d) 321 at 352.

Thailand Court Decision No. 16/2542 (1999).

Supreme Court of Thailand's Decision No. 2817/2543 (2000).

Yu v. Court of Appeals, 217 SCRA 328–333 (1993).

U–Bix Corporation v. Ariancorp International Inc. CA – G.R. No. 41260, 1995.

Société Anonyme des Manufactures de Glaces v Tilghman's Patent Sand Blast Company (1883) 25Ch. D1 (CA).

Dunlop v Longlife (1958) R.P.C. 473 and Goodyear v Lancashire Batteries (1958) L.R. 1 R.P. 22 at 35.

Beecham Group Ltd. v International Products Ltd., (1968) R.P.C. 129 and FSR 162.

United Wire Ltd. v Screen Repair Services (Scotland) and Others, House of Lords, 4 All E R 353 (2000).

GlaxoSmithKline Services Unlimited v Commission of the European Communities, Case No. T-168/01 [2006] E.C.R. II-2969.

National Phonograph Co. of Australia v. Menck [1911] 28 R.P.C. 229.

Lever Brothers Co v United States of America, eta al., 877 F.2d 101 (D.C. Cir. 1989).

Lever Brothers Co v United States of America, eta al., 981 F. 2nd 1330 (D.C. Cir. 1993).

The HAG case in EU Case C 10/89, SA CNL – SUCAL NV v HAG GF AG.

Consten SaRL and Grundig GmbH v Commission of EEC (1966), Case 56/64.

Consten S.à.R.L. snd Grundig-Verkaufs-GmbH v. Commission of the European Community, Joined cases Nos. 56/54 and 58/64, (1966) ECR 299.

GlaxoSmithKline Services Unlimited v Commission of the European Communities, Joined Case Nos. C-501/06 P, C-513/06 P, C-515/06 P, E.C.R. I-9291, 2009.

Usedsoft GmbH v Oracle International Corp, Case No. C 128/11, 3 C.M.L.R. 44, 2012.

Merck & Co. Inc. v Stephar BV and Petrus Stephanus Exier, Case No. 187/80, July 14, 1981.

Centrafarm BV v. Sterling Drug Inc., 87 Case No. 15/74, 31st October 1974 [1974] 2 CMLR 480, [1974].

Centrafarm BV v. Winthrop BV, Case 16/74, ECLI:EU:C:1974:115.

Bayer AG v Commission of the European Communities, Joined Cases Nos. C-2/01P C-3/01P, (T-41/96) [2000] E.C.R. II-3383; [2001] 4 C.M.L.R.

Polydor Limited and RSO Records Incorporated v Harlequin Record Shops Ltd. and Simons Records Limited, Case 270/80 [1982], ECR 329.

Mag Instrument Inc. v California Trading Company Norway, Case E-2/97 [1997], EFTA Ct. Rep. 129.

Deutsche Grammophon Geselischaft mbH v Metro-SB Grossmarkte GmbH & Co. KG, Case No. 78/70, 1971 ECR 487, 1971 CMLR 631.

Parke, Davis and Co. v Probel, Reese, Beintema-Interpharm and Centrafarm, Gerechtshof's-Gravenhage-Netherlands, Case 24/67, 1968, ECLI:eu:c:1998:11.

Pharmon BV v Hoechst AG, Case No. 19/84, ECR 2281 (1985).

Merck & Co. Inc., Merck Sharp & Dohme Ltd. and Merck Sharp & Dohme International Services BV v Primecrown Ltd., Ketan Himatlal Mehta, Bharat Himatlal Mehta and Necessity Supplies Ltd. and Beecham Groupp PLC v Europharm of Worthing Ltd., Joined cases, C 267/95 and C 268/95, ECRI 6285 (1996).

Silhouette International Schmied GmbH and Co. KG v. Hartlauer Handelsgesellschaft mbH, Case C-355/96, ECLI:EU:C:1998:374.

Websites

http://www.gersterconsulting.ch/docs/TWN_Patents_and_Development.pdf

https://constitution.congress.gov/browse/article-1/section-8/

https://cambridge.dlconsulting.com/cgi-bin/cambridge?a=d&d=Sentinel19420926-01.2.46

http://www.philly.com/philly/blogs/TODAY-IN-PHILADELPHIA-HISTORY/Samuel-Hopkins-granted-first-patent-in-the-United-States.html

http://www.patentstation.com/mdm/tractionwheels.htm

https://founders.archives.gov/documents/Jefferson/03-06-02-0322

https://www.thefederalistpapers.org/wp-content/uploads/2012/12/Two-Treatises-of-Government-by-John-Locke.pdf

https://www.utilitarianism.com/bentham.htm

https://scholarship.law.duke.edu/cgi/viewcontent.cgi?article=2648&context=faculty_scholarship.

https://www.researchgate.net/publication/285855355_Intellectual_property_and_human_rights.

https://www.india.gov.in/my-government/constitution-india/amendments/constitution-india-forty-fourth-amendment-act-1978.

https://www.un.org/development/desa/indigenouspeoples/wp-content/uploads/sites/19/2018/11/UNDRIP_E_web.pdf

https://giuseppecapograssi.files.wordpress.com/2014/08/rawls99.pdf

http://www.law.nyu.edu/sites/default/files/upload_documents/Kitch.pdf.

https://lib.dr.iastate.edu/cgi/viewcontent.cgi?Article=1317&context=card_workingpapers.

https://socialsciences.mcmaster.ca/econ/ugcm/3ll3/ricardo/Principles.pdf.

http://files.libertyfund.org/files/1410/Pigou_0316.pdf.

https://eur-lex.europa.eu/legal-content/EN/TXT/PDF/?uri=CELEX:61964CJ0056&from=EN.

https://eur-lex.europa.eu/legal-content/EN/TXT/?uri=CELEX:61980CJ0270

https://eftacourt.int/cases/e-02-97/

www.admin.ch/opc/en/classified-compilation/19540108/201904010000/232.14.pdf

https://ustr.gov/sites/default/files/uploads/agreements/fta/morocco/asset_upload_file797_3849.pdf

https://www.supremecourt.gov/opinions/16pdf/15-1189_ebfj.pdf

https://www.dbba.com.br/wp-content/uploads/empresarial09.pdf

https://www.aippi.fr/upload/Totonto2014/sumrep_q240_e_120814.pdf

http://www.wipo.int/edocs/mdocs/scp/en/scp_21/scp_21_7.pdf

https://www.dwt.com/advisories/Chinese_PatentLaw_and_Implementation_Amendments_Bring_Key_Changes_Interpretive_Challenges_02_22_2011/
http://patentblog.kluweriplaw.com/2018/05/29/beijing-high-court-upholds-chinas-first-ever-sep-injunction-iwncomm-v-sony/
www.nber.org/papers/w10159
http://www.wto.org/english/thewto_e/minist_e/min01_e/mindecl_trips_e.htm
http://www.wipo.int/wipolex/en/text.jsp?file_id=256035
www.dgip.go.id
https://adipven.com/en/2016/09/06/indonesia-massive-amendments-to-the-patent-law/
http://www.myipo.gov.my/wp-content/uploads/2016/09/PATENT-ACT-1983-ACT-291.pdf
http://www.wipo.int/wipolex/en/text.jsp?file_id=128830#P63_4459
https://www.worldbank.org/en/country/singapore/overview#1
https://sso.agc.gov.sg/Act/PA1994?ValidDate=20171030&ProvIds=pr66-
https://ustr.gov/sites/default/files/uploads/agreements/fta/singapore/asset_upload_file708_4036.pdf
http://www.asianlii.org/th/legis/consol_act/pa199991/
https://www.lawphil.net/judjuris/juri1993/jan1993/gr_86683_1993.html
http://vcci-ip.com/wp-content/uploads/2017/06/Agreement_between_the_United_States_of_America_and_the_Socialist_Republic_of_Vietnam_on_Trade_Relations.pdf
http://asean.org/?static_post=asean-intellectual-property-right-action-plan-2004-2010
https://www.wto.org/english/docs_e/legal_e/27-trips_04_e.htm
https://www.lawgazette.co.uk/law/law-reports/4308.Article
https://www.wto.org/english/res_e/booksp_e/trips_agree_e/chapter_4_e.pdf
https://www.researchgate.net/publication/228122380_From_Punta_Del_Este_to_Doha_and_Beyond_Lessons_from_the_TRIPS_Negotiating_Processes
https://www.wto.org/gatt_docs/English/SULPDF/91240226.pdf
www.admin.ch/opc/en/classified-compilation/19540108/201904010000/232.14.pdf
http://www.eurasiancommission.org/ru/act/finpol/dobd/intelsobs/Documents/WTO%20Compartibility%20of%20Exhaustion%20Regimes_EEC_SkHSEreport.pdf
https://wipolex.wipo.int/en/text/287556
https://www.unido.org/sites/default/files/2014-04/Paris_Convention_0.pdf
http://curia.europa.eu/juris/showPdf.jsf?docid=96580&doclang=en
https://www.epo.org/law-practice/unitary/unitary-patent/start.html

https://www.nyulawreview.org/wp-content/uploads/2018/08/NYULawReview-76-6-Gitter.pdf

https://www.wto.org/english/tratop_e/trips_e/factsheet_pharm02_e.htm#art30

https://www.wto.org/english/tratop_e/dispu_e/7428d.pdf

https://papers.ssrn.com/sol3/papers.cfm?abstract_id=391540

https://msfaccess.org/why-article-30-will-work-why-article-31-will-not

https://www.wto.org/english/tratop_e/dispu_e/98abr.pdf

https://www.wto.org/english/res_e/booksp_e/gatt_ai_e/art1_e.pdf

https://www.wto.org/english/tratop_e/dispu_e/91nruber.pdf

https://www.un.org/en/about-us/un-charter/full-text

https://docs.wto.org/dol2fe/Pages/SS/directdoc.aspx?filename=Q:/WT/DS/27ABR.PDF&Open=True

https://www.wto.org/english/tratop_e/dispu_e/400_401abr_e.pdf

https://www.wto.org/english/docs_e/legal_e/havana_e.pdf

https://www.wto.org/english/res_e/booksp_e/gatt_ai_e/art3_e.pdf

https://docs.wto.org/dol2fe/Pages/SS/directdoc.aspx?filename=Q:/WT/DS/8ABR.pdf&Open=True

https://www.wto.org/english/tratop_e/dispu_e/gatt_e/91alcohm.pdf

https://www.wto.org/english/tratop_e/dispu_e/456abr_e.pdf

https://www.wto.org/english/tratop_e/dispu_e/363abr_e.pdf

https://law.unimelb.edu.au/__data/assets/pdf_file/0007/1687786/Harris-and-Moon.pdf

https://img1.wsimg.com/blobby/go/05156989-4612-4459-967b-0b66817b7a32/downloads/04_henrik_andersen.pdf?ver=1557336870890

https://www.eajournals.org/wp-content/uploads/Meaning-Of-the-Terms-%E2%80%9CArbitrary-or-Unjustifiable-Discrimination%E2%80%9D-In-the-Chapeau-of-Gatt-Article-XX.pdf

https://www.wto.org/english/res_e/publications_e/ai17_e/gatt1994_art11_gatt47.pdf

https://www.wto.org/english/tratop_e/dispu_e/87semcdr.pdf

https://www.wto.org/english/tratop_e/dispu_e/90abr.pdf

https://files.pca-cpa.org/pcadocs/bi-c/1.%20Investors/4.%20Legal%20Authorities/CA172.pdf

https://www.wto.org/english/tratop_e/trips_e/nonviolation_background_e.htm

https://www.investopedia.com/ask/answers/050615/what-are-fabless-chip-makers-and-why-are-they-important-semiconductor-market.asp

https://www.iatp.org/sites/default/files/MFN_and_the_GATS.htm

https://www.academia.edu/5518155/Most-Favoured-Nations_MFN_and_National_Treatment_NT_principles_under_GATT_and_GATS

https://www.wto.org/english/tratop_e/dispu_e/27abr.pdf

https://papers.ssrn.com/sol3/papers.cfm?abstract_id=979481

https://www.wto.org/english/tratop_e/dispu_e/cases_e/ds27_e.htm

https://papers.ssrn.com/sol3/papers.cfm?abstract_id=1280215

https://papers.ssrn.com/sol3/papers.cfm?abstract_id=1951549

https://www.wto.org/english/res_e/publications_e/ai17_e/gatt1994_art5_gatt47.pdf

https://www.wto.org/english/tratop_e/dispu_e/512r_e.pdf

http://asean.org/?static_post=rcep-regional-comprehensive-economic-partnership

https://www.wto.org/english/tratop_e/dda_e/meet08_e.htm

https://www.wto.org/english/news_e/news13_e/mc9sum_07dec13_e.htm

https://www.wto.org/english/news_e/news15_e/mc10_19dec15_e.htm

https://eur-lex.europa.eu/LexUriServ/LexUriServ.do?uri=OJ:L:2012:361:0001:0008:en:PDF

http://www.europarl.europa.eu/ftu/pdf/en/FTU_2.1.2.pdf

https://eur-lex.europa.eu/legal-content/EN/TXT/HTML/?uri=CELEX:61974CJ0015&from=EN

https://eur-lex.europa.eu/legal-content/EN/TXT/HTML/?uri=CELEX:61980CJ0187&from=EN

https://eur-lex.europa.eu/legal-content/EN/TXT/HTML/?uri=CELEX:61967CJ0024&from=LT

https://eur-lex.europa.eu/legal-content/EN/TXT/HTML/?uri=CELEX:61984CJ0019&from=EN

https://eur-lex.europa.eu/legal-content/EN/TXT/HTML/?uri=CELEX:61995CJ0267&from=EN

http://curia.europa.eu/juris/showPdf.jsf;jsessionid=9ea7d2dc30dbc81efbb3c3ea4e3e9551d7ffed674088.e34KaxiLc3qMb40Rch0SaxqTbNn0?text=&docid=100690&pageIndex=0&doclang=en&mode=req&dir=&occ=first&part=1&cid=18338

https://eur-lex.europa.eu/legal-content/EN/TXT/HTML/?uri=CELEX:62001CJ0002&from=EN

https://eur-lex.europa.eu/legal-content/EN/TXT/PDF/?uri=CELEX:62001TJ0168&from=EN

http://curia.europa.eu/juris/document/document.jsf?docid=124564&doclang=EN

https://www.researchgate.net/publication/228154939_TRIPS-Plus_Provisions_in_FTAs_Recent_Trends

https://law.anu.edu.au/sites/all/files/users/u9705219/236-artprometheus fta.pdf
https://www.trade.gov/usmca
https://oaktrust.library.tamu.edu/bitstream/handle/1969.1/172747/V9-5%20Why%20We%20Need%20USMCA%20NAFTA.pdf?sequence=1&isAllowed=y
https://www.academia.edu/73049957/Digital_Trade
https://ustr.gov/trade-agreements/free-trade-agreements/united-states-mexico-canada-agreement
https://www.heritage.org/sites/default/files/2019-01/BG3379_0.pdf
https://ustr.gov/sites/default/files/files/agreements/FTA/USMCA/Text/20%20Intellectual%20Property%20Rights.pdf
http://asean.org/asean-economic-community/
http://www.gcc-sg.org/en-us/AboutGCC/Memberstates/pages/Home.aspx
http://www.austlii.edu.au/au/journals/SCULawRw/2013/4.pdf
https://ipmall.law.unh.edu/sites/default/files/hosted_resources/IDEA/idea-vol47-no4-raslan.pdf
https://idosi.org/wjihc/wjihc7(3)17/1.pdf
http://www.wipo.int/treaties/en/ShowResults.jsp?country_id=ALL&start_year=ANY&end_year=ANY&search_what=C&treaty_id=15&treaty_id=2
https://www.gccpo.org/
http://www.kadasa.com.sa/news/181?type=END_TO_UNITARY_PATENT_SYSTEM_IN_THE_GCC
https://www.rouse.com/magazine/news/gulf-co-operation-council-countries-patent-landscape/
https://wits.worldbank.org/GPTAD/PDF/archive/MERCOSUR.pdf
https://www.mercosur.int/en/https://www.mfat.govt.nz/assets/Trade-agreements/CPTPP/Comprehensive-and-Progressive-Agreement-for-Trans-Pacific-Partnership-CPTPP-English.pdf
https://www.international.gc.ca/trade-commerce/trade-agreements-accords-commerciaux/agr-acc/cptpp-ptpgp/index.aspx?lang=eng
https://www.dfat.gov.au/trade/agreements/in-force/cptpp/comprehensive-and-progressive-agreement-for-trans-pacific-partnership
https://www.international.gc.ca/trade-commerce/trade-agreements-accords-commerciaux/agr-acc/tpp-ptp/text-texte/18.aspx?lang=eng
https://ec.europa.eu/trade/policy/in-focus/ceta/ceta-explained/
https://www.lawsocieties.eu/viewpoint/the-ceta-opinion-of-the-cjeu-right-of-access-to-an-independent-tribunal-by-emily-hay/5067617.article
https://ec.europa.eu/trade/policy/in-focus/ceta/ceta-chapter-by-chapter/
http://www.ipindia.nic.in/history-of-indian-patent-system.htm

www.idei.fr/doc/conf/pha/scherer.pdf
https://www.statista.com/statistics/265645/ranking-of-the-20-companies-with-the-highest-spending-on-research-and-development/
https://www.wipo.int/edocs/mdocs/mdocs/en/wipo_gc_ip_ge_16/wipo_gc_ip_ge_16_brief.pdf
https://www.hrw.org/legacy/backgrounder/hivaids/ungass0806/3.htm
http://www.unaids.org/sites/default/files/sub_landing/files/aidsdeclaration_en_0.pdf
www.unaids.org
https://www.wto.org/english/tratop_e/dispu_e/cases_e/ds199_e.htm
www.wto.org/english/news_e/news01_e/dg_trips_medicines_010620_e.htm
https://www.wto.org/english/tratop_e/trips_e/paper_develop_w296_e.htm
https://www.wto.org/english/thewto_e/minist_e/min01_e/mindecl_trips_e.htm
https://www.wto.org/english/res_e/booksp_e/roadtodoha_e.pdf
https://www.wto.org/english/tratop_e/trips_e/implem_para6_e.htm
https://www.wto.org/english/tratop_e/trips_e/factsheet_pharm02_e.htm#importing
http://www.wto.org/english/tratop_e/trips_e/amendment_e.htm
https://www.wto.org/english/docs_e/legal_e/31bis_trips_annex_e.htm
http://unctad.org/meetings/en/SessionalDocuments/ciclpd27_en.pdf
https://www.internationalcompetitionnetwork.org/about/
https://www.wto.org/English/tratop_e/comp_e/history_e.htm
https://www.wto.org/English/thewto_e/minist_e/min03_e/min03_14sept_e.htm
https://www.wto.org/English/tratop_e/dda_e/draft_text_gc_dg_31july04_e.htm
https://www.wto.org/english/res_e/reser_e/ersd201812_e.pdf
https://www.wto.org/english/forums_e/ngo_e/iisd_singapore_e.pdf
https://docs.wto.org/dol2fe/Pages/FE_Search/FE_S_S009-DP.aspx?language=E&CatalogueIdList=7356,1998,2060,46167,1625,25828,54923,83896,68482,80668&CurrentCatalogueIdIndex=6&FullTextHash=&HasEnglishRecord=True&HasFrenchRecord=True&HasSpanishRecord=True

All web-links have been last visited on 10th January 2023.

Index

www.ingramcontent.com/pod-product-compliance
Lightning Source LLC
LaVergne TN
LVHW010542300926
849162LV00002B/213